Hesychasm and Art

Hesychasm and Art

The Appearance of New Iconographic Trends in Byzantine and Slavic Lands in the 14th and 15th Centuries

Anita Strezova

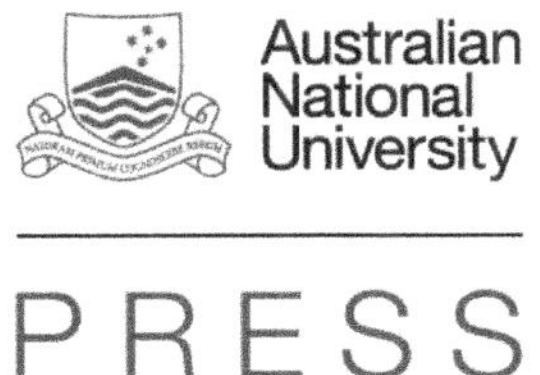

PRESS

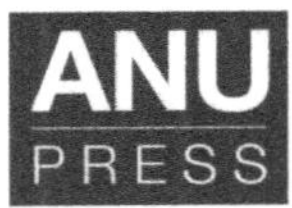

Published by ANU Press
The Australian National University
Canberra ACT 0200, Australia
Email: anupress@anu.edu.au
This title is also available online at http://press.anu.edu.au

National Library of Australia Cataloguing-in-Publication entry

Author:	Strezova, Anita, author.
Title:	Hesychasm and art: the appearance of new Iconographic trends in Byzantine and Slavic lands in the 14th and 15th centuries / Anita Strezova.
ISBN:	9781925021837 (paperback) 9781925021851 (ebook)
Subjects:	Hesychasm--In art. Mysticism and art. Christianity and art.
Dewey Number:	759.022

The subchapter 'Doctrinal Positions of Barlaam of Calabria and Gregory Palamas' is republished here with permission of St. Vladimir's Seminary Press. An earlier version appears under the heading 'Doctrinal Positions of Barlaam of Calabria and Gregory Palamas during Byzantine Hesychast Controversy' in *St. Vladimir's Theological Quarterly*, vol. 2 (2014).

Cover photo: *Christ Pantokrator (surrounded by saints and signs of the zodiac)*, c. 1347-1349, fresco, the central cupola, painted by Michael of Lesnovo, Church of St Archangel Gabriel, Monastery of Lesnovo, Probistip (Macedonia).

Cover design by Nic Welbourn and layout by ANU Press

Contents

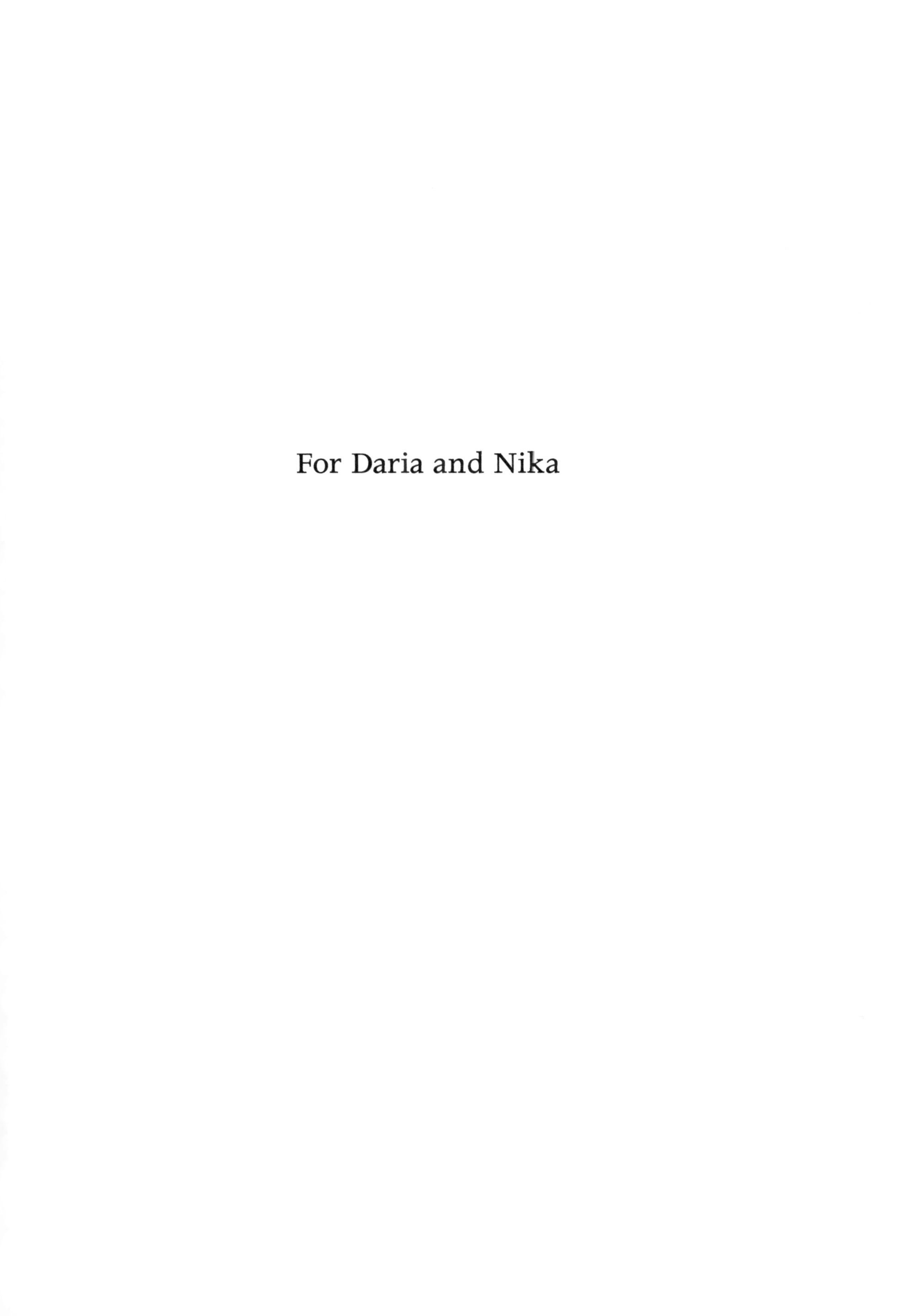

For Daria and Nika

Acknowledgements

I express my gratitude to the many people who saw me through the writing of this book; to all those who provided support, read, wrote, offered comments, allowed me to quote their remarks and assisted in the editing, proofreading and design. I thank ANU Press for enabling me to publish this book. I sincerely thank Professor Sasha Grishin from The Australian National University for his patience, timely advice and careful attention to countless drafts. In a world of increasingly rapid change and compromise, Sasha is an inspiring example of the traditional values of academic rigour, professionalism and critical enquiry. I feel privileged to have been part of such an academic environment.

I extend my deepest thanks to individuals and institutions that assisted me with this research by offering either guidance or support. I thank the staff at the Byzantine Library at the College of France, as well as those working at Gabriel Millet Archives, Paris, for granting me access to rare bibliographical material. Without their assistance, this research would not have been possible. Also, I extend my gratitude to Dr Catherine de Leve for providing me with networking support around France. My appreciation also goes to Dr Nikolay Nenov, the director of the Rousse Regional History Museum (Bulgaria) for his extraordinary initiative in securing my access to frescoes at the rock-hewn churches of Ivanovo. I also thank Professor Emmanuel Mutafov from Bulgaria for his warm hospitality and assistance.

I extend my gratitude to Archbishop Hilarion of the Serbian Orthodox Church, Diocese of Australia and New Zealand, for arranging permission for me to take photographs of frescoes and icons in the churches of Serbia. Special acknowledgement goes to members of the Macedonian Orthodox Church who assisted me in taking photographs of paintings in many Macedonian churches. I am also grateful to staff of the Museum of Skopje for allowing me to access their permanent exhibition of Byzantine icons. I also feel in debt to Dr Zoja Bojic and her parents for arranging permissions to access collections in Serbia. I thank Frédéric Buret for taking photographs of frescoes on my behalf at the monastery complex of Göreme. I thank Associate Professor Vladimir Strezov, who provided assistance during my fieldwork trip around Europe. He made photographs of frescoes in remote churches of Serbia, Bulgaria, Macedonia and Mount Athos. I extend my gratitude to the brotherhood and sisterhood of all monasteries I visited. Finally, I wish to acknowledge the help of the Russian Government in the Kremlin for allowing me to visit their monuments.

I acknowledge my immediate family members, especially my mother Zhana, who assisted with care of my daughters Daria and Nika. Your tremendous help and support during difficult times in my life have ensured I finished my book on time.

Dr Anita Strezova

List of illustrations

Foreword

Although many of the iconographic traditions in Byzantine art formed in the early centuries of Christianity, they were not petrified within a time warp. Subtle changes and refinements in Byzantine theology did find reflection in changes to the iconographic and stylistic conventions of Byzantine art.

This is a brilliant and innovative book in which Dr Anita Strezova argues that a religious movement called Hesychasm, especially as espoused by the great Athonite monk St Gregory Palamas, had a profound impact on the iconography and style of Byzantine art, including that of the Slav diaspora, of the late Byzantine period. While many have been attracted to speculate on such a connection, none until now has embarked on proving such a nexus. The main stumbling blocks have included the need for a comprehensive knowledge of Byzantine theology; a training in art history, especially iconological, semiotic and formalist methodologies; extensive fieldwork in Macedonia, Bulgaria, Serbia, Greece, Turkey and Russia, and a working knowledge of Greek, Old Church Slavonic, Macedonian, Russian, Serbian, Latin as well as several modern European languages, French, German, Russian and Italian. These are some of the skills which Dr Strezova has brought to her topic.

This is a ground breaking study which examines essentially the Christological cycle in predominantly murals, manuscript illuminations and portable panel icons from the Paleologue period across the territory of the Byzantine Empire. The material preserved in the literary sources is dense, but the author treats it with a degree of lucidity and arrives at a convincing conclusion. Although the focus is quite specific, as is appropriate for a book of this nature, the imagery which it touches on becomes canonical in subsequent religious art of the diaspora of the Orthodox Church throughout the world, including Australia.

Professor Sasha Grishin AM, FAHA
Adjunct Professor of Art History
School of Literature, Languages and Linguistics
The Australian National University

Epigraph

As we ascend to that which is more perfect, He who is without form or shape comes no longer without form or without shape. Nor does He cause His light to come to us and be present with us in silence. But how does He come? He comes in a definite form indeed, though it is a divine one. Yet God does not show Himself in a particular pattern or likeness, but in simplicity, and takes the form of an incomprehensible, inaccessible, and formless light. We cannot possibly say or express more than this; still He appears clearly and is consciously known and clearly seen, though He is invisible. He sees and hears invisibly and, just as friend speaks to friend face to face (cf. Ex. 33:11), so He who by nature is God speaks to those whom by grace He has begotten as gods. He loves like a father, and in turn He is fervently loved by His sons.

Symeon the New Theologian, *The Discourses*, 365, C.J. de Catanzaro (ed. & trans), (Toronto 1980)

Introduction

The extant monuments in Byzantium and the Orthodox Slavic territories from the Palaeologan period show evidence of stylistic and iconographic changes in icon painting, murals and book illumination. There is, however, no scholarly consensus on the reasons for these transformations. What initiated the development of an innovative style of Christian art in Byzantine and Slavic lands in the 14th and 15th centuries? What caused the interruption of the 'pre-renaissance' in Byzantium, which was, admittedly, only incipient? Was the development of a new artistic style during this period the result of a revived interest in late-Byzantine society in classical antiquity?[1] Alternatively, were these changes in Byzantine and Slavic art caused by the 'triumph of monastic rigorism', which Palamites supported in the 14th and 15th centuries?

No written document offers evidence for the relationship between the appearance of new artistic trends in the 14th and 15th centuries and the spread of mystical trends during the Palaeologan era. Nevertheless, the two spiritual and theological movements of the 14th century, namely hesychasm and humanism, had some bearing on artistic development during the so-called Palaeologan renaissance.[2]

Urgency to reinforce religious identity by rediscovering the Byzantine roots in Hellenic culture, education and philosophy, underlined the humanist thinking of the Palaeologan era.[3] The followers of this trend in Byzantium interpreted dogmatic truths with the aid of natural reason, adopting Aristotle and neoplatonic philosophy as an essential criterion of Christian thought. This resulted in an increase in literary editions and commentaries on classical texts, the development of secular-humanistic treatises and rhetoric, and the establishment of a new conception of art.[4] This period nurtured a great flowering of arts and culture.

Parallel to humanism, an enigmatic movement known as hesychasm reappeared in Byzantine consciousness at the end of the 13th century. The central tenet of this mystical spirituality was the development of *hesychia*, a term denoting tranquility and stillness, and a psychosomatic technique (consisting of repetition

---

1 J. Meyendorff also posed these questions in his book *Byzantium and the Rise of Russia: A Study of Byzantino-Russian Relations in the Fourteenth Century* (Crestwood 1989) 95–128.

2 T. Velmans, 'Le Portrait dans l'Art Religieux à l'Époque des Paléologues et son Témoignage sur la Société Byzantine', *Art et Société à Byzance sous les Paléologues: Actes du Colloque Organisé par l'Association Internationale des Études Byzantines à Venice en Septembre 1968* (Venice 1971).

3 D.M. Nicol, 'The Byzantine Church and Hellenic Learning in the Fourteenth Century', *Studies in Church History*, vol. 5 (London 1972) 23–57.

4 C.N. Tsirpanlis, 'Byzantine Humanism and Hesychasm in the Thirteenth and Fourteenth Centuries: Synthesis or Antithesis, Reformation or Revolution?', *The Patristic and Byzantine Review*, vol. 5, no. 12 (1993).

of the Jesus Prayer)[5] to achieve knowledge and experience of the divine. The art of *hesychia* existed since the beginning of Orthodox monasticism in the 3rd century, and the monastic elders commonly transmitted this tradition to their spiritual children. In the 14th century, however, Gregory Palamas summarised hesychast teaching and came to its defence against attacks by Barlaam of Calabria, a leader of the humanist movement in Byzantium. The theological debate between Barlaam and Palamas escalated into the hesychast controversy.[6] This dispute concluded with a reaffirmation of the theological doctrines of Palamas and a sanctioning of the dogma of the real distinction between the essence and the energies of God.[7]

The two different iconographic tendencies of the Palaeologan period, did not exclude the plethora of interwoven trends (hesychasm and humanism) as found in the monuments of north Russia (Novgorod, Pskov, Vladimir Suzdal and Moscow), as well as in Romania (Walachia and Moldavia), Bulgaria, Serbia and Macedonia.[8]

The Byzantine art of the 14th and 15th centuries, a period often wrongly referred to as Palaeologan or the Last Byzantine renaissance,[9] was not uniform, therefore, and its evolution cannot be defined in clear stages. The ideas and tastes of each stage are variously reflected in the original symbolic iconography and the addition of new stories and songs. A multiplicity of interpretations and stylistic choices for a particular subject reveals a close relationship between art and theological dogma.

The first trend in the art of Palaeologan era began at the beginning of the 14th century. The religious art in Byzantium showed changes guided by a profusion of humanist ideas. There was a tendency towards adopting classical artistic traits, an increase of new symbolic images, appearance of a temporal element and tendency towards emotionalism. Scholars have studied this phase in detail.

A second spiritual trend appeared in Palaelogan art in the middle of the 14th century. No scholarship is solely devoted to this subject of the possible impact of Byzantine hesychasm on religious art in Byzantine and Slavic lands during the

---

5 I. Brianchaninov & K. Ware, *On the Prayer of Jesus* (Boston 2006); P.O. Sjögren, *The Jesus Prayer: Lord Jesus Christ, Son of God, Have Mercy upon Me* (Minneapolis 1975).

6 Meyendorff, 'Introduction a l'Etude de Grégoire Palamas', *Patristica Sorbonensia*, vol. 3, no. 38 (Paris 1959) 178; Tsirpanlis, 'Byzantine Humanism and Hesychasm'; Meyendorff, A Study of Gregory Palamas, G. Lawrence (trans) (London 1964) 27. M.B., 'Hesychasm: Its Development and Basic Characteristics', *Canadian Catholic Review* (June 1988) 228.

7 I. Ševčenko, 'The Decline of Byzantium Seen through the Eyes of its Intellectuals', *Society and Intellectual Life in Late Byzantium* (London 1981) 171–172.

8 G. Mathew, *Byzantine Aesthetics* (New York 1971).

9 M.M. Vasic, 'L'Hésychasme dans l'Eglise et l'Art des Serbes du Moyen Age', *Recueil Th. Uspensky*, vol. 1 (Paris 1930) 110–123.

Palaeologan renaissance.[10] Some researchers have claimed that hesychasm had a stifling effect on the arts, and it was detrimental to the development of new artistic trends.[11] Seemingly, the modest artistic growth of the preceding centuries had ceased and no new development occurred. Hesychasm was supposedly responsible for a decline in art production in Byzantium in the 14th century. Moreover the Palamite theology, presumably, reduced the Christian experience of direct contemplation of divine light and destroyed the main Christological basis of the iconography, thus introducing a 'de facto iconoclasm'.[12]

Would it be proper, then, to assert that hesychasm had a negative effect on art? What about the fact that this ascetic movement was influential in Byzantine society long before the triumph of Palamas? Moreover the chief promoters of hesychasm, such as Patriarch Arsenus and Athanasius, dominated the Byzantine church during the flourishing of the renaissance?[13] Finally, how is it possible that the artistic trends to which the monastic millennium was supposedly hostile or indifferent flourished in the Slavic lands, where hesychast ideals and literature were widely accepted and propagated? A scholarly consensus on the reasons behind these transformations is yet to be reached.

The corpus of Byzantine art in the late-13th and the early 14th centuries was, above all, the product of a refined humanistic culture; e.g., a culture faithful to artistic traditions rooted in the past.[14] Also, towards the end of the century, classical trends in painting began to wane, and the new idealistic tendencies became pronounced in art. Certainly, as art historians have identified, exactly in the middle of the 14th century variations in artistic patterns and style began to develop.[15] The art of this period showed the world as wondrously animated by the divine essence 'alive to natural beauty, but consecrated to sacred aims'.[16] Instead of the sensible realism, which characterised the art of the late-13th and early 14th centuries,[17] new styles appeared and assumed spiritual rather than temporal qualities.[18] The art of this period often featured a depiction of historical events, such as the victory of hesychasm, represented by the icon of the

---

10 G.A. Ostrogorsky, 'Афонские Исихасты и их Противники', *Записки Русского Научного Института в Белградее* (Belgrade 1931); Arhimandrite Cyprian, *Антропология Св. Григория Паламы* (Moscow 1996); V. Lossky, *Мистическое Богословие* (Kiev 1991); Meyendorff, *О Византийском Исихазме и его Роли в Культурном Историческом Развитии Восточной Европы: История Церкви и Восточно-Христианская Мистика* (Moscow 2003).

11 V.N. Lazarev, *История Византийской Живописи*, 2 vols. (Moscow 1947–1948) 225–235.

12 H.G. Beck, 'Von der Fragwurdigkeit der Ikone', *Scripture Bulletin*, Philosophie & Historie, KL, vol. 7 (Munich 1975).

13 Meyendorff, *Byzantium and the Rise of Russia*.

14 M. Chatzidakis, *Hellenike Techne: Byzantina Psephidota* (Athens 1994).

15 A. Grabar, 'The Artistic Climate in Byzantium during the Palaeologan Period', in P.A. Underwood (ed.), *The Kariye Djami*, vol. 4 (Princeton 1975) 7–8.

16 K. Weitzmann, *The Icon: Holy Images—Sixth to Fourteenth Century* (New York 1978).

17 J.F. Hamburger, *St John the Divine: The Deified Evangelist in Medieval Art and Theology* (Berkeley 2002).

18 Chatzidakis, *L'Icone Byzantine, Saggi e Memorie di Storia dell Annie*, vol 2 (Venice 1959) 11–40.

Sunday of Orthodoxy.[19] Important hesychast protagonists such as Palamas and John Kantacuzenos were also portrayed.[20] Under the influence of this spiritual ascetical tradition, narrative scenes from the lives of hermits occupied the space previously assigned to the warrior saints.[21] New compositions appeared in the 14th century, such as *Barlaam and Iosaphat*, the *Vision of Ezekiel* as well as various interpretations of the Akathist Hymn.[22] The iconostasis (templon) was also fully developed during this time. These iconographic changes occurred due to the 14th-century formulation of the hesychast doctrine of uncreated light.[23]

The geographical spread of the mystical spirituality of hesychasm outside Byzantium influenced the development of new artistic trends in the Slavic lands. Nevertheless, the definite installation of Christian art informed by hesychasm in the Slavic lands remained remarkable for its continued ability to apply the shared formulae of its past.[24] The art of Theophanes the Greek and Manuel Eugenicos, whose iconographic techniques are permeated with the hesychast thought, strongly reaffirms this view.[25] Hence, one may witness an appearance of fleshless, idealised figures animated by a religious lyricism and an exalted spirituality. Such iconographic and stylistic changes can also be traced in the churches of south of Macedonia, and the Aegean islands.[26] The monasteries of Serbia, Bulgaria and Romania also bear witness to this trend.[27] Moreover, the characteristics of Palaeologan art of the second half of the 14th century are the elegant and decorative effects, virtuosity of drawing, and rich and refined agreement of the colours. Such characteristics are present in the fresco cycles of the churches of Ivanovo, Mistra, Kastoria, Manasija, Kalenić, among others.[28] An increase in the number of churches dedicated to the Transfiguration of Christ in the 14th and 15th centuries reveals the hesychast influence on art

---

19 A. Cutler, 'Main Sources of Patronage in Byzantium', *Jahrbuch der Ostereichiscen Byzantinisk*, vol. 31 (Vienna 1981).

20 R. Cormack, *Byzantine Art* (Oxford 2000) 150–156.

21 S. Petkovic, 'The Lives of Hermits in the Wall Painting of the Katolikon of the Monastery at Josanica', in C. Moss & K. Kiefer (eds), *Byzantine East and Latin West, Art Historical Studies in Honor of Kurt Weitzmann* (Princeton 1995) 289–298.

22 S.E.J. Gerstel, 'Civic and Monastic Influences on Church Decoration in Late Byzantine Thessalonike: In Loving Memory of Thalia Gouma-Peterson', Symposium on Late Byzantine Thessalonike, *Dumbarton Oaks Papers*, vol. 57 (2003) 225–239; A. Karthsonis, *The Anastasis: The Making of an Image* (Princeton 1986).

23 M. Cheremeteff, 'The Uncreated Light: Hesychasm, Theophanes the Greek and Russian Iconostasis', *Записки Русской Академической Группы в США* (Moscow 1988) 125–162.

24 Grabar, Byzantium: Byzantine Art in the Middle Ages (London 1966) 188–200.

25 N.K. Goleizovskii, 'Заметки о Феофане Греке', *Византийский Временник*, vol. 24 (1964) 139–149.

26 S.E.J. Gerstel, 'Civic and Monastic Influences on Church Decoration in Late Byzantine Thessalonike: In Loving Memory of Thalia Gouma-Peterson', Symposium on Late Byzantine Thessalonike, *Dumbarton Oaks Papers*, vol. 57 (2003) 225–239.

27 D.J. Deletant, 'Some Aspects of the Byzantine Tradition in the Rumanian Principalities', *Slavonic and East European Review*, vol. 59, no. 1 (January 1981).

28 Chatzidakis & Grabar, *Byzantine and Early Medieval Painting* (New York 1965) 22–29.

in the Slavic lands.[29] Noteworthy is the impact that the hesychast theology of uncreated light had on the development of iconography of Transfiguration, not just among Slavs, but also in Byzantium and the West.[30]

Hence, this book aims to establish the possible relationship between the re-emergence of hesychasm in the 13th century and the development of new artistic trends in Byzantine and Slavic lands during the Palaeologan period (1261–1453). It investigates the background currents, circumstances and individuals impelling the outbreak of the hesychast controversy. It further examines the doctrinal views of both hesychasts and humanists and considers the iconographic and stylistic changes in the Christian art of the 14th and 15th centuries. The compositions of the Transfiguration, the Anastasis (the Ressurection of Christ) and the Trinity are selected to illustrate the iconographic changes during this period. Broad sociological and theological methods are used to analyse the three selected artfacts. There is an emphasis on several key issues: the cultural context, the thematic content, and the aesthetic status and role of images within the theological discourse. Nevertheless, formal and iconographic analysis are the principal means for the study of objects of art in their historical development and stylistic contexts.

Within a basic art historical framework, and drawing extensively on theology, this manuscript interprets the changes in Byzantine and Slavic art and iconography in the 14th and 15th centuries. The first chapter of the book explores the spiritual movement of hesychasm, starting from its conceptual beginnings in the 3rd century up until the 14th century. In addition, this section examines the historical and sociological background of the hesychast controversy. A subchapter is devoted to Gregory of Sinai, who established hesychasm in the Slavic lands, and also to Palamas, the main expounder of the hesychast theology in the 14th century. A separate section observes the doctrinal positions of both Palamas and Barlaam.

After a thorough analysis of the subject of hesychasm, the next two parts of the book examine the possible impact of Byzantine hesychasm on religious art in the 14th and 15th centuries. The first of these two sections, observes the general changes that occurred in religious art of Byzantine and Slavic lands. This section serves as an introduction to understanding the basic characteristics of Byzantine and Slavic art in the Palaeologan period, and their relation to social and spiritual trends, chiefly, hesychasm and humanism.[31]

29 D. Obolensky, *The Byzantine Commonwealth: Eastern Europe 500–1453* (Crestwood 1971) 460–461.

30 A. Andreopoulos, *Metamorphosis: The Transfiguration in Byzantine Theology and Iconography* (Crestwood 2005) 215–217.

31 R. Nelson, *Later Byzantine Painting: Art, Agency, and Appreciation* (Ashgate 2007).

The possible affinity between hesychasm and art is explored in the second section through the study of three compositions: the *Anastasis*, the *Transfiguration* and the *Trinity*. These figurative scenes serve as examples of the impending changes in art and they reflect three media: a manuscript illumination (the *Transfiguration*), a fresco painting (the *Anastasis*) and an icon (the *Trinity*). In addition, the chosen works of art are from three different locations and periods (the *Transfiguration* image is from the second half of the 14th century, the *Anastasis* from the beginning of 14th century, and the icon of the *Trinity* comes from the 15th century). Finally, the *Transfiguration*, the *Anastasis* and the *Trinity* serve as paradigms of theological teaching about the three ways of union with or within God as described by the hesychasts. There is a hypostatic union of the divine and the human nature in Christ (Transfiguration). In addition, there is a union according to energies or grace between God and the saints (Anastasis); and, finally, there is the union between the three divine hypostases of the Triune God (Trinity).

A Byzantine manuscript illumination of the Transfiguration (*Parisinus Graecus* 1242),[32] which provides the viewer with a dramatic visual narrative is the main subject of the first chapter in this cycle.[33] The *Parisinus Graecus* miniature is a composite and captivating image of the Transfiguration, eloquently illustrating the release of the uncreated light of God on Mount Tabor. It reflects changes in the iconography of the event, characterised by development of a new 'hesychast' mandorla, a tripartite representation of Mount Tabor, and variations in the overall reaction of the apostles to the Metamorphosis.

The second chapter is dedicated to one of the most accomplished images of the Anastasis in Byzantine art. It occupies the apse of the parekklesion (a side chapel, in this case a funerary chapel) of the Church of the Holy Saviour in Chora (Kariye Djami), built and decorated under the patronage of Theodore Metochites, 'the real father of Hellenic paidaia' in Byzantium.[34] This figurative scene reflects the gradual shift from the humanistic[35] to the theocentric[36] spiritual trends in art of the 14th and 15th centuries.

The third chapter in this cycle reflects the impact of the hesychastic dispute on art production in the Slavic lands, where the iconography of the figurative scene

---

32 'Refutationes Duae Prochori Cydonii et Disputatio cum Paulo Patriarcha Latino Epistulis Septem Tradita Nunc Primum Editae Curantibus', *Iohannis Cantacuzeni Opera*, E. Voordeckers & F. Tinnefeld (eds), Corpus Christianorum. Ser. Graeca, vol. 16 (Belgium 1987) 3–105.

33 S. Ćurčić, 'Divine Light: Symbol and Matter in Byzantine Art', lecture, Alexander S. Onassis Public Benefit Foundation, Athens (Greece) 2 Jul. 2007; http://www.onassis.gr/enim_deltio/foreign/08/lecture_07.php (accessed 25/08/2010).

34 D.M. Nicol, *The Last Centuries of Byzantium 1261–1453* (Cambridge 1972) 166.

35 Meyendorff , 'Spiritual Trends in Byzantium in the Late Thirteenth and Early Fourteenth Centuries', *Art et Societe a Byzance sous les Paleologues* (Venice 1971) 56.

36 V. Lossky, *Theology of the Icon* (New York 1996) 243.

commonly known as the Hospitality of Abraham acquired a Trinitarian rather than Christological connotation. Andrei Rublev's icon of the Hospitality of Abraham (Old Testament Trinity) is the best example of this iconographic trend.

The closing chapter relates the findings of the assessment concerning the impact of Byzantine hesychasm on the development of new artistic trends in Byzantine and Slavic lands during the Palaeologan period.

1. Byzantine Hesychasm in the 14th and 15th Centuries

In the last two centuries of its existence, the Byzantine Empire, which was restored after the Latin conquest of Constantinople, was politically and economically weak. Nevertheless, its intellectual and cultural influence had a widespread impact upon religious, literary and artistic development in the Slavic lands and Italy.[1] Economically, the split empire was dependent on Genoese and Venetian interests, which were affected by the relationship between Italian and Ottoman authorities around the Black Sea. Politically, the Byzantine state was reduced to a minimum.[2] Sociologically, a significant number of the Byzantine population died from the Black Death, and the power of the state was reduced due to the constant wars between the emperors Andronicus II and III.[3] Given these circumstances, it is not surprising a resurgence of interest in late antiquity occurred that was associated with a new, specifically ethnic consciousness, marked by nostalgia and longing for the past.[4] Humanist scholars Theodore Metochites and Nikephoros Gregoras often refer to this period as 'pre-Renaissance'.[5] The phase was characterised by an increase of literary editions and commentaries on classical texts, the development of secular treatises and rhetoric, as well as the establishment of a new conception of art, with new motifs and subjects.[6]

While Byzantine intellectuals propagated humanism, a renewed interest in ascetic and mystical theology occurred in the Byzantine Empire, under the influence of the mystical movement of hesychasm. In the 14th century, Gregory Palamas synthesised hesychast teaching[7] and came to its defence against the notorious monk Barlaam of Calabria, the leader of the humanist movement in Byzantium.[8] The Palamite Council of 1351 accepted the doctrine of hesychasm as an official dogma.[9]

---

1 L. Chadd, 'From Byzantium to El Greco', MA thesis, Courtald Institute of Art (2004) 5.

2 ibid., 5.

3 D.M. Nicol, 'The Byzantine Church and Hellenic Learning in the Fourteenth Century', *Studies in Church History* (Leiden 1969).

4 J. Meyendorff, 'Society and Culture in the Fourteenth Century: Religious Problems', in M. Berza & E. Stanescu (eds), *Actes du XIV Congres International des Etudes Byzantines, Bucarest, 6–12 Septembre, 1971* (Bucharest 1974) 111–124, 54.

5 D. Geanokoplos, *Constantinople and the West: Essays On the Late Byzantine (Palaeologan) and Italian Renaissances and The Byzantine and Roman Churches* (Wisconsin 1989) 3.

6 C.N. Tsirpanlis, 'Byzantine Humanism and Hesychasm in the Thirteenth and Fourteenth Centuries' *The Patristic and Byzantine Review*, vol. 5, no. 12 (1993) 13–23.

7 I. Ševčenko, 'The Decline of Byzantium Seen through the Eyes of its Intellectuals' *Society and Intellectual Life in Late Byzantium* (London 1981) 171.

8 ibid., 171.

9 ibid., 172.

Even though the Orthodox Church established Palamas's essence–energies distinction as dogma at the 1351 synod under the presidency of Emperor John VI Kantacuzenos,[10] no systemic struggle against the Hellenic heritage of Byzantine civilisation was present in Byzantium. Polarisation between the promoters of the philosophical learning of Hellenes, frequently designated as 'humanists', and the followers of the ascetic tradition of hesychasm, had been a permanent element in the intellectual life of Byzantium since the ninth century. The subject of 'humanism' appeared during the dispute between Barlaam and Palamas because Barlaam attacked the practices of hesychasm.[11] Moreover, from 1351 on, Byzantine humanists could stimulate the revival of Classical Greek literature without interruption. Many scholars and intellectuals, such as Georgios Gemistos Plethon and Basilius Bessarion, were influential in Byzantine society after the Church accepted hesychasm as official dogma.[12] A similar conclusion can be drawn from the fact that the Palamites of the 14th century expressed respect for such authorities as Metochites and Gregory of Cyprus. The brief tension between the two theological and cultural trends resulted in a civic dispute, the hesychast controversy.

Before the historical background of the hesychast controversy is examined, it is necessary to define the meaning of the word 'hesychasm' in the context of the Byzantine tradition.

The meaning of hesychasm

The issue of hesychasm has concerned scholars in the fields of history, theology and art. The interdisciplinary character of the hesychast debate resulted in important findings, but no proper method for studying the controversy has been developed. In addition, there is no agreement on the meaning of the term 'hesychasm'.[13] Nevertheless, the semantic shifts characterising this term, which cannot be used without reservation in the context of Byzantine history,[14] point to four distinct but interrelated meanings of the word hesychasm.[15]

---

10 Meyendorff, 'Introduction à l'Etude de Grégoire Palamas', *Patristica Sorbonensia*, vol. 3, no. 38 (Paris 1959) 178.

11 C. Tsirpanlis, 'Byzantine Humanism and Hesychasm in the Thirteenth and Fourteenth Centuries: Synthesis or Antithesis, Reformation or Revolution', *The Patristic and Byzantine Review*, vol. 5, no. 12 (1993) 13–23.

12 Meyendorff, *A Study of Gregory Palamas*, G. Lawrence (trans.), (London 1964) 27.

13 Meyendorff, 'L'Hésychasme: Problêmes de Sémantique', *Mélanges D'Histoire des Religions Offerts à H.-Ch. Puech* (Paris 1973) 543–47.

14 Meyendorff, 'Introduction', *Byzantine Hesychasm: Historical, Theological and Social Problems: Collected Studies* (London 1974).

15 Meyendorff, 'О Византийском Исихазме и его Роли в Культурном и Историческом Развитии Восточной Европы в 14в', *Труды Отдела Древнерусской Литературы*, vol. 29 (Moscow 1974).

Christian ascetic treatises emanating from Egypt from the 4th century refer sparingly to the concept of hesychasm, although the *Apophthegmata Patrum* from the 5th century does not contain any clear references to this practice.[16] The Egyptian fathers used the term hesychast to designate the life of solitude and contemplation (*anchoretis*), by differentiating it from the practice of a living in a convent or community (*cenobitism*).[17] For example, Gregory of Nyssa designated the monks who lived isolated from human society for more than 40 years as 'hesychast'.[18]

In the 4th and 5th centuries, the definition of hesychasm broadened in Asia Minor, Egypt and Palestine to incorporate anyone who practised 'prayer of the heart' or 'prayer of the mind'. In this context, the term hesychasm appeared in the writings of Evagrius of Ponticus and Macarius the Great, but each writer focused on a different aspect of hesychast spirituality. Both were responsible for formulating the fundamental doctrine of prayer, which inspired the hesychasts of later centuries.[19] A threefold path of spiritual ascent involving purification from passions (*praxis*), contemplation of nature as the work of God (*physike theoria*), and the vision of God (*theologia*) as light formed the basis of Evagrius's doctrine of imageless prayer.[20] The later Byzantine fathers transformed his doctrine of the imageless prayer in the context of the Christocentric spirituality; it became closely connected to the practice of the 'Jesus Prayer'.[21]

The writings of the unknown author with the pseudonym of Macarius the Great affected the evolution of the hesychast spirituality away from a neoplatonic scheme into the realms of Christocentrism (which occurred in the late-5th century). He emphasised the place of the heart instead of the 'mind'.[22] Macarius also elaborated a hesychast anthropology that was more in keeping with a Semitic understanding of the body and soul as an integrated whole.[23] Moreover, the transfiguration of the entire person–soul and body through the presence of the incarnated God and divine grace, which took possession of the heart, was the main goal of the Macarian prayer.[24] It was a mysticism of the consciousness of grace, of divine sensibility, where gnosis took on the meaning of consciousness, without which the search for union with God would be futile.

16 'Apophthegmata Patrum', *The Catholic Encyclopedia*, online version http://www.newadvent.org/cathen/01623c.htm (accessed 18/05/2012).

17 I. Hausherr, 'L'Hesychasm: Etude de Spiritualite', *Orientalia Christiana Periodica*, vol. 22 (1965) 5–40, 247.

18 Gregory of Nyssa, 'In Psalmos', in J.P. Migne (ed.), *Patrologia Graeca (electronic version)* (Stone Mountain, Ga. 2003); *Patrologia Graeca* 44, 298–434; 456B; G.M. Prokhorov, 'Исихазм и Общественная Мысль в Восточной Европе в 14в', *Литературные Связи Древних Славян*, vol. 23 (1968).

19 V. Lossky, *The Vision of God* (Beds 1963) 95; Lossky, *The Mystical Theology of the Eastern Church* (London 1957) 201.

20 G. Maloney, *Pseudo-Macarius: The Fifty Spiritual Homilies and the Great Letter* (New York 1992).

21 Evagrius of Pontikus, *The Praktikos: Chapters on Prayer*, J.E. Bemberger (trans.), (Spencer 1970) 53–69.

22 Meyendorff, *Orthodox Theology in the Modern World* (New York 1981) 175.

23 Maloney, *Pseudo-Macarius*, 115–16.

24 Macarius the Great, 'Homily' 15, 20, in H. Dorries & E. Klostermann (eds), *Die 50 Geistlichen Homilien des Macarius* (Berlin 1964) 139.

Later writers, such as Diadochos of Photiki, attempted to synthesise both Evagrian and Macarian spiritualism, by equating the nous with the heart (a main locus for the experience of God).[25] Diadochos thought that, through the unceasing invocation of the name of Jesus, the intellect could be purified and illuminated with the light perceived within the heart. The main effect of the illumination of the heart was spiritual transformation, leading to acquisition of the likeness of God (*theosis*).[26]

The influence of John Climacus and his masterpiece *The Ladder of Spiritual Ascent* on the later hesychast tradition has been at once extensive and impressive.[27] Although, in this work, he focused on the practical aspects of spiritual life, mostly avoiding the ascetic's goal of actual transformation as well as his vision of the divine light, his teachings were fully hesychastic. The work illustrates the hierarchical ladder of spiritual progression leading to union with God by grace (*theosis*).[28]

Apart from Climacus, it is necessary to mention the contribution made to the development of hesychasm by the Cappadocian fathers, as well as the later theologians, such as Dionysius the Areopagite and Maximus the Confessor, who offered a metaphysical basis for the hesychast 'theology of light'. The Cappadocian distinction between essence and energies provided a corrective to the experience of God in monastic practice.[29] Dionysius's affirmation of the apophatic and kataphatic theology voiced a paradigm for the monastic experience of divine vision.[30] Maximus, on the other hand, clarified the meaning of energy in the context of Christology and Soteriology.[31]

From the 10th to the 14th century, the term hesychasm affirmed the synthesis between the early Christian spirituality of the desert fathers and the hesychast tradition of the middle Byzantine period. It emphasised the acquisition of the knowledge of God through the work (grace) of the Holy Spirit. In the writings of Symeon the New Theologian, there is a more charismatic emphasis on the experimental side of deification, equating the acquired (personal) state of *theosis*

---

25 Nikiphoros the Monk, 'On Watchfulness and the Guarding of the Heart', *The Philokalia*, vol. 4 (Athens 1961) 206.

26 Diadochos of Photiki, 'On Spiritual Knowledge', *The Philokalia*, vol. 1 (London 1983) 288.

27 There are 13 citations from John Climacus's 'Ladder of Divine Ascent' in the writings of Gregory of Sinai and 25 quotations from the treatise in the writings of Palamas; see J. Chryssavgis, *John Climacus: From the Egyptian Desert to the Sinaite Mountain* (London 2004) 10–11.

28 Mark the Hermit, 'Sermons', *Patrologia Graeca* 65, 893–1140; *Patrologia Graeca* 65, 921D, 1064B; John Climacus, 'Ladder of Divine Ascent', *Patrologia Graeca* 88, 1095–1130; 'Ladder' 27, 17; *Patrologia Graeca* 88, 112A.

29 A. Strezova, 'Knowledge and Vision of God in the Cappadocian Fathers', *Theandros*, vol. 5, no. 1 (2007) http://www.theandros.com/cappavision.html (accessed 20/3/2009).

30 B. Krivocheine, *In the Light of Christ: Saint Symeon the New Theologian* (Crestwood 1987) 47–48.

31 D. Payne, 'The Revival of Political Hesychasm in Greek Orthodox Thought: A Study of the Hesychast Basis of the Thought of John S. Romanides and Christos Yannaras', PhD thesis, Baylor University (2006) 154.

with that experienced by Christ's disciples during the Transfiguration.[32] Symeon highlighted the importance of obligatory obedience to a spiritual father, and he also provided detailed descriptions of his private visions of the divine light.[33] Above all, he had no interest in discussions concerning the nature of God; rather, his concern was in how an individual may come to know God.[34]

Symeon is often classified as a major representative of the hesychast tradition in Byzantium, despite having made no reference to prayer of the mind or having insisted on a clearly formulated distinction between essence and energies in God. He stood, rather, as a unique exemplar of the personal mysticism of light, a position he shared with his fellow hesychast Nikephoros the Hesychast.[35]

A new stage in the line of visionary mysticism began at the end of the 13th century with Theoleptus, Metropolitan of Philadelphia. While discussing the relationship between the practical and contemplative aspects of monastic spirituality, he placed the practice of unceasing prayer into the context of Christological and ecclesiological frameworks.[36] Moreover, he incorporated the Dionysian description of the apophatic ascent to God into the spiritual experience of *theoria*.

Hesychasm and Gregory of Sinai

Gregory of Sinai's arrival on Mt Athos at the end of the 13th century initiated a new hesychast revival in Byzantium. He seemingly created 'hesychast international', a universal vocation of asceticism aimed at all people regardless of their ecclesiastical position.[37] He brought the practice of the Jesus Prayer to Athos and later transmitted it to his followers in the Slavic lands.

Gregory of Sinai was born at Koukoulos on the western shores of Asia Minor; during the reign of Andronicus II Palaeologos (1259–1332), the Turks imprisoned him, and sent him to Laodicea on the Syrian coast. After the local Christians had ransomed him, Gregory of Sinai embarked on a lifelong odyssey impelled by his search for God, or by force of circumstances.[38] Later, he became a monk at the Monastery of St Katherine, Sinai, where his ascetic zeal proved to be exemplary,

32 Krivocheine, *In the Light of Christ*, 15.
33 H.G. Beck, *Kirche und Theologisch Literatur im Byzantinischen Reich* (Munich 1959) 360ff.
34 Symeon the New Theologian, *The Discourses*, C.J.D. Catanzaro (ed. & trans.) (Toronto 1980) 245–46 [XXI.4].
35 Symeon the New Theologian, 'Catéchèses', in B. Krivocheine (ed.) *St Symeon the New Theologian* (Crestwood 1986) 358–368.
36 Payne, 'The Revival of Political Hesychasm', 167.
37 Obolensky, *The Byzantine Commonwealth: Eastern Europe 500–1453* (Crestwood 1971) 389; G. Ostrogorsky, *History of the Byzantine State* (New Brunswick 1986) 512.
38 K. Ware, 'The Jesus Prayer in St Gregory of Sinai', *Eastern Churches Review*, vol. 4 (1972) 4.

and his accomplishments were outstanding. Travelling to Crete in search of a spiritual director, Gregory of Sinai learned the method of pure prayer, the guarding of the mind, and the manner of true vigilance from Arsenius of Crete.[39]

This encounter was of supreme importance, for it turned out to be a milestone in the great hesychast movement, which swept through the monastic world. After learning the hesychast method of prayer and contemplation, Gregory of Sinai embarked on a voyage to Magoula at Mt Athos. On the holy mountain, he encountered monks whose zeal was concentrated on practical asceticism and not on *hesychia* and guarding of the mind. Here, he lived a semi-eremitic life and became the spiritual father of a number of chosen disciples.[40] Despite the fact Nikephoros promulgated this method in the 13th century, when Gregory of Sinai settled on Mt Athos there were only three practitioners of the hesychast method of prayer. Gregory of Sinai and his contemporary, Theoleptus, Metropolitan of Philadelphia changed this situation by initiating a renaissance of hesychast spirituality.[41]

Faced with constant attacks from the Turks, Gregory of Sinai left Athos and, together with his disciples, including the future patriarchs Isidore and Kalistos, he moved to Thessaloniki. Later, he wandered through Chios and Lesbos and contemplated returning to Mt Sinai. He never reached Sinai, however, but journeyed to Mytilene, and thence to Constantinople. At around 1335 he and his disciples settled in the mountains of Thrace, in Paroria, where they were under the protection of Czar John Alexander. Gregory of Sinai dwelt in the mountainous terrain of Bulgaria and took no part in the hesychast controversy. Nevertheless, his followers frequently visited other parts of the Byzantine commonwealth, exerting a greater influence than that of Palamas and his followers in the sphere of spiritual life in the Slavic lands.

Gregory of Sinai's dogmatic system was mainly a theological synthesis of the speculative and intellectual mysticism of Evagrius and Symeon.[42] His doctrine of hesychasm was predominantly practical, with an emphasis on outward exercises, manual labour and ascetic prayer. He often reaffirmed the importance of the hesychast life, not just for monastics and clergy, but for all people, regardless of their status in society. To reaffirm the universal character of the hesychast movement, Gregory of Sinai sent Isidore on a mission to teach the

39 I. Pomyalovskiy, 'Житие Святого Григория Синаит'а, *Записки Ист.-Филол. Фак* (St Petersburg 1894–1896) Chapter 35, 21.

40 P.A. Sirku, *Житие Григория Синаита, Составленное Константинопольским Патриархом Каллисто: Жития по Рукописи XVI в. и Ист.-Археол. Введ* (St Petersburg 1909); Житие Григория 15 (33, 7–8); Житие Григория 5 (9, 3–4).

41 Gregory of Sinai, 'On Stillness: Fifteen Texts', in G.E.H. Palmer (ed.), *The Philokalia: Eastern Christian Spiritual Texts*, vol. 4 (Athens 2006).

42 Anonymous, *Orthodox Spirituality* (Crestwood, N.Y. 1997) 131–134.

hesychast method to laity.[43] He did, however, limit the visionary experience of light to those more advanced in spiritual matters, and stressed the need for beginners to exercise obedience to a spiritual father.[44]

Gregory of Sinai initiated an ascetic model based on patristic doctrine of the creation of man in the image and likeness of God. By insisting on the cosmological event of Christ's incarnation, he also addressed the deification of man.[45] The Fall and expulsion from Paradise is recounted in Genesis 3, and in New Testament passages such as Romans 5 and 2 Corinthians 15:22. Gregory of Sinai went beyond scripture and added other teachings drawn from tradition and philosophy. The Sinaite insists on the importance of 'spiritual senses', the role of perception in the program of spiritual discipline, and of the faculty of reason in controlling the senses.[46] He taught that the human soul, involved in the Fall through forgetfulness of God's commandments, became corrupt. Its natural and spiritual senses were distorted, inoperative and incapable of their usual function, that is, participation in the mysteries of the Spirit.[47] This defined the principal spiritual goal of humanity in this life: merging of the natural and spiritual powers of the soul into a single perception under the influence of the Holy Ghost. Gregory of Sinai juxtaposed those who achieved this aim with 'the wise in the word' who have succumbed to their rationality.[48] This affirmed the ideal that if human beings were in better exercise of their mental faculties by shouting out their thoughts using hesychast practice, there was a higher probability of acquiring the supernatural knowledge that comes straight from God.[49] On the other hand, those who were devoted to worldly wisdom could not proceed to the higher stage of reasoning.[50]

In such a framework, intellectual knowledge was a point of transition, from which one could move in two directions: either towards the wisdom of the world or to the supernatural wisdom of grace. Moreover, the acquisition of abstract knowledge was for the 'wise of the world', who failed to control their desire for knowledge and repeated the same error as Adam and Eve did in Paradise.[51] On the other hand, knowledge of God as an effect of divine grace was preserved for those practicing the hesychast method of prayer. The divine simplicity and

43 Ware, *Act out of Stillness: The Influence of Fourteenth-Century Hesychasm on Byzantine and Slavic Civilisation* (Toronto 1995) 9–11.

44 Gregory of Sinai, 'Opera', *Patrologia Graeca* 150, 1240–1345; 1340–1341.

45 Gregory of Sinai, 'On Prayer: Seven Texts', *The Philokalia: The Eastern Christian Spiritual Texts*, G.E.H. Palmer (ed.), vol. 4 (Athens 1961) 207–285.

46 ibid., 220.

47 ibid., 223–40.

48 Gregory of Sinai, 'Words', *Patrologia Graeca* 150, 1240; 1240A.

49 ibid., *Patrologia Graeca*, 150, 1245C.

50 ibid., *Patrologia Graeca*, 150, 1262BC.

51 ibid., *Patrologia Graeca*, 150, 1240A.

unity reflected in the brief and repetitive Jesus Prayer permitted the possibility of divine vision, whereas the intellectual pursuits of Christians associated with the demonic spirit of the world, lead to multiplicity and division.[52]

Gregory of Sinai wrote several prayer manuals, which he addressed to various Athonite monks. These manuals are evidence of the spread of hesychasm on Athos. One of his treatises, *On Stillness and Two Methods of Prayer*, gives concrete details about hesychast prayer practices.[53] Here, Gregory of Sinai mentioned the two ways that can be utilised to confirm baptismal grace.[54] The first way in which the grace of baptism and the presence of the indwelling Godhead was achieved, was through fulfilment of the commandments (the active life). The second way was through the enduring divine memory, permanently entrenched in the hesychast practices of the Jesus Prayer combined with constant remembrance of God under the guidance of the spiritual father.[55]

The full version of this prayer is 'Lord, Jesus Christ, son of God, have mercy on me, a sinner'. In practice, however, hesychasts recite a shorter chant: 'Lord Jesus Christ, have mercy on me.'[56] Other elements are associated with this prayer, such as a low chair on which the monk leaned to concentrate his intellect. The control of breathing involved sitting, the resting of the chin or beard against the chest while the eyes and attention are brought to the centre of the belly, the navel. In addition, a darkened place is required to keep the mind from distractions. The Jesus Prayer contains two parts, and it is repeated either silently or aloud, and the breathing is through the nostrils.[57] Opponents of the hesychasts often criticised this technique and referred to hesychast as 'navel-psychics',[58] with the clear intention of slandering and offending them, as Palamas noted. The psychosomatic technique of inward and outward control of the breath is recommended as a tool to recollect the mind until such a time that the mystic is able to maintain inner quiet.[59] There remained, however, the physical labour, constraint and pain, on which the Sinaite set more store. The kingdom of heaven demanded that violence be suffered, and violence here means the feeling of bodily distress in everything, both physical and spiritual.

Gregory of Sinai introduced a tripartite system of spiritual ascent. Starting in the world of action and ascending to the world of contemplation, it culminated

---

52 M. Angold, 'Eastern Christianity', *The Cambridge History of Christianity*, vol. 5 (Cambridge 2006) 118.

53 Gregory of Sinai, 'Opera', in *Patrologia Graeca* 150, 1240–1345; 1313–1329.

54 Gregory of Sinai, 'On Prayer', 275.

55 Gregory of Sinai, *Opusculum* III, in J. Gouillard, *Petite Philocalie* (Seuil 1978) 241, 244.

56 Gregory Palamas, *The Philokalia: The Eastern Christian Spiritual Texts*, G.E.H. Palmer (ed.), vol. 4 (Athens 1961) 337.

57 ibid., 276–77.

58 V. Antonov, *Classics of Spiritual Philosophy and The Present* (Santa Fe, N.M. 2008) 413–415.

59 Gregory Palamas, 'Triads', *Gregory Palamas: The Triads*, J. Meyendorff (ed.), (New Jersey 1983); 'Triad' II, 2, 7.

in the stage of union with God. The three steps of spiritual ascent were: *ethike* or *praktike*, *physike* and *theologike*. The first stage was that of the grammarians, or those physically engaged in the world of action, who occupied themselves with the purification of the soul. The second stage was that of divine orators, who applied apodictic logic to the universals in the spirit, and recognised the causes of things through reading the creator's handwriting.[60] This was the so-called 'natural contemplation', understood as a symbolic interpretation of natural phenomena, such as the capacity to perceive traces of God's wisdom and beauty in visible realities.[61] The reading of the divine Logos in created things leads to *theologike*, the state of ultimate contemplation or 'the vision of God', realised through the state of the intellect itself (the soul finds its native land, within itself, by recovering its primitive state).[62] This was the final stage in spiritual development, the moment of inner transformation of the person, resulting in inner divine warmth. In other words, a stage of a philosopher, manifested in a vision of uncreated light, when the human person achieves the state of union with God (*theosis*).[63]

Gregory of Sinai also gave an account of the three stages of spiritual life by elaborating on the symbolic meaning of the Feast of the Transfiguration of Christ.[64] His account of the feast clarifies his approach to the theological concepts of *praxis* (struggle to cleanse passions from the soul) and *theoria* (a state of inner concordance between the human soul and God) and adds a new element that was never clearly expressed in the teachings of his predecessors.[65] Following the earlier patristic tradition, Gregory of Sinai claimed that the Transfiguration happened six days after the apostle Peter confessed the divine nature of Christ. This period of six days was a time of silence. No other events of Christ's life were mentioned by the evangelist in relation to either Peter or Christ during this period of six days. After that time had passed, Christ took the three apostles and climbed Mt Tabor and the Transfiguration occurred after a set period of prayer.[66] These are the three periods of the spiritual life, which correspond to the stages of purification, illumination and deification.[67] The first stage begins with the confession, which embodies a complete knowledge of faith and an understanding of the commandments and the meaning of the divine Word.

---

60 Gregory of Sinai, 'Words', 1292D.

61 Angold, 'Eastern Christianity', 121.

62 Gregory of Sinai, 'On Commandments and Doctrines, Warnings and Promises'; 'On Thoughts, Passions and Virtues'; 'On Stillness and Prayer: One Hundred and Thirty Seven Texts', in G.E.H. Palmer (ed.), *The Philokalia*, vol. 4 (Athens 1961) 57, 39–58, 4; 57, 33–38; 60, 8–9.

63 Gregory of Sinai, *Discourse on the Transfiguration* l, 18, in D. Balfour (ed.), *St Gregory the Sinaite: Discourse on the Transfiguration* (Athens 1985) 217–218.

64 Gregory of Sinai, *Discourse on the Transfiguration* l, 98, in Balfour (ed.) *St Gregory the Sinaite*, 275; Palmer, *The Philokalia*, vol. 4; 47, 35–37.

65 E. Hisamatsu, 'The Significance of the Transfiguration for Hesychasm', *Kobe Kaisei Review*, vol. 44 (2005) 129–140.

66 Gregory of Sinai, *Discourse on the Transfiguration* 2, 24; in Balfour (ed.), *St Gregory the Sinaite*, 672, 384.

67 Palamas, 'On Prayer and Purity of Heart', *Patrologia Graeca* 150, 1117D.

The second stage is the knowledge of the mysteries of creation; it incorporates the practising of prayer and commandments. This is essentially an ascent of the body and soul by way of catharsis or purification into the darkness where God resides. It is the period of purifying one's self; a realm of praxis or the struggle for apatheia and love. The third and final stage is when the Christian no longer sees images or concepts, but meets God directly, face to face, in an unmediated union of love. This stage is sanctification or deification, or the time of the vision of God — *theoria*. The apostles perceived this final stage of Transfiguration of Christ on Mt Tabor.[68] In turn, the feast of the Transfiguration is a biblical actualisation of the mystical vision, and the criterion for a legitimate dogma which affirmed the unity of the Trinity and the unity of divine and human nature in Christ.[69] Moreover, the Transfiguration on Mt Tabor was a final and complete theophany of what was indicated symbolically in the previous theophanies of Elijah on Mt Horeb (I Kings 19:1–13) and of Moses on Mt Sinai (Exodus 33: 20, 23), 'the pledge of eternal beatitude in the other world'.[70]

Gregory of Sinai and Gregory Palamas

A number of scholars assert that there was rivalry between the hesychast movements of Palamas and Gregory of Sinai. Others, on the contrary, have affirmed Palamas was a disciple of Gregory of Sinai whom he met while residing on Mt Athos. Both lived in the Monastery of Vatopedi and later transferred to the Great Lavra of St Athanasius.[71] Gregoras, one of the chief exponents of the anti-hesychast movement recorded this fact in his *Romaike Historia*. He claimed that Palamas had as his teacher Gregory the Sharp, who propagated the hesychast teaching on the uncreated light.[72] The historical data was disputed by eminent scholars, such as Meyendorff, who recounted that although Palamas was under the guidance of Gregory the Great, the bibliographical details of that person do not correspond with those of Gregory of Sinai.[73] Similarly, Papamichael states that the biographical details of Gregory the Wise do not parallel those of Gregory of Sinai. Staniloae shared the opinion of his predecessors[74] while Mayer presented the famous ascetic Gregory from Byzantium as a teacher to Palamas.

68 J. Touraille, *Philocalie Des Peres Neptiques: Fascicule 7 Thalassius l'African, Jean Damascene, Abbe Philemon, Theognoste, Philothee le Sinaite, Elie l'Ecdicos, Theophane le Climaque* (Kidderminster 1991) 626.

69 Gregory of Sinai, *Discourse on the Transfiguration* 2, 3, in Balfour (ed.), *St Gregory the Sinaite*, 646, 4.

70 Gregory of Sinai, *Discourse on the Transfiguration* 2, 1, in Balfour (ed.), *St Gregory the Sinaite* , 658, 211.

71 Meyendorff, *St Gregory Palamas and Orthodox Spirituality*, A. Fiske (trans), (New York 1974) 52.

72 Nikephoros Gregoras, *Romaike Historia*, L. Schopen & I. Bekker (eds), (Bonn 1829–1830) 19, 1; 2, 10.

73 Meyendorff, *Study of Gregory Palamas*, 33–34.

74 Balfour, 'Was St Gregory Palamas St Gregory the Sinaite's Pupil?', *St Vladimir's Theological Quarterly*, vol. 28 (1984) 116.

Bones did not exclude the possibility that both Gregorys met on Mt Athos,[75] but Ware declared that the direct contact between Palamas and Gregory of Sinai, while it seems probable, cannot be proven.[76]

Balfour also provided several proofs in support of the claim that 'Gregory the Great' was identical with Gregory of Sinai and that Palamas was formally under his spiritual direction[77] until their arrival in Thessaloniki in 1325, when the two men became, to some extent, estranged. The possible reason was the supposed vision Palamas had in his sleep of Demetrius, patron of Thessaloniki.[78] On the basis of this vision he persuaded many monks to stay with him. Following the patristic tradition of 'imageless prayer', Gregory of Sinai often warned his disciples against visions, and could not stand the company of self-willed men; he preferred to remove himself from that situation and move to a designated place that was suitable for contemplation.[79]

Balfour claimed the personalities of these two hesychasts were different. Palamas became a spiritual leader in own right and began a career as a theological author and a leading champion of hesychasm against Barlaam, whereas Gregory of Sinai embarked on a painful odyssey ending with his second or final establishment in the wilderness of Paroria. While Gregory of Sinai was more cosmologically oriented, Palamas was a Byzantine universalist with a nationalistic Greek orientation. Moreover, the theological system of Gregory of Sinai was for the simple monks and laity, and the theological teaching of Palamas was for the educated monks. Though not a good systematic theologian or an accurate exegete, Gregory of Sinai left a body of spiritual writing, which influenced many of his followers, especially in Slavic lands. He was the prime inaugurator of a mystical renaissance that started in the 3rd century and which Palamas fully systematised during the hesychast controversy.

The hesychast controversy

In the 14th century an acrimonious controversy erupted in the Byzantine Empire, leading to a redefinition of traditional Trinitarian dogma as formulated in the late antiquity. Beginning in 1330, the debate reached its climax at the church council held in Constantinople in 1351, and reverberated in eddies and echoes until the end of the century. The controversy started when Barlaam, under the influence of Western scholastic theology, attacked the ascetic practices

75 K. Bones, 'Gregory Palamas, der Letze der Grossen Byzantinischen Theologen 1296–1359', *Theologia* (Athenes 1979).

76 Ware, 'Jesus Prayer', 3.

77 Balfour, 'Was St Gregory Palamas St Gregory the Sinaite's Pupil?', 117.

78 Philotheos, 'Enkomion', in *Patrologia Graeca* 151, 558–717; 151, 569D.

79 Balfour (ed.), *St Gregory the Sinaite: Discourse on the Transfiguration*, 127.

and theological ideas of the hesychast community in Thessaloniki and Mt Athos; in particular, he criticised their claims to have seen the same light that the apostles saw on Mt Tabor during Christ's Transfiguration. Barlaam was bilingual in Latin and Greek and came to Constantinople from South Italy in 1330. He made an impression in the imperial court by challenging many intellectuals in order to demonstrate his knowledge. Barlaam served as a negotiator for the church union with Rome. He also headed the Byzantine embassy to Avignon in 1339.[80]

In the course of a few years, he produced treatises defending the Byzantine position on the Holy Spirit against the question of the *filioque*.[81] The main error of Barlaam was the use of Aristotelian logic to avoid the theological point that divided East and West for years. Palamas found Barlaam's syllogistic method disturbing and wrote several letters to counter these arguments.

Palamas was born to an aristocratic court family in 1296. His education at the University of Thessaloniki provided him with a considerable knowledge of Aristotle. In his Encomium, the patriarch Philotheus Kikkinos states that the Grand Logothete [Megas Logothetēs, an official supervising all the sekreta (or the fiscal departments) of the Byzantine Empire] Metochites was so favourably impressed by the skill of Palamas in handling Aristotelian methods of argument that he stated 'Aristotle himself … would praise Gregory beyond measure'.[82] After an early humanistic education, Palamas was mentored in the use of syllogistic argumentation in theology by his teachers, and he went on 'to develop into a rigorous champion of monastic anti-intellectualism'.[83] When his father died, Palamas decided to follow a monastic vocation and, after spending two decades in study and ascetic labours, he became a monk at Mt Athos, the centre of all Orthodox monasticism in the 14th century. Soon after Turkish raids affected Athos, Palamas went to Thessaloniki, where he entered the priesthood. He stayed there before founding a hermitage at Veroia. Around 1331 Serbian raids were constantly ravaging the area of Veroia, and Palamas returned to Athos. He learned the techniques of the guardian of the heart (*nepsis*) and the noetic prayer from practising hesychasm on Athos, but his teacher par excellence was his personal devotional practice, and the empirical knowledge he procured through this devotion.[84] Palamas engaged in a bitter dispute with opponents of hesychasm, above all with Barlaam and his associate Gregory Akindynos. Other eminent personalities supported the opposition to Palamas, including Eulogia Choumnaina. Although she was related to the imperial family

80 G.V. Gianelli, *Un Progetto di Barlaam per l'Unione delle Chiese* (Vatican 1946) 185–201.

81 Filioque is Latin for 'and (from) the Son'; G. Schiro (ed.), *Barlaam Calabro Epistole Greche I Primordi Episodici e Dottrinari delle Lotte Esicaste, Instituto Siciliano di Studi Byzantini e Neogreci, Studi e Testi*, vol. 1 (Palermo 1954) 24–26.

82 Philotheos, 'Enkomion', Patrologia Graeca 151, 558D–560A.

83 G. Podskalsky, *Theologie and Philosophie in Byzanz* (Munich 1977) 47.

84 Palamas, *Triad*, 'Homily' 1, 2, 8, in Meyendorff (ed.), *Gregory Palamas: The Triad.*

and was a spiritual daughter of one of the leaders of hesychasm — Theoleptus, she objected to these teachings, together with Manuel Kalekas and Joannes Kyparissiotes.[85] Palamas, however, had strong support from Patriarch Kalistos of Constantinople and the well-known theologian Joseph Calaothetus.[86] Secular authorities also intervened in the dispute, including emperor Andronicus III (1328–1341) and Emperor John VI Kantacuzenos (1347–1354).[87]

Unhappy with the response he received from Palamas, in 1340 Barlaam went to Constantinople to register his complaint against the monks and Palamas. He came armed with his treatises titled *Against the Messalians* (a deragotory term used for Palamists).[88] Palamas was summoned to Constantinople for an official hearing. In his treatise against Barlaam, Palamas made a distinction between the wisdom of the Greeks, on which Barlaam relied, and Christian grace, which could not be generated by intellectual knowledge. He emphasised the role of experience against the use of intellectual wisdom by developing a doctrinal distinction between the divine essence and divine energies.[89]

The patriarch redirected his summons only after the intervention of Akindynos on behalf of his old friend Palamas. Faced with the shocking charges that Barlaam was making against the hesychast monks with regard to illegal conventicle, ditheism and polytheism, and not wanting the dogmatic issue to surface, the patriarch and the emperor tried to bring Palamas and Barlaam together, in order to get them to settle their dispute quietly. After this attempt had failed, a council was called and met on 10 June 1341, in the Church of Saint Sophia.[90] Barlaam, permitted to explain the reason why he had taken the matter up, produced the book he wrote, before he began to condemn the monks. His first claim against the hesychast was his conclusion about the light of Tabor (the uncreated light), arguing it was not uncreated, but created.[91] The second charge was of Messalianism;[92] he exaggerated the implications of the hesychast use of the unique and special monastic prayer, the Jesus Prayer.[93] After these

85 Meyendorff, 'Is "Hesychasm" the Right Word? Remarks on Religious Ideology in the Fourteenth Century,' *Harvard Ukrainian Studies*, vol. 7 (1983) 447–456.

86 D. Angelov,'Към Историята на Религиозно-Философската Мисъл в Средновековна България: Исихазьм и Варлаамитство', *Известия на Българското Историческо Дружество*, vol. 25 (1976).

87 V.S. Kiselinkov, 'Житието на Св. Теодосий', *Търновски Като Исторически Паметник* (Sofia 1926) 29–30.

88 Meyendorff, 'Introduction', *Gregorie Palamas, Defense des Saints Hesychastes* (Louvain 1959).

89 Palamas, *Dialogue Between an Orthodox and a Barlaamite* (1999) 3–4; A. Carile, *Η Θεσσαλονίκη ως Κέντρο Ορθοδόξου θεολογίας-Προοπτικές στη Σημερινή Ευρώπη* (Thessaloniki 2000) 131–140.

90 T. Ouspensky, *Ocerki po Istorii Vizantiskoi Obrazovanosti* (St Petersburg 1892); J. Bois, 'Le Synode Hesychaste de 1341', *Echos D'Orien*, vol. 6 (1903) 50–60.

91 G.D. Dragas, 'The Synodical Procedure followed in the Hesychastic Disputes', *The Greek Orthodox Theological Review*, vol. 45 (2000) 631–646.

92 A piedistic mendicant sect which held that, because of Adam's sin, everyone has a devil substantially united to his soul. This demon is partially expelled at baptism, and can be completely driven out only by ceaseless prayer and asceticism.

93 'Conciliar Tome of 1341', *The Philokalia*: *The Eastern Christian Spiritual Texts*, G.E.H. Palmer (ed.), *The Philokalia*, vol. 4 (Athens 1961) 418–425.

charges were made, the monks, led by Palamas, were permitted to defend themselves. Palamas refused to employ syllogism as Barlaam did. Instead, Palamas chose clear and reliable arguments against Barlaam, which he borrowed from the treatises of the fathers.[94]

After the council, which convoked in June, supported Palamas's refutation of Barlaam, the *Hagioritic Tome* was produced under its guidance condemning the wicked doctrines of Barlaam.[95] This extraordinary document was the result of a meeting at Mt Athos in August 1341, after Barlaam had written his notorious 'Against the Messalians'. The *Hagioritic Tome* presented a new doctrine of the distinction between essence and energies, as well as a new revelation and a new religious age. In the interests of peaceful necessity, Barlaam was ordered to abandon and even to repudiate his position, and the monks were to be freed from further abuse. Being a sympathiser of the Latins, Barlaam returned to the west after his condemnation at the council of Constantinople in 1341 and immediately converted to Catholicism.[96]

The meaning of the complicated period beginning with the departure of Barlaam cannot be examined on one level alone. With the onset of hostilities between the regency of Kantacuzenos and the Grand Logette (the commander-in-chief of the Byzantine army), the hesychast controversy was swept into the arena of Byzantium's powerful political and socio-economic forces.[97] When the emperor Andronicus I Komnenos died suddenly, his heir John V was only a child. The patriarch John Kalekas became a designated guardian of the dynasty, and its chief authority alongside Anne of Savoy and Alexios Apokaukus, stood against the regency of Kantacuzenos, who used the hesychast controversy for political purposes.[98] Moreover, since Palamas was a supporter of Kantacuzenos, he yoked his religious position to the political position of the emperor. Unsympathetic to the doctrines of Palamas, Kalekas worried about the political significance of their aggressive sponsorship of the Kantacuzenos. Thus, due to Kalekas's policy, 'hesychasm suffered eclipse and disgrace during the regency years'.[99] Popular works often make hesychasm out to be an active ingredient in the Byzantine civil war, but this interpretation is unwarranted, and the lines were not clear-cut. Kantacuzenos's camp was anti-hesychast, whereas Apokaukos, who was the major opponent of Kantacuzenos, showed sympathy for Palamism,

---

94 John Kantacuzenus, *Historiarum Libri IV* (Nabu Press2010) I, 551–552.

95 ibid., I, 552.

96 Akindynos, 'Report to the Patriarch', in F. Uspenskii, 'Синодик в Неделю—Православия', *Известия Русского Археологического Института в Константинополе*, (Odessa 1893) 87.

97 L. Clucas, 'The Hesychast Controversy in Byzantium in the Fourteenth Century: A Consideration of the Basic Evidence, PhD thesis, University of California (1975).

98 G. Weiss, *Joannes Kantacuzenos, Aristokrat, Staatsmann, Kaiser und Mönch, in der Gesellschaftsentwicklung von Byzanz im 14* (Munchen 1969) 29.

99 J. Van Antwerp Fine, *The Late Medieval Balkans: A Critical Survey from the Late Twelfth Century* (Michigan 1994) 437.

in spite of political differences between the two parties. Nevertheless, since Palamas was a political supporter of Kantacuzenos, he could no longer either discuss the issue or write about hesychasm. Although one of the regents, the Empress Anna had sympathy for the ideas of Palamas, she had to succumb to Kalekas's policy.

Kalekas provided support to Akindynos, yet another opponent of Palamas, and elevated him to episcopal rank, whereas Palamas received the support of the regent Kantacuzenos, who wrote a set of Three Antirrhetici against Akindynos and another set of Seven Discourses against Akindynos.[100] Akindynos was an Orthodox monk and theologian. He was critical of the teaching of Palamas on spiritual enlightenment, although he had been his disciple. Akindynos was more inclined towards scholarship, philosophy and scholastic theology and was closer to humanistic ideals of the future renaissance than to Byzantine theology and monastic mysticism.[101] He initially tried to mediate the dispute between Palamas and Barlaam, but later criticised Palamas for abandoning the long-established tradition of the fathers and developing an innovative approach to defining the practices of the hesychast.[102] After Barlaam, the instigator of the dispute, returned to Italy, Akindynos carried on the battle against Palamas's doctrines, showing a willingness to stand by what he considered the orthodox traditions.[103] He wrote approximately 76 letters, which dwelt heavily on the hesychast dispute.[104] Unlike later anti-Palamites, he was not interested in the political aspects of the conflict, did not support the union with West, and regarded Greek philosophy in the truly Byzantine tradition as ancillary to theology, and inferior to the revealed wisdom of God.[105] Palamas often designated Akindynos with the term 'chameleon' because he frequently gave in under pressure and signed agreements of submission that he immediately retracted.[106] If God were absolutely transcendent, but could also be experienced and seen as uncreated, one had to speak of a transcendent divine essence and uncreated energies. This is the teaching that Akindynos refuted. Claiming that God is identical with his essence, he affirmed if any vision of God is to be admitted a possibility, that vision could only be a vision of the divine essence itself and its created manifestation. To make this claim would constitute heresy according to Akindynos.

100 Akindynos, 'Letter' 10.34, in A.C. Hero (ed.), *Letters of Gregory Akindynos* (Washington D.C. 1983) 87.

101 Nicol, 'Thessalonica as a Cultural Centre in the Fourteenth Century', *Studies in Late Byzantine History and Prosopography* (London 1986) 126.

102 J.M. Hussey (trans), *The Orthodox Church in the Byzantine Empire* (New Brunswick 1969) 259.

103 T. Hart, 'Nicephoros Gregoras: Historian of the Hesychast Controversy', *Journal of Ecclesiastical History*, vol. 2 (1951) 171.

104 Hero, 'Some Notes on the Letters of Gregory Akindynos', *Dumbarton Oaks Papers*, vol. 36 (1982) 225.

105 Akindynos, 'Letter to a Follower', in Hero (ed.), *Letters*, Letter 19, Marc. 155, fol. 40; H.V. Beyer, 'Nichephoras Gregoras als Theologe und sein Crstes Auftreten Gegen die Hesychasten', *Jahurbuch Osterricichen Byzantinisti*, vol. 20 (1971) 171–188.

106 Hero, 'Some Notes', 226.

When Palamas openly refuted the anti-hesychast sentiments of Akyndinos, Kalekas sent Palamas to jail. A synod was convoked which excommunicated Palamas.[107] He remained in exile until the civil war ended in 1347. Kantacuzenos became a co-emperor, sharing power with the legitimate heir, John Palaeologus. The triumph of Kantacuzenos also led to the revival of the hesychast movement. Serving as a mediator between the two opposing sides in the controversy, Empress Anna released Palamas from jail and appointed him as archbishop of Thessaloniki.[108] Kalekas was deposed, and replaced by Isidore.[109] The Council of 1351 reaffirmed the theological doctrines of Palamas and proclaimed anathemas against Akindynos, Barlaam and Gregoras. The *Synodikon of Orthodoxy*, which was created once the hesychast controversy concluded, contains these documents.[110]

The theology of Palamas was for a time opposed by Gregoras, the Byzantine patrician and chronicler who published several works, including a commentary on *Synesius* ('On Dreams') and a plan for the reform of the calendar. Gregoras was known as a late-Byzantine Christian humanist. He drew some confidence from the wider support of the Orthodox Church represented by Arsenius, Bishop of Tyre (1351–1366), a vigorous opponent of the new mystical theology of Palamas.[111] Gregoras devoted five books of his *Romaike Historia* (books 30–35) to the hesychast controversy; these are identical in context with his theological 'refutations'. Despite his vast encyclopaedic knowledge, Nikephoros Gregoras had no understanding of the Palamites' theological distinction between the essence and energies of God. He spent at least five years focusing his attention on clarifying two main expressions used by Palamas. The first was the word 'divinities' as an alternative term for the energies of God, which, according to Gregoras, implied polytheism. The second expression was the description of human beings in the state of *theosis* as 'uncreated by grace' which implied Messalianism.[112] Gregoras stressed the negative theology, which implied that the only knowledge of God that can be attained by humanity is awareness of all the supreme qualities we attribute to God, is inappropriate because they

107 ibid., 438.

108 G.T. Dennis, 'The Deposition of the Patriarch Calecas', *Jahrbuch der Österreichischen Byzantinistik*, vol. 9 (1960) 51–55.

109 J.S. Nadal, 'La Critique par Akindynos de l'Herméneutique Patristique de Palamas', *Istina*, vol. 19 (1974); J.S. Nadal (ed.), *Gregorii Acindyni Refutationes duae Operis Gregorii Palamae cui Titulus Dialogus inter Orthodoxum et Barlaamitam* (Louvain 1995).

110 R. Mihajlovski, 'A Sermon about the Anti-Palamite Theologian Gregory Akindynos of Prilep', www.ni.rs/byzantium/doc/zbornik6/PDF-VI/10%20Robert.pdf (accessed 15/05/2010); ibid, 438.

111 R.E. Sinkewicz, 'Christian Theology and the Renewal of Philosophical and Scientific Studies in the Early Fourteenth Century: The Capita 150 of Gregory Palamas', *Pontifical Institute of Mediaeval Studies*, vol. 48 (1986).

112 Akindynos, 'Letters' 10, 197–99: 33, 47–49; 42, 81; 44, 81–83, in Hero (ed.), *Letters of Gregory Akindynos*; Palamas, *Triads* II,1.31, in Meyendorff (ed.), *Gregory Palamas: The Triad*.

cannot be attributed to his infinite essence.[113] To believe that anyone could behold the divine, nameable energies to God, distinct from his essence, was not only to exaggerate man's access to the divine, it was to misrepresent Byzantine patristic tradition, the negative theology of the church fathers.[114] Gregoras held actual knowledge of God to be the result of illumination, though, in his case, he interprets this as a mind freeing itself from material images, rather than escaping from a vision of some object other than itself. For Gregoras, the Taboric Light was no more than a symbolic enigmatic manifestation of uncreated light, analogous to the light mentioned in other theophanies.[115] In addition, he often charged Palamas with iconoclasm and accused him of forgetting the importance of the sacred liturgy and the Eucharist.[116]

In the course of a distinguished career, Metochites, who had earlier taken the young Gregoras into his household, warned Gregoras to have nothing to do with the hesychast doctrine. Moreover, because Gregoras upheld the views of some visiting western astronomers, he had fallen into disgrace with the empress Anne of Savoy. In 1351 Gregoras and his supporters were allowed to state their case against the orthodoxy of Palamas, but they did not succeed in convincing the bishops and senators present that Palamas was heretic. Instead, the *Synodical Tome* affirmed the validity of the doctrine of hesychasm, which was in accordance with decisions of synods in 1341 and 1347, and condemned the teachings of Gregoras.[117] Kantacuzenos refused to execute or blind him, as was the customary punishment for such offences, but he went to prison at the Chora church (monastic community at that time) and was forbidden to write and receive letters. At this time, he finished his *Romaike Histora* and dealt with the theological debates of 1351 at considerable length. Gregoras was liberated after the abdication of Kantacuzenos and the assumption of power by Palaeologus.[118] When he died in 1360, however, a mob broke into his house and dragged his body through the streets.[119]

The second phase of hesychast controversy began when Kantacuzenos abdicated in 1354. Another anti-hesychast, Prochoros, raised questions concerning the nature of visions of God and the meaning of participation in the divine essence that subjected them to rational analysis by means of Aristotelian syllogisms.[120] The issues raised were instrumental in bringing the hesychast teaching to its

113 Nikephoros Gregoras, *Antirrhetika*, in B.H. Veit (ed.), (Vienna 1999); *Antirrhetika* I, 1, 8, 23.

114 ibid., 32–35.

115 Nicephoros Gregoras, *Corpus Scriptorum Hist. Byz.*, L. Schopen & I. Bekker (eds.) (Bonn 1829–1830); *Hist. Byz.* 33, 21 (iii, 414).

116 ibid., 25, 1 (ii, 1136).

117 Nicephoros Gregoras, *Hist. Byz*, 19, I (ii, p. 919).

118 E. Fryde, *The Early Palaeologan Renaissance 1261–1360* (Leiden 2000) 379.

119 John Kyparissiotes, 'Palamicarium Transgressionum' 4, 10, *Patrologia Graeca* 152, 734D–736A.

120 Patriarch Philotheos, 'Synodical Tome of 1368', *Patrologia Graeca* 151, 693–715, 698B–699B.

full maturity.[121] The first essential difficulty was the temporary nature of the disciples' experience of the Transfiguration. Prochoros claimed that the light shining from the face of Christ was divine only in a manner of speaking.[122] Prochoros's writings also raised the issue of the nature of Christ's glory, seen at the Last Judgment by the unjust and the wicked.[123]

Examining the treatises written by Prochoros, the patriarch Philotheus concluded that they were full of heterodox teaching and, therefore, he initiated legal proceedings against Prochoros.[124] The legal actions against Prochoros resulted in his excommunication and deposition from priesthood.[125] The emperor Kantacuzenos and Theophanes, the metropolitan of Nicaea, refuted his teachings. In the course of this refutation, Kantacuzenos examined the question of how human beings can participate in the divine, as well as the proper understanding of the concept of light and the problem of the eschatological vision of God. Theophanes examined the distinction between participation and communion and the tripartite division of knowledge attained on the level of the senses, the imagination and the intellect.[126] The teachings of Palamas were reaffirmed and, once again, Palamas was acquitted of heresy. The Turks captured Palamas and he spent a year in Asia Minor, but the Serbs ransomed him. Afterwards, he returned to his episcopal see, where he died in 1357. His cult was confirmed in 1368. The Council of Trnovo in 1360 confirmed the decisions from the previous councils, and hesychasm became an official dogma of the Byzantine church. This period of internal struggle of rivals in Byzantium permitted the rise to power of the Serbian ruler Stephan Dushan, who took control of more than half of the old Byzantine territories.

Hesychasm in the Slavic lands

The takeover of the patriarchate of Constantinople by the Athonite monastic party after 1347 had an undeniable impact upon an area beyond the narrow limits of the Byzantine Empire itself. The ecclesiastical policy sustaining hesychasm and ensuring its influence on Slavic lands came from Constantinople, but the spiritual practice that was widely accepted outside Byzantine borders originated from the monasteries of Mt Athos, where followers of hesychasm, including Gregory of Sinai, Palamas, Philotheus and Kalistos, Nil Sorsky and

121 N. Russell, 'Prochoros Cydones and the Fourteenth-Century Understanding of Orthodoxy', in A. Louth & A. Casiday (eds), *Byzantine Orthodoxies* (Durham 2006).

122 Patriarch Philotheos, 'Synodical Tome', 706A.

123 ibid., 707B–D.

124 ibid., 705B.

125 ibid., 712D.

126 Theophanes of Nicae, 'Refutation' I, 6 (9–10); 'Refutation' II, 1 (109–12), in E. Voordeckers & F. Tinnefeld (eds), *Ioannis Cantacuzeni Refutationes Duae* (Turnhout 1987).

St Sava, spent prolonged periods of spiritual practice.[127] When this spiritual movement became available to Slavs, they selected practices and beliefs from among its component elements, accepting, rejecting or transforming them.

Many scholars agree that hesychasm was a part of a pan-Slavic renewal process, but exactly how remains elusive. Through hesychasm, however, different parts of the Byzantine Empire were linked with each other and to its centre.[128] In a way, hesychasm became a cultural tradition common to Greeks, Slavs and Romanians and assumed the role of an intermediary, analogous to the role played by the Cyrillo-Methodian movement of the 9th, 10th and 11th centuries.[129] On the other hand, Byzantine humanists had neither the means nor the interest to promote their ideals amongst the Slavs, who knew no Greek and were far from sharing Hellenistic ideas and principles.

Adoption of hesychast principles resulted in an interesting collision in the spiritual realm of Bulgarian society that found itself simultaneously under the influence of two opposing ideological currents: hesychasm and humanism.[130]

The beginning of the hesychast revival in Bulgaria has been associated with Gregory of Sinai as previously stated. When he died, his disciples travelled to various places, especially Athos. From Paroria, hesychasm also moved to the rest of the Balkans. Theodosius of Trnovo was one of the most prominent disciples of Gregory of Sinai. He travelled first to Athos, Thessaloniki and Veroia, before establishing a prominent monastic community near Kilifarevo under the patronage of Czar John Alexander of Bulgaria in 1350. Theodosius was fluent in Greek, and he translated the works of Gregory of Sinai into Bulgarian, thus making them accessible in a Slavonic language. This monastery became a new hesychast translation centre. The translations included: liturgical works, writings of the early church fathers, and treatises from contemporary Byzantine theologians. It also contained many vitae of the saints as well as accounts of ecumenical councils. Byzantine chronicles, popular tales such as the *Fall of Troy* and stories of the medieval Alexander were also translated. Moreover, Czar John Alexander commissioned an encyclopaedia and produced the famous *London Gospel*, illustrated with 366 miniatures showing biblical subjects and portraits of the imperial family. Under the patronage of Alexander's daughter-in-law Anna of Savoy (the second wife of Andronikos III Palaiologos), the lives of 13 women were included in *Bdinski (Vidin) Sbornik* (Codex Gandavensis Slavicus 408).

After Theodosius had relocated to Kilifarevo, where he remained for nearly a decade, many of his followers from Bulgaria, Serbia, Hungary and Romania

127 ibid., 478.

128 Obolensky, *Byzantine Commonwealth*, 390.

129 ibid., 476.

130 Angelov, 'Hesychasm in Medieval Bulgaria', *Bulgarian Historical Review*, vol. 14, no. 3 (1989) 41.

settled around him, creating a monastic establishment.[131] The accepted rule of this monastery was the Sinaitic (brought by Gregory of Sinai from Monastery of St Katherine on Sinai). In addition, the Bulgarian monks who travelled back and forth to Mt Athos introduced hesychast practices to the fellowship of the Kilifarevo monastery. Those proficient in Greek translated important spiritual writings by John Chrysostom and John Climacus into Old Bulgarian.[132] The Slavic version of the *Vita of Theodosius* by Kalistos contains references to the international character of hesychasm.[133]

Theodosius was a zealous fighter for orthodoxy against heretics, such as Theodoret, a known anti-hesychast and a magician. Irene, a nun from Thessaloniki, was another of his opponents. She was a follower of the heresy of Bogomils, which, according to two passages found in the *Life of Saint Theodosius*, was synonymous with Messalianism.[134] Due to the individualistic and mystical nature of her ideas, Irene converted a large portion of the aristocracy and clergy to Bogomilism, which severely affected even the monastic communities on Mt Athos. A church council held in 1344 and 1360, condemned and exiled these heretics. Later on, Theodosius fought the heresy of the Adamites, whose exponents advocated shedding of clothes as a means for the return of humankind to a paradisiacal state. Cyril Bosota, a known Adamite, preached the dissolution of marriage. Lazarus, on the other hand, walked out naked and urged the necessity of castration.

After the condemnation of the Bogomils, Theodosius fought against Judaising Christians who attacked various aspects of Christian life, such as the practice of image veneration, and the institution of the monks.[135] An important aspect of the hesychast movement in Bulgaria was the close links between its leading members and Byzantine hesychasts, especially those of Constantinople. Theodosius was a strong supporter of the ecclesiastical primacy of Constantinople over the Bulgarian patriarchate. Thus, when the Bulgarian primate discontinued the practice of commemorating the name of the patriarch of Constantinople in the liturgy, Theodosius protested against this action and sought help from his hesychast friend, Kalistos. Sharing a close bond, when Theodosius felt his end was approaching, he went to visit Kalistos in Constantinople accompanied by

131 V.N Zlatarski, Житие на Теодосий Търновски (Sofia 1962) 65–67.

132 K. Konstantinova, 'Някои Моменти на Българо-Византийските Связи', in *Старобългарска Литература* (Sofia 1971) 209–42.

133 Van Antwerp Fine, *Late Medieval Balkans*, 440.

134 The Euchites or Messalians were a sect that was first condemned as heretical in a synod of 383 AD. The sect of Messalians taught that once a person experienced the essence of God he was freed from any moral obligations or ecclesiastical discipline (church); H. Wice & W. Smith, *A Dictionary of Christian Biography, Literature, Sects and Doctrines* (1880) 258–261; Kiselinkov, 'Житието на св. Теодосий', 1–11, 32.

135 Obolensky, *Bogomils: A Study of Balkans Neo Manichaeism* (Cambridge 2004) 262.

four disciples.[136] Kalistos wrote the biography of Theodosius; the Slavic version of this *Vita* served as a link between the monastic brotherhood in Bulgaria with their fellow hesychasts in the empire.[137]

Euthymius, the last patriarch of Bulgaria, succeeded Theodosius. He was not just one of the outstanding supporters of hesychasm in Bulgaria, but also one of the most prolific writers in the second half of the 14th century, producing eulogies, vitae and epistles in support of this mystical spirituality.[138] Euthymius's spiritual and moral influence was strongly felt amongst his disciples. They regarded him as a 'physician who healed spiritual fevers by his wisdom and most skilfully exorcised other passions and sins right from the depth'.[139] He founded the Trinity monastery near Trnovo, which became a significant literary centre modelled on the Zographou monastery on Athos. Euthymius developed linguistic reforms and established literary standards, modelled on the Old Church Slavonic language of Cyril and Methodius. He replaced the old Slavonic versions of the sacred texts with a corpus of translations from Greek that was new in all matters of style, grammar and orthography.[140] He also introduced new terms into the Slavonic language and subjected translated liturgical and theological texts to rigorous checking. He corrected and revised several Greek texts and banned copies of corrupted translations. Since these translations were not like the spoken Bulgarian of the time, or any other Slavonic dialect, some Slavic hesychasts sensed a tension between the history of Slavic scripture and the new appreciation of scripture that they were gaining from the hesychast teachers. Nonetheless, because Euthymius's changes to literary style were dependent on the Greek liturgical text and syntax, a new sense of universalism arose between Byzantines and Slavs.[141] Euthymius wrote a number of saint's vitae and undertook revisions of liturgical texts.[142] He also engaged in the practice of copying and editing liturgical text, which assisted in the distribution of hesychast practices in Bulgaria.[143]

Euthymius battled against heretics, especially against the representatives of the Barlaamite heresy, such as Piron, who came from Constantinople to Trnovo, and his disciple Fudul. He also refuted other heretics who attacked the

---

136 Zlatarski, *Житие на Теодосий Търновски*, 12.

137 ibid., 31–33.

138 E. Kałužniacki,'Werke des Patriarchen von Bulgarien Euthymius (1375–1393)', *Nach den besten Handschriften hrsg* (Munich 1901) 131–150.

139 R. Picchio, 'Hesychastic Components in Gregory Camblak's Eulogy of Patriarch Euthymius of Trnovo', in R. Lenček et al. (eds), *Proceedings of the Symposium on Slavic Cultures, Columbia University, November 14, 1980* (Sofia 1983).

140 P. Rusev et al., Търновска Книжовна Школа 1371–1971, *Международен Симпозиум Велико Търново, 11–14 Октомври 1971* (Sofia 1974); Rusev et al., *Похвално слово за Евтимий от Григорий Цамблак* (Sofia 1973) 140–142.

141 H.R. Cooper, Slavic Scriptures: The Formation of the Church Slavonic Version (Boston 1981) 109.

142 P. Sirku, *Литургические Труды Патриарха Евфимия* (St Petersburg 1890) part 2.

143 Sirku, *К Истории Исправления Книг в Болгарии в 14th веке* (St Petersburg 1898) part 1, 416.

ecclesiastical structure of the church and the cult of holy images. Euthymius was a restless figure, moving from one place to another, and entered as many as ten monasteries during his life, including those across borders in Byzantium, Bulgaria and Russia. When Bulgaria fell to the Turks, Euthymius was sentenced to death, but later exiled to the Backovo Monastery, where he formed a new school that continued to function after his death. He died at the beginning of the 14th century.[144]

After the fall of Bulgaria, many intellectuals immigrated to Russia and Slavic lands, bringing with them not only Bulgarian culture, but also hesychast ideas and texts. Scholars often refer to this phenomenon as the 'Second Slavic influence' on Russia. Important figures were Cyprian Tsamblak and Constantine the Philosopher. Cyprian, who became a metropolitan of Lithuania in 1375 and of Kiev and all Russia in 1390, made a significant effort to correct Russian texts and to revise Russian canon law. He was also a prominent hesychast representative of the Trnovo School.[145] He brought with him the *Corpus Areopagitum*, which was translated into Slavonic by a Serbian monk, Isaac, in 1371.[146] His cousin, Gregory Tsamblak, went to Serbia and became an abbot of the famous monastery Visoki Decani. Gregory Tsamblak presented a biography of Decanski, who erected the monastery and was subsequently canonised. In one of the pages of his *Eulogy*, the names of Gregory of Sinai, Theodosius of Trnovo and Euthymius are mentioned, thus linking Bulgarian and Byzantine hesychasm.[147]

The Trnovo School lost its creative impulse after the passing of Euthymius and Cyprian, and many disciples of Gregory of Sinai and Theodosius eventually immigrated to Serbia, Romania and Russia. Two of them, Constantine and Cyprian were the principal propagators of hesychasm, bringing the spiritual practices of this movement to Slavic Lands.

Constantine was a monk and supporter of hesychasm under the guidance of Euthymius's disciple Andronicus. He immigrated to Serbia in 1411 and established a school in Belgrade. Constantine served Stefan Lazarevic as a diplomat and, in 1430, he wrote the biography of this monarch. Constantine also instituted the linguistic reforms Euthymius proposed and enforced in his work *On Letters*. Cyprian was a Bulgarian by birth and a man of action, deeply involved in ecclesiastical matters and politics. As a diplomat, he was also a mediator between Lithuania and Moscow. He was to administer the Russian metropolis after the death of the incumbent, the Russian Alexei. His appointment was contested

144 Van Antwerp-Fine, *Late Medieval Balkans*, 443.

145 M. Hepell, 'The Hesychast Movement in Bulgaria: The Turnovo School and its Relations with Constantinople', *Eastern Churches Review*, vol. 7, no.1 (1975).

146 Prokhorov, 'Послание Титу Иерарху Дионисия Ареопагита в Славянском Переводе и Иконография Премудрость созда себе Дом', *Труды Отдела Древнерусской Литературы*, vol. 38 (1985) 11–12.

147 Grigorii Camblak, *Похвала Слово за Евтимий [похвала за Евтимий]* (Sofia 1971) 140.

in Moscow by the grand Prince Dmitri, who held a grudge against Cyprian for having opposed Alexei; he accordingly assigned a Russian metropolitan who could be controlled. Dmitri sent his father-confessor Mitiai for consecration, but he died before reaching Constantinople.[148] His companions chose to conduct a forgery by placing the name of abbot Pimen on the petition. Prince Dmitri soon learned about the forgery regarding the placement of Pimen's name on the list and decided to assign the Metropolitan see of Russia to Cyprian. It was not until 1390, however, that Cyprian secured his administrative position as metropolitan of Moscow and all Russia, and he took part in the politics of the Byzantine patriarchate in Lithuania and Muscovy, thus dividing the Russian church. Cyprian ruled over both parts of the Russian Church until his death in 1406. Later on, due to Constantinople's double dealing in the affairs of Russian church, a separation between the churches was inevitable. When Metropolitan Isidore betrayed orthodoxy and submitted himself to the pope, Byzantium and Russia broke all ties.[149] Cyprian spent much energy in translating Greek texts, copying manuscripts and transmitting Byzantine ideas and usage.[150] On his deathbed, he dictated a unique testament, which he was unable to sign, instructing his disciples to follow the hesychast lifestyle.[151]

The extent to which hesychasm influenced Russia is a matter for extended debate, as is its impact on the technique of icon painting and 'word weaving'.[152] It is true, however, that many Russian theologians from the 14th century were unfamiliar with the writings of Palamas. This is even the case with Sorsky, the Russian exponent of the doctrine of безмолвийе (state of silence).[153] Scholars generally agree, however, that hesychast teachings were accepted in Russia in the middle of the 14th century, influenced by the teachings of Gregory of Sinai, as well as the proliferation of translated patristic sources made available to Russian Christianity from Byzantium. These translations included the works of Climacus, Symeon, Gregory of Sinai, Nicholas Cabasilas, Kalistos and Patriarch Ignatius Xanthopoulos.[154] Also, many Russian monks who were acting as translators and copyists in Constantinople and Mt Athos disseminated *sborniki* (compilation of texts) composed of passages of the works of Isaac the Syrian, Symeon, Climacus, Abba Dorotheus, Peter of Damascus and Philotheus Sinaites,

148 D. Pospielovsky, *The Orthodox Church in the History of Russia* (Crestwood N.Y. 1998) 3.

149 ibid., 44.

150 I. Ivanov, 'Bulgarskoto Българското Книжовно Влияние в Русия при Митрополит Киприан', *Izvestiya na Institut za Bulgarska literature* (Sofia 1958) T.I, C. 56.

151 G.P. Majeska, *Russian Travelers to Constantinople in the Fourteenth and Fifteenth Centuries* (Washington D.C. 1984) 59.

152 Prokhorov, 'Исихазм и Общественная Мысль в Восточной Европе в 14в'.

153 ibid., 106–107.

154 F.J. Thomson, 'Corpus Slavonic Translations Available in Muscovy: The Cause of Old Russia's Intellectual Silence and a Contributory Factor to Muscovite Cultural Autarky', in *Christianity and the Eastern Slavs*, vol. I, B. Gasparov & O. Raevsky-Hughes (eds), *Slavic Cultures in the Middle Ages* (Los Angeles 1993) 184–185.

mixed with writings of the scholars of the Apocrypha and canonical gospels.[155] Several hundred manuscripts containing these texts have survived. A profound change occurred in the content and form of the writings available to Russians in Slavonic Church translations from Greek, under the influence of southern Slavs upon Russia, usually referred to as the 'Second Slavic influence'.[156]

The ideas and patterns of Byzantine civilization poured into Russia through other channels.[157] Mt Athos was a permanent point of encounter between monks and travellers from Constantinople, with an equally strong impact upon Greeks, Slavs, Georgians and Arabs. Furthermore, the patriarchate of Constantinople exercised its administrative powers in immense territories and countries such as Russia, which would certainly not have felt any commitment to the ideas of antique Hellenism, but continued to hold Christian baptism in great esteem.[158]

The elitist character of Byzantine humanism precluded any transmission of secular Greek culture to the Slavs. On the contrary, the mass of translated literature was religious (chiefly hesychastic) and ecclesiastical. The library of the Church of the Trinity at the Monastery of St Sergius contained a number of the classics of hesychast spirituality, as did that of St Kirillo-Belozerskii Monastery.[159] Sergius of Radonezh (St Sergius) began his monastic career at a time when Russian monasticism found itself with few examples of spiritual greatness. At the age of 23, Sergius left the world to live an eremitic life and brought the 'monasticism of the desert' to 14th century Russia. As a boy, he was miraculously taught to read. Later he dedicated his church to the Holy Trinity.[160] Leading a semi-eremitic life of absolute humility, rejection of worldly cares and fasting, Sergius thought that, by praying silently to Christ, one could overcome the limitation of the flesh through the divine energies perceived in the form of the light of Tabor.[161] Sergius's mystical teachings are analogous to Palamas's teachings on the uncreated light (the light of Mount Tabor or the Taboric light),[162] as well as Iosif Volotsky's writings on the spiritual discipline of practicing silence.[163] In fact, a number of Greek manuscripts containing hesychast texts of authors such as Symeon and Gregory of Sinai were found in the library of Holy Trinity. Moreover, two of his disciples, namely, Sergius of

---

155 Prokhorov, *Памятники Переводной и Русской Литературы XIV–XV веко* (St Petersburg 1987) 5.

156 D. Bogdanovic, *Јован Лествичник у Византијској и Старој Српској Књижевности* (Belgrade 1968) 27–30, 194–200.

157 Meyendorff, *Byzantium and the Rise of Russia: A Study of Byzantino-Russian Relations in the Fourteenth Century* (Crestwood 1989) 120.

158 ibid., 121.

159 ibid., 105.

160 S. Bulgakov, *Благодатные Заветы Преп. Сергия Русскому Богословствованию* (Moscow 1926) 3–19.

161 G.A. Hosking, *Russia and Russians* (2003) 76.

162 D.M. Goldfrank, *The Monastic Rule of Iosif Volotsky* (Kalamazoo 1983).

163 L. Muller, 'Epiphanius, Die Legenden des Heiligen Sergij von Radonez', *Slavische Propylaen*, vol. 17 (Munich 1967).

Naroma and Athanasius came from Mt Athos, where hesychasm was flowering. Sergius and two of his contemporaries were proficient in Greek. St Stephen, the missionary of pagans, created the Russian alphabet and afterwards he translated the liturgy into Russian. The Metropolitan Alexis translated the New Testament from Greek into the Slavic language.[164]

This testifies to the fact Sergius and his contemporaries were fully aware of the hesychast movement, had direct connections with Mt Athos and had close connections with Constantinople, in particular with the hesychast Philotheus.[165] In addition, literary evidence found in the *Vitae of Sergius* points to the fact he had visions of the uncreated light. Interestingly, during his life, his disciples Isaac and Simeon saw Sergius surrounded by the divine light during the celebration of the divine liturgy. Hence, Sergius was the first Russian monk to experience visions of light. It is significant to note that visions of light emerged in Russia at precisely the same time hesychasm made inroads onto Russian soil. Soon after Sergius's death, his most dedicated disciples left the Trinity monastery in search of solitude by forming *sketes* (small monastic communities consisting of an elder and a small group of monks). The trans-Volga *startsy* (elders) would also play an important role in the development of Russian hesychast spirituality.

Another prominent hesychast who rose to fame in Russia in the latter half of the 15th century was Nil Sorsky; he learned the practice of inner prayer under the guidance of Paisij Jaroslavov, a monk who was a follower of Athonite monasticism. He immersed himself in spiritual life according to the highest hesychastic ideals. When he returned to Russia in 1478, he noted a decrease in the quality of ascetic life practiced in some monasteries and a lack of monastic observances.[166] He embarked on a journey to the desert, but soon found himself surrounded by monks who wanted to be his disciples. To entrench the *skete* as a permanent feature of Russian spirituality and to govern the monastic community, he developed the *Ustav* (rule), consisting of quotes by such authors as Isaac the Syrian, Climacus, Symeon, and Gregory of Sinai.[167] While he focused much of his rule on practical observances of monastic laws, he considered the practice of the Jesus Prayer as the most advantageous means of achieving union with God. The frequent references to the Taboric light in Sorsky's writings affirm his connection to the hesychastic practice, something he became familiar with through his readings of ascetic fathers and his experiences on Mt Athos.[168]

164 Pospielovsky, Orthodox Church, 46.

165 O. Kovalevsky, *Saint Sergius and Russian Spirituality*, E.W. Jones (trans.) (Crestwood 1976) 100–120.

166 Maloney, *Russian Hesychasm: The Spirituality of Nil Sorsky* (Hague 1973) 37.

167 G.P. Fedorov, *The Russian Religious Mind* (Harvard 1946) 269.

168 Nil Sorskij, 'The Tradition to the Disciples', in G.A. Maloney (ed. and trans.), *Nil Sorsky: The Complete Writings* (Paulist Press 2003) 100.

Other notable hesychasts became representative witnesses of Byzantine and south Slavic ideas, and of literary forms adopted in Russia. An immigrant from the Balkans, Pachomius the Serb, who completed translations of the Old and the New Testaments, made frequent references to the hesychast doctrine of the divine light.[169] Stephen of Perm was a scholar and missionary who acquired the reputation of a good copyist, and translated scripture and liturgical books for the benefit of the Slavs.[170] He assembled a collection of Greek books. Stephen also invented the Zyrian alphabet so he could translate essential books for Zyrian people.[171] Philotheus also wrote a special liturgical office in honour of Palamas, whom he canonised in 1368,[172] and David Dishypatos adjudicated the debates between Palamas and his adversaries.[173] Libraries were established, with more than 200 manuscripts in the library of the Kirillo-Belozerskii Monastery, and more than 300 at St Sergius Holy Trinity Monastery Library.[174]

The hesychast teaching concerning the light of Mt Tabor made a profound impact on the doctrine of the image in Russia in the 14th century. This epoch became a golden age for Russian art, an era that gave birth to such artists as Theophanes the Greek, Andrei Rublev and Dionysius, each of them embodying this doctrine in their own way.[175]

The influence of hesychasm on Russia lessened after the victory of the Josephites in 1504; this compromised the reliance of mysticism on the mystical theology promulgated by Sergius and Sorsky. Outward ritualistic monasticism replaced the contemplative mysticism of the hesychast, and invocation of the name of Jesus was abandoned.[176]

Cultural and intellectual development in Serbia occurred at the same time as the hesychast movement spread to Serbian territories. The mystical movement of hesychasm affected monasteries in Serbia through the influence of the Monastery of Chilandar on Mt Athos. In terms of the production of manuscripts, this monastery superseded Zographou, its Bulgarian counterpart.[177] The influence of

---

169 Prokhorov, 'Pakhomii Serb', in D.S. Lixačev (ed.), *Slovar' Knizhnikov i Knizhnosti Drevnei Rusi*, vol. 2, (Moscow 1987–1993) 167–177.

170 D. Chizhyevskiy, 'Житие Стефана Пермского, Епископа Пермского', *Apophoreta Slavica* II (Gravenhage 1959) 9.

171 Fedorov, *The Russian Religious Mind: Kievan Christianity, the Tenth to the Thirteenth Centuries* (Harvard 1966) 230–245.

172 Meyendorff, 'Introduction à l'Etude de Grégoire Palamas', 168–169; Meyendorff, *Study of Gregory Palamas*, 112.

173 Prokhorov, *Памятники Литературы Византийско-Русского Общественного Движения Эпохи Куликовской Битвы* (St Petersburg 1977) 25–26.

174 Pospielovsky, Orthodox Church, 49.

175 Prokhorov, 'Гимны на Ратные Темы Эпохи Куликовской Битвы', *Труды Отдела Древнерусской Литературы*, vol. 37 (Moscow 1983).

176 L.V. Betin, 'Митрополит Киприан к Феофан Грек', *Etudes Balkaniques*, vol. 1 (Sofia 1977).

177 V. Moshin, 'О Периодизации Русско-Южнославянских Литературных Связей X-XV вв', *Труды Отдела Древнерусской Литературы* (St Petersburg 1963) 94.

Mt Athos spread to Serbia by other channels. Fostered by Athos, St Sava brought the practice of hesychasm to Serbia. He was a Serbian prince and Orthodox monk, the first archbishop of the Serbian Church, the founder of Serbian law and literature, and a diplomat. His biographer Theodosius stated that St Sava had a strong yearning to live a life of solitude and contemplation, and thus followed a strict routine of psalmology and prayers. He took his monastic vows on Mt Athos, where he resided before returning to Serbia. His gift for writing is mainly apparent in autobiographies and poetical works.[178]

St Sava's earlier works, *Karyes* and *Chilandar Typikon*, were a reference for the hesychastic monastic lifestyle.[179] In addition, when Czar Dushan succeeded to the throne and Athos fell under Serbian rule, the hesychast influence spread to the Serbian state. It was not until Prince Lazar opened the doors to many monks, writers and artists, however, that hesychasm played a decisive role in Serbia, where the writings of Palamas were translated into Slavonic for the first time.[180] The constant wars on Byzantine territories led many monks, artists and writers to seek refuge in Serbia. In the last quarter of the 14th century, a new hesychast colony of so-called Sinaite monks of Serbian, Greek and Bulgarian descent formed in the Kučaj Mountains in central Serbia. One of these monks, Romil of Vidina, who was of mixed Greek and Slav descent, joined the exodus of monks who fled the Turkish raids on Athos, and relocated to the Albanian coast.[181] He retired to the monastery of Ravanica and died there. He was a catalyst for the transmission of hesychasm to medieval Serbian monasteries.[182] When Prince Lazar moved the state and spiritual centre to Moravia, hesychasm influenced this part of Serbia, with centres rising in Ljubostinja, Resava and Lazarica. The so-called Moravian school of painting was a creative and contemporary example of art that was inspired by hesychasm. In his *Life of Gregory*, Kalistos mentioned a disciple of Gregory of Sinai named Jacob who brought hesychast ideology to medieval Serbia.[183] He sent several hesychast writings to the monastery of Mt Sinai in 1360. During Đurađ Branković's reign (1427–1456), the constant wars on the territory of the Byzantine Empire lead to a further increase in the number of monks, religious and cultural figures entering Serbia, with the hesychast tradition becoming particularly influential around Zeta, under the auspices of Balsica Helena, the daughter of Prince Lazar.[184]

---

178 B. Žikić, 'Културни Херој као Морални Трикстер: Свети Сава у Усменом Преда у Срба из БиХ', *Bulletin of the Ethnographical Institute SASA*, vol. 46 (1997) 122–128.

179 N. Velimirović, *The Life of St Sava* (Platina 1989) 41–49.

180 Obolensky, *Byzantine Commonwealth*, 482.

181 M. Barthusis et al., 'Days and Deeds of a Hesychast Saint: A Translation of the Greek Life of Saint Romylos', *Byzantine Studies/Etudes Byzantines*, vol. 9, no. 1 (1982).

182 P. Devos, 'La Version Slave de la Vie de S. Romylos', *Byzantium*, vol. 31 (1961).

183 Palmer, *The Philokalia*, vol. 4, 210–12.

184 F.R.V. Miklosich, *Monumenta Serbica: Spectantia Historiam Serbiæ Bosræ Ragusii* (Vienna 1858) 227; L. Tachiaos, 'Le Mouvement Hesychaste Pendant les Dernières Décennies du XIVe Siècle', *Kleronomia*, vol. 6, no. 1 (1974) 122–125.

Hesychasm prevented the formation of a permanent rift in the structure of the Byzantine commonwealth by withstanding the forces of nationalism in Serbia. When Kalistos excommunicated the Serbian tsar and his religious subjects and leaders, the hesychast monk Isaiah mediated between Prince Lazar and the patriarch and managed to repair the broken ties between Constantinople and Serbia.[185] He persuaded the patriarch to lift the excommunication of the Church of Serbia, and Byzantine ecclesiastical primacy was restored under hesychast guidance. When peace was reestablished, Prince Lazar opened the doors to many writers, translators and artists, which contributed to the spread of hesychasm in Serbia. This resulted in the acceptance of Jeremiah, a Bulgarian, as the first Serbian canonical patriarch in 1379. Under the influence of hesychasm, the development of hagiographical literature flourished, more in-depth translations of the liturgical texts were created, and liturgical reforms started with the translation of the *Jerusalem Typika*. The monk and diplomat Isaiah made a translation of works by Dionysius the Areopagite that were the basis of the Byzantine theology. Writings of Palamas and Gregory of Sinai were also translated into Serbian. Despite the gradual weakening and political disintegration of the state after the battle of Kosovo in 1389, hesychasm fortified the Orthodox self-consciousness of the Serbian people and brought to them the spirit of resistance in the Christian philosophy of life, and in universal spirituality.[186] Therefore, the existential spirituality of hesychasm, a spirituality which stressed the importance of experiencing the divine, became widespread throughout Eastern Christendom among monk and laypeople alike.

Doctrinal positions of Barlaam of Calabria and Gregory Palamas[187]

A balanced historical and theological inquiry into the hesychast controversy necessitates an analysis of doctrinal positions of Barlaam, the leader of the humanist movement in Byzantium during the Palaeologan era, as well as of his opponent Palamas, the main expounder of hesychast theology in the 14th century. This study reveals the theological and philosophical standpoints of both authors and finds that they did not differ in principle, as both were followers of the traditional Orthodox dogma. Their respective views on the doctrine of knowledge and vision of God, however, differed significantly. Barlaam insisted

185 Tachiaos, 'Le Mouvement', 123.

186 A. Jevtic, *The Heavenly Kingdom in Serbias Historic Destiny*, B. Dorich & B.W.R. Jenkins (eds), (Kosovo 1992) 63–69.

187 The subchapter 'Doctrinal Positions of Barlaam of Calabria and Gregory Palamas' is republished here by permission of St. Vladimir's Seminary Press. An earlier version appears under the heading 'Doctrinal Positions of Barlaam of Calabria and Gregory Palamas during Byzantine Hesychast Controversy' in *St. Vladimir's Theological Quarterly*, vol. 2 (2014).

upon the absolute intelligibility of the divine essence. He also argued against the use of demonstrative science (a concept borrowed from Aristotle) in theology. Moreover, Barlaam rejected the possibility of direct vision of God. Contrary to this view, Palamas defended the metaphysical antinomy of the Absolute, both visible and invisible at the same time (essence–energies distinction). On the contrary, Palamas defended the antinomy of the transcendent Christian God, invisible in his essence and visible in his energies. In turn, the distinction between the essence and energies of God was the basis for development of the new Christian humanism founded on the hesychast concept of *theosis* (the attainment of *likeness to* or *union with* God).

1. Knowledge

The different backgrounds and intellectual formations of Palamas[188] and Barlaam led them to assign different values to the subject of natural contemplation. Attacking the ascetic practices of Athonite hesychasts as well as the Palamite theological understanding of the parameters of human knowledge of God, Barlaam proclaimed *physike theoria* (contemplation of the world around us via scripture and the physical universe) as a condition for, and not a consequence of, illumination by grace.[189] He believed the hesychast experience was essentially emotional and irrational; it did not lead to knowledge, but to mental and physical states about which theologically confused conclusions were formed.[190] Fascinated by the divine inspiration of the great pagan philosophers, as well as the apostles and classical theologians, Barlaam reasoned a spiritual ideal that represented the ethical dimension of the life in Christ.

While raising questions concerning the nature of the vision of God and the meaning of participation in the divine, which enters into rational analysis by means of Aristotelian syllogisms, Barlaam equated the philosophical learning of the Hellenes with that of theological revelation. He even proposed Hellenic philosophers might have experienced some type of enlightenment by God and were worthy of high appraisal.[191] Furthermore, he claimed that only those who have entered into communion with Pythagoras, Aristotle and Plato and learned from them the laws of nature could arrive at the truth. Moreover, since every vice and passion had its root and foundation in ignorance, Barlaam believed knowledge of Greek antiquity could expel all evils from the soul and all passions. This view, based on a high evaluation of the rational principle and of the achievements of the scientific thought of antiquity, was clearly charged with

188 Balfour, 'Was St Gregory Palamas St Gregory the Sinaite Pupil?', 116.

189 Ostrogorsky stated that 'Barlaam's Rationalistic and Aristotelian Approach Found no Response with the Byzantine Public (*History*, 512).

190 Lossky, *Mystical Theology*, 220–21.

191 Barlaam, 'First Letter to Palamas', in G. Schiro (ed.), *Barlaam Calabro Epistole Greche*, 262.

marked humanism.[192] Barlaam insisted on the existence of uncreated divine ideas in the essence of God, reflected in created images, and on the analogical method of arriving at knowledge of God based on the existence of those ideas and their reflections.[193] According to Barlaam, knowledge through science — understood as a cleansing of the mind from ignorance — became a mode of access to the divine.[194] In a sense, this *habitus* was a condition for and not a consequence of illumination by grace.

Barlaam also insisted on the use of universal truths against the inferior knowledge of individuals in the quest for knowledge of God. In addition, he taught that static divine ideas or universals had been placed by God within the human soul from birth and were reflected in created images.[195] Moreover, he claimed knowledge of God through philosophical science and through revelation could be regarded as two ways of arriving at a vision of God.[196] Revelation through intellect was superior to that received by created stimuli. It was received through imagination, intellectual work, methods of discrimination, syllogistic reasoning and analysis, all of which served as aids that could raise men to God, confirming them to be in the image and likeness of Jesus.[197] Barlaam criticised the hesychasts for the unique way in which they employed the terms and categories of Hellenistic philosophy, thus adapting them to the context of their theology.

Barlaam thought the *filioque* clause was not a matter of an apodictic demonstration. Because the issue was beyond the reaches of reason and of demonstrative proof in either philosophy or revelation, he relegated it to mere theological speculation.[198] Hence, if it was accepted that the Holy Spirit is from the Father and the Son *tanquam ab uno principo* this could perhaps be considered a justifiable consideration. But if these two principles of the Holy Spirit were understood not as opposed to or distinct from one another, but as one principle subordinate to the other, then there was no need for the use of any methods of demonstration.[199] This statement was a simple affirmation of the position of the Latin Church and not an expression of Barlaam's opinion, as Palamas thought.[200] Palamas reacted to Barlaams's attempt to subject divine truths to examination

192 D. Angelov, 'Hesychasm in Medieval Bulgaria', *Bulgarian Historical Review*, vol. 14, no. 3 (1989) 41–61.

193 Meyendorff, 'L'Origine de la Controverse Palamite: La Premiere Lettre de Palamas a Akindynos', *Theologia*, vol. 25 (1954) 602–630.

194 Palamas, *Triad* I, 1, 5; 469, in Meyendorff (ed.), *Gregory Palamas: The Triad.*

195 Palamas, *Defense*, Tr. II, 3, 34; 455 in Meyendorff, *Defense.*

196 ibid., Tr. II, 1, 26; 277.

197 Palamas, *Che Cos'e L'Ortodossia: Capitoli, Scritti Ascetici, Lettere, Omelie Testo Greco a Fronte*, in E. Perella (ed.) , *Che Cos'e L'Ortodossia* (Rome 2006) 272.

198 J.S. Romanides, 'Notes on Palamite Controversy and Related Topics', *The Greek Orthodox Theological Review*, vol. 6, no. 2 (1960/61); vol. 9, no. 2 (Winter 1963/1964).

199 Palamas, 'Akindynos' I, 203, in Hero (ed.), *Letters of Gregory Akindynos*, 15–17; Meyendorff, 'Les Debutes de la Controverse Hesychaste', *Byzantion*, vol. 23 (1953) 104–108.

200 Sinkewicz, 'A New Interpretation of the First Episode in the Controversy Between Barlaam the Calabrian and Gregory Palamas', *Journal of Theological Studies*, vol. 31 (1980) , 489–490.

by Aristotelian logic.[201] Barlaam could not permit the use of demonstrative syllogism in theology because he believed that primordial knowledge could not be applied to God.[202] Instead, Barlaam attempted to prove the highest form of knowledge possible to men in this life is attainable only by leaving the light behind and entering into Dionysian darkness, which is the apophatic form of intellectual knowledge.[203]

In contrast, the major point made by Palamas in his *Triads* was precisely that the darkness of the cloud surrounding God was not an empty darkness. The 'divine unknowability' was a preliminary step for contemplation and transfiguration of man. Further, he argued on the basis of patristic text and scriptures, and wrote a treatise against the philosophy of Plato and Aristotle regarding matters of theological truth. He strongly depreciated the value of intellectual effort, maintaining the primacy of direct illumination over scientific reasoning. He allowed for philosophical work and scientific research within their scope, but believed that when trying to explain elements of faith, this study was perfidious and deceived those who practised it.[204] Indeed, certain passages in the writings of Palamas, also found in the *Conciliar Tomes* of the pro-hesychast councils, which began in 1341, make it obvious that for the hesychasts; their doctrinal argumentation was not so much a rational proof as it was a defence and an act of witness to their experience.[205]

While discussing the use of demonstrative syllogism, Palamas reminded Barlaam that dialectical syllogism, which functions within the four elements of gender, form, term and accident, could not be applied to uncreated God, whose qualities exist only for God's self.[206] Instead, Palamas proposed the use of the demonstrative method in theology. Theological demonstrative syllogism came, however, from the Holy Scriptures and writings of the fathers. It was not in the form of dialectic and did not have as its starting point the principles of possibility and probability, but only pursued truths through proven premises.[207] These premises were always true to their subject.[208] Palamas clarified that the universal axioms and laws of demonstrative syllogism could not be used in regard to divine essence, but they could be applied to things surrounding the divine essence.[209]

201 Barlaam, First Letter to Palamas II, 1–160, 262.
202 Palamas, ' Barlaam', B' 17, 269–70, in Gregory Palamas, Tomus Contra Barlaam et Acyndinum', *Patrologia Graeca* 151, 679–693, 717–763.
203 Palamas, *Defense*, Tr II, 3, 34; 455 in Meyendorff, *Defense*.
204 Palamas, 'Akindynos' 6, 98; 149V.
205 Palamas, *Triads* I, 3, 34, in Meyendorff (ed.), *Gregory Palamas: The Triad.*
206 Palamas, 'Akindynos' A' 9, 213.
207 ibid., A' 13, 217–18.
208 Palamas, *Triad* III, 2, 18–19, in Perella (ed.), *Che Cos'e L'Ortodossia*, 873–882.
209 Palamas, 'Against Akindynos' A 10, 214; 'Against Barlaam' A 52, 255–266.

Palamas opposed Barlaam's contention that human knowledge is of equal or higher value than the knowledge of Holy Scriptures and the patristic writings. He rejected the view that monks need to trust their reason in distinguishing delusional thoughts from the truth.[210] Instead, he claimed only a contemplative commitment to the disciplines of *hesychia*, of solitary contemplation and vision under the guidance of a spiritual father, would result in a Christian religious experience that would transform the whole person.[211] No other knowledge is equal or approximate to this mystical knowledge of God.

Palamas supposed that application of the mind to the higher sphere of knowledge of God or true philosophy is pointless and superfluous. Even if external philosophy could refer to objects of a perfect nature separated from matter and could bring man closer to the truth, it was still far away from seeing God or entering into communion with him.[212] 'He that has in his heart the knowledge of beings,' Palamas stated, 'does not have God inside himself [but] he who believes in the Lord Jesus in his heart, has God enthroned in his heart'.[213] Moreover, since Barlaam simply manipulated the equivalent of geometric corollaries in his theological argumentation, it was obvious that he had 'no experience of the energies of the divine mystery of the Holy Spirit'.[214]

The theological principle presupposed by Palamas was that a vision of God does not depend on human knowledge, and no worthy conception could be attained by intellection. Worldly wisdom, according to Palamas, is not worthy of the name 'human' since it is inconsistent, mindless and foolish.[215] It seems that Palamas preferred to approach the Ancient Greek philosophical tradition as an aid to natural wisdom before Christ's coming required the need for baptismal rebirth, a condition for integration into the tradition of the Church.[216] Palamas rejected the Platonite tendency to undervalue sensory experiences in favour of the intellect and sought knowledge of God not in the metaphysical system of understanding but in the realm of mystical experience.[217] He claimed that

210 Palamas, *Defense* 1 15, 22–30 in Meyendorff, *Defense*; see also, Palamas, *Triads* I, 1, 4, in Meyendorff (ed.), *Gregory Palamas: The Triad.*

211 Palamas, 'Hagioretic Tome', 1228 CD, in Gregory Palamas, 'Hagioretic Tome', *Patrologia Graeca* 150, 1225–1236.

212 Krivocheine, 'Аскетическое и Богословское Учение Святого Григория', *Seminarium Kondakovianum*, vol. 8 (Praga 1931) 102.

213 Palamas, *Defense* 2. 3. 44. 477, in Meyendorff, *Defense*.

214 Palamas, *Triads* III, 3, 3, in Meyendorff (ed.), *Gregory Palamas: The Triad.*

215 ibid., I, 1, 18–26.

216 Palamas did not deny the relative achievements of Greek philosophy or the participation of natural human functions such as the body or the heart in perceiving divine presence, but he perceives this presence itself as not the simply result of natural efforts but as a gift of divine communion (*Triads* I, 1, 21, in Meyendorff (ed.), *Gregory Palamas: The Triad*).

217 P. Miquel, 'Gregoire Palamas, Docteur de l' Experience', *Irenikon*, vol. 37 (1964).

those who are devoted to worldly wisdom could not proceed to a higher degree of intellection, because such wisdom originates in demons and corrupts the 'discursive and divisible character of thought processes of the soul'.[218]

Taking passages from Holy Scriptures and from Basil the Great and Gregory of Nyssa, Palamas distinguished between 'demonic' knowledge and divinely inspired knowledge that was accessible to both educated and illiterate. These types of wisdom were mutually exclusive, and the engagement of one precluded ascent to the other. So-called profane knowledge was generally knowledge of the creator through his creatures and a true knowledge of God. Divine knowledge was supernatural. It could be attained with the use of man's natural faculties under the guidance of divine grace. Whereas profane knowledge was seen as a gift of God accorded to all, spiritual knowledge was taken to be a supernatural gift accorded only to those who were worthy of it.[219] It surpassed every intellectual expression and intellectual light, and could only begin by a divine act providing direct knowledge of God, which restored divine nature to its original state.[220] When God was approached through symbols, concepts and negations, his incomprehensibility was not readily manifested. When God was approached through the spiritual vision itself, however, his transcendent nature was fully affirmed.[221]

In his monastic stance against the Byzantine humanists, Palamas placed negative theology in its traditional ascetical-mystical context, where negation was part of the ascent to paradoxical contemplation of God as 'hidden light', and the most appropriate language to give an account of the experience.[222] Various commentators have remarked on the possible 'existentialism' of the Palamite theological method.[223] While Palamas's theology was not a model of clarity, Anastos suggests a reason for this, namely his awareness of the inadequacy of theological language when speaking about God.[224]

Palamas's appeal to mystical experience involved a rejection of the Platonic tendency to undervalue sensory experience — and the life of the senses in general — in favour of the life of the intellect.[225] Knowledge acquired through the intellect alone could not lead to any worthy concept of God, because this knowledge was acquired through the contemplation of the natural world or

218 Palamas, *Defense* 1. 243.22–25, in Meyendorff, *Defense*; *Triad* I, 1, 9, in Meyendorff (ed.), *Gregory Palamas: The Triad.*

219 Palamas, *Triads* II, 1, 25, in Meyendorff (ed.), *Gregory Palamas: The Triad.*

220 ibid., 1, 3, 4.

221 ibid., II, 3, 31.

222 ibid., 141.

223 M. Aghiorgoussis, 'Christian Existentialism of the Greek Fathers: Persons, Essence and Energies in God', *The Greek Orthodox Theological Review*, vol. 23, no. 1 (Spring, 1978).

224 T.L. Anastos, 'Gregory Palamas's Radicalization of the Essence, Energies and the Hypostasis Model of God', *The Greek Orthodox Theological Review*, vol. 38, no. 4 (1993) 335.

225 P. Evdokimov, *L' Orthodoxie, Delachaux et Niestle* (Paris 1959) 159–161

general knowledge of the creator through his creatures.[226] Ultimately, however, both apophatic and kataphatic theology were subordinate to the vision of God, because God was beyond both affirmation and negation.[227] This did not mean God was understood to be unknowable to the mind, but the mind acted as an intuitive religious disciple and as the organ of spiritual inspiration. His revelation is also a mystery of a most extraordinary kind, since divine manifestations, even if symbolic, remain unknowable because of their transcendence.[228] Ascent through the negative way did not transform the soul and bestow angelic dignity upon it, but the purity of the passionate part of the soul liberates the mind from all things and unites it through prayer to the grace of God.[229]

Thus, Palamas ascribed only a relative value to negative theology. Once absolutised as the summit of what we know of God, for him, the contemplation of God was not simply an abstraction but also a participation in divine things, which was beyond negation.[230] Apophatic discourse was a preparation for apophatic experience, and the most appropriate language to give an account of that experience.[231] The progress of contemplation was infinite — it had a beginning — but there was no end to revelation.[232]

Palamas reaffirmed that the perception of God only goes as far as the contemplation of created things would allow. Knowledge of God, however, procured by the vision of light according to the receptivity of the sinner, was above all other knowledge, since it elevated one towards the spiritual mysteries.[233] Palamas also drew Barlaam's attention to a major inconsistency of his argument: despite the fact the divine was supposedly beyond demonstration, the Greek philosophers to whom Barlaam refers developed a system of theological concepts that cannot serve as an argument for divine transcendence. These are the self-existing ideas of Platonic *eros*, the golden epic of Pythagoras, the spiritual enlightenment of Proclus.[234]

Confronted with Barlaams's denial of apodictic elements in our knowledge of God, Palamas feared the loss of the efficacy of unmerited illumination ensured by the Incarnation, which was central to the hesychast theory of personal

---

226 Palamas, *Triads* I, 1.3; II, 2, 3–15, in Meyendorff (ed.), *Gregory Palamas: The Triad*.

227 ibid., I, 3, 4.

228 ibid., 1, 3, 4.

229 ibid., 1, 3, 20.

230 B.G. Bucur, 'The Theological Reception of Dionysian Apophaticism in the Christian East and West: Thomas Aquinas and Gregory Palamas', *The Downside Review*, vol. 125, no. 439 (April 2007) 140.

231 The hesychast had no need to go out from himself in order to theologise negatively, whereas to enter into union with God he had to go out of himself; ibid., 141.

232 Palamas, *Triads* II, 3, 35, in Meyendorff (ed.), *Gregory Palamas: The Triad*.

233 Palamas, *Defense*, Homily 2, 3, 17, in Meyendorff, *Defense*.

234 S. Yangazoglou, 'Philosophy and Theology: The Demonstrative Method in the Theology of Saint Gregory Palalmas', *The Greek Orthodox Theological Revew*, vol. 41, no. 1 (1996).

transcendence.[235] If God had not become incarnate, according to Palamas, we could only contemplate him in his creatures, as argued by Barlaam and Akindynos.[236] The significance of the incarnation was not only that it bridged the gap between man and God, but also it focused and projected the energies of God, so that they were accessible not just through the sacraments but also through the hesychast route.[237] This ontological gap between the creator and creatures is crossed in deification, when humanity is united to God by grace.[238] Transformation or deification, the vision of uncreated light, and the vision of God must be understood only in the context of human salvation, which is a factual and non-symbolic vision of God. John Romanides maintains Barlaams's theological formulation was old-fashioned and entirely Western and Augustan.[239]

2. Vision

Palamas spoke about the uncreated light of the Transfiguration on Mt Tabor, whereas Barlaam perceived this light as being created. On the basis of a simplistic understanding of the apophatic theology of Dionysius, Barlaam argued that it was impossible to make any claims with respect to the inner life of the Trinity, and that any revelation — anything that can be seen — must be a creation of God, and not God himself.[240] He also denied the reality of divine energies and claimed anything that was outside the essence had a beginning and was created in time.[241]

Barlaam maintained it was impossible to obtain vision of the Taboric light because it was a temporary phenomenon, like all God's creations. If the hesychast were affirming this phenomenon was permanent, they were supposedly claiming to see the Godhead, which is impossible. His belief 'God makes himself known only through his creatures' predicated that if the apostles on Mt Tabor, through the light of Christ, knew God then that light had to be sensory and created.[242] He also posited that if we love those activities, which are common to the passionate part of the soul, the body thus nails the soul to the body and fills it with darkness.[243] Barlaam believed revelations in the Old and New Testaments were not a vision of divinity, but were rather temporary revelations, which

235 G. D'Onofrio & B. Struder, *The History of Theology: Middle Ages* (2008) 496.

236 Palamas, 'Homily 16', *Patrologia Graeca* 151, 204A, in Gregory Palamas, 'Operum Coninuatio', *Patrologia Graeca* 151, 9–551.

237 ibid., *Defense*, II, 3, 29, 46, 54; III, 1, 10, 16, 17, 19, 20; III, 3, 5; I, 1, passim, in Meyendorff, *Defense*.

238 Palamas, *Triads* II, 3, 52, in Meyendorff (ed.), *Gregory Palamas: The Triad.*

239 Romanides, 'Palamite Controversy'.

240 Bucur, 'Dionysian Apophaticism', 140.

241 Palamas, *Triad* III, 2, 3, in Perella (ed.), *Che Cos'e L'Ortodossia*, 852.

242 Palamas, *Triads* II, 3, 64, in Meyendorff (ed.), *Gregory Palamas: The Triad.*

243 ibid., II, 2, 12.

symbolised divinity. Barlaam stated that the incomprehensible nature of God cannot be recognised in the immediate vision of God, but rather can only be approached and mediated through symbols, abstract concepts and negations.[244]

Barlaam had a different perception of the status of symbols than Palamas; for him the symbol was something other than the reality it represented. He considered any illumination to be a symbolic creation and imaginary illusion, which was inferior to the revelation of truth through the intellect alone.[245] Following the thought of Augustine and Thomas Aquinas, Barlaam distinguished between created glory, in which the elect had the opportunity to see the divine essence, and uncreated glory, which the divine essence represented.[246] From this premise, he claimed that the lights manifested by God to the saints were only symbolic visions, illusions of immaterial and intelligible realities, which made themselves known through the imagination in particular circumstances. In effect, in each separate case of revelation, a created glory came into existence and passed out of existence. Barlaam even thought the illumination on Tabor at the time of the saviour's Transfiguration, and the one when the Holy Spirit descended, were clearly perceivable by the senses.[247] Both were created and sensible symbols of divinity, visible through the medium of air to the senses of the apostles and later disappearing.[248] Proof of the created nature of the light was the fact that the intellect became aware of the vision of the Transfiguration only after abstraction from the imagination was achieved.[249] Barlaam thought it was impossible for a reality which was immaterial, unchangeable and transcends the senses and the mind not to be the super-essential essence of God, for only the divine nature bears these characteristics.[250]

The term symbol, on the other hand, had a different meaning for Palamas: it could either be derived from the nature of the object of which it was a symbol, or belong to a different nature. A natural symbol always accompanied the nature that manifested it, whereas the symbol that derived from another nature existed before and after the object it symbolised. Finally, the symbol lacking independent existence appeared as soon as the object appeared; it disappeared as soon as the object disappeared.[251] Therefore, if the light of Tabor was a symbol, either it had its own existence or it was a phantom without substance. When Christ was transfigured on Mt Tabor, however, he did not put on a quality that he did not previously possess, rather, he revealed to his disciples who he truly was:

244 ibid., II, 3, 57.
245 Romanides, 'Palamite Controversy', 194.
246 Palamas, *Defense*, *Triad*, III, 1, 13, 667, in Meyendorff, *Defense*.
247 Palamas, *Triads* I, III, 31, in Meyendorff (ed.), *Gregory Palamas: The Triad*.
248 ibid., III, 1, 12.
249 ibid., I, 3; II, 3, 5; 395, 409.
250 ibid., II, 2, 25.
251 ibid., III, 1, 13.

> The true light and the radiance of glory. For if this light was an independent reality separate from the nature of Christ, than he would be composed of three natures and three essences: the human, the divine and the nature of the light.[252]

Even though the light of Transfiguration existed from the beginning and will remain in existence for eternity, a transformation of the senses occurred at the time of the event and produced change in the eyes of the apostles. As the need for symbols in one's knowledge of God is done away with only during the supra-rational union with and vision of God by deification, the experience of these men who were taken up into God's glory was expressed by symbolic words and imagery. Those who attain this state of glorification transcend all created words and concepts and experience an ineffable contact with God, who is an indescribable *Hyper-Icon*. When they communicate their revelation to human beings, however, they do use words and concepts.[253]

Palamas tried to prove that the glory revealed to prophets, apostles and saints was identical with the eternal light of God's eschatological glory; hence these lights were uncreated. Moreover, there was no question about this light's visibility in the future age by means of air or any created light. It was only within the uncreated light that one could see the deified and divinised glory.[254] This vision transcended the senses and the intellect, and Barlaams's contention that this glory was directly experienced by the senses alone was utterly wrong.[255] In fact, the revelatory experiences of the saints, that of the apostles on Tabor and all visionary experiences of light before and after the Resurrection, were identical.[256] Yet, all these visions of the glory of God could be seen only by means of grace. The light was not an essence of God, for that was incommunicable; it was not an angel, for visions of angels take place in various ways according to the capacity of those who behold them; nor was it the very essence of the mind under the form of light, because the mind beheld other mystical and supernatural inexpressible ways, and his expressions about God are not conjectures, but are based on having true vision and practical experience of Him.[257] He reaffirmed the Dionysian view that during the super-rational union with and vision of God in *theosis*, the need for created symbols is abolished. This union takes place by virtue of a cessation of all intellectual activity; it is something that goes beyond abstraction.[258]

252 ibid., III, 1, 16.

253 A. Giakalis, *Images of the Divine: The Theology of Icons at the Seventh Ecumenical Council* (New York1994) 60.

254 Palamas, *Triad* I, 3, 36, in Perella (ed.), *Che Cos'e L'Ortodossia*, 189; III, 1, in Perella (ed.), *Che Cos'e L'Ortodossia*, 591.

255 ibid., II, 3, 34; 455; 51–52; 491ff.

256 ibid., I, 3, 5; 117.

257 Palamas, *Triads* III, 1, 12, in Meyendorff (ed.), *Gregory Palamas: The Triad*.

258 ibid., I, 3, 17.

Against Barlaam, Palamas demonstrated that Dionysian darkness was another name for the unapproachable light in which God dwells. It was often referred to as both knowing and unknowing, seeing and not seeing, and not a subject of knowledge in general.[259] For Palamas, the Taboric light was not simply an external phenomenon but an *enhypostatic symbol*, that is, it was both a symbol of the divinity and the divine. It had no independent hypostasis or existence of its own and occupied the space between the self-subsistent and the accidental.[260] It was enhypostatic not because it went beyond not having a hypostasis of its own, but because the Spirit sent it into the hypostasis of another in which it was contemplated.[261] He perceived, however, a certain duality in the contemplation of the light: in one aspect, it was the apprehension of the power, wisdom and providence of God (knowledge of God through the creatures), and in another, it was the contemplation of the glory of his nature bestowed on all who have manifested their faith through their works.[262] The second type of contemplation was not a form of 'knowledge', since nothing surpassed the indwelling and manifestation of God in men because of its transcendence.[263]

One of the keys to the vision of God, according to Palamas, was the notion of realised eschatology, which is the link to various aspects of his theology.[264] The light of Mt Tabor, the glory, splendour, power, kingdom and divinity of the Holy Trinity is 'the mystery of the eighth day',[265] the vision of the resurrected and ascended person of Christ in glory and the vision of the kingdom of God having come into its power.[266] The uncreated light was not sensible or intelligible, but spiritual and divine, and far away from all created cognitive faculties in its transcendence.[267]

Palamas distinguishes between three classes of Christians: those who possess direct personal experience of divine energies; those who do not have such experience but trust those who have it; and those who, due to lack of experience of their own, refuse to believe that such knowledge is possible.[268] He also differentiates between the light apprehended by the senses (which shows us objects perceivable by the senses), the light of the intellect (which makes clear the truth about our thinking), and the uncreated light transcending both

259 Palamas, *Triad* II, 3, 34, in Perella (ed.), *Che Cos'e L'Ortodossia*, 455; 53, 493.
260 Palamas, *Triads* III, 1, 18, 802, in Meyendorff (ed.), *Gregory Palamas: The Triad*.
261 ibid., III, 1, 9.
262 ibid., II, 3, 15.
263 ibid., II, 3, 18.
264 Meyendorff, *A Study of Gregory Palamas*, 126.
265 D. Rogich, 'Homily 34 of Gregory Palamas', *The Greek Orthodox Theological Review*, vol. 33, no. 2 (1988).
266 ibid., 147.
267 Palamas, *Triads* III, 2, 14, in Meyendorff (ed.), *Gregory Palamas: The Triad*.
268 A.M. Allchin, 'The Appeal to Experience in the *Triads* of St Gregory Palamas', in F.L. Cross (ed.), *Studia Patristica*, vol. 8 (Berlin 1966).

(which was known only to God and those who had experience of this grace). It was only by becoming God by grace that one saw God by means of God, not only in the future age but also in this life, both before and after the Incarnation.[269]

For Palamas, the cessation of all intellectual activity and the resulting union with the light is granted solely to those who have purified their hearts and received grace.[270] The vision is granted, however, in proportion to the practice of what is pleasing to God, assiduity in prayer and the longing of one's soul for God.[271] Palamas upholds the view that the capacity for divine illumination in the faithful is always dependent on the receptivity of the seer, resulting in the illumination of divine grace, a constant vision of light and vision of things in the light.[272] Palamas recognised the restrictions and limitations of theological knowledge about God. He went so far as to state that God so transcends the senses that men cannot possibly model God's characteristics after created beings.[273] Humanity beholds God as light, not in his essence or as He is reflected in created beings. Rather, through purification of the senses, the intellect enters the heart and God is seen noetically through a spiritual facility.[274]

The illumination of this light is less bright for beginners, whereas in those reaching the highest state of mystical contemplation, the light is perceived as brightness by which the mind has been enriched through the grace of God as a deifying gift.[275] *Theosis*, as grace of the Holy Spirit, coincides with the kingdom of God, and the light of Transfiguration on Mt Tabor, along with the light experienced by the saints here on earth, is the light of the future age.[276] It is experienced as the apocalyptic knowledge of righteousness, holiness and freedom, not visible to those who have not transformed their senses.[277] Although divine grace was always present in saints as supernatural and divine participation, this grace is manifested only when it is necessary. Because *theosis* presupposes full union of man with God, it is considered to be far superior to any other vision of light.[278]

Similar arguments were found in the *Five Discourses on the Taboric Light* written by Theophanes, the third bishop of Nicaea during the latter stage of the hesychast

---

269 Palamas, *Triad* II, 3, 52, in Perella (ed.), *Che Cos'e L'Ortodossia*, 491–93.

270 Palamas, *Triad* 1, 3, 17 in Meyendorff (ed.), *Gregory Palamas: The Triad* 35.

271 ibid., I, 3, 22.

272 ibid., I, 3, 17.

273 ibid., *Triad* I, 3, 5.

274 ibid., *Triad* I, 3, 15.

275 Palamas, *Defense*, Homily, 2, 3, 11, in Meyendorff, *Defense*.

276 ibid., 2, 2, 14.

277 D. Tselengidis, 'The Contribution of Saint Gregory Palamas to Hesychasm: Theological Pressumposition of the Life in the Holy Spirit', http://www.saintnicodemos.org/documents/Final_Tselengides_Word.pdf (accessed 10/09/2011).

278 Palamas, 'Περί Θείας και Θεοποιού Μεθέξεως 7', in P. Chrestou (ed.), *Gregory Palamas: Works*, vol. 3 (Thessaloniki 1962–1972) 212–261.

controversy. These are sophisticated treatises on the nature of our participation in God. Theophanes argues that to deny the reality of the vision of the Taboric light is equivalent to denying the reality of divine communion in the body and blood of Christ in the Eucharist. The second issue Theophanes addresses is the nature of the divine light, which, according to him, is not a symbol of the Godhead but rather a symbol of the incomprehensibility of the Godhead.[279]

3. Body

Much of Barlaams's initial attack took the form of *ad hominem diatribes* against the practices and mentalities of the hesychasts, not merely against their views on knowledge and the vision of God. On one occasion, Barlaam encountered a hesychast in Thessaloniki, who claimed a body participating in the hesychast method of prayer could sense divine grace in the form of a vision of uncreated light. Barlaam became indignant with this, and often referred to hesychasts as being *'omphalopsychoi'* — having their soul in their navel — and accused them of trying to see the invisible God by visual means. Barlaam ridiculed hesychasts as people who were trying to get the essence of the intellect into the body, while according to him, the two are not separate.[280] He argued the mind, being that part of man most characteristically made in the image of God, was bodiless.[281] His critique of the visionary mysticism of hesychasm was drawn from patristic sources, which supported the idea that perception of the highest realities is reserved to a higher faculty of the soul (*nous*). Barlaam was scandalised by the idea that the human body could be transfixed by the mind and dismissive of hesychast bows, prostrations, incense and breathing techniques.[282] He had a negative view of both the emotions and the body,[283] which played an important role in the hesychast experience, and accused the hesychasts of believing the essence of God to be a perceivable light.[284] Barlaam believed that human beings must first awaken their dormant rationality through exposing their analytical and logical faculties to all kinds of knowledge before they can transcend the purely human level and ascend to God.[285]

Fully aware of the vulnerability of his position, Palamas visited Constantinople to inform himself of the charges of Messalianism, and responded to the accusation

279 Louth, 'Light, Vision and Religious Experience in Byzantium', *The Presence of Light: Divine Radiance and Religious Experience* (Chicago 2004) 100.

280 Palamas, *Triad* I, 2, 71–73; II, 2, 25; 373–75, 35, in Meyendorff (ed.), *Gregory Palamas: The Triad*.

281 Barlaam, First Letter to Palamas, 5, 316.

282 R.H. Schmidt, *God Seekers: Twenty Centuries of Christian Spiritualities* (Grand Rapids 2008) 129.

283 Palamas, *Triad* II, 3, 12, in Meyendorff (ed.), *Gregory Palamas: The Triad*.

284 Schiro, Barlaam, 302, 303, 566–570.

285 Barlaam did not accept the hesychast contention that the heart, or the mind in the heart, was the organ for potential perception of the divine light (Sinkewicz, 'The Doctrine of the Knowledge of God in the Early Writings of Barlaam the Calabrian', *Mediaeval Studies*, vol. 44 (1982) 210, 238–239).

with the treatises *On Theosis*, making up the third of his *Triads*.[286] Irrespective of their social preferences for 'inner perfection', the Byzantine hesychasts were not Messalians and did not reject the need for ecclesiastical authority or observance of the rites, which made up the cult of the Church.[287]

In comparison to the Greco-Roman dualistic anthropology of division between the body and soul, the Palamite anthropology was characterised as a positive one because, together with the soul, it integrates the body into a holistic transformation of human beings. This system took its substance from the affirmation of Christ being human so that, by grace, human beings might restore the image of God within them; for that image had been sullied by the disobedience of Adam and Eve and this sin was passed on as an 'ancestral curse' to all mankind.[288] When freed from passion and sinful inclinations, body and soul were given great powers according to Palamite theology, for they become the vessel of the *nous*. The *nous* was perceived to be a spiritual intellect that has the potential for direct apprehension of the eternal truths about God and the meaning of the created world (*gnosis*) and not simply a discursive rationality grounded in sense perception.[289] The correct use of the body and the mind allows the soul to acquire divine love.

Palamas strongly objected to Barlaams's conception of the body as the prison of the soul, and that man's salvation is the soul's liberation from the body. He made a new theological observation that the return of the *nous* from the outside world to the heart and its ascent from the heart to God is the only way for man to acquire pure knowledge of God.[290] In addition, he restored the notion of the body as God's created vessel of the Spirit, and thought that human spirituality could be achieved only through harmony between the spirit and the body, which is accomplished through the discipline of subjecting the body to the mind, thus allowing the soul to acquire love.[291] Palamas corrected Barlaam by stating the noetic faculty was energy of the soul, which must be fixed within the body and guarded against the wanderings of contemplation, which are the root of all heresies.[292]

---

286 Meyendorff, *Gregorie Palamas, Defense des Saints Hesychastes* (Louvain 1959) 30–31.

287 Messalianism held that the persons of the Trinity were visible to the human eye and many of them believed that they had direct experience of God, receiving divine energy as a gift (Angelov, 'Hesychasm', 67).

288 Archbishop Chrysostomos & Hieromonk Patapios, 'Comments on the Transformation of Hellenistic Philosophic Nomenclature in the Byzantine Patristic Tradition', *Glossa: An Ambilingual Interdisciplinary Journal*, vol. 2, no. 1 (December 2006) 12.

289 M. Bakić-Hayden, 'Two Methods of Contemplation: Yoga and Hesychast Prayer', *Гласник Етнографског Института САНУ*, vol. 56, no. 2 (2008) 4.

290 Metropolitan Hierotheos of Nafpaktos, 'Saint Gregory Palamas as a Hagiorite', http://www.pelagia.org/htm/b16.en.saint_gregory_palamas_as_a_hagiorite.03.htm (accessed 24/10/2010).

291 Macarios of Corinth and Nicodemos of the Holy Mountain, *The Philokalia*, vol. 4 (Athens 1977).

292 Palamas, *Triad*, I, 2, 4, 83, in Meyendorff (ed.), *Gregory Palamas: The Triad*.

The question arises: what did Palamas assert as being the part of the body that constitutes the mind? He stated the mind uses one of the bodily organs, the heart, as an instrument in its operation. The heart then directs the entire organism and reigns over all thoughts of the soul and all members of the body. Thus, when the mind is allowed to go out of the body with the aim of contemplating intelligible visions, it falls into error and receives demonic illusions. When the mind is enclosed within the body, however, grace takes possession of the body and inscribes in it the laws of the spirit.[293] In general, however, Barlaam and Palamas had different understandings about the way in which the soul is attached to the body. Palamas saw the heart as a means of attaching the soul to the body, and Barlaam believed that the soul is attached to every part of the body.[294]

Palamas recognised two different movements of the mind: the direct movement that sees and observes visible things, and the circular movement, when the mind returns and operates within God.[295] Contemplation of God in his glory is carried out in a spiritual fashion, for the mind becomes super-celestial and mysteriously united to God, being filled with all immaterial knowledge and supernatural and ineffable visions.[296] Thus, even though Palamas considers the soul to be a unique reality possessing multiple powers, but which uses the body as an instrument that coexists with it, the sanctity of the body too is essential for the return of the intellect to the heart, and the body assumes an active role in prayer and salvation.[297] Palamas was not concerned with the dangers of mystical experience, and eliminated the need for discretion and independent moral judgment when embarking on the journey of spiritual ascent.[298] Palamas also made a link between faith and ignorance, and listed them as preconditions for salvation.[299]

4. Hesychast life

In the course of the Hesychast controversy, Barlaam rejected the Palamite conception of purity and dispassion (*apatheia*) as well as the mortification of the passions (*nekrosis*), because he thought that the experience of a vision was simply an exaggerated emotional condition. Nevertheless, he revived that level of mystical ascent known to classical Greek theology and mysticism as *physike theoria*, the contemplation of God through nature. His theology also lacked

293 ibid., II, 2, 4.
294 Palamas, *Defense*, Tr. II, 2, 27; 377, in Meyendorff, *Defense*.
295 ibid., I, 2, 5; 85.
296 Palamas, *Triad*, I, 3, 5; 33, in Meyendorff (ed.), *Gregory Palamas: The Triad*.
297 ibid., II, 2, 3.
298 ibid., I, 3, 48–49.
299 ibid., II, 3. 43.

the doctrines of the centrality of Christ and the personal necessity of grace. Having been preoccupied with the intellectual perception of God's essential unknowability, he placed no emphasis on *praxis*.

Palamas structured the hesychast life as a ladder, with the steps going from repentance and conversion (*metanoia*) via 'unseen warfare' or a fight with the passions, to the struggle for *apatheia*, which culminates in the actual transformation of human corporeality or *theosis*. In the first step, the monk was to develop an extreme repugnance for sin, and an aversion to and rejection of worldly cares.[300] A struggle against passions and vices by self-restriction and self-punishment, such as fixing heavy burdens to one's body, weeping and prostrations also formed a part of this step. The second ontological mover of the spiritual process consists of two interrelated practices: attention and prayer (the latter taking the form of the Jesus Prayer). Both were shaped by the rules relating to the postures of prayer and rhythms of the breath, aimed at reorganising all human beings into an integral system that becomes involved in the spiritual process.[301] The main task of the hesychast in this stage is the keeping of commandments that help with the guarding of the *nous*, the spiritual purity achieved through the virtues of temperance, love and sobriety, and participation in the sacramental life.[302] Having separated himself from threads of the world and of his own ego, the hesychast was to enter the stage of passive purification, marking the transition from the human to the divine dimension.[303] The presence of free will was declared by Palamas to be a positive quality of man, a gift bestowed on him by the heavenly creator as a spiritual weapon against the devils. At the same time, attacks were directed against the manifestation of free will, and it was condemned as the original cause for the disobedience, which brought about the tasting of the fruit of the forbidden tree. This peculiar contradiction is inherent in the theory of hesychasm.[304]

Palamas accepted the patristic teaching affirming that even those who have an unclean heart acquire knowledge of God. He affirmed, however, that in order to receive illumination from God, the heart must first be purified, and the passionate part of the soul transformed from the lower to the higher. The heart is the chief intellectual organ of the body and all impulses of the soul are located

300 John Climacus, 'Ladder of Divine Ascent' XV, 17, *Patrologia Graeca*, 88, 1095–1130.

301 Palamas, *Defense*, Homily 1, 3, 12, in Meyendorff, *Defense*.

302 ibid., Homily 1, 3, 46.

303 N. Corneanu, 'The Jesus Prayer and Deification', *St Vladimir's Theological Quarterly*, vol. 39 (1995) 19.

304 In fact, Palamas often stated that only those who have presented to God a mind purified by prayer and made an occasion of virtue from his wishes and desires can acquire knowledge of the glory of God in the face of Jesus Christ (Palamas, *Triad* II, 2, 2, in Meyendorff (ed.), *Gregory Palamas: The Triad*).

there.[305] Since the mind constantly wanders off once embarked on the spiritual path, the practice of hesychast prayer is utilised to continuously reunite the mind with the heart.[306]

In the highest stage of the ladder, the hesychasts reached *synergia*, in which their uncreated energies enter into contact and collaboration with the divine energy or uncreated grace of God. At this point, one starts to perceive a vision of the divine light with all 'spiritual senses', and one is united to God by grace of the Holy Spirit, who accomplishes man's deification 'not by created means or through the essence of humanity but by means of grace and energy natural to it'.[307] Thus, it was reasonable to say that in the noetic sense the divine light became visible within the monks spiritually, and acted in them without being separated from the Holy Spirit.[308] This was the stage of cognition through deification, which could be reached by the means of love for God and the soul's elevation to God. In the teaching of the hesychasts, the celestial regions and 'Upper Jerusalem' was their home and not their actual country on earth.[309] In the hesychast literature, the first stage is *praxis*, the second stage *theoria* and the final stage is *theologia*.

In spite of his affirmation of the three-stage process of ascent, in reality Palamas placed no decisive value on *praxis* (ethical self-purification) or on *physike theoria* (contemplation of God through nature), but instead, he emphasised the final mystical stage, namely *theologia*.[310] His ultimate concern was the transformation of human nature by the divine energies of God, which, as uncreated light, invisibly filled the world. The most direct way to achieve this experience is through the practice of hesychast prayer and focused concentration.[311]

5. Image and likeness

Barlaam did not appreciate the single psychosomatic technique of prayer as a method for re-establishing unity between spirit and body. He had no taste for Biblical anthropology, and preferred Platonic terminology and ideas affirming the opposition between spirit and matter.

Palamas, on the other hand, held a strong Christocentric and sacramental view of the Church, in contrast to the spiritualistic views that had been apparent

305 Palamas, *Defense*, 1. 2. 3. 81, in Meyendorff, *Defense*.
306 ibid., 2. 2. 2. 323.
307 Palamas, 'Answer to Akindynos', 5. 24. 96, in Chrestou, *Works*, vol. 3, 359.
308 Palamas, *Defense*, Homily, 2, 3, 37, in Meyendorff, *Defense*.
309 Grigorii Camblak, *Похвала Слово за Евтимий*, 140.
310 Palamas, *Triad*, I, 3, 42; II, 3, 52; II, 3, 16; III, I, 37, in Meyendorff (ed.), *Gregory Palamas: The Triad*.
311 Palamas, *Defense*, 1, 2; 1–12; 3, 2, 1–30, in Meyendorff, *Defense*.

in the hesychast tradition in earlier centuries.[312] This approach to the issue of experience of God implied the basic anthropological presupposition that man was capable of transcending his own nature, as well as the main theological principle that God — even when he communicates himself — remains transcendent. Thus, he frequently referred to the doctrine of the image and likeness to God. The claim that Adam and Eve had free will, enabling them to act in accordance with choice and wish, was the starting point in his doctrine of knowledge of God.[313]

Palamas proposed that having been created in the image and likeness of God, in the Fall, humanity lost the likeness but retained the image, which was darkened (Genesis 3:1–24). Since the darkening of the image happened through sin, when man practised the commandments and inner unceasing prayer and attained visions of God, his sin was removed and likeness to God restored.[314] Thus, Palamas conceived of Christian life as a process of restoration of the lost likeness to those redeemed and recreated in Christ.[315] The pre-Lapsarian image of God was restored and renewed in the human person, whose individuality was not only retained but also enhanced.[316]

Palamas emphasised that the aim of humankind was to progress from the image to the likeness through Christ's commandments and the power of the Cross. Created in the image and likeness of God in virtue of his freedom, man had the capacity to transcend his own nature and to know God in love. This could not occur mechanically, but as an opportunity to cooperate with the free grace of God that was bestowed to the person in baptism, and more specifically, during the mystery of Holy Chrism. Through baptism he was offered the opportunity to wash his image and to start his imitation of Christ. Through the Eucharist, he was given the ability to be renewed and deified with the grace of Christ.[317] The keeping of commandments offered not only knowledge of God but also charismatic *theosis* emanating from the mystical vision of God. Those who acquired this state could attain visions in their hearts similar to the apostles' experience of the Transfigured Christ on Mt Tabor, if they followed a prayer routine involving a sitting position, breathing control and invocation of the name of Jesus.[318] This communion was possible through the Holy Spirit, who

312 Clucas, 'Eschatological Theory of Byzantine Hesychasm: A Parallel to Joachim de Fiore', *Byzantinische Zeitschrift*, vol. 70, no. 2 (October 1977).

313 Prokhorov, 'Исихазм и Общественная Мысль в Восточной Европе в 14в', 23, 90.

314 Meyendorff, 'О Византийском Исихазме и его Роли в Културнсм и Историческом Развитии Восточной Европы в 14в'.

315 K. Barth, 'The Christian Life', *Church Dogmatics*, vol. 4, part 4 (Grand Rapids 1982) 28.

316 C. Cavarnos, *Byzantine Thought and Art* (Belmont 1986) 28.

317 J. Rait et al. (eds). *Christian Spirituality: High Middle Ages and Reformation*, vol. 2 (1987) 210.

318 Nicephorus the Italian (Callistus), 'On Sobriety', *Patrologia Graeca* 147, 962A, in Nicephorus the Italian, 'Tractatus de Sobrietate et Cordis Custodia', *Patrologia Graeca* 147, 945–967.

leads human beings to empirical knowledge of Christ as a person, according to the paradigm of synergy (*synergia*).[319] Yet, human cooperation was necessary for the grace of the sacraments to have any effect.[320]

It is clear from this that human beings could not achieve *theosis* through their own efforts, but only if they participated freely in the process through synergy, which is possible only if the body is subordinated to its consciousness.[321] Palamas thought this process of human transformation begins with baptism but reaches fulfilment after the Resurrection of the dead, through which the whole person of man is mysteriously reconstructed and transformed from the state of sin to that of incorruption and glory with the aid of divine energies (*duvnamei*). This was the condition of *hesychia*, an eschatological reality reserved in its fullness for the future life in heaven, when humanity will confine its incorporeal being within the bodily house, paradoxical as this may sound.

6. The Jesus Prayer

It is unknown whether Barlaam met hesychasts who made use of the simple breathing technique as a way of acquiring permanent vigilance in prayer, but his stance against this method was unambiguous. He frequently attacked the hesychast practitioners as fixing their mind on the navel, and protested the body could assume any position in prayer. Barlaam believed that Christians pray unceasingly when they acquire conscious knowledge about the important Christian paradigm that 'nothing can be done without the will of God'.[322] He grew indignant at the thought that the mind could dwell in the body, which he considered to be in a subordinate position to the soul.[323]

To counter this hesychastic theological preposition, Barlaam made a clear distinction between unceasing prayer in terms of activating a state of grace, and noetic prayer in terms of mystical non-discursive ecstatic experience. In the latter, according to Barlaam, there was no room either for 'discursive prayer or for those experiences common to the irascible and concupiscent passions'.[324] It is important to note that both Barlaam and Palamas believed that in ecstasy, faculties of body and soul are transcendent; however, whereas Palamas regarded this experience as supra-intellectual, Barlaam understood this experience to be non-discursive and intellectual.[325] In effect, Barlaam claimed those who strove

319 C.S. Calian, *Theology without Boundaries: Encounters of Eastern Orthodoxy and Western Religion* (Louisville 1992) 59.

320 Palamas, 'Against Akindynos' 3.6.13.

321 Palamas, *Triad* I, 2. 9; 47, in Meyendorff (ed.), *Gregory Palamas: The Triad*.

322 Romanides, 'Palamite Controversy', 231.

323 Palamas, *Triad* II, 2, 1, in Meyendorff (ed.), *Gregory Palamas: The Triad*.

324 Palamas, *Defense*, Tr. II, 2, 11, 339, in Meyendorff, *Defense*; Romanides, 'Palamite Controversy', 227.

325 George Mantzaridis, 'Spiritual Life in Palamism', in J. Raitt et al. (eds), *Christian Spirituality: High Middle Ages and Reformation*, vol. 17 (New York 1987) 217.

towards God in prayer had to reject the perception of corporeal and intellectual things and had to leave behind the divine lights and elevation towards the summit of God.[326] On the contrary, the supporters of the hesychast spirituality led by Palamas held the view that prayer is an expression of a human existence.[327] Unceasing prayer, in particular, was not only for monks, but for all Christians.[328]

To explain how the concept of hesychasm could be applied to the spiritual life, Palamas divided it into three levels. The first level, the ethical, is primarily purification of the heart. The second is the illumination of the *nous*. Finally, the theological is the vision of uncreated light, and it was believed man could be united to God either through communion with the divine virtues or through supplications during prayer to God.[329] These three stages corresponded to the stages of purification, illumination and deification. A lack of worries (*amerimnia*), attention or guarding of the mind (*nepsis*) and of the heart, and finally, unceasing prayer were the accompanying elements of exterior hesychasm.

Palamas devoted only two short treatises (I, 2; II, 2) to a defence of the psychosomatic methods of prayer. Fixity of physical posture combined with mechanical repetition of the same words of the Jesus Prayer induced a receptive state, in which the mind perceives the divine light.[330] More clearly, this technique involved a progressive self-emptying, in which the mind was stripped of visual images and devised concepts, and so contemplated in purity the realm of God.[331] With the mind centred in the heart, the hesychast repeated the words of the Jesus Prayer aloud, and then unceasingly in thought, until the prayer was no longer initiated by the person but became the vehicle of the Holy Spirit, affecting every conscious and unconscious response. The hesychast was told to restrain the drawing in and out of his breath, to avoid breathing deeply or quickly. Control of breathing was only an accompanying technique to keep the mind from wandering.[332]

Palamas considered the gift of unceasing prayer and noetic prayer as an identical reality, not to be confused with non-discursive ecstatic intuition of ultimate reality. In this state of prayer, the physical and intellectual facilities no longer exercised an influence on the noetic faculty, but were dominated by the noetic

326 Palamas, *Triad* II, 2, 8, in Meyendorff (ed.), *Gregory Palamas: The Triad*.

327 ibid., II, 1.30–31.

328 Palamas affirmed a way of prayer that was free from all visual pictures and intellectual concepts and that had the ability to apprehend the divine through the immediate sense of presence and unintuitive awareness. It was not only an outward and physical condition but state of soul where, with the mind in the heart, the hesychast is standing before God day and night (Philotheos, 'Enkomion', 573–574).

329 Palamas, 'De Hesychasti', *Patrologia Graeca* 150, 1101–1118; 1117D.

330 I. Hausherr (ed.), 'La methode d'Oraison Hesychaste', *Orientalia Christiana Periodica* , vol. 2, no. 2 (Rome 1927) 101–209.

331 Gregory of Sinai, 'On Prayer', 1333B.

332 Palamas, *Triads*, I, 2, 7 (87, 17–18) in Meyendorff (ed.), *Gregory Palamas: The Triad*.

faculty's unceasing prayer in such a way that they were cleansed and inspired.[333] This experience was characterised neither by sensual emotionalism nor by a transcendent Gnostic exercise independent of liturgical and sacramental life.[334] It was, rather, a ladder connecting the creator with the creatures. In the course of prayer, one became illuminated with the radiance of inexpressible light, which was beyond the senses, words and intellect.[335] This was the stage of ignorance superior to knowledge, when the mind does not pray a definite prayer but finds itself in ecstasy in the midst of incomprehensible realities.[336] As for those not yet arrived to this degree of spiritual contemplation, but seeking to attain it, they had to gain mastery of every sensual pleasure and reject the passions. To mortify the body's inclination to sin, physical suffering in the form of fasting, vigils and prayer had to be imposed; through these disciplines, the stain of past faults was washed away and, above all, divine favour was attracted.[337] For Palamas, the purification of the passionate part of the soul liberated the mind from all things and united it through prayer to the grace of the Holy Spirit, and the entire person became deified through the power of the Spirit.[338]

7. Essence and energies

The third issue between hesychasts and anti-hesychasts centred on the distinction made by the hesychasts between essence and energies.[339] In fact, the real issue during the hesychast debates was the notion of *theosis* — deification or participation in the very being of God. If *theosis* was perceived as being participation in the essence of God, then God ceased to be unique in his personal existence and transcendence. If *theosis* was only a paraphrase to designate psychological experience perpetuating the Neoplatonist concept, then the affirmation 'God became man so that man can become God' was lost.[340] The theory of *theosis* revolved around the distinction between essence and energies (essence of God is invisible but he is manifested in his energies), but the hypostatic element used by Palamas's predecessors (especially the Cappadocian

333 Palamas, *Defense*, Tr. II, 2, 9; 335, in Meyendorff, *Defense*.

334 As P. Meyendorff has stated, 'Liturgy is itself a source of theology. Just like Scripture, the liturgy is a revelation, which implies a multiplicity of meanings, and indeed offers the possibility for participation in divine life'; P. Meyendorff, *St Germanus of Constantinople: On the Divine Liturgy, Trans., Introduction And Commentary* (Crestwood 1984) 41.

335 D. Rogich, 'Homily 34 of Gregory Palamas', 143.

336 Palamas, *Triads*, I, 3, 22, in Meyendorff (ed.), *Gregory Palamas: The Triad.*

337 ibid., II, 2, 6.

338 ibid., F, III; B, I.3, 22:39; F, III. 2.9:106.

339 C. Yannaras, 'The Distinction between Essence and Energies and its Importance for Theology', *St Vladimir's Theological Quarterly*, vol. 19 (Summer 1975).

340 Meyendorff, 'Mount Athos in the Fourtheenth Century, Spiritual and Intellectual Legacy', *Dumbarton Oaks Papers*, vol. 42 (1988) 157–165.

fathers) to model God's Trinitarian existence and the union of divine and human nature in Christ were always implicitly present.[341] This in turn provided a mechanism for explaining the vertical movement of man to God and vice versa.

Barlaam objected to the distinction between essence and energies in a philosophical way, unable to grasp the implications of Christological controversies giving clear support to this doctrine. He was prepared to accept the mental distinction between energies and essence, but the hesychasts insisted God's attributes could be detached from God in such a way that they would be perceivable.[342] In fact, Barlaam did not deny the reality of *theosis*, but only the supposed participation in some created reality and not in the divine essence, which is the only uncreated reality.[343]

Followed the teaching of Dionysus, Barlaam accused hesychasts of impiety when they glorified God according to his essence since, he declared, the divine essence transcends all affirmation and all negation. He distinguished between the glory of God that is beyond participation (an eternal reality), and the participatory glory that receives its existence from the principal cause and is not eternal and different from the essence. Consequently, Barlaam concluded the divine powers are not eternal, since God has granted existence to them.[344] He supported this thesis by claiming that because the divine essence is the only unoriginated reality, everything else having a beginning is a creation of God.[345]

Palamas's response to this attack involved a broad discussion of the nature of Christian faith. It affirmed the possibility of direct knowledge of God and the primacy of incarnational, eschatological and sacramental values over secular values. To maintain the basic antinomy of Eastern Christian understanding of the God–man relationship, he established at length the patristic doctrines of 'deification' or communion with God as representing the only acceptable context for a Christian epistemology, and he developed the distinction between 'essence' and 'energies'. Palamas made this distinction to reconcile the reality of mystical experience with traditional theology, which stressed the inaccessibility of God and rejected all claims to a vision of God's being. This is in contrast to Oriental mysticism — the total absorption of the self in union with the divine essence — as it also is anathema to Occidental sensual mysticism. Palamas, on the other hand, often stated that vision and union with the energy of God deifies angels and men and that Christ receives his deification from the divine essence.[346]

341 Palamas, *Triad*, III, 1 in Meyendorff (ed.), *Gregory Palamas: The Triad*, 34, 89.
342 Barlaam, Letter, I, 260–61; *Letter* III, 290–294.
343 Palamas, *Dialogue*, 7, 1132.
344 Palamas, *Triad* III, 2, 13, in Meyendorff (ed.), *Gregory Palamas: The Triad*.
345 ibid., III, 2, 8.
346 Romanides, 'Palamite Controversy', 231–270.

Palamas linguistically dramatised the inaccessibility of God by replacing the term essence with 'super-essence', that is, the incommunicable, inaccessible, inparticipable aspect of God, which was not to be identified even with those energies that were without a beginning. While the Cappadocian fathers asserted the inaccessibility of the divine essence, Palamas's incorporation of the adjective 'super-essential' designated the radical transcendent essence of God's form as 'identically in-acted by the divine hypostasis of the Father, the Son and the Holy Spirit'.[347] He claimed the term 'essence' was misleading and could not properly be used to indicate the absolute inaccessibility of God. The word 'nature' in relation to God cannot be applied, because it designates one of his divine energies, the substantifying one that came down to humans, creating substance, giving life and bestowing wisdom.[348] If we admit this power of God to be uncreated, then we have to admit that all other powers of God are uncreated, or alternatively accept all powers of God are created.[349]

Palamas claimed the divine attributes were not effects foreign to the divine essence; they were not acts exterior to God and dependent on his will, like the creation of the world or acts of providence, but natural processions of God himself, a mode of existence which was proper to him.[350] They belonged at the same time to the domains of *theologia* and *oikonomia* because, on the one hand, they were eternal — an inseparable force of the Trinity existing independently of the created act — and on the other hand, they manifested the infinite variety of God-loving acts towards creation.[351] If the powers or energies were not eternal realities, as Barlaam claimed, the deifying grace of the Holy Spirit would be created and incapable of deifying the believer. If Barlaam thought the divine energy was necessarily created, he had to admit Christ did not possess, in accord with his two natures, energies both created and uncreated, but only created or single energies, as Monophysites and Monothelites held.[352] According to Palamas, even if divine essence signifies God's absolute transcendence, and humans will never participate in it either in this life or in the age to come, the divine energies by which God comes out of himself and reveals himself to humanity to permeate all of creation are uncreated,[353] and men participate in them through grace.[354] The divine energies act through the deified subject,

347 Anastos, 'Gregory Palaamas's Radicalization of the Essence', 347.

348 Palamas, *Triad* III, 2, 11, in Anastos, 'Gregory Palaamas's Radicalization of the Essence', 335–349; 346.

349 Palamas, *Triad* III, 2, 11, in Meyendorff (ed.), *Gregory Palamas: The Triad*.

350 Aghiorgoussis, 'Christian Existentialism'.

351 In his 'Letter to Amphilochios of Ikonium', Basil the Great synthesises the two aspects when he speaks of the many facets of knowledge of God. This knowledge is at the same time 'understanding of our creator, comprehension of His marvellous things, observance of His commandments, and familiarity with Him'; Basil the Great, Epistulae 235, 3; *Patrologia Graeca* 32, 873C, in Basil the Great, Epistulae, *Patrologia Graeca* 32, 67–113.

352 Palamas, *Triad* III, 2, 7, in Meyendorff (ed.), *Gregory Palamas: The Triad*.

353 Louth, *Denys the Areopagite* (London 1989) 90.

354 Palamas, *Triad*, *Patrologia Graeca* 151, 723C.

'energies to energies', making him, by adoption, all that God is by nature.[355] Palamas affirms the famous patristic dictum that it is impossible to find a name to manifest the nature of the uncreated Trinity, but that names belong to the energies.[356]

Hence, to be in communion with the divine energies means to be united with God in his totality, though one can never know his essence or become identical with either the divine essence or one of the three Divine Persons.[357] The energies of God, Palamas claimed, are active in the world and manifested in many different ways, one of them being the light seen on Tabor. Hesychasm, by providing a means to see the light, was therefore a means to bridge the gulf between man and God.

Although Palamas perceived the Trinitarian divine energies, which proceed from all three divine hypostases at once — as being supernatural, eternal and uncreated — that which the energies affected and produced was in effect created. Through the energies of God, we know the beauty, order and splendour of created beings, and we behold the magnificent names of God: Wisdom, Life, Power, Justice, Love, Being, God, and the infinity of other names unknown to humanity.[358]

The ontology of the divine essence or personhood, or even the energy of the three-in-one God was not affected by the incarnation, and what was seen on Mt Tabor were the uncreated energies, and not the essence of God the Logos. Palamas quickly responded to this opposing argument of Barlaam by introducing Christological doctrine in support of the view that divine energies are uncreated.[359] He attacked his opponents, who claimed the divine light is created to introduce a third nature in Christ — the nature of the divine light, in addition to his divine and human nature.[360] The feast of the Transfiguration on Mt Tabor showed the Word of God deified human nature.[361] The supreme significance of this event was that it focused and projected the energies of God into this world, making it accessible not only through the sacraments but through the ascetic piety of the hesychasts, whose ultimate Scriptural paradigm was the apostles' vision of the Transfiguration of Christ. This was to become a paradigm for the doctrine of *theosis*.

Palamas affirmed that during the Transfiguration of Christ on the Mount, spiritual grace in the heart of the faithful was not produced by the imagination

355 Palamas, *Triad* III, 1, 33, in Meyendorff (ed.), *Gregory Palamas: The Triad*.
356 ibid., III, 2, 10.
357 Meyendorff, *A Study of Gregory Palamas*, G. Lawrence (trans.) (London 1964) 293ff.
358 Dionysius the Areopagite, *Divine Names and Mystical Theology*, C.E. Rolt (ed.) (London 1957) 20–191.
359 Palamas, *Triad* III, 2, 10, in Perella (ed.), *Che Cos'e L'Ortodossia*, 1132.
360 Rogich, 'Homily 34 of Gregory Palamas', 151.
361 Palamas, 'On the Transfiguration', Homily 34, *Patrologia Graeca* 151, 433B.

and did not originate with us, nor did it appear only to disappear; rather, it was a permanent energy united to the soul, liberating it from material things.[362] The grace of God transformed the body and made it spiritual. It was not visible through the medium of air, because in the 'age to come', humanity will no longer need air. Instead, this light was visible to the eyes of the heart, and was seen by the apostles after they transcended every sensible and intellectual perception.[363] The grace of God descends from the mind into the body, which it transforms and deifies, by the blessed activities of the passionate aspect of the soul, and makes capable of becoming praiseworthy and divine.

Palamas derived his view on *theosis*, or the acquisition of divine grace, from the clear outline of the doctrine in 2 Peter 1:3–4, where participation in divine power was portrayed as the highest gift of God: a gift which made it possible for the faithful to escape the destructive pleasures and desires of this world, and partake in the divine.[364] It was also perceived as a present possibility and a future hope, based on the restoration of the capacity for grace through the person of Christ and the Holy Spirit, who communicated to us the energies of God himself so that we may become gods by adoption and grace.[365] Moreover, *theosis* was seen as a direct enhypostatic illumination of those worthy of comprehension, manifesting itself in creatures that have acquired the grace of the Spirit. This illumination is achieved through ontological purification in the active acquisition of human virtue, while still acknowledging the potential dominance of sin over the flesh and the fallen world, and humanity's essential imperfections.[366] Participation in God is a gift. It is given to those who live a Christian life according to their spiritual aptitude.[367] Hence, the deifying gift and *theosis* are one and the same, and not something apart from God, for it is the Spirit himself in his mode of self-giving.

The transmission of the Spirit takes place not only during the practice of mental prayer, but at those moments when the body is operating towards the end for which God created it. The light, on the other hand, becomes visible spiritually with noetic sense, but it becomes an effulgence of hypostatic light in the souls of the faithful.[368]

---

362 Palamas, *Triad*, II, 2, 9, in Meyendorff (ed.), *Gregory Palamas: The Triad*.

363 ibid., II, 2, 23, in Meyendorff (ed.), *Gregory Palamas: The Triad*.

364 P. Bilaniuk, 'The Mystery of Theosis or Divinization', in D. Nieman & M. Schatkin (ed.), *The Heritage of the Early Church. Essays in Honor of the Very Reverend Georges Vasilievich Florovsky*, Orientalia Christiana Analecta, vol. 195 (Rome 1973) 337–359.

365 Palamas, *Triad*, II, 3, 32, in Meyendorff (ed.), *Gregory Palamas: The Triad*.

366 Auxentius of Photiki, 'The Humanist Quest for a Unity of Knowledge and the Orthodox Metaphysics of Light', http://www.orthodoxinfo.com/inquirers/meycorr.pdf.14 (accessed 8/09/2011).

367 Palamas, *Theophanes* 15, in Perrella (ed.), *Che Cos'e L'Ortodossia*, 1272.

368 D. Rogich, 'Homily 34 of Gregory Palamas', *The Greek Orthodox Theological Review*, vol. 33, no. 2 (1988) 135–166.

Conclusion

The main arguments brought up by Barlaam against Palamas and his supporters were threefold.

Firstly, Barlaam prohibited the use of demonstrative science in theology. In turn he suggested the use of dialectical syllogism in all matters concerning the transcendent nature of God. Moreover, Barlaam applied only one aspect of the theological–philosophical program, as found in Dionysian writings — namely the *apophatic* theology — while he neglected the value of positive or *kataphatic* theology. Barlaam also made use of Aristotelian logic, particularly concerning the transcendent nature of the divinity.

Secondly, Barlaam considered the acquisition of knowledge of God through baptism and other sacraments as a mere symbolic participation in truths that cannot be reached by reason. Hence, he refuted the central hesychast tenet that humans can acquire vision of God through prayer. Such revelations, he thought, could only be fragments of imagination or demonic illusions.

Finally, Barlaam promoted the neoplatonic dualistic view of the subordinate role of the human body as compared with the soul and the intellect. Instead, he perceived the mind to be inseparable from the soul — but inferior to it — and questioned the possibility of recalling the wondering of the mind within the body. As a consequence, he ridiculed the hesychast psychosomatic technique accompanied by the repetition of the Jesus Prayer, and accused monks of following the practices of Messalianism.

The theological propositions of Palamas, on the other hand, were founded on four important principles. First, he opposed Barlaams's contention that human knowledge was of equal or higher value than knowledge of Holy Scriptures and patristic writings. He rejected the Platonic tendency to undervalue sensory experiences and the life of the senses in general in favour of the intellect, and sought knowledge of God in the realm of mystical experience. Palamas emphasised the role of the *nous* or spiritual understanding, whereas his opponents put their trust in the διάνοια or *discursive thinking*. Palamas further distinguished between profane knowledge and divinely inspired wisdom. The two types of wisdom were mutually exclusive, and engagement of one precluded ascent to another. Yet the contemplative commitment to the art of *hesychia* was the way in which one could acquire this spiritual knowledge of God.

Second, one of the key principles governing Palamas's theology was the ineffable distinction between the divine essence and the divine energies. Palamas introduced this doctrine to reconcile mystical experience with traditional theology as well as to defend the antinomy of God, visible and invisible at the same time. The transcendent essence of God or 'super-essence' (as designated by Palamas) signified the incommunicable, inaccessible, inparticipable aspect of his divinity. On the other hand, the divine attributes were the activities and actions of God. They were his manifold presence, as it were, the way God makes himself to humanity.

Third, the doctrine of immanent energies implied vision of the relationship between God and the world and the divine energies were often experienced in the form of light that, though beheld through bodily eyes, was in itself non-material, 'intelligible' and uncreated. This was the uncreated light manifested to the apostles at the Transfiguration on Mt Tabor, seen during prayer by saints, symbolically represented by the halo in icons and the light of the age to come.

Finally, the main doctrinal difference between Palamas and Barlaam was their respective views on Christian anthropology. Whereas Barlaam defined man as a spiritual mind that acquires knowledge of divine realities through natural contemplation, Palamas affirmed the function of man as a psychosomatic creature capable of direct experience of the divine. Moreover, in contrast to the scholastic dualism and rationalism propagated by his opponent, Palamas instigated a new Christocentric humanism founded on the hesychast concepts of *theosis*, *synergia* and *theologia*. Moreover, Palamas restored the notion of the human body as God's created vessel of the spirit, and considered that the state of union with God could be achieved only through the discipline of subjecting the body to the mind (*nous*), which in turn allowed the soul to acquire love (*agape*). Finally, the new humanistic presuppositions developed by Palamas affirmed three different movements of the mind: the direct movement that sees and observes visible things, the circular movement, when the mind returns and operates within God, and the movement from the ego-centred state (one dominated by senses) to the ego-transcendent consciousness (God-centred state) according to the paradigm of *synergia*. The third movement was the stage of cognition through deification, which could only be reached by means of love for God. Hence, the originality of Palamism towards essentialist conceptions of God does not consist in adding a foreign divine reality, but in relating to God in an existential and agaptic way, while maintaining his absolute transcendence.

2. General Iconographic Changes in the 14th and 15th Centuries

At different times, the subject of the re-emergence of hesychasm in the Byzantine world was related to new trends in the Palaeologan era of the 14th and 15th centuries in Byzantine and Slavic lands. Hesychasm supposedly affected the 'pre-renaissance' in Byzantium by stifling its development. Fruitful in itself, this hypothesis must be used with caution. Although it is possible that there were circumstances in which the monastic rigor of the 14th and 15th centuries was detrimental to artistic development, there is no stark contrast between the theology of Byzantine hesychasm and the most creative aspects of Palaeologan art. If the hesychast movement represents a consistent world view, then as well as a renewal of personal religiosity, individual prayer and a better understanding of Christianity, it is probable it could create an atmosphere of artistic creativity. The matter of the appreciation, collection and study of Byzantine art in the Palaeologan period and its relation to social and spiritual trends in Byzantium is, however, a complex topic, and it does not allow for a definitive answer.[1]

Two conflicting, but interwoven, cultural trends influenced the development of orthodox dogmas as well as artistic production during the Palaeologan period, namely, hesychasm and humanism. These tendencies in iconography did not, however, exclude the development of a plethora of private, complicated and interwoven trends as well.

The humanistic or descending (antique) trend of naturalisation (which had the characteristic of temporality) reduced the canon of icon painting and placed it in the ranks of secular painting. Hence, a love of the ancient past, the study of various works of ancient classical literature and art, and their imitation, characterised the Byzantine art of the late 13th and early 14th centuries.[2] The subject of this art, of course, was the church; the attraction to antiquity was only in style and form, for which the classical model became almost mandatory. Theatrical scenes appeared in mosaics and frescoes and iconographic programs expanded to contain complex allegories, symbols and allusions to the Old Testament, as well as texts of liturgical hymns. Complete theological preparation and intellectual erudition was a general requirement in the commission of iconographers and the contemplation of works of art. The form and content of frescoes reflected this renewed wave of reflection on classical ideas and subjects.[3]

---

1 R. Nelson, *Later Byzantine Painting: Art, Agency and Appreciation* (Ashgate 2007).

2 N.L. Okunev, 'Арилье: Памятник Сербского Искусства XIII в', *Seminarium Kondakovianum*, vol. 8 (Prague 1936); K. Specieris, *Изображения Эллинских Философов в Церквах* (Athens 1964).

3 J. Meyendorff, 'Humanisme Nominaliste et Mystique Cretienne a Byzance au XIVe Siecle', *Nouselle Revue Theologique*, vol. 79, no. 9 (Louvain 1957).

Many Byzantine paintings that were executed around 1300 bear an imprint of humanism, with their light and jagged architectural landscape, animated and graceful scenes, with frequent personifications and draped figures with expressive and elegant gestures.[4]

Parallel to this naturalist or descending trend in Palaeologan art, a second or rising trend arose in the art of the 14th century, informed by the spiritual and mystical tradition of hesychasm.

Hesychasm and Christian art of the 14th and 15th centuries

When hesychasm became a universally accepted doctrine in 1375, not only in monastic life but also in the Byzantine Church, art experienced changes that were different from those occurring at the beginning of the 14th century. The aim of this art was to contemplate transfigured flesh and matter, the shading of divine light, the fullness of ascent by the divine presence to ethereal heights where everything was perfect.[5] The spiritual ideal of a contemplative monastic life, as expressed in the theology of Gregory Palamas, supported the essence of Byzantine culture, in particular its doctrine of the transfiguration of human nature and the inseparable connection between heaven and earth. Palamite hesychasm denied Platonic spiritualism and taught the positive value of the body: its ideal was the transfiguration, not the destruction of the flesh (Figs 1–4).[6]

Even in this context, dramatic changes began to transpire in art that reflected changes in all parts of life.[7] First, the main trend of the new style, which reached a peak in the 14th century, was a gradual shift away from painting expressing psychological states. Small exquisite mosaics that were created during the early Palaeologan renaissance disappeared, and icons increased in size. Large images with full-length silhouettes were easy to read in the church's interior. Together with theological treatises and sermons, painted images expressed the essence of the doctrine of divine energy, a state of vision reserved for those in an advanced spiritual state of ascesis.[8]

4 A. Grabar, *Byzantium: Byzantine Art in the Middle Ages* (Holland 1966) 84.

5 M.M. Vasic, L'Hesychasmedans l'Église et l'Art des Serbes du Moyen Age', *L'Art Byzantin Chez les Slaves, Les Balkans: Mélanges Théodore Uspenskij*, vol. 1 (Paris 1930).

6 C.N. Tsirpanlis, 'Byzantine Humanism and Hesychasm in the Thirteenth and Fourteenth Centuries: Synthesis or Antithesis, Reformation or Revolution', *The Patristic and Byzantine Review*, vol. 5, no. 12 (1993) 18–21.

7 G. Ruzsa, 'Une Icone Inconnue Representant les Apotres Pierre et Paul et la Question del'Hesychasme', *Jahrbuch der Osterreichischen Byzantinistik*, vol. 32, no. 5 (1982).

8 Vasic, *Жича и Лазарица: Студије из Српске Уметности Средњег Века* (Belgrade 1928) 163–237; L. Brehier, 'La Renovation Artistique sous les Paleologues et le Mouvement des Idees', in *Melanges Charles Diehl* vol. 2 (Paris 1930) 2.

Dense, bold, dramatic brush strokes that expressed emotion framed painting technique during this period. The surface was unusually lively and included expansive movement, finicky gestures with hands and fingers outstretched, conveying a striking specificity of character and personality.[9] Figures had sharp flashing eyes, thick red lips and fleshy noses. Overall, a movable light blazed a harsh glare on their faces and hands. All this created a unique imaginative and artistic operation, which was active and temperamental

The religious art of Byzantine and Slavic lands at this time used expressive colours, which depicted high emotional states and also enhanced the mystical mood of the icon. The expression of the faces in these icons was more emotional than previously, depicting different mental states, from the lyrical to the dramatic. Especially strong was the attachment to dark blue hues. There was a tendency to create a deep mysterious glow to arouse heavenly associations in the viewer. Larger surfaces were painted in a spectrum of colours.

A prominent feature of this new style was heightening the emotion and expression while maintaining the dynamism of heightened spirituality. Thus, the gesturing of figures was impulsive, robes began to flap, and figures turned to the sides, suggesting a freer and more bold perspective.[10] The iconography was complex, some images were close to genre scenes, and the colour range was softer, lighter, and dominated by blue-grey and greenish-yellow hues. These stylistic devices were reminiscent of the humanist trends of the Palaeologan era. Restoration of the classicism of previous centuries, however, or its natural extension, was on a different basis.[11] The central goal of this art was not to imitate ancient models, but rather to reflect their unique beauty by saturating the figures with divine light.[12]

Byzantine art of the early 14th, and later, centuries did not engage in literal reproduction of classical elements. Over time, more expressive options appeared, and love for the classical past lost its value. The figurative scene evolved to be characterised by a number significant artistic nuances. The emission of light from one point or central compositional axis revitalised the dynamic centre of

---

9 N.K. Goleizovskii, 'Послание Иконописцу и Отголоски Исихазма в Русской Живописи на Рубеже XV–XVI вв,' *Византийский Временник*, vol. 26 (1965); idem, 'Исихазм и Русская Живопись XIV–XV вв', *Византийский Временник*, vol. 29 (1968); M.V. Alpatov, 'Искусство Феофана Грека и Учение Исихастов', *Византийский Временник*, vol. 33 (1972); G.I. Vzdornov, *Фрески Феофана Грека в Церкви Спаса Преображения в Новгороде* (Moscow 1976) 236–58; O. Vopovz, *Ascesi e Trasfigurazione: Immagini dell'Arte Bizantina e Russa nel XIV Secolo* (Milan 1996).

10 For the scholarly approach that locates the influence of hesychasm in the domain of iconography, see E. Bakalova, 'Към Вы і Роса за Отраженной! На Исихазма Върху Изкуството 1371–1971', in P. Rusev et al. (eds), *Търновска Кяижовна Школа* (Sofia 1974); T. Velmans, *La Peinture Murale Byzantine la Fin du Moyen Age* (Paris 1977) 54–57.

11 Velmans, 'Le Rôle de l'Hésychasme dans la Peinture Murale Byzantine du XIVe et XVe Siècles', in P. Armstrong (ed.), *Ritual and Art: Byzantine Essays for Christopher Walter*, (London 2006) 182–226.

12 E. Tachiaos, 'Hesychasm as a Creative Force in the Fields of Art and Literature', in D. Davidov (ed.), *L'Art de Thessalonique et des Pays Balkaniques et les Courants Spirituels au XIVe Siècle* (Belgrade 1987).

the icon. There was an aesthetic inversion (antinomian) in the painting, opposed to the canons of outer and inner beauty. It reflected spiritual peace, silence and exultation, and a combination of 'earthly' and 'heavenly' realities and, finally, a spiritual ecstasy, all fruits of the fruit of hesychast concentration. The sacred symbolism of colours emphasising the expressiveness and semantics of complex shades supported the mystical mood and inspiration of religious images. Icons were concise in detail; their semantic structure was centralised and had a transcendent vector to overcome emotional and psychological expression.[13] The process of spiritual rebirth was opened; the individual in transition was hypostatic. Many religious images created in a portable format (icons) reflected the increasing hesychast mood. They straightened the timelessness and allegorical physical space of Christian gnosis, with its address to inner peace, and metaphysical interpretation of the universe.

The religious art of the Palaeologan period marked an emergence of new iconographic subjects manifesting temporal and expressive elements in a figurative scene. The volume and the space of the buildings increased to have clear and rhythmic arrangements. The ancient mapping of the human figure changed, and it was accompanied by columns and soft drapes. Asymmetrical and small-scale facial features appeared in oblique view and were psychologically subtle. A soft rolling light illuminated the anxious facial expression, which gave an impression of the peace being unstable and unusually personal. The architectural forms were overly abundant and their bulk was drenched with energy, thereby reducing the space and dynamics of the figurative scene.[14]

Finally, the classical art of the Commnenian and Palaeologan periods acquired new features, such as enhanced spiritual focus, new religious symbolism, iconicity, and timelessness. All these elements referred to a new manifestation of the icon and its primary function — to be a prayerful mediator between humanity and God. The 'techniques and methods of such iconography were to be understood only in the context of the doctrine of the uncreated light.'[15] Nevertheless, iconographers had the liberty to uniquely embody doctrinal topics in paintings, which proves that canonical Orthodox art did not detract from the individual vision of the artist.

---

13 G. Peterson, 'The Parekklesion of St. Euthymius in Thessalonica: Art and Monastic Policy under Andronicus II', *Art Bulletin*, vol. 58 (1976).

14 Velmans, 'Infiltrations Occidentales dans la Peinture Murale Byzantine au XIVe et au Début du XVe Siècle, in V. Duric (ed.), *L'École de la Morava et son Temps: Symposium de Résava 1968* (Belgrade 1972).

15 P. Florensky, 'Иконостас', Собрание Сочинений, vol. 1 (Paris 1985) 221.

After the victory of hesychasm in 1375, idealistic tendencies became more pronounced. The sense of monumentality slowly diminished while the scenes came to have affinities with the portable icon. Works of art were complex and the architecture and landscapes assumed unprecedented importance.[16]

General iconographic changes in the art of the 14th and 15th centuries

One of the key objectives of Byzantine art in the 14th and 15th centuries was to communicate spiritual (invisible) realities by physical means. Contemporary scholars have yet to enunciate the way in which this aspect of Byzantine art was achieved.[17]

In order to discern hesychasm in art, it is important to define the new message that hesychasm brought to the age and to see to what extent it brought renewal and change into spiritual life in the Byzantine Empire and the Slavic lands. The paintings of Theophanes the Greek gave art historians pause, mainly because he came to Russia from Constantinople at the time the hesychast influence was at large.[18] Was Theophanes influenced by hesychasm or humanism?[19] There is an apparent contradiction. Similar problems appear when one surveys monuments, which have a number of contrasts. Such is the case in the Monastery of Ivanovo, Bulgaria (1341–1370).[20] There is a series of naked human figures in frescoes of Ivanovo (a rare detail in art of the Christian East) as well as tonal gradations, shadows, and white highlights that symbolise the rays of divine light.[21] A diligent art historian faces challenges when analysing artworks by either Manuel Panselinos, from the Monastery of Protaton (14th century), or Manuel Eugenikos, from the Church of Calendžicha (Georgia). The frescoes of Panselinos represent a fusion of both humanistic and hesychastic artistic traits. For example, the light illuminating Christ (as circumscribed by Panselinos) is simultaneously a natural illumination and a visual language for the participation (of Christ) in the divine light. The expression of the eyes shows the compassion

16 M. Chatzidakis, *Studies in Byzantine Art and Archaeology* (London 1972).

17 Bakalova, 'La Societe et l'Art en Bulgarie au XIVe Siècle, L'Influence de l'Hesychasme sur l'Art', *Actes du 14th Congress International des Etudes Byzantines II* (Bucharest 1975).

18 Tachioaos, 'Hesychasm'.

19 N.K. Goleizovskii, 'Заметки о Творчестве Феофана Грека', *Византийский Временник*, vol. 24 (1969) 139–143.

20 S. Dimitrieva, 'Rospisi Hrama Spasha Preobrazenija na Kovaleve (1380) v Novgorode', PhD thesis, Lomonosov Moscow State University (2003) 489–497.

21 Grabar, 'Les Frescoes de Ivanovo et le Art de la Palaeologes', *Le Art de la Fin du l'Antiquiti at du Moyen Age* vol II (Paris 1968) 842; S. Jordanov, *Skalniot Manastir Sv. Archangel Michael pri Selo Ivanovo* (Varna 2009) 70–72.

and mercy of a God who condescended to become human.[22] These features confirm the enduring importance of a coherent picture of the unity or synergy of the Byzantine world.

Nevertheless, a limited number of monuments, such as the Church of St Nikolas at Chilli, Tilos, contain paintings with such a distinctive style they could be interpreted only in the context of hesychasm. Inclusion of frescoes of eight monastics and 13 hesychast leaders in the middle zone of the church is a new element not found in art of the region. The technique is peculiar and the palette austere and limited. The facial features are rendered with swift, irregular and bold brushstrokes of white paint that was applied during preparation.[23] Arms and fingers receive a similar simplified treatment; modelled freely and concisely, they do not follow anatomical guides. The drapery is traced with thick white paint, which also covers large expanses of the body, creating the sense of plasticity through contrast between lit and shadowed areas. These troubled forms of lighting allow the painter to avoid excess in his rendering of movement and to select restrained poses. The same feeling animates the work of Eugenikos.[24]

Even though no particular hesychast influence could be assigned to a monument, icon or a subject, a set of iconographic changes occurred in the 14th century, which could only be interpreted as occurring in that context. No circumscription of a work of art represents the reciprocal influence of hesychasm on art more than a painting representing Palamas. Since the veneration of Palamas, took hold over the cities in which he lived and preached, that is Thessaloniki, Veroia and Kastoria, icons with his portrait appeared at the same time as his cult spread to these areas.[25] The Monastery of Christ Pantokrator, Vladaton (constructed around 1339), contains the earliest icon depicting Palamas. Brothers Markos and Dorotheos Vlates, two important supporters of Palamas, resided in this monastery.[26] The figurative scene of the Transfiguration, placed just below the image of Palamas, affirms the hesychast connection.[27] Another well-preserved example comes from the Monastery of Vatopedi (1371). Both images were created during the hesychast controversy (Fig. 5).

---

22 S. Skliris, 'The Person of Christ and the Style of Icons, A Mystery Great and Wondrous', *Byzantine and Christian Museum. Exhibition of Icons and Ecclesiastical Treasures 28 May – 31 July 2001* (Athens 2001).

23 A. Katsioti, 'Ηεσυcηασμ ανδ τηε ΩαλΛ Παιντινγσ ιν τηε Cηθρcη οφ Στ. Νικολασ, Cηελι, Νικοσ'; *Αρcηαελογιcον Δελτον*, vol. 54 (1999) 327–342.

24 H. Belting, 'Le Peinture Manuel Eugenicos de Constantinople en Georgie', *Cahiers Archéologiques*, vol. 28 (1979).

25 G.V. Popov, 'Икона Григория Паламы из ГМИИ и Живопись Фессалоник Поздне-Византийского Периода', *Искусство Западной Европы и Византии* (Moscow) 197.

26 C. Mauropoulou-Tsioumē, *Vlatadon Monastery* (Thessaloniki 1987).

27 The image of Palamas is also represented on the opposite side of the same church, closer to the south parakklesion which dates from the last quarter of the 14th century. Here Palamas is shown together with John Chrysostom, Symeon the New Theologian, Gregory the Theologian and Gregory Archbishop of Thessaloniki (S.E.J. Gerstel, 'Civic and Monastic Influences on Church Decoration in Late Byzantine Thessalonike: In Loving Memory of Thalia Gouma-Peterson', Symposium on Late Byzantine Thessalonike, *Dumbarton Oaks Papers*, vol. 57 (2003) 236).

The story of conversion of the young Indian prince named Iosapath by the monk Barlaam of Calabria was another influential image.[28] Important monuments depicting this scene are in the north-west chapel of the Protaton Church on Mount Athos (1290), the Peribleptos Church in Ohrid (1294/5), and the Church of St George at Omorphokklesia near Kastoria.[29] The Cathedral of the Deposition of the Robe, in Moscow's Kremlin contains the important example of the possible influence of hesychasm on art. The fresco in question represents the story of the appearance of an angel to the monk Pachomios. This composition often accompanied that of Barlaam and Iosaphat (Fig. 6) in churches.

With illustrations of individual moments of the liturgy, abstract symbolic images of the *Sophia* (the wisdom of God), the Communion of the Apostles (Fig. 7), and many others appeared to reveal the meaning of the sacrament. These images represent a figurative transmission of the Biblical text of Proverbs (Prov. 9:1–7) and express two subjects. The image of an angel symbolises the concept of *Sophia*. Christ is also depicted as Wisdom, but in the guise of the angel of the great council.[30] Wisdom was one of the subjects discussed during the hesychast controversy, resulting in a symbolic image of *Sophia*.[31] The inconsistencies, which occur in the use of the image of the Wisdom prior to the 14th century, reflect the various interpretations of the notion of Sophia among church fathers. During the hesychast controversy, both hesychast and humanists used the theme of Wisdom in support of their cause. The supporters of Palamas, however, interpreted the meaning of *Sophia* in the context of their Christology, to support Palamite doctrine of Christ as the Wisdom of God (Fig. 8). The followers of hesychasm applied other iconographic features to express the meaning of Wisdom as a manifestation of God's action in the world.[32] An unusually shaped halo, which surrounds the angel of wisdom, clearly expresses this concept. Many Russian icons contain the image of the angel of wisdom, such as that from the Monastery of Kirillo-Belozerskii (1548), which is currently in the Tretyakov Gallery, Moscow.[33] In this work, the angel stands in front of the temple with seven columns, all representing the

---

28 R. Janin, *Les Eglises et les Monastires des Grands Centres Byzantins Bithynie, Hellespont, Latros, Galesios, Tribizonde, Athines, Thessalonique* (Paris 1975) 386–388.

29 E.G. Stikas, 'Une Église des Paléologues aux Environs de Castoria', *Byzantinische Zeitschrift*, vol. 51 (1958) fig. 5; C. Mavropoulou-Tsioume, *Buzantinhv Qessa* (Paris 1927) pl. 55.1; Stikas, 'Une église des Paléologues', 100–112, figs 5, 6.

30 Meyendorff , 'L'iconographie de la Sagesse Divine dans la Tradition Byzantine', *Cahiers Archeologiques*, vol. 10 (Paris 1959).

31 Okunev, 'Арилье, Памятник Сербского Искусства XIII в'.

32 G. Florovsy, О Почитании Софии Премудрости Божией в Византии и на Руси, *Труды 5-го Съезда Русских Академических Организаций за Границе*, vol. 1 (Sofia 1932); Meyendorff, 'L'iconographie', 10.

33 Meyendorff, 'Wisdom-Sophia: Contrasting Approaches to a Complex Theme', *Studies on Art and Archeology in Honor of Ernst Kitzinger on His Seventy-Fifth Birthday*, vol. 41 (Washington D.C. 1987) 391–401.

'home' of *Sophia*. The symbolic representation of Wisdom affirms the opposition between the concept of *Sophia* as the wisdom of God and the concept of *Sophia* — the wisdom of the philosophers.[34]

In contrast to the hesychasts, the humanists, lead by Barlaam, have identified wisdom with the divine essence. Hence, two opposing concepts of divine wisdom prevailed in Byzantine and the Slavic lands, which contributed to the growth of this representation during the second half of the 14th century.[35] Consciously or unconsciously, however, the image of wisdom breached conciliar decrees. Similar violations occurred when iconographers used symbols to represent the Eucharistic story. In particular, Canon 82 of the Trullo Council eliminated symbols as a substitute for the direct image of the incarnate word of God: 'Honouring the ancient imagery and the shadow, as signs of destiny and truth … , we prefer grace and truth, accepting them as judges do when fulfilling the law.'[36]

Other iconographic changes evolved in the late-14th century and many compositions were either reintroduced or redeveloped. The compositions of the Akathist Hymn, the Prayer of John Chrysostom and the Heavenly Ladder[37] became frequent. Moreover, there was an increase in the number of images representing monks, hermits and stylites, as well as images of other followers of the hesychast tradition.

New objects of art emerged in the 14th century showing images of prominent saints, such as John Chrysostom, Basil the Great, Gregory the Theologian and Athanasius the Great. An image of Athanasius at the Church of the Archangel Gabriel in Lesnovo (1341–1348),[38] accompanied by an angel, the personification of divine wisdom, is an important exemplar of this trend, as noted by Velmans. The most interesting detail is the head of the saint touching the angel's halo, suggesting the saint's participation in divine energies. The presence of this creation within the church stems from the desire to provide a visual narrative

---

34 Palamas defined Wisdom as an attribute of God common to the Father, the Son and the Holy Spirit, through which God created the universe. In addition, he only approved signs that Old Testament prophets used as symbols for depicting higher realities, such as the Scythe of Zechariah (Zech. V, 1–2) and the Axe of Ezekiel (Ezek. IX, 1–2); reference to the image of the Divine Wisdom has been found in several Palamite texts (Meyendorff, 'Spiritual Trends in Byzantium in the Late Thirteenth and Early Fourteenth Centuries', in P. Underwood (ed.), *Kariye Dzami* (Princeton 1975) 103–106).

35 Dimitrieva, 'Rospisi Hrama Spasha Preobrazenija', 489–497, 495.

36 H.R. Percival, *The Seven Ecumenical Councils, Second Series of Philip Schaff and Henry Wace, Nicene and Post-Nicene Fathers*, vol. 14 (1956) http://www.ccel.org/ccel/schaff/npnf214.txt (accessed 20/02/2012).

37 E. Miner, 'The Monastic Psalter of the Walters Art Gallery', in Weitzmann et al (ed.), *Late Classical and Mediaeval Studies in Honor of Albert Mathias Friend*, (Princeton 1955) 2.32.–53; A. Cutler, 'The Marginal Psalter in the Walters Art Gallery: A Reconsideration', *Journal of Walters Art Gallery*, vol. 35 (1977).

38 G. Millet & T. Velmans, *La Peinture du Moyen Age en Yougoslavie: Serbie, Macédoine et Monténégro*, vol. 4 (Paris 1969) 49.

of a Palamite doctrine, the topic of the wisdom of God. The placement of this representation on the spandrels of the dome, however, was an unusual feature; it replaces the usual decoration of the dome with images of evangelists.

Also, the proliferation of paintings of healing miracles reflected the hesychast atmosphere of the Palaeologan period. It relates directly to the anthropological teaching of the hesychast, which perceives the body and soul as an integrated whole.[39] The union of the divine and human nature in Christ reveals and recreates authentic humanity, which is in fact, divine humanity. Christ grants the possibility of participation in that which frames his life: true humanity and true divinity in a single hypostasis.[40]

The image of Theotokos (the Mother of God) the Life-Giving Spring (Fig. 9). appeared in the 14th century due to the changes in liturgy and the introduction of a new liturgical office in honour of the Virgin Mary in 1335. It is difficult, however, to ascertain whether hesychasts contributed to this vast outpouring of Marian piety.[41]

Palamas expressed a personal attachment to the Virgin Mary, and he devoted several sermons and hymns to her; he often called the Virgin the source of life.[42] The first images of the Virgin as the source of life appeared in the middle of the 14th century, shortly after new liturgical services were composed in her honour in 1335, following the introduction of the Marian month. In this work, Theotokos assumes a frontal pose and emblem of Christ is visible on her chest. The meaning of the image is clear: salvation and eternal life were available to the Virgin after she willingly became an instrument of the incarnation. A few iconographical variants of the Virgin as the source of life exist and are distinguished not only for their iconographical subtlety, but also for a refined pictorial interpretation of the subject, indicating the high degree of freedom that Byzantine artists used in structuring holy images.[43] It is superfluous to question whether the above-quoted representations exhibit theologically explicable differences. Diversity of poetic formulations, both in poetry and in painting, arises from theological reflection on a topic; it is a result of subtle contemplation about its place, role and meaning within the economy of deliverance. According to Maglovski, this composition (*the Theotokos of the Life-giving Spring)* in art coincided with discussions during the hesychast controversy on the nature of light Three types

39 T.B. Roussanova, 'Painted Messages of Salvation: Monumental Programs of the Subsidiary Spaces of Late Byzantine Monastic Churches in Macedonia', PhD thesis, University of Maryland (2005).

40 J. Breck, 'Reflection on the Problem of Chalcedonian Christology', *St Vladimir's Theological Quarterly*, vol. 33, no. 2 (1989).

41 Velman, 'L'Iconographie de la Fontaine de Vie dans la Tradition Byzantine a la fin du Moyen Age', *Synthronon: Bibliotheque des Cahiers Archeologiques*, vol. 2 (Paris 1968) 121.

42 A. Kniazeff, 'La Theotocos dans le Offices du Temps Paschal', *Irenikon*, 1 (1961) 30ff.

43 D. Medakovic, 'Bogorodica Zivonosni Istocnik u Srpskoj Umetnosti', *Zbornik Radova Vizantološkog Instituta*, vol. 5 (Belgrade 1958).

of images bear the title the Virgin as the source of life: the Virgin Orant with or without the Christ-child, and with a legend; the Virgin Orant (other, later types as well) with the fountain and a legend; and, finally, the Virgin Orant with Christ painted 'as a fountain' on her chest, without a legend.[44]

Two striking Serbian examples are those of Lesnovo (1349) and Ravanica (1387).[45] They reveal one of the many mystical names for Theotokos, most notably the 'Spring', expanded at Lesnovo to 'the Spring of Life', and later to 'the Life-Giving Spring' in Ravanica. The Lesnovo example constitutes an iconographical minimum which developed further and reached its fullest form in Džefarovic, in a printed icon of 1744.[46] Unlike the Lesnovo type, the one from Ravanica, along with examples from the Afendico, Mystra, from 1313–1322 and the Chora church, Istanbul, 1340–1375, belong to the type where the epithet is the only iconographical connection with the fountain depicted. The example from Ravanica testifies to this, with its contrast of a dark, but starry, night on which an image of Oranta is depicted; the title reads Theotokos, the Life Giving Spring.[47]

The appearance of this figurative scene also testifies to the role of Theotokos in salvation, a representative of those who acquired true vision of light. According to the teaching of Palamas, she has, in fact, brought the light into the world.[48] Besides the two iconographical types which occurred in Serbian and Macedonian painting, there is an older type which has no legend. In the Patriarchate of Peć, there is such example, created in 1330.[49] The image of the *Virgin, the Spring of Life*, from the church of St Cosmas and Damian, Ohrid, which bears the inscription 'not made by hand' dates to 1340. From 1365 on, this Mariological composition found a place in the apses of the churches. The

44 J.D. Maglovski, 'The Virgin as the Fountain of Life: Gems of a Late and Post-Byzantine Motif', *Zbornik Matice Srpske za Likovne Umetnost*, vol. 1, no. 32–33 (2002).

45 Okunev, 'Lesnovo', in P. Lemerle (trans), *L'Art Byzantin Chez les Slaves: Mélanges Théodore Uspenskij*, vol. 1 (Paris 1930) 252, pl. 35; J. Babić, 'Портрет Данила II изнад Улаза у Богородичину Цркву у Пеħи', *Данило II и Његово Доба* (Belgrade 1991).

46 T. Starodubcev, 'Богородица Живоносни Источник у Раваници-Питања Порекла Слике' (unpublished paper) accessed 5/06/2011, in situ (Belgrade 2011).

47 G. Millet, *Recherches sur l'Iconographie de l'Evangile aux XIVe, XVe et XVIe Siècles d'Après les Monuments de Mistra, de la Macédoine et du Mont Athos* (Paris 1960) chpt I, 95; P. Underwood, *The Kariye Djami* (New York 1966) 207; V.J. Djurić, *Манастир Раваница и Раванички Живопис 1381–1981: Spomenica o Šestoj Stogodišnjici* (Belgrade 1981) 53–60.

48 The examples from Afendico, Mistra (1313–1322), and the Chora church, Istanbul (1340–1375), belong to a type where the epithet 'spring' is the only iconographical connection with the depicted fountain (Maglenovski, *Theotokos-Zivonosni Istocnik: Dragulj Jedne Kasne i Postvizantiske Teme* (Belgrade 2003) 188–192.

49 M. Tatic-Djuric, 'Image et Message de la Theotokos Sorce de Vie', *Association Internationale d' Etudes du Sud-Est Europeen Buletin*, vol. 19. no. 23, 1–2 (Bucarest 1993). This example, which has no legend, precedes an unpublished example from the Church of Virgin Peribleptos in Ohrid, more or less of the same type (Velmans, 'Le role de l' Hesychasm', 192–195).

image of the *Virgin the Spring of Life* from Psaća is one of those paintings placed in apses; it bears no inscription, but it exhibits the iconographical features of the type.[50]

The intellectual climate prevailing in the Church in the middle of the 14th century, and for which the hesychasts were partly responsible, made an impact upon the growth of the composition 'Jesus Christ the King of Kings'. In this figurative scene, Christ wears imperial robes, and he is surrounded by the Virgin and other saints. The main examples are found at the Church of St Athanasius, Kastoria (1384), the Monastery of Theotokos, Trescavec[51] (1342–1343), as well as at the Church of the Transfiguration, Kovalevo (1380),[52] and the Dormition Church, Kremlin. According to Millet, this creation depicts Palamas's interpretation of Psalm 44, 9 and gives a narrative prefiguration of Christ as King and Theotokos as Queen. Similarly, a text written by patriarch Philotheus Kokkinos, a known hesychast proponent, described one of Palamas's dreams in which the saint had a vision of Christ as King surrounded by a group of servants (St Demetrius being one of them).[53] Even though Djurić and Grozdanov disputed this hypothesis, claiming that Palamas could not have had such a public influence before 1347, the influence of hesychasm was widespread before 1347 under the guidance of Gregory of Sinai.[54] Furthermore, Palamas's teachings spread to monastic circles long before he was sent to prison. Finally, it is difficult to ascertain the date of creation of frescoes in the few monasteries containing these themes.[55]

The addition of song VI of the *Akathistos Hymn* at the end of the 13th century informed its representation (Virgin Olympiotissa, Elasson, for example). The purpose of this image was to reject the changes brought by the Western doctrine of *filioque* (Fig. 10). In addition, the aim of this representation was to validate the double nature of Christ (human and divine) as well as to confirm the role of the Virgin Mary in the incarnation. The *Akathist Hymn* at the Trinity Church, Cosia, symbolises Palamas's concepts regarding the role of the Virgin in the history of salvation. She is endorsed with a complex mandorla that is commonly reserved for Christ. While the neighbouring Church of Panagia Kanakaria, Lithrankomi, (6th century) contains precedents for this image, such models are rare.

50 Velmans, 'Fontaine', f. 11.

51 S. Smolčić-Makuljević, 'The Treskavac Monastery in the 15th Century and the Programme of Fresco Painting of the Nave in the Church of the Dormition of the Mother of God', *Zbornik Matice Srpske za Likovne Umetnosti*, vol. 37 (2009).

52 D.M. Fiene, 'What is the Appearance of Divine Sophia?', *Slavic Review*, vol. 48, no. 3 (Autumn 1989).

53 A. Xyngopoulos, 'Seint Demetre le Grand duc Apocafkos', *Ellenica*, vol. 15 (Thessalonica 1957).

54 C. Grozdanov, 'Христос Цар, Богородица Царица, Небесните Сили и Светите Воини во Живописот од XIV и XV век во Трескавец', *Културно Наследство* (1985–86) (Skopje 1998).

55 V.J. Djurić, *Византијске Фреске у Југославији* (Belgrade 1974) 218; C. Grozdanov, 'Христос Цар', 7–11.

An interesting example is in the illustrated program of *Stichera for Christmas* (6th century). The Church of the Virgin Peribleptos, Ohrid, from the 13th century, contains a similar figurative scene.[56]

The metaphorical title of the Virgin as *'kandilo svetlonosno'* (light-emitting lamp) used in XI Ikos (part of the hymn) advanced the Mariological cycle in the churches of Decani, Matejce, Koxija as well as in manuscripts of Thomas's Psalter and the Escorial. All these artistic creations contain an image of Theotokos with a candle placed above her head or behind her neck. In some Byzantine lead seals, the body of Theotokos assumes the shape of a candle, and the space around her is painted bright red to symbolise the bright light that comes from 'tongues of fire' (divine energies).[57]

Finally, due to the spread of hesychasm in Byzantium, the pictorial representation of the Eucharist incurred alterations. In principle, the composition commonly known as the Communion of the Apostles, which was usually placed in the apse of the church, was a symbol of the liturgy, celebrated by Christ and the angels in heaven. This was frequent in the middle of the 14th century, when the figure of Christ in this work recalls in a concrete way the parallelism between the heavenly and earthly Church, as in Decani and Matka (1496–1497).[58] Despite the presence of this image in the apse, the dome was decorated with a related composition, the Divine Liturgy. Both compositions refer to the service celebrated in heaven, yet each has a different context: Communion of the Apostles was a liturgical version of the Supper; the Divine Liturgy, on the other hand, illustrated the sacramental rites as acts of God.[59] Many fathers of the Eastern Christian tradition affirmed the parallelism between the two offices (heavenly and earthly liturgy), but Nicolas Cabasilas advanced this doctrine even further.[60]

In terms of symbolism, important novelties were the introduction of complex mandorla, the appearance of eight rays of light, the appearance of the 'O'ΩN ('I am who I am') monogram on the halo of Christ, and the introduction of three-dimensional rainbows. Other significant features were the use of zigzag

---

56 G. Babic, 'Le Iconographie Constantinopolitane de l'Catiste de la Vierge i Valachie', *Zbornik Radova Vizantiskago Institute* (Belgrade 1973) fig. 13.

57 J. Cotsonis, 'The Virgin with the Tongues of Fire on Byzantine Lead Seals', *Dumbarton Oaks Papers*, vol. 48 (1994).

58 G. Millet & A. Millet, *La Peinture du Moyen Âge en Yougoslavie: Serbie, Macédoine, et Monténégro*, vol. 3 (Paris 1962) fig. 116.

59 F.E. Brightman, 'The Hystorica Mystagogica and Other Commentaries on the Byzantine Liturgy', *Journal of Theological Studies*, vol. 9 (1908) 255–256, 390–394.

60 This composition is interesting as it represents figures of officiating prelates accompanying the procession of angels to emphasise their mystical union, the effect being that behind the liturgy, which takes place in the bema, is its model, which takes place in heaven. A. Jevtic, 'Recontre De la Scholastique et de l'Hesychasme dans l'Oeuvre de le Nilus Cabasilas', *L'Art de Thessalonique et des Pays Balkaniques et les Courants Spirituels au XIVe Siècle Recueil des Rapports du IVe Colloque Serbo-Grec 1987: Éditions Spéciales: Balkanološki Institut*, vol. 31 (1987) 149–157; D.P. Miquel, 'L'Experience Sacrementelle selon Nicolas Kabasilas', *Irenikon*, 2 (1965) 130.

patterns on murals, consisting of red and blue bands within a circular band, fanlike highlights on figures, and the use of monochrome colours (red, ochre and dark shades of blue). The painted surfaces were illuminated with white strokes (on the face, neck and hands) representing the rays of the divine light. Given the widespread changes in style and iconography arising in the 14th and 15th centuries, it can be affirmed that iconographic trends during Paleologan era were shaped by mystical spiritual currents, one of them being the Byzantine hesychasm. Detailed analysis of three compositions of the Transfiguration, the Anastasis and the Trinity will provide evidence for this assertion.

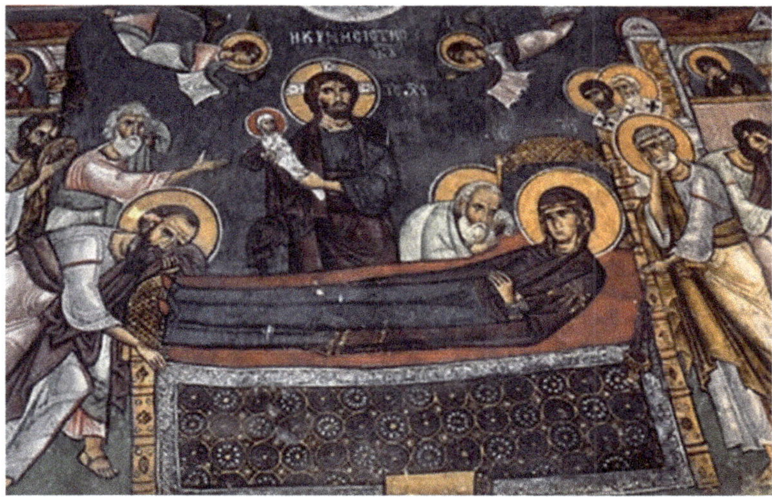

Figure 1. *The Dormition of the Virgin*, c. 1105–1106, fresco, west door of the nave, Church of Panagia Phorbiotissa, Asinou (Cyprus)

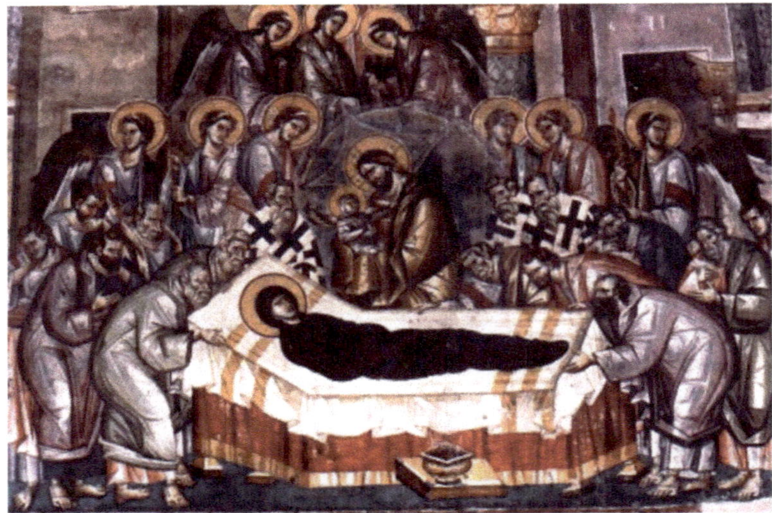

Figure 2. *The Dormition of the Virgin*, c. 1294–1295, fresco, west wall of the nave, painters Eutychios and Michael Astrapas, Church of St Clement Ohridski (Church of the Virgin Peribleptos), Ohrid (Macedonia)

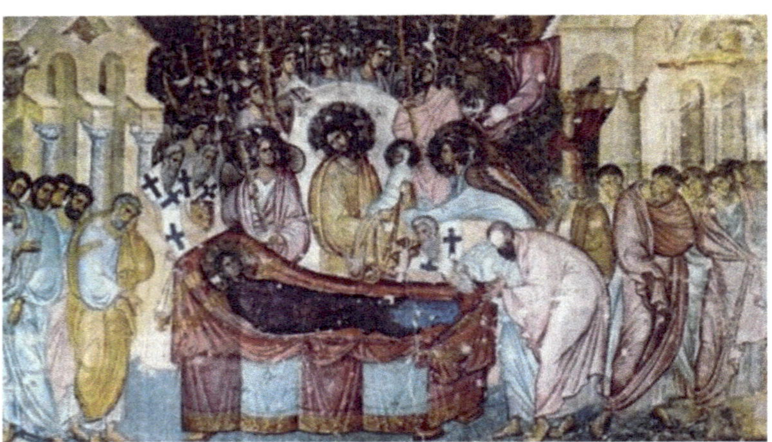

Figure 3. *The Dormition of the Virgin*, c. 1265, fresco, west wall of the nave, Monastery of Sopočani, Raška (Serbia)

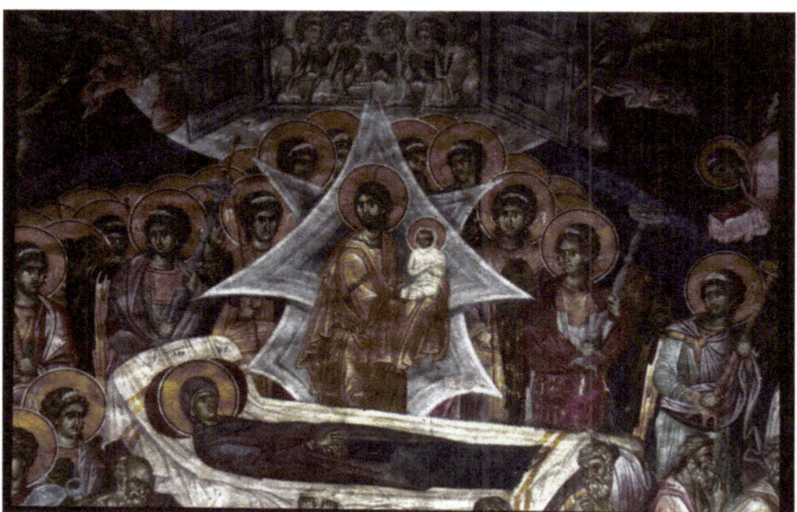

Figure 4. ***The Dormition of Virgin*****, c. 1321, fresco, west wall of the nave, Monastery of Gračanica (Serbia)**

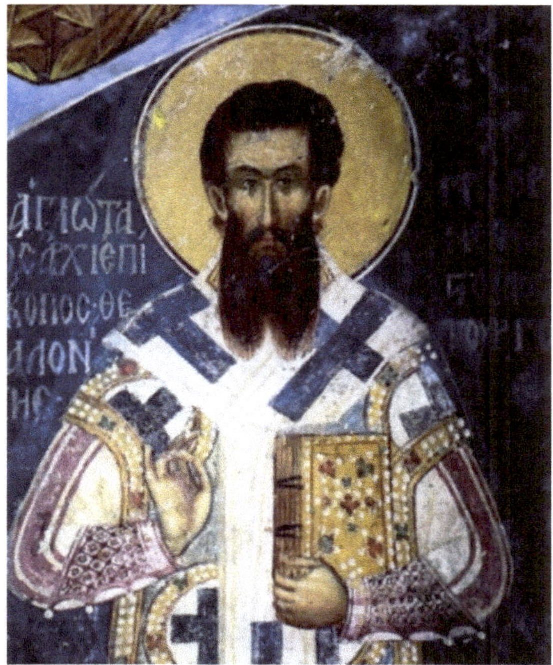

Figure 5. ***Gregory Palamas*****, c. 1371, fresco, eastern wall of the nave, Monastery of Vatopedi, Mt Athos (Greece)**

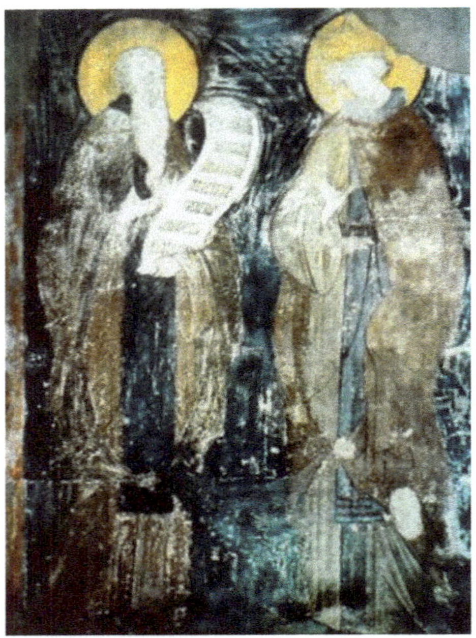

Figure 6. *Barlaam and Iosaphat*, c. 1400, fresco, painter Andrei Rublev, Church of the Dormition of the Virgin Mary, Gorodok, Zvenigorod (Russia)

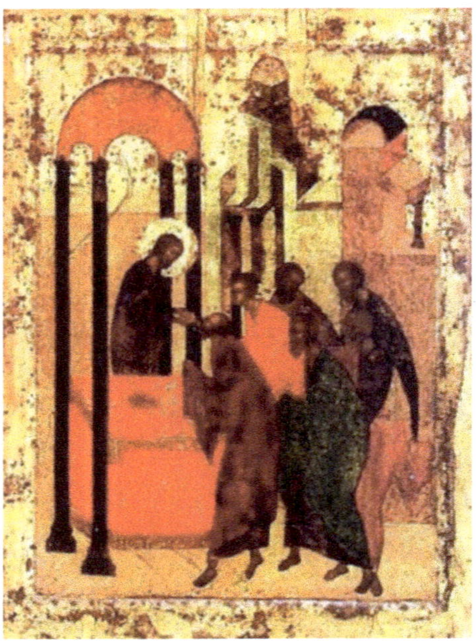

Figure 7. *The Communion of the Apostles*, c. 1425–1427, tempera on wood, 87.5 x 67 cm, Cathedral of the Trinity, Trinity-Sergius's Lavra, Sergiev Posad (Russia), inv. no. 3050

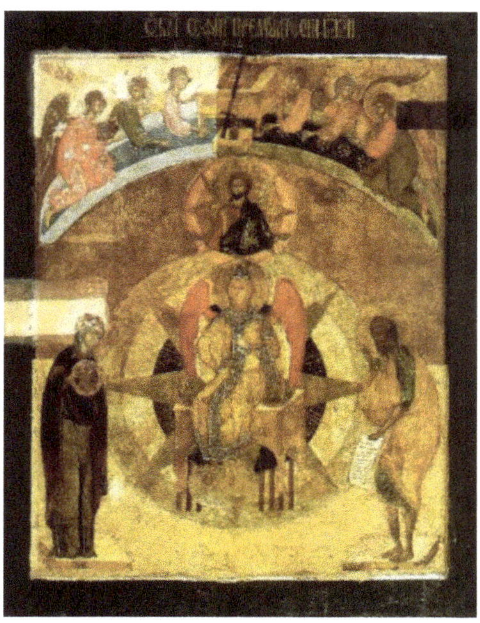

Figure 8. *The Wisdom of God (Sophia)*, mid-15th century, tempera on wood, 69 x 54.5 cm, Church of the Annunciation, Kremlin, Moscow (Russia), inv. no. 480 соб

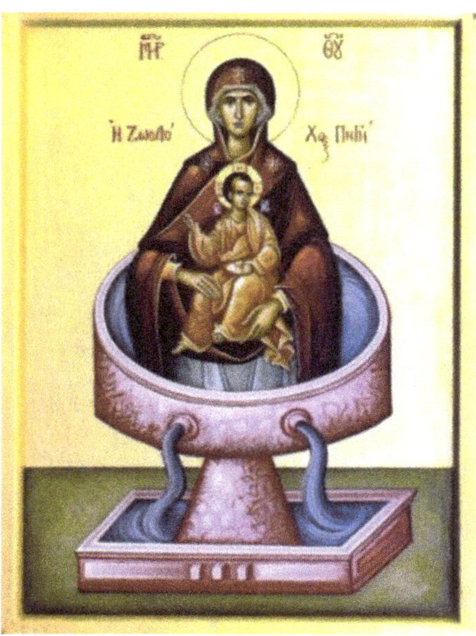

Figure 9. *The Theotokos of the Life-giving Spring*, c. 2012, tempera on wood, 69 x 54.5 cm, painter Anita Strezova, private collection (Sydney)

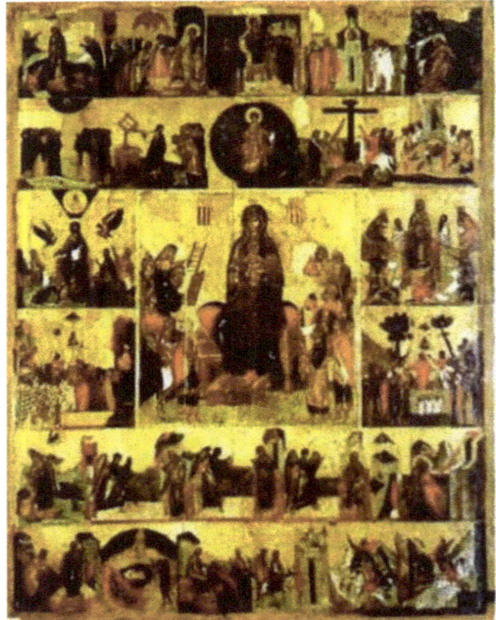

Figure 10. ***The Akathistos Hymn*****, 14th century, tempera on wood, 198 x 153 cm, Cathedral of the Dormition, Kremlin, Moscow (Russia)**

3. The *Transfiguration* Miniature of *Parisinus Graecus* 1242

The subject of Christ's Transfiguration appears regularly in a doctrinal context in the writings of the hesychasts, connected with the vision of the 'age to come'. The event of the Transfiguration represents the vision of Christ in His glory, the deified state of being in God's Kingdom. For the 'Son of God became man so that we might become gods'.[1] It is a doctrine underlining Byzantine aesthetics and the theory of the image (*icon*) in representational arts; the inaccessible and invisible Triadic God imparts himself directly to his creation through his incarnation and in his uncreated glory or energies.[2] Hence, the doctrine of the Taboric light provides evidence for establishing an iconographic and aesthetic argument for the existence of God.[3]

The acceptance by the Byzantine Church of the theology of the uncreated light as an official dogma in 1375 motivated the advancement of a new and complex image of the Transfiguration in the 14th and 15th centuries.[4] Byzantine manuscript illumination of the Transfiguration accompanying the *Theological Works of John VI Kantacuzenos* (*Parisinus Graecus* 1242)[5] verifies this trend. The miniature is a dramatic and captivating image of the Transfiguration that eloquently illustrates the release of the uncreated light of God on Mt Tabor (Fig. 11). Three new elements appear in this luxurious work of art: a new 'hesychast' mandorla, a tripartite representation of Mt Tabor, and overall change in the positioning of the apostles.

The theological background of the Transfiguration

The composition of the Transfiguration is the traditional Byzantine image of the feast of the Metamorphosis of Christ. This event is a theophany, a manifestation of God and a display of His uncreated light on Mt Tabor.[6] It has a pivotal place

1 V. Lossky, *The Vision of God* (Beds 1963) 34.

2 Nikephoros of Constantinople, Antirrheticus II, 16; *Patrologia Graeca* 100, 367 ABC, in Nikephoros of Constantinople, 'Antirrhetici Tres Adversus Constantinum Copronymus', *Patrologia Graeca* 100, 206–574.

3 P. Evdokimov, *The Art of the Icon: A Theology of Beauty* (Crestwood 1998) 231–238.

4 A. Andreopoulos, *Metamorphosis: The Transfiguration in Byzantine Theology and Iconography* (Crestwood 2005) 215–217.

5 John Kantacuzenos, 'Refutationes Duae Prochori Cydonii et Disputatio cum Paulo Patriarcha Latino Epistulis Septem Tradita Nunc Primum Editae Curantibus', in E. Voordeckers & F. Tinnefeld (ed.), *Iohannis Cantacuzeni Opera*, Corpus Christianorum. Ser. Graeca, vol. 16 (Belgium 1987) 3–105.

6 M. Smith, 'The Origins and Significance of the Transfiguration Story', *Union Seminary Quarterly Review*, vol. 36 (1980).

in the New Testament and is described in the three Synoptic Gospels (Matthew 17:1–13, Mark 9:2–13 and Luke 9:28–36). It refers to the occasion when Christ appeared in glory during his earthly life. Shortly before his suffering on the cross, Jesus left Capernaum and, accompanied by his three apostles John, James and Peter, he ascended Mt Tabor, where he experienced a metamorphosis.

While the three evangelists give separate accounts of the event of the Transfiguration, their descriptions of the feast are similar.[7] When Jesus and his disciples climbed up Mt Tabor, the clothes of Jesus 'became shining and exceeding white as snow, such as no launderer on earth could whiten them' (Mark 9:3). At this point, the three apostles saw Christ conversing with Moses and Elias about his forthcoming suffering at Golgotha, and the fact that the blood of the Saviour would redeem the sins of humanity. When the apostles fell to the ground, a cloud overshadowed them, and from the cloud a voice was heard: 'This is my beloved Son, in whom I am well pleased' (Matthew 3:17). Peter's response to witnessing this miracle was to build three tabernacles, one for Jesus, one for Moses and one for Elias. The other Synoptic Gospels are slightly different. According to Luke, the apostles were heavy with sleep and, when they awoke, they saw His glory and the two men who stood with Him (Luke 9:32). When the apostles heard God's voice, 'they fell on their faces and were greatly afraid' (Matthew 17:6). After the Transfiguration, Jesus returned to Capernaum with his disciples.[8] The event of the Transfiguration is also mentioned in II Peter 16–18, but the emphasis is on the reality of Christ's Transfiguration, making known His divine power and majesty.[9] This text also refers to the doctrine of the hypostatic union of divine and human natures in Christ (*communicatio idiomatum*), which introduces a close relationship between the Transfiguration and deification.[10]

Written evidence of the Transfiguration also comes from the apocryphal treatises from the 2nd century, such as the Acts of John, the Apocrypha of John, and the Apocalypse of Peter 15–17.[11] The sources present the episode of

---

7 John Chrysostom, On Mathew, Homily 56; *Patrologia Graeca* 56, 552–553, in John Chrysostom 'Spuria Contra Theatra', *Patrologia Graeca* 56, 517–564.

8 The Troparion of the Transfiguration similarly summarises the meaning of the feasts: 'You were transfigured on the mount, O Christ God, revealing your glory to your disciples as they could bear it. Let your everlasting light shine upon us sinners, through the prayers of the Theotokos, O Giver of Light, and Glory to you', The Troparion of the Transfiguration, http://orthodoxkansas.org/HolyTransfiguration.html#troparion (accessed 3/09/2012).

9 L. Thuren, 'Style Never goes out of Fashion: 2 Peter Reevaluated', in S.T. Porter & H. Olbricht (eds), *Rhetoric, Scripture and Theology: Essays from the 1994 Pretoria Conference* (Sheffield 1996) 341.

10 M. Aghiorgoussis, 'Orthodox Soteriology', in J. Meyendorff (trans), R. Tobias (ed.), *Salvation in Christ: A Lutheran Orthodox Dialogue* (Augsburg 1992) 42.

11 R. Bauckham, '2 Petar and the Apokalipse of Peter', *The Fate of the Dead: Studies on the Jewish and Christian Apocalypses* (Leiden 1998) 290–293; See also D.H. Schmidt, 'The Peters Writing: Their Redactors and Their Relationships', PhD thesis, Northwestern University (1972) 115–116.

the Transfiguration in the light of *Parousia*, (the Second Coming of Christ),[12] though in many different ways and against many false teachers and messiahs. The apocryphal writings, however, refer to the final destiny of righteous martyrs, rather than discussing the vision of the uncreated light on Mt Tabor.[13]

Interpretation

The homilies and sermons of ecclesiastical writers, such as John Chrysostom, Ephraim the Syrian and Cyril of Alexandria, affirm that the origins of the feast of the Transfiguration go back to the first centuries of Christianity. When Empress Helena erected a church on the site of the Transfiguration, religious authorities added the feast of the Transfiguration to the Church calendar.[14] The Eastern Church celebrated this feast on 6 August, well before the 8th century, when John of Damascus gave the feast canonical status.[15] The four gospels refer to the Transfiguration as occurring 40 days before the Crucifixion (possibly in February). Church authorities, however, transferred the celebration to August because, amidst the sorrow and repentance of Lent, the full glory and joy associated with the Transfiguration could not be celebrated. The writings of St Nicodemus Hagiorite and Eusebius of Caesarea contain references that support this hypothesis.[16] A celebration on 6 August is proper given that it is 40 days before the Feast of the Exaltation of the Cross (14 September in the Julian calendar), when the Eastern Church remembers Christ's passion for the second time during the liturgical year. Both *Kontakion of the Transfiguration* and the *Service of the Vespers* affirm the link between the Transfiguration and the Crucifixion, which share a common theological basis. A proper understanding of both Christological events is only possible in reference to the Resurrection.[17]

Pope Kallistos III introduced the feast of the Transfiguration in the West in 1457 to commemorate the victory over the Turks at Belgrade on 6 August 1456. The essentially Roman calendar of the Supplicationes does not include the event of the Transfiguration, which is a festival of the second rank (without octave of the feast).[18]

---

12 D. Farkansfalvy, 'The Ecclesial Setting of Pseudepigraphy in Second Peter', *The Second Century*, vol. 5, no. 1 (1985–1986).

13 V. Hills, *Parables, Pretenders and Prophecies: Translation and Interpretation in the Apocalypse of Peter 2, Revue Biblique*, vol. 98 (1991) 572–573.

14 P.B. D'Alsace', *La Mount Tabor* (Paris 1900) 58–61, 133–154.

15 John of Damascus, 'Homilae on the Transfiguration', *Patrologia Graeca* 96.

16 P.B. Paschos, 'La Θεολογίας de la Μεταμόρφωση', *Ερως Ορθοδοξίας εκδ Αποστολικής Διακονίας* (Athens 1978) 51–57.

17 For isolated instances of the celebration of the feast of the Transfiguration in Europe before the fifteenth century, see W. Kroning, 'Zur Transfiguration der Cappella Palatina in Palermo', *ZKunstw*, vol. 9 (1956).

18 K. Ware, 'La Transfiguration du Christ et la Souffrance du Monde', *Soperim*, no. 294 (January 2005).

Irenaeus was the first Christian father to provide an explanation of the meaning of the Transfiguration and he set the pattern for all future patristic exegesis about this event. Emphasising the eschatological and soteriological meaning of this feast, Irenaeus claimed that by participating in the uncreated light we acquire the state of incorruptibility or deification.[19] Clement of Alexandria regarded the Transfiguration as a sign of the transformation of human nature and the reality of salvation.[20] He focused on the experience of light as revealed to the apostles according to their spiritual state and their ability to receive the divine grace. Origen interpreted the event of the Metamorphosis of Christ in the light of eschatology, where only those living beyond the sixth day could see the transfigured Christ. According to Origen, the bright cloud, Jesus' shining face and the whiteness of his garments revealed Christ as God. The words of God the Father, which came from the cloud, signalled that Jesus is a beloved Son. The manifestation of the Holy Spirit in the form of dazzling light indicated the same. Moreover, the presence of Moses and Elijah alongside Christ bore witness to the fact that Christ was the Messiah of the Old Testament.[21]

Similarly, in one of his interpretations on the subject of the Metamorphosis of Christ, Basil the Great affirmed the eschatological character of the Transfiguration, especially in the presence of Elias during the miracle. Elias was the prototype and prophet of the Second Coming of Christ because he received a vision of God on Mt Sinai while he was still embodied (I/III Kings 19:1–14, especially vs. 8–14). He achieved the state of transfiguration by virtue of his holiness in such way that God placed him within the divine aura of his holiness, in which Elias shared, participating in God's energies without compromising the divine essence.[22]

Moses, on the other hand, had two major theophanies on Mt Sinai. In the first revelation, the angel of the Lord appeared to Moses in a bush that burned, but was not consumed (Exod. 3:1–2). The manifestation of God on Mt Sinai was a spectacular demonstration of God's power and majesty (Exodus, 3:lf; 33:19–23). The two revelations of God to Moses led Christian scholars to understand theophany as an unambiguous manifestation of God to man.

Athanasius of Sinai claimed that Christ banished all doubts concerning the *Parousia* when he gave Peter, John and James a vision of his glory and foreshadowed the kingdom of heaven.[23] More significant, however, was the

---

19 Lossky, *The Vision of God*, 34.

20 Clement of Alexandria, 'Stromateis II', 22, in O. Stählin (ed.) *Stromateis I–VI* (Berlin 1960).

21 A. Chemberas, 'The Transfiguration of Christ: A Study in the Patristic Exegesis of Scripture', *St Vladimirs Theological Quarterly*, vol. 14, no. 1–2 (1970) 48–65; R.P. Moroziuk, 'Origen and Apophaticism: The Case of Asomaton in I, 1.1–9 of the Peri Archon', *Logos*, no. 34 (1993) 587–600.

22 K. Onasch, *Icons* (New York 1969) 107 & 142f.

23 Anastasius of Sinai, 'Sermon on the Transfiguration 6–10', *Melanges d'Archeologie et d'Histoire*, vol. 67 (1955).

revelation of the change his body experienced during the Transfiguration. Christ did not depart from his divinity when he became man, nor was his human nature lost when it became part of the Godhead. On the contrary, the two natures in Christ remained unconfused, and their properties retained their integrity even after the union. Consequently, by virtue of the hypostatic union of his two natures, Christ gave humanity a share in the divine honour, as shown during his Metamorphosis on Mt Tabor.[24]

Maximus the Confessor affirmed that the uncreated light on Mt Tabor was without beginning and end and belongs to the mystical realm of apophasis, which means that it remains uncircumscribed and unperceivable by the senses.[25] John of Damascus stated that 'in the Transfiguration Christ did not become something He was not before, but appeared to his disciples as God and man'.[26] In other words, Christ was the same person with whom they usually conversed every day. It was during the Transfiguration, however, that Peter, John and James received the faculty of contemplating him in his eternal glory.[27]

Gregory Palamas (1296–1359) was the greatest exponent of the doctrine of the Transfiguration, which he progressed in response to the attacks of Barlaam of Calabria.[28] His doctrinal position on this issue, which formed the basis of the Byzantine understanding of the Transfiguration, is discussed in detail in Chapter One.

Even though there are many different interpretations of the event of the Transfiguration in the writings of church fathers, symbols reveal the essence of the events. This allows for more than one explanation to be entertained across three literary genres: an epiphany that dealt with the revelation of Jesus' two natures, an apocalyptic vision of Christ referring to his *Parousia*, and a soteriological revelation of the Son of God with an emphasis on the restoration of the lost image in humankind.[29]

The iconography of the Transfiguration

Scholars distinguish five different stages in the development of the iconography of the Transfiguration. The earliest preserved images of the Transfiguration are

24 Leo the Great, 'Homily delivered on the Saturday before the Second Sunday in Lent: On the Transfiguration, Matthew 17:1–13'; http://www.newadvent.org/fathers/360351.htm (accessed 10/03/2010).

25 Maximus the Confessor, 'Ambiguorum Liber 10', *Patrologia Graeca* 91, 1168A, Cf. K. Parry, *Depicting the Word: Byzantine Iconophile Thought of the Eighth and Ninth Centuries* (Leiden 1996) 123.

26 John of Damascus, 'Homilae on the Transfiguration', 564.

27 Gregory Palamas, *Triads, Patrologia Graeca* 151, 433B, in Gregory Palamas, Operum coninuatio, *Patrologia Graeca* 151, 9–551.

28 Please refer to the Chapter I on Hesychasm.

29 D.A. Lee, *Transfiguration* (Chicago 2004) 122.

from the 4th–5th century. These are the images threaded on an ivory casket from Brescia, Italy;[30] manuscript illuminations of the Rabbula Gospels;[31] and, the woodcarving of a scene from the doors of Santa Sabina in Rome.[32] Artistically speaking these examples are not well developed, with the common feature being the depiction of only three characters: Jesus, Moses and Elijah. It is possible they express one of the central concerns of the early doctrinal conflicts — the unity of Old and New Testament.

The inclusion of all the elements of the Biblical story of the Transfiguration, such as Moses and Elijah (standing next to Christ) and Peter, John and James witnessing the event, characterises the second stage of development of Transfiguration iconography. Among the best-known examples from this period are two mosaics of the Transfiguration in the Basilica of St Apollinaire in Classe, Ravenna (Fig. 12), and the apse of the Monastery of St Katherine on Mt Sinai (Fig. 13).

The symbolic composition which covers the top part of the apse of the Basilica of St Apollinaire in Classe clearly symbolises the Transfiguration of Christ on Mt Tabor.[33] Moreover, this figurative scene is an allegorical interpretation of the eschatological glory of God's presence through the depiction of the cross, the martyrdom of apostles represented as lambs, the death of St Apolliniarie and, finally, through the mystery of the Eucharist (the mosaic extends to the area above the altar where priests celebrate the Eucharist).

The mosaic of the Transfiguration in the apse of the Church of the Virgin Mary in the Monastery of St Katherine (Fig. 13), on is the most majestic of preserved ancient examples of early images of the Transfiguration.[34] This type reflects the influence of the new theology of the Transfiguration that reached its full development with Maximus the Confessor.[35] The inclusion of the three apostles

---

30 C.B. Tkacz, *The Key to the Brescia Casket* (Notre Dame 2001) 42.

31 M. Bernabò, *Il Tetravangelo di Rabbula: Firenze, Biblioteca Medicea Laurenziana, Plut. 1.56: l'Illustrazione del Nuovo Testamento nella Siria del VI Secolo* (Roma 2008); M. Jeremias, *Die Holtur des Basilika S. Sabina in Rom* (Tubingen 1980) 77–80.

32 The three earliest images — from Brescia, Santa Sabina and illustration of the Rabula Gospels are commonly known as pre-Sinaitic images of the Transfiguration of Christ (J.M. Spieser, 'Le Programme Iconographique des Portes de Sainte-Sabinem', *Journal des Savants* (1991) 63–69.

33 E. Dinkler, *Das Apsismosaik von S. Apollinare in Classe* (Cologne 1964) 32–34.

34 Apocalyptic notes are combined with the image of the Holy Cross in the centre of heaven, which in turn points out the historical incident during the victory over Rome, the founder of the Byzantine Empire — St Constantine the Great. The presence of a symbol of the Lamb of God is like the lamb used for Christ as depicted in the first three centuries when Christians were persecuted (in this case depicted as a substitute for the image of 12 Apostles). It seems that the artist did not try to recreate a segment of physical reality, but rather used complex symbolism to convey the fully developed Christian dogma (G. Schiller, *Iconography of Christian Art*, J. Seligman (trans), vol. 1 (London 1971) 147.

35 Andreopoulos, 'The Mosaic of the Transfiguration in St Katherine's Monastery on Mount Sinai: A Discussion of its origins', *Byzantion*, vol. 72, no. 1 (June 2002); G.H. Forsyth & K. Weitzmann, *The Monastery of Saint Catherine at Mount Sinai* (Princeton 1973) 11; G. SedRajna, *L'Art Juif: Orient et Occident* (Paris 1975) 105.

in the lower part of the icon, the placement of Christ surrounded by Moses and Elias at the top of the image, and the portrayal of Christ inside the mandorla surrounded by rays of light, confirm this fact.[36]

The next stage in the developing the iconography of the Transfiguration appeared during the Iconoclastic controversy of the 8th and 9th centuries. Two types of Transfiguration images florished at this time. In the first, Christ appears in the centre of a circular mandorla, with Moses and Elijah encompassing him. In the second, the oval mandorla belongs to Christ alone. Although the two types often appear in one monument, for example, in the churches of St Prassede, St Nereus and St Achilleus in Rome,[37] they in fact represent two separate stages in the development of the iconography of the Transfiguration.

Circular mandorlas behind Christ appeared in images of the Transfiguration from the 9th to the 11th centuries, whereas from the 11th to the 14th centuries an oval mandorla surrounds Christ (Fig. 14). Often, to create an illusion of standing in front of luminous stars, iconographers added the luminous rays of light, which shone forth from the mandorla (Fig. 15). The depiction of the witnesses of the event of the Metamorphosis, as well as the representation of the mount of the Transfiguration, is of particular importance. Within this scheme, there was room for variation in the grouping and the relationship between various figures, the placement and gestures of the apostles, the shape of the mandorla, the representation of Mt Tabor, and Christ's relationship with his apostles.

The appearance of a narrative type of image in the late-13th century marked the intermediary stage in the developing iconography of the Transfiguration. Images of the three disciples, accompanied by Christ ascending and descending, supplemented the regular iconography of the Transfiguration. A contributing feature was the elevation of John, James and Peter above the ground, which is not depicted in earlier or later images of the Metamorphosis.[38]

A rise in the popularity of the subject of the Transfiguration parallels the spread of the hesychast movement in the 14th century. Patterson observed an increased interest in the theme of the Transfiguration during the second half of the 14th century, as well as changes in iconography in contemporary medieval Romania. A parallel development, persisting until the 17th century, was also noticeable in

36 O. Demus, *Byzantine Mosaic Decoration* (London 1948) 9–10; For St Katherine, see J. Miziolek, 'Transfiguratio Domini in the Apse of Mount Sinai and the Symbolism of Light', *Journal of the Warburg and Courtauld Institutes*, vol. 53 (1990) 42–60; and the pages devoted to this mosaic in J. Elsner, *Art and the Roman Viewer* (Cambridge 1995) 99–123.

37 A Transfiguration image from the Chuldov Psalter consists of a round mandala in which the figures of Moses and Elijah are enclosed; M.B. Mauck, 'The Mosaic of the Triumphal Arch of S. Prassede: A Liturgical Interpretation', *Speculum*, vol. 62, no. 4 (October 1987).

38 There is an abundance of variations in the mandorla type: circular mandorla, oval mandorlas, mandorlas that envelope the Old Testament prophets and others that just stop just short from including them fully, mandorlas with or without rays; V.N. Lazarev, *History of Byzantine Art*, vol. 19 (1986) 46.

Russia (Fig. 16). The increase in the number of churches dedicated to the feast of Transfiguration affirms that the hesychast doctrine of the Transfiguration spread outside Byzantine borders around this time.[39]

Emphasis on the psychological reactions of the disciples, appearance of the complex mandorla and tripartite representation of Mt Tabor exemplifies the new iconography of the Transfiguration that formed under the impact of hesychasm. The best example of this trend is the miniature of the *Parisinus Graecus*.

The *Transfiguration* miniature of the *Parisinus Graecus* 1242

It was not common for Byzantine scribes of the late Palaeologan period to produce illuminated manuscripts of theological treatises and, in the 'surviving corpus of late Byzantine manuscripts the Paris Codex is a rarity'.[40] The manuscript *Parisinus Graecus* (1242) contains the theological works of the Byzantine Emperor John VI Kantacuzenos who died at Mystra in 1383.[41]

The library of the monastery of St Athanasia on the Holy Mountain held the manuscript before it was deposited in the Bibliothèque nationale de France. Kantacuzenos created this book as a gift for Nicolas Cabasilas, an eminent theologian and active participant in the hesychast controversy.[42] The first part of the manuscript dates from 1370, and the final colophon is from 1375. The illuminations were long believed to be a product of the noble author who, after his abdication in 1354, took the monastic name of Ioasaph; however, this is not the case.[43] The scribe was another person, also named Ioasaph, one of the most outstanding Byzantine calligraphers.[44] He was a monk and eventually a hegumen of the monastery of the Hodegon at Constantinople between 1360 and 1405.[45] Ioasaph died in 1406, leaving behind him a legacy of around 30 signed and dated illuminated manuscripts.[46]

---

39 J. Patterson, 'Hesychast Thought as Re-evaluated in Byzantine, Greek and Roumanian Church Frescoes: A Theory of Origin and Diffusion', *Revue des Études Sud-Est Européennes*, vol. 16, no. 4 (1978).

40 I. Drpic, 'Arts, Hesychasm and Visual Exegesis', *Dumbarton Oaks Papers*, vol. 62, (2008) 236.

41 The *Parisius Graecus* 1242 is luxurious. The leaves of parchment are set vertically and horizontally and form two columns of 25 lines each. The titles and the initials which are from the hand of the same scribe are gilded.

42 A. Omont, *Miniatures des Plus Anciens Manuscripts Grecs de la Bibliotheque Nationale du VIe au XIVe Siecle* (Paris 1929) 38.

43 H. Buchthal, 'Toward a History of Palaeologan Illumination', in K. Weitzmann (ed.), *The Place of Book Illumination in Byzantine Art* (Princeton 1975).

44 L. Politis, 'Jean-Joasaph Cantacuzène fut-il copiste?', *Revue des Études Byzantines*, vol. 14 (1956).

45 G.M. Prokhorov, 'Публицистика Иоанна Кантакузина 1367–1371', *Византийский Временник*, no. 27 (1968).

46 Omont, *Miniatures*, 58–59, pl. 126; Buchtal, 'Toward a History', 165.

It is more likely that Kantacuzenos commissioned the production of the *Parisinus Graecus,* which contains images of him and theological writings as well as his expositions against union with the Church of Rome.[47] The theological treatises start with strong patriarchal orthodoxy, referring to the doctrine of the uncreated energies of Palamas; they continue with a political statement against the circumstantial union with the Church of Rome; and finally, they outline Christian attitudes towards Jews and Muslims.[48] Kantacuzenos's authorship of the theological treatises contained in the *Parisinus Greaecus* has never been challenged.[49] Apart from the theological texts, however, the manuscript is better known for its illuminations, which are a subject of interest for both theologians and art historians.[50] Buchthal identified the painter of the miniatures (based on the style) as the same individual who painted the *Lectionary of Koutloumousi* (*Codex 62*), kept at Hodegon monastery. He also decorated the *Vatican Gospel* (*Codex Graecus* 1160).[51]

The first miniature is an image of the emperor presiding over a council. Folio 123V contains the second miniature, which in a striking and solemnly confrontational way shows two portraits of Kantacuzenos side by side: one of him as an emperor (dressed in an imperial regalia), and one of him as a monk named Ioasaph.[52] The offset on folio 70v, and the stubs of two missing leaves, suggest that someone removed at least one more page of miniatures accompanying the theological text. An inscription on folio 70 provides a hint: this page contained an excerpt from the writings of the holy fathers.[53]

On the left page of the diptych (v. 92 f.), the dramatic scene on Mt Tabor is depicted, whereas a three-quarter folio on the opposing page, 93v, shows the portrait of Gregory the Theologian with an inscription 'Holy Gregory'. Gregory's thought was a precursor to the essence and energies distinction, which was affirmed as dogma by the Palamite Council of 1375.[54] Moreover, he received the title *Theologus,* or Theologian, a designation that was given to no other Christian writers except John the Apostle and Symeon the New Theologian. Many other liturgical texts referred to Gregory Palamas with the title the 'New Theologian', to emphasise the importance and mystique of his work reflected

---

47 K. Weitzmann, 'The Selection of Texts for Cyclical Illustration in Byzantine Manuscripts', *Byzantine Books and Bookmen: A Dumbarton Oaks Colloquium* (Washington D.C. 1975).

48 The treatises are written against: Isaac Argyre (8 books, ff. 9–70), the Latin patriarch Paul (7 books, ff. 71–119V), Islam (22 books, ff. 120–292) and Jews (18 books, ff. 293–436).

49 Buchthal, 'Toward a History'.

50 E. Voordeckers, 'Examen Codicologique du Codex Parisinus Graecus 1242', *Scriptorum,* vol. 21 (1967).

51 It seems that the miniaturist belonged to a group of painters whose style is recognisable also in the Peribleptos Church at Mystra and which re-emerges fully developed in the works of Theophanes the Greek, a native of Constantinople who worked in Russia; see Buchthal, 'Toward a History', 164ff.

52 ibid., 290.

53 ibid., 1, 29.

54 John Kantacuzenos, *Johannis Cantacuzini Imperatoris Historiarum Libri IV,* L. Schopen (ed.), vol. 2 (Bonn 1830) 438–439.

through his spiritual vision of the uncreated light. This view is supported by the representation of Gregory the Theologian in the *Parisinus Graecus* miniature. There is also a visual connection between the text written by Kantacuzenos and the miniature representing the event of Transfiguration.[55] The text elaborates on the nature of divine light, interpreted as divine energy or grace as seen on Mt Tabor. Three quotations by Gregory the Theologian and numerous lengthy excerpts from other ecclesiastical writers accompany the miniatures.

The first quotation starts with the initial Phi. Taken from Gregory the Theologian's oration *On Baptism*, this citation equates the scriptural revelation of the divine light received 'during baptism in illumination with the light seen by the apostles during the Transfiguration'.[56] Starting with the golden letter Omicron and referring to the apostle's vision of light (the sole reason for the Transfiguration), the second quote comes from the treatise *On Discipline in Discourse* by Gregory the Theologian.[57] Specifically, Peter, John and James climbed up the mountain to witness Jesus 'shining forth in his bodily form, reveal the divinity and bare the one who was hidden in the flesh'.[58] The final quotation stems from the First Letter of Gregory the Theologian to Kledonios, in which Gregory talks about the reality of the incarnation and the impending event of *Parousia*. Kantakuzenos used this sentence as a proof that the divine light of the Transfiguration of Christ was equal to the eternal light of the Godhead.[59] The light revealing Christ as the Son of God is furthermore an anticipation of the *Parousia*, the final coming of Christ in all his glory. Kantacuzenos, therefore, quoted the Cappadocian father to validate and endorse his own teachings, and to support the hesychast doctrine he promoted.[60] The page contains an image of Gregory pointing at the scene of the Transfiguration; this gesture further advances Kantacuzenos's doctrinal views.[61]

---

55 The visual connection between the written word and the miniatures as well as that between the two miniatures is quite extraordinary. The manuscript's reduced visual program serves as an autonomous medium of theological reflection. In the illustration, Gregory the Theologian wears the liturgical garments of a bishop. He sits on a backless throne set against a uniform background of gold leaf. He holds a large codex and gestures towards the image of Metamorphosis on the opposite page.

56 Drpic, 'Art, Hesychasm', 228; Drpic's observations about the Paris miniature are similar to my conclusions that were reached when researching the *Parisinus Graecus* 1242 during a fieldwork trip in 2008 and also in 2010 (the manuscript is held at Bibliothèque Nationale de France). Drpic's paper was published prior to this volume and Drpic's observations inform this text. See also Gregory the Theologian, 'Oration 40', 5–6 in C. Moreschini (ed.) & P. Gallay (trans) *Gregory the Theologian, Discourse 38–41*, SC 358 (Paris 1990) 204–208.

57 Drpic, 'Art, Hesychasm', 228.

58 Gregory the Theologian, Or. 32.18 3–12; in Gregory the Theologian,'Orationes' 27–45, *Patrologia Graeca* 36, 9–623, in C. Moreschini (ed.), *Gregory the Theologian*, 112.

59 Gregory the Theologian, Epist. 101, 25–29, in C. Moreschini (ed.), *Gregory the Theologian*; Drpic, 'Art, Hesychasm', 228–229.

60 P. Guran & B. Flusin, 'L'Emperour Hagiographe: Culte des Saints et Monarchie Byzantine et Post-Byzantine', *Actes des Colloques Internationaux, L'Empereur Hagiographe (13–14 Mars 2000) et 'Reliques et Miracles (1–2 Novembre 2000) Tenus au New Europe College* (Bucharest 2001).

61 The Paris miniature depicts the spectacular moment on Mt Tabor when the apostles Peter, John and James witnessed Christ's Transfiguration (cf. Mt 17:1–6, Mk 9:1–8, Lk 9:28–36); Drpic, 'Art, Hesychasm', 228.

This example shows the emperor Kantacuzenos being a diligent follower of Palamas's hesychast tradition. He fought for the hesychast cause during his reign and, when he abdicated voluntarily from the throne, he maintained a friendship with supporters of this movement, such as Philotheus Kokkinos and Nikolas Cabasilas.[62] Hence, Kantacuzenos was instrumental in making hesychasm part of wider Orthodox doctrine at the patriarchal council of 1351. The miniatures in *Parisinus Graecus* that show Kantacuzenos presiding over a council, and the miniature of the Transfiguration, provide clear evidence of this claim.

Description

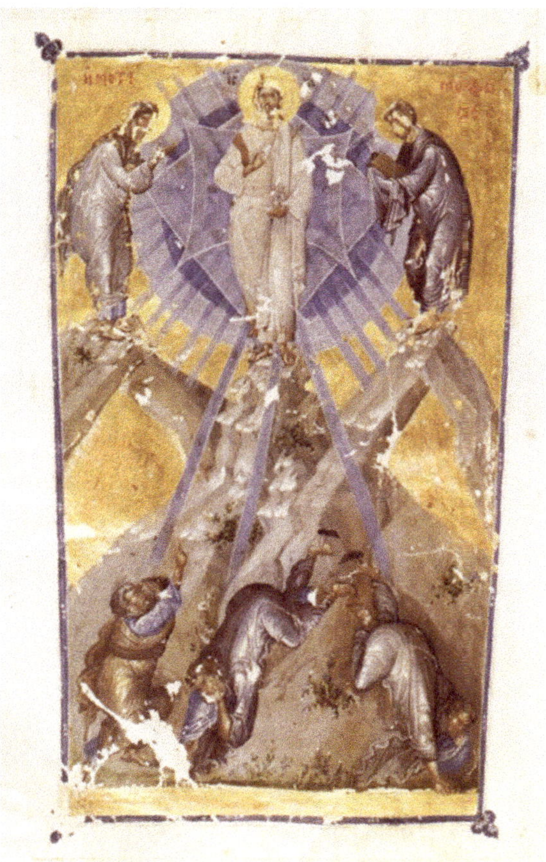

Figure 11. *The Transfiguration of Christ*, c. 1375, book illumination, scribe Ioasaph, in J. Katacuzenos, *Disputatio cum Paulo Patriarcha Latino*, Bibliothèque Nationale de France, (*Parisinus Graecus* 1242), fol. 92V

62 See B. Laourdas, *Νικολάου Καβάσιλα προσφώνημα καὶ ἐπιγράμματα εἰς ἅγιον Δημήτριον* (Athens 1952) 100–101; Also Palamas, Operum Coninuatio, *Patrologia Graeca* 151, 9–551; 536–558; Laourdas, 'Φιλɔqενοθ Πατριανρcοθ Κωνσταντινοπονλεω': ΔΕγκωνμιον ειј' το;ν 'Αγιον Δημηντριον', *Μακεδονικα*, vol. 2 (1941–1952).

Dressed in a white vestment and surrounded by a blue-white circle of glory and octangular star, Jesus Christ stands on top of the mountainous peak. He raises his right hand in blessing and holds a scroll in his left hand, which is perhaps symbolic of his authority and role as the Living Word of God. Two men in profile rest upon their own respective mountains, to the right and left side of Christ. On the right, Moses keeps the tablets (of the law) and, on the left, the prophet Elijah points towards Christ; both make a sign of supplication to Christ. Elijah wears a greenish robe with dashes of ochre and blue, which are highlighted with white. He shows his attention to Christ by a gesture of his right hand. The slightly younger figure of Moses wears a reddish-brown robe with highlights in light grey. While Moses and Elijah are on the same level as Christ, they do not divert the viewer's attention from Jesus, who is the central point of the composition. The three apostles stand, kneel and collapse in a half circle below the figure of Christ, their postures are reflective of their response to the Transfiguration. With short curly hair and a beard, the apostle Peter rests against the hills, to the left. While he falls headfirst to the ground, he uplifts his right hand and gestures towards Christ the Transfigured Lord, but is unable to look upon his radiating body and he shields his eyes with his left hand. John lies on the bare ground in a foetal position with his face turned downwards. His chin is resting on his left hand, as if he is contemplating the meaning of the miracle, while he stretches his right hand in front, as if he is trying to protect himself from falling. Furthest to the right is James, who has collapsed to the ground face first; with his right hand he touches the ground and his left hand covers his face, protecting his eyes from the light. The disarray manifested in the postures and garments of the apostles indicates the dramatic impact of the vision. The rays of light radiate in different directions, connecting the apostles to Jesus by means of a triangular composition (Jesus, placed above, is the highest point, and the apostles below are the lowest points of the triangle). A complex, geometrically shaped mandorla surrounds the figure of Christ, consisting of two superimposed and overlapping shapes, a concave square and a rhombus inscribed within two concentric circles. The octagonal mandorla provides a complex rendition of the vision of the uncreated light of God (Fig. 17).[63] Moses and Elijah are not fully enveloped within the mandorla; rather, they stand at the corners of the circle. Both, however, touch the edges of the rhombus, hence, they share in the glory of God. This aspect of the iconography directs the viewer's attention to the divine energies revealed by Christ during the Transfiguration.

---

63 More often than not the iconographic vision of the uncreated light included the use of luminous colours, especially in the garments of sacred personages (pure and transparent colours that are frequently enhanced by reflected or self-generated light). White and gold were most frequently used to epitomise spiritual light. This effect is especially apparent on folds of clothing and is seen as patterns of white or gold ovals, rectangles and triangles. Also, hatching lines were used as accent lights and were seen as stars at the edges of clothing, thrones, seats, angels, wings and around halos. Glass tesserae reflected irregular light that was transmitted from one plane to another with mercurial effect (E. Terzian, *The Aestethics and Poetics of Art in Eastern Christian Iconography: A Mythopoetic Perspective* (Carpinteria 2003) 141–147.

Although geometrically shaped mandorlas, aureoles and haloes are commonly found in compositions, such as the Anastasis, the Ascension of Christ, the Dormition of the Virgin Mary and the Pantokrator, the proliferation of the octagon or star-shaped doxa in Byzantine and Slavic art was mainly due to the icon of the Transfiguration.[64] Mandorlas contained many colourful layers, usually between three and seven, from the centre of which rays of light shone forth. According to Pseudo-Dionysius the number of layers in the mandorla reflected the three levels of ascent of the mystic (the darkness, the cloud and the divine light), as well as the three levels of hierarchy in the celestial sphere.[65] The Dionysian notion of hierarchy established that not everyone can contemplate and participate equally in the supreme cause (God); there is, therefore, a sophisticated and far-ranging hierarchy of the different images and representations that exist in heaven and on earth. The higher levels, which also possess the illuminations and powers of the lower ranks, receive a more direct illumination, and they can spread the divine light to the lower ranks at the level they are able to perceive the divine energies. The lower ranks, however, do not participate equally with those above them, but they guide other inspired hierarchs to the divine brightness. The same conclusion can be reached when considering the different levels of the spiritual journey as detailed by Palamas and Gregory of Sinai.

The colours and shapes of mandorlas varied; they often passed from the stages of darkness to the light, from the edge toward the centre, behind Christ, the Virgin or the saints. After the hesychast controversy, however, some compositions showed a new trend, with the core of the mandorla being translucent, or sometimes white or gold.[66] The preferred option, however, was a mandorla with three blue concentric circles (sometimes in green or silver-white). Predominately painted in white (at the time of hesychasm the frames of the mandorla were black), the borders of this mandorla were of varying thickness.[67] Before the 14th century, iconographers placed the figure of Christ within the space reserved for the mandorla, with the aim of affirming the hypostatic union of his two natures.

---

64 And finally, the uncreated light was represented as a nimbus or mandorla. The major difference between the nimbus and the mandorla lies not only in form, but in their symbolic value. The nimbus is a visual record of the indescribable idea of uncreated light emanating from God, and His grace and angels and saints. The mandala represents a 'cutting' in substantive space through which one can see a mystical event and spiritual reality (M. Raushenbah, *Пространственные Построения в Живописи* (Moscow 1980) 154–159.

65 Dionysius the Areopagite, 'Celestial Hierarchy VI', 1, 2, in G. Heil & A.M. Ritter (eds), *Pseudo-Dionysius Areopagita: De Coelesti Hierarchia, De Ecclesiastica Hierarchia, De Mystica Theologia, Epistulae* (Berlin 1991); R.G. Todorova, 'Mandorla in Eastern Orthodox Iconography — Light or Space', http://www.sustz.com/Proceeding08/Papers/THEOLOGICAL%20STUDIES/Todorova_Rostislava.pdf (accessed 10/03/2011).

66 I.K. Jazikova, 'Учение о Фаворском Свете и Иконография, Богословие Иконы: Учебное Пособие', http://nesusvet.narod.ru/ico/books/yazyk/yazyk9.htm (accessed 31/01/2012).

67 Todorova, 'Mandorla in Eastern Orthodox Iconography'.

In the middle of the 14th century, however, iconographers depicted the body of Christ outside the mandorla to affirm the separate properties of his divine and human nature.[68]

From the second half of the 14th century up until the late-17th century, an acute-angled quadrangle superimposed over a rhomboid formed an octagon-shaped mandorla behind Christ. The eight-sided mandorla was circumscribed within a circle, from the centre of which rays of light shone forth.[69] The mandorla had many layers, the darkest at the centre and growing progressively lighter towards the edges, 'precisely the opposite of what we expect from the source of light, and whose effect grows weaker the further it extends from the centre'.[70] Wherever the beams of light touched Peter and James, their pale-chocolate brown or purple garments changed to pale shades of blue.[71]

The use of black and blue for the centre of the mandorla reflects the teaching of Pseudo-Dionysus regarding the essence of God, which he often refers to as 'luminous darkness'.[72] Similarly, the hesychasts described the essence of God as the 'unknowable darkness hidden by the profusion of light'.[73]

Under the influence of hesychasm, the iconographers chose the dark mandorla with aberrant thick black borders and dark edges as the most brilliant expression of the uncreated light, seen during the Transfiguration. To symbolically affirm the differences between the three hypostases of the Trinity, the iconographers used different methods, such as the interplay of light and darkness to suggest the progress of the light from the whole (the unity of the Trinity) to part (hypostases of the Trinity). It is a movement from the illuminated volume of the sphere (God) towards the single point of a surface (the historical Jesus).[74]

---

68 W.C. Loerke, 'Observations on the Representation of Doxa in the Mosaics of S. Maria Maggiore, Rome, and St Katherine's, Sinai, Essays in Honor of Harry Bober', *Gesta*, vol. 20, no. 1 (1981).

69 Lazarev, *Storia della Pittura Bizantina* (Torino 1967) fg. 542.

70 J. Cage, *Color and Meaning: Art, Science and Symbolism* (University of California Press 2000) 76.

71 Many elements in the Gospel account of the Transfiguration support the view of Nikola Mesarites that the union of God and man in the transfigured Christ was productive of darkness and was a phenomenon beyond understanding (Mark (9, 7) and Luke (9, 34)) (G. Downey, 'Description of the Church of the Holy Apostles at Constantinople', XVII, *Transactions of the American Philosophical Society*, vol. 47, part 6 (1957).

72 The blue in Byzantine art has always been identified with transcendence. Dionysius the Aeropagite called it 'mysterious' because it creates an impression of depth and serenity that are the domain of the world — other than material. Therefore, the use of blue in Orthodox iconography was reserved mostly for displaying garments of the Almighty, the chiton of the Theotokos, certain clothes of Holy Apostles, and the spiritual space in which God dwells. Hence the blue of the mandorla is the visual expression of the mystery of the divine existence. E.N. Trubetskoi, *Умозрение в Красках: Три очерка о Русской Иконе* (Moscow 1991) 52: R.G. Todorova, 'Mandorla in Eastern Orthodox Iconography'.

73 Dionysius the Areopagite, 'De Divinis Nominibus' 7, *Patrologia Graeca* 3, 586–997; 869D–872A; also P. Rorem, *Pseudo-Dionysius, A Commentary on the Texts and an Introduction to their Influence*, (New York 1993).

74 L. Mavrodinova, *Stenata Zivopis v Balgaria do Kraja na XI vek-Sofija* (Sofia 1996) ill, 97; P. Hunt, 'The Wisdom Iconography of Light: The Genesis, Meaning and Iconographic Realization of a Symbol', *Byzantinoslavica*, vol. 67, no. 1 (2009) 12.

The emergence of two superimposed rhomboid or star shapes behind the Transfigured Christ in the *Parisinus Graecus* miniature is not a novelty. This feature appeared for the first time in an unrelated miniature of the 6th-century *Codex Dioscourides* (folio 6.v). Subsequent versions of the Transfiguration, such as the 6th-century apse mosaic of Sinai and the Monastery of Daphne contain the same detail.[75] This mandorla was identified as being a hesychast type in the late-14th century.[76] The miniature of the Transfiguration, which is the most prominent composition containing the octagon mandorla, accompanied the theological writings of Kantacuzenos, a known supporter of hesychasm.[77] The iconographers commissioned on Mt Athos and Mystra in the late- and post-Byzantine period also used the octagon mandorla.[78] It appears that the hesychasts adopted the eight-pointed mandorla as a principle means of expressing the vision of divine light, as claimed by Patterson and Belting.[79] Ouspensky and Lossky mention the possible connection between the use of complex mandorlas and the spread of hesychast doctrine in the Palaeologan era,[80] but they do not confirm or reject this assumption. Dufrenne defended the same argument, in the absence of convincing refutation of the hesychastic theory.[81]

Although the real reasons behind the introduction of this complex symbolism in the 14th century remain unknown, the hypothesis proposed below is is plausible based on the available evidence.

The hesychast mandorla appeared at the same time that Trinitarian dogma was challenged by the Western Church, perhaps emerging as a response to the *filioque* clause. Recognition of three geometric forms as symbols for the three hypostases is probable,[82] though associating the three shapes (two rectangles and a circle) with the concrete hypostasis is problematic. The circle is a symbol of the Father;

75 In this miniature the prince Juliana Anticia, a well-known philanthropist and sponsor of the Church in the 5th and 6th centuries coming from Constantinople is pictured in two crossing squares which are included in a circle situated among two personified virtues, Magnanimity and Prudence (F.I. Walther, *Codices Illustres: The World's Most Famous Illuminated Manuscripts, 400 to 1600* (Cologne 2005) Folio 6 of Vienna Dioscorides, from Honorata (near Turkey) 512; at Österreichische Nationalbibliothek).

76 F. Gerke, *La Metamorphosi nell'Arte Protobyzantine*, vol. 7 (Rome 1960) 99–111.

77 For Emperor John VI Kantakouzenos see G. Weiss, *Joannes Kantakuzenos: Aristokrat, Staatsmann. Kaiser und Mönch, in der Gesell Schaftsentwicklung on Byzanz im 14* (Munchen 1969); D.M. Nicol, *The Reluctant Emperor: A Biography of John Cantacuzene, Byzantine Emperor and Monk, c. 1295–1383* (Cambridge 1996); Nicol, *The Byzantine Family of Kantakouzenos (Cantacuzenus) ca. 1100–1460: A Genealogical and Prosopographical Study* (Washington D.C. 1968) 35–103.

78 S. Makseliene, 'The Glory of God and its Byzantine Iconography', MA thesis, The Central European University Budapest (1998) 65.

79 Patterson, 'Hesychast Thought', 663; H. Belting, *Des Illuminierte Buch in der Spatbyzantinischen Gesellschaft* (Heidelberg 1970) 15.

80 L. Ouspensky & V. Lossky, *The Meaning of Icons* (1982) 73; J. Meyendorff, 'Introduction', *Defense de Saints Hesychasts, Texte Critique, Traduction et Notes*, 2 vols (Louvain 1959) 218.

81 S. Dufrenne, 'La Manifestation Divine dans l'Iconographie Byzantine de la Transfiguration, in Nicee II, 787–1987', in B. Boespflug & N. Lossky (eds) (Paris 1987) 202.

82 G. Millet, *Recherches sur l'Iconographie de l'Évangile aux XIVe, XVe et XVIe Siècles d'Après les Monuments de Mistra, de la Macédoine et du Mont Athos* (Paris 1916).

the two rectangles are emblems for the hypostases of the Son and the Holy Spirit, signifying their relation to the Father (of either birth or procession). Andreopoulos asserts that the Holy Spirit takes the form of a vertical square while the Son is the horizontal rhombus.[83] Maxilene, on the other hand, proposes that the square represents Christ (it is behind Christ), and the rhombus suggests the Father (according to visions of both Isaiah and Ezekiel, the tetramorphous surrounds the throne of the Father). The sphere around the two rhombi is the symbol for the Spirit, (according to the patristic identification of the bright cloud with the Spirit).[84] Although both interpretations are contradictory, they in fact reveal the tripartite stage in the evolving Christian symbolism of light. Delivering from the spatial realisation, it incorporates the three-stage development of the light symbolism involving the 'multiplication of the triad and quaternion' (the plane and volume). The 'action of the cone that identifies the seer and the Seen reflects the first stage in the development of the symbolism of light. It reveals the unity of the Trinity as reflected in the creation'.[85] Stages two and three represent the mirroring rhombi integrated by the cone and show the antinomical nature of God. This evolution in light symbolism contributed to the development of the mandorla's geometrical forms of star and protostar.[86]

An inscription of a sacred triangle within a divine sphere, supplemented with a single ray of light coming out of the upper triangle (signifying the essence of God), formed a star shape. As the ray emanates from the star, it divides into three, symbolising the participation of the three hypostases in the economy of salvation. The ray also connects the star with the part of the sphere which went beyond the limits of the icon.[87] This star also represents the return spiral of mental ascent. Moses and Elijah stood within circles of light, and they touched the rhombus of accessible divinity. They occupied individual mountains and were both interiorised into the circle of light, both acquiring the state of mental participation in Chris's mystical body.[88] The emergence of the star symbolism, as well as the introduction into the iconography of the Transfiguration of a mandorla of three layers, reflected the renewed impact of the writings of Dionysius in the development of hesychastic spirituality.[89] A passage from the Christmas liturgy provides a reference to the star symbolism. In this text, Christ is the 'light of spiritual knowledge' in front of whom monks prostrate themselves as before the

83 Andreopoulos, Metamorphosis, 209–245.

84 Maksiliene, 'Glory of God', 68.

85 Hunt, 'The Wisdom Iconography of Light'.

86 ibid., 12.

87 On the symbolism of the numbers in the Transfiguration see M. Didron, *Iconographie Chretienne. Historie di Dieu* (Paris 1843), E. J. Millington (trans), (New York 1851) 117f.

88 B. Bucur, 'The Theological Reception of Dionysian Apophatism in the Christian East and West, Thomas Aquinas and Gregory Palaamas', *The Downside Review*, vol. 125, no. 439 (April 2007) 131–146.

89 Bucur, 'The Theological Reception of Dionysian Apophatism', 137.

'sun of sightlessness'.[90] The Bible contains other references; for example, verses in Revelation: star out of Jacob in 24:17; and 2 Peter 1:18–19, in particular, refers to the day of the Transfiguration as the 'day of the Star'.[91]

The star-shaped mandorla representing the dual nature of Christ vanished by the end of the 14th century, when the octagon mandorla emerged. A vertical rhombus superimposed on the expanding circles of light evoked the intellectual form of Christ's divinity (a double triangle represents the dyadic communication of the Godhead — the essence and energies distinction).[92] The horizontal rhombus, on the other hand, symbolised the divine self-identity communicated externally in Christ's glorified body.[93] The octagon itself was a symbol of cosmogony emerging from the two manifesting the One.[94] It represented the world itself, so that when the mystic stood at the centre, he could identify himself with the force that governs the universe, or alternatively take the figure of Christ as a centre point of his meditation.[95] 'Iconographers integrated the vertical and horizontal rhombi as modelled by the opening cone so that they could show with symbols the immaterial, indivisible, simultaneous form of unity of the material, divisible and plural world'.[96] The sphere was both a 'Wisdom mirroring process between God and his creation, and a modelling system for representation of the uncreated light'.[97] Wisdom of God (*Sophia*) was one of the main doctrines clarified by Palamas during the hesychast controversy.[98]

The symbolism of numbers six and eight as expressed in the scriptural account of the Transfiguration[99] had some bearing on the emergence in iconography of the star and octagon mandorlas.[100] While the number six signified the number of days taken to create the universe, the number eight symbolised the final, heaven-like stage of history (*eschaton*).[101] Moreover, the eight (octagon) directly expressed the transcendence of the created world.[102] Finally, as an ecclesiastical

90 F. Walzl, 'The Liturgy of the Epiphany Season and the Epiphanies of Joyce', *Publications of the Modern Language Association of America*, vol. 80, no. 4 (Sep., 1965) 436–450.

91 J. Danielou, 'The Star of Jacob', *Theologie du Judeo-Christianisme* (Paris 1958) 237–247.

92 D. Fiene, 'What is the Appearance of Divine Sophia', *Slavic Review*, vol 48, no. 3 (Fall 1989).

93 Hunt, 'The Wisdom Iconography of Light', 15.

94 ibid., 15–16; also T. Mathews, *Byzantine Aesthetics* (New York 1971) 31.

95 J. & M. Arguelles, *Mandala* (London 1972) 21.

96 Dionysius the Areopagite, 'Divine Names', IV, 3–10; 73–80, in Dionysius the Areopagite, 'De Divinis Nominibus', *Patrologia Graeca* 3, 586–997; 697A–708D.

97 Dionysius the Areopagite, *Divine Names*, IX, 9; *Patrologia Graeca* 3, 915D, 119; D. Burrell & I. Moulin, 'Albert, Aquinas, Dyonisus', *Modern Theology*, vol. 24, no. 4 (October 2008); Hunt, 'The Wisdom Iconography of Light', 15–17.

98 A.G. Sakovic, *Narodnaja Gravirovannaja Kniga Vasilija Korenja 1692–1696* (Moscow 1983) 19–21.

99 Six or eight days passed between the times the apostles had a discussion about Christ and the the Transfiguration.

100 E. Baldwin Smith, *Architectural Symbolism of Imperial Rome and the Middle Ages* (Princeton 1956) 46–47 and figs 42–43.

101 H. Rahner, 'The Christian Mystery of the Sun and Moon', *Greek Myths and Christian Mystery*, B. Buttershaw (trans), (London 1963) 154ff.

102 D. Fideler, *Jesus Christ, Sun of God: Ancient Cosmology and Early Christian Symbolism* (New York 1993) 128.

emblem, the octagon stood 'for the resurrection' and marked cosmic equilibrium and immortality.[103] For this reason, in centrally planned churches, the shape of baptismal fonts is often octagonal.

The shape of an octagon, or sometimes a spiral, also constituted the great vision of the light of the Transfiguration of the Lord on the eighth day (eschatological connotation).[104] According to Gregory the Theologian, if the first Christians referred to the Resurrection as the 'eighth day', it was because 'it is the first of those that follow and the eighth of those that precede it, a glorious day among all others'.[105] Maximus the Confessor stated that Luke's eighth days included the beginning and end: the first day was the one in which the Lord spoke, and the last that of the Transfiguration.[106] Palamas stated that the great vision of the light at the Transfiguration of the Lord was the mystery of the eighth day; that is, after the termination of creating the world in six days. It represents the excess of the senses, which are six in number: 'We have five senses,' Gregory claimed,

> but the word was uttered significantly, and the six energies of our sensation were added; conversely, this number not only symbolises the sensations but also represents a sign of the Kingdom of God promised to those who are worthy. Hence, the Age to come would happen on the eighth day after the suspension of these beautiful energies which are six, and after the seventh day when the wealth and dignity of God through the creation of humanity was shown.[107]

Palamas provided three different, but interrelated, interpretations of the meaning of the 'eighth day'. First, in two of his homilies (16 and 931) he confirmed that the eighth day came on earth when Christ rose from dead. Second, Palamas claimed that the number of people present during the Metamorphosis, that is, eight (five men and the Trinity) was a numerical reference to the 'eighth day'.[108] Finally, in a continuation of the preceding passage, Palamas referred to the eighth day as an age that is yet to come.[109] Two other passages in Palamas's *Homily of the Transfiguration* served as a source for the iconography of this episode.

---

103 Quoted by M. Reynolds, 'The Octagon in Leonardo's Drawings', http://markareynolds.com/?p=89 (accessed 10/03/2012).

104 O.A.W. Dilke, 'Cartography in the Ancient Word: A Conclusion', in J.B. Harley & D. Woodward (eds), *History of Cartography*, vol. 1 (Chicago 1987).

105 Gregory the Theologian, 'Oration 44', in Gregory the Theologian, 'Orationes 27–45', *Patrologia Graeca* (Paris 1886) 36, 9–623; 36, 612C.

106 G. Gianelli, 'Una "Edito Maior" delle "Quaestiones et Dubia" di S. Masimo il Confessore', a paper given at the Ninth International Congress of Byzantine Studies, Thessaloniki, 1953, *Scriptora Minora: Studi Byzantine et Neollenici*, vol. 10 (1963).

107 Palamas, *Douze Homélies Pour les Fêtes*, Jérôme Cler (trans) (Paris 1987) 189.

108 J. Meyendorff, 'Introduction à l'Étude de Grégoire Palamas', *Patristica Sorbonensia*, vol. 3, no. 38 (Paris 1959) 267.

109 Palamas, 'Pour la Vénérable Transfiguration de Notre Seigneur, Dieu, et Sauveur Jésus-Christ; Où il est Démontré que la Lumière qui y est Apparueest Incréée', Homélie 34, *Patrologia Graeca* 151, 425C, in *Douze Homélies pour les Fêtes*, Jérôme Cler (trans) (Paris 1987) 188.

The first passage affirms the light seen by the disciples as an expression of Christ invisible.[110] The second quote acknowledges the vision of the uncreated light on Mt Tabor as an expression of the Trinity.[111] In other words, the event of the Transfiguration is, in fact, a theophany that reveals God's glory and the divine nature of Christ, and also presents him as Kyrios elevated by God the Father.[112]

A new interpretation of the symbolism of light came from from the writtings of Metropolitan Theophanes III of Nicaea, a known defender of hesychast practice in the 14th century. He observed the mandorla surrounding Christ as representing the light of his *prosopon* (person) while the light reflected on the garments came from the hypostasis of the Godhead.[113] In addition, he claimed that the octagon mandorla emphasises two notions: firstly, the holiness of Christ, manifesting his divine nature during the Transfiguration, and secondly, it affirms the trans-temporal nature of the occasion, since, during the Metamorphosis, the notion of historical time was no longer in practice.[114]

Deliberate groupings of three apostles and prophets with Christ, as well as the use of a triangular shape for the mountain and the appearance of light beams radiating from Christ, provides the miniature with a Trinitarian accent that was always inherent in the generic iconography of light (Jesus as the light of the Father). The vision of the Trinitarian glory culminates in the inscription of a circle around two squares, which form the octagon mandorla.[115] This, in turn, creates a connection between two miniatures of *Parisinus Graecus*, the Transfiguration and the Double Portrait of Kantacuzenos (containing the image of the Holy Trinity).

Andreopoulos claims that the appearance of the hesychast mandorla in the 14th century coincided with developments in the fields of geography and cartography.[116] The visual language of individual 14th-century portolan charts, which were instrumental for European travel between the 13th and 14th centuries, consists of elements appropriated from Byzantine maps of Ptolemy's *Geography*, Medieval Latin world maps, regional maps from Islamic societies, and

---

110 Millet, *Recherches*, 230: Palamas, Homily 35, Migne, *Patrologia Graeca* 151, 441 B, in Gregory Palamas, 'Operum coninuatio, *Patrologia Graeca* 151, 9–551.

111 Guran, P. & Flusin, B., 'L'Emperour Hagiographe', 30–41.

112 Dufrenne, 'La Manifestation', 195–197.

113 I. Polemēs, *Theophanes of Nicaea: His Life and Works*, vol. 20 (Vienna 1996) 100.

114 The diamond nimbus is a sign of pre-existing Christ at St Clement in Ochrid (1295) and in Rila Monastery (1335). After 1540 only the pre-existent Christ or the Ancient of Days were represented with an eight-pointed nimbus. In the later iconography of the sixth day of creation, Christ, as an angel of great council, is shown with an eight-pointed nimbus. The same phenomena occurs in the icon 'On the Seventh day God Rested', in A.A. Saltkov, *Музей Древнерусского Искусства Имени Андрея Рублева* (St Petersburg 1989) 243, fig. 18, 19. Didron, *Iconographie* Chretienne, 31, 60 ff; see also Polemēs, *Theophanes of Nicaea*, 99.

115 The sun as a circle with eight rays, or an eight-pointed star, has often been depicted in the art of the ancient east (old Babylonian relief in Louvre, Neo-hititte stela from northern Syria, now in Berlin (G. Contenau, 'La Representation des Divinites Solaires en Babylonie', *Revue Biblique*, vol. 12 (1917) 4f.)).

116 Andreopolis, *Metamorphosis*, 145.

art works from 13th-century Arabic and 14th-century Iranian provenance.[117] Moreover, the principle of the four cardinal directions supplemented by four secondary ones, sometimes even 16 directions, was used to arrange geographical space after the 9th century.[118]

As a cosmogram, the mandorla represents the world reduced to an essential pattern; it was a sign of the whole universe in its essential plan, in its process of emanation and reabsorption. The octagonal mandorla was also a psycho-cosmogram, presenting in a symbolic fashion not only the 'disintegration of one to many, but also the reintegration from the many to the one'.[119] The central part of the mandorla represented the unity, peace and stability of the divine and human nature in Christ. The centre was also a point of breakthrough between the material–mental world of space and time, and the calm, peace and stability of the heavenly reality ... an *axis mundi* for macrocosm and microcosm.[120]

Within the octagon mandorla, the feet of the Old Testament prophets form the axis of an equilateral triangle; the two sides of the triangle extend towards the three apostles and finish at the edges of the icon. The dominant blue of the triangle separates the lower part of the miniature that is the vision of the apostles, represented in an earth-bound perspective of terror and incomprehensibility, expressed towards the upper part, where the glory of Christ during the Transfiguration appears (Mark 9:6; Mathew 17:6). The blue enflames the middle section of the miniature; see, for example, the greyish-brown mountain rocks beneath Moses and Elijah.[121]

Even though the Biblical text does not describe the relative position of Elijah and Moses in relation to Christ during the Metamorphosis, the painters invariably deployed them in a symmetrical triad. Unlike the signficance of their placement on the peaks of Mt Tabor, it does not seem to have been important whether Moses and Elijah stand on the right or left side of Christ. This disposition of the figures of Christ, Moses and Elijah, would remain more or less fixed in Byzantine art.[122] In a few instances the composition of the

---

117 An example from the Cathalan atlas from 1375 is interesting — Bibliothèque Nationale de France, Ms. Esp. 30; Ibid. 145–146.

118 Similar designs were found in Bede's 9th-century manuscript of *De Natura Rerum* which demonstrates the relationship between four cardinal virtues and superimposes one square onto another (hot, cold, wet and dry with four sides of the world east, south, west and north). This shape also forms a part of Islamic cartography, such as in the four Qiblas' Dar al-Katub in Cairo, which symbolise the word around the axes mundi (G. Gabra, *The Treasures of Coptic Art and Architecture in the Coptic Musum and Churches of Old Cairo* (Cairo 2007) 235).

119 Andreopouos, *Metamorphosis*, 238–241.

120 Z. Grover, 'Mandala Symbolism and Use in the Mysticism of Hugh of St Victor', *History of Religions*, vol. 12, no. 4 (1973) 317.

121 Some compositions of the Transfiguration have the images of Moses and Elijah symmetrically positioned on each side of Jesus and enveloped within the mandorla, hence, forming a circle around Jesus.

122 On the composition and iconography of the Transfiguration, see J. Myslivec, 'Verklarung Christi', in E. Kirschbaum & W. Braunfels (eds), *Lexikon der Christlichen Ikonographie* vol. 4, 416–421; Schiller,

Transfiguration included images of angels taking Moses and Elijah from the place of the Transfiguration up to the clouds (this is the case in the icon of the Transfiguration at the Cathedral Pereslavl-Zaleski).[123]

Moses and Elijah appeared together in the Transfiguration of Christ as witnesses of his glory or the heavenly kingdom coming to power. In the same manner, iconographers adopted various streams of Old Testament thought and patristic traditions[124] about the role of Moses and Elijah as eschatological prophets.[125] Basil the Great described the figures of Moses and Elijah as prophets appearing in the last days before the dawn of the kingdom of heaven.[126] Ephraim the Syrian claimed both Moses and Elijah affirmed the state of human transfiguration: God took Elijah alive to heaven in a transfigured state; Moses, on the other hand, received a new life at his Resurrection, just like Christ's people will obtain at his return. Hence, Moses and Elijah are representatives of both worlds — the dead and the living: Moses represents the dead, and Elijah the living, because he never saw death; he went by a whirlwind 'into heaven' (2 Kings 2:1).[127]

The appearance of Moses and Elijah alongside Christ at the Transfiguration provided another site for typological analysis, closely connected with the teachings of the hesychasts. Both Moses and Elijah were specifically connected with a mountain where the direct vision of God was denied.[128] In regard to the theophanic visions that both Moses and Elijah experienced, it is necessary to note that Moses received two revelations on Mt Sinai. Prior to the Exodus, God appeared to Moses in the Burning Bush. Moses, however, received another vision when he saw God's glory from the back with God's face remaining hidden (Exodus 33:18f.). The prophet Elijah, on the other hand, had one sighting of God in a revelation of Him when he climbed Mt Horeb (I Kings 19:11–15). Both Gregory of Nyssa and Dionysius the Areopagite took Moses as an exemplar of a mystic who entered divine darkness, whereas Gregory of Sinai and Palamas described the various postures and gestures assumed by Elijah as embodying

---

Iconography of Christian Art, vol. 1, 145–52; Changes in situation and context, however, have altered the significance of the composition. See Elsner, 'Image and Iconoclasm in Byzantium', *Art History*, vol. 11 (1988) 471–491.

123 N.K. Goleizovsky, 'Notes on the Work of Theophanes the Greek', Византийский Временник, vol. 24 (Moscow 1964).

124 C.E. Carlton, 'Transfiguration and Resurrection', *Journal of Biblical Literature*, vol. 80, no. 3 (Sept. 1961) 233–240.

125 The Old Testament testifies the assumption and return of Elijah (II Kings, 2:11; Mal 3:23) while the evidence for either of those in the career of Moses is uncertain at best. Yet, there is a reference in the New Testament to both Elijah and Moses being eschatological prophets (Rev 11:6), and many church fathers support this assertion.

126 Basil the Great, Homily, Psalm 44, 5; *Patrologia Graeca* 29, 400, in Basil the Great, 'Basilii Opera Omnia', *Patrologia Graeca* 29 (Paris 1886).

127 N.V. Pokrovsky, *Notes on Monuments of Russian Iconography and Art* (St Petersburg 1900) 356.

128 Palamas often mentions the prophet Elijah as an exemplum for his fellow hesychasts. See Gregory, *Triad* 1.3.24, in Meyendorff (ed.), *Gregory Palamas: The Triad*, 160–162.

the 'hagiographical topos of the solitary hesychast'.[129] In particular, Elijah's theophanic vision on Mt Sinai was described as an earthquake of the heart and fire of such force that it purifies, illuminates and sometimes destroys the initiated in the hesychast practice.[130] In the *Parisinus Graecus* miniature, however, Moses and Elijah serve as 'models of ascetic monasticism, rather than operating as Old Testament archetypal visionaries'.[131]

The typological link between mounts Sinai and Tabor, as privileged sites for theophanic visions, recurred in exegesis and liturgical poetry and became a frequently narrated topic in the hesychast literature.[132] Writers of these treatises found several parallels between the theophanies of Sinai and Tabor. Both revelations of God occurred on the mountain only when the prophets left the non-initiated majority behind; both served as initiations for the missionary works of Moses and Elijah. Finally, the sightings of God on Sinai and Tabor showed that his essence is unknowable and unperceivable.[133] What Moses and Elijah saw was not the essence of God but his energies.[134]

The contrast between Sinai and Tabor also offered an opportunity to consider the interplay of doctrines of apophaticism and deification, the way of darkness and the way of light, the ambiguity of silence and the clarity of articulation.[135] Sinai was a symbol of the elusive, aniconic quality of the divine being, where Moses met God in the darkness of unknowing. Sinai also served as a symbol to remind people of God's utter freedom and inaccessibility. It showed that no permanent guarantee of the divine presence could be assigned. Tabor, by contrast, incorporated the uncreated light, allowing the light of the divine presence to be experienced by humans. In turn, while participating in the event of the Metamorphosis, the disciples not only received a vision of the uncreated light, but they also saw themselves anew.[136]

The ecclesiastical writings of the Christian fathers mentioned the interplay between darkness and light, Sinai and Tabor. Some of them, such as John Chrysostom,[137] Gregory of Nyssa,[138] Maximus the Confessor[139] and

129 V. Lossky, 'La Théologie Négative dans la Doctrine de Denys l'Aréopagite,' *Revue des Sciences Philosophiques et Théologiques*, vol. 28 (1939); J. Williams, 'The Apophatic Theology of Dionysius the Pseudo-Areopagite', *Downside Review*, vol. 117 (1999); Drpic, 'Art, Hesychasm', 233.

130 Palamas, *Triad* 1.2. 10; Palamas, *Defense des Saints Hesychastes*, J. Meyendorff (ed. & trans), 2 vols (Louvain 1959) 1, 92–94.

131 M. Corbin, *La Vie de Moise selon Grégoire de Nysse (2008);* Drpic, 'Art, Hesychasm', 233.

132 B.C. Lane, 'Sinai and Tabor: Apophatic and Kataphatic Symbols in Tension', *Stoicorum Veterum Fragmenta*, no. 13–14 (1992–1993) 192.

133 Dionysius the Areopagite, 'De Divinis Nominibus', 1045–1048B.

134 Loerke, 'Observations', 21.

135 Lane, 'Sinai and Tabor', 199.

136 ibid., 190.

137 John Chrysostom, 'Expositio in Psalmum' 143, 2–3, *Patrologia Graeca* 55, 459; John Chrysostom, *On the Incomprehensible Nature of God*, P.W. Harkins (trans) vol. 72 (Washington, D.C. 1984).

138 Gregory of Nyssa, 'Quod non Sunt Tres Dei', *Patrologia Graeca* 45, 132.

139 Maximus the Confessor, 'Ambiguorum Liber 10', 1168A.

Pseudo-Dionysius the Areopagite,[140] took Moses as a model of a mystic who ascended to Mt Sinai to encounter God in a thick cloud (darkness). Other Christian apologists, however, such as Irenaeus, Origen, Gregory the Theologian, Symeon and Palamas took the light seen during Christ's Transfiguration on Mt Tabor as a goal for their mystical ascent.[141]

Tabor is the place where both *apophasis* and *kataphasis* meet: God came down to earth so that humanity could be lifted from its earthly baseness and be transformed in the same way that Christ was transfigured.[142] Bringing the experience of God closer to the human realm, however, the hesychast, in fact, underplayed the significance of the Resurrection.[143]

The event of the Transfiguration is not only a revelation of things to come (with a reference to the future Apocalypse), but also a fulfilment of the promise given by God to Moses on Mt Sinai.[144] Hence, Tabor has absorbed the mystical tradition associated with Mt Sinai, but in some ways, it served as symbol for Sinai. The image of human participation in God as light, and images of divine transcendence as darkness, do not present mutually irreconcilable views of God.[145] Dionysius the Areopagite reconciled both symbols, calling the vision of God 'dazzling darkness outshining the brightest light'.[146] In other words, what the darkness is to the light, Mt Sinai is to Mt Tabor.[147]

Conversely, the mount of the Transfiguration was a culmination of the events that took place on all Old Testament mountains, which is a symbol of spirituality that is not limited to Tabor, Hermon or Sinai, and which transcends all historical realities and foreshadows the unending process of human transformation.

An interesting detail in the *Parisinus Graecus* miniature of the Transfiguration affirms the parallelism between Sinai and Tabor. The apostles John and James are literally thrown out of their sandals as they fall headlong down the mountain. This iconographical marker of losing sandals is an allusion to the episode of the Burning Bush, when Moses took off his sandals at God's command (Exodus, 3:2–5).[148] In his celestial hierarchy, Dionysius the Aeropagite presented this episode as a symbol of the apophatic nature of God. He claims the brilliance of the fire of

140 J. Meyendorff, *Byzantine Theology: Historical Trends and Doctrinal Themes* (New York 1983) 3–12.

141 K. Ware, 'La Transfiguration du Christ et la Souffrance du Monde', *Soperim*, no. 294 (January 2005) 20–26.

142 Gregory of Sinai, 'On the Transfiguration', in D. Balfour (ed.), *St Gregory the Sinaite, Discourse on the Transfiguration, Theologia*, vol. 52, no. 4 (1981) 647–651; Palamas, Homily 34, *Patrologia Graeca* 151, 426, in Gregory Palamas, Operum coninuatio, *Patrologia Graeca* 151, 9–551.

143 H.P.L. Orange, 'Luc Aeterna: L'Adorazione della Luce nell'Arte Tardoanica el Alto Mediveale', *Rendiconti della Pontifica Accademia Romana di Archeologia*, no. 67 (1974–1975) 78–142.

144 C. Jones et al., The Study of Spirituality (Durham 1986) 240–253.

145 C. Charalampidis, 'The Representation of the Uncreated Light (Lux Increata) in the Byzantine Iconography of the Transfiguration of Christ', *Arte Mediveale*, vol. 1 (2003).

146 Dionysius the Areopagite, 'Mystical Theology 1', in *Patrologia Graeca* 3, 997–1065, 997B.

147 Balfour, *Discourse on the Transfiguration*, 75, 22–23.

148 Drpic, 'Art, Hesychasm'.

the Buring Bush revealed the divine energies or the proper operation of God.[149] The essence of God, on the other hand, remained forever uncircumscribable and unknown in the Burining Bush.[150]

The 5th- and 6th-century representation of Mt Tabor in the figurative scene of the Transfiguration was only minimal. Starting from the 9th century onwards, however, Mt Tabor was given prominence in the composition. Around the 12th century, images of the disciples ascending and descending from the mountain, led by Christ, enriched the composition.[151] Also, there are instances when the mandorla surrounding Christ assumes the shape of a star (Fig. 18). Finally, in the icons of the Transfiguration of the 13th and 14th centuries, Mt Tabor was easily identifiable and it became personalised. Sometimes there was a single mountain, at other times the mountain had three parts, with Moses and Elijah standing on their own respective rocks. Rarely, the entire mountain had only two levels, with the apostles standing at the foot of the mountain, while Christ stood at the top (Ex. 24:12–18; Ex. 33:11–23; 34:4–6, 8).

The *Parisinus Graecus* miniature shows Mt Tabor as steep, inaccessible and harsh; its appearance differs from the vertical mountain seen in the Chludov Psalter illumination. The most prominent change, however, is the introduction of a mountain consisting of three peaks joined at the base, instead of one angular and rocky landscape. This accentuated the unity of all previous mystical ascents to Christ, with the incessant upwardly aimed spirituality represented as a triangular mountain.[152]

Moreover, Mt Tabor assumed the shape of an upward triangle, stressing the upward movement of the soul towards God, as well as reaffirming the division between heaven and earth. The overall trapezoid shape of the miniature further affirms these aspects. The illusion of a gap (*diastema*), between the creation and the creator was a common feature in all earlier compositions of the Transfiguration.[153] For example, the mosaic from the Monastery of St Katherine, Mt Sinai, and the manuscript illumination of the Rabula Gospel, show the Transfiguration being divided in two parts. Christ and prophets are confined to the upper part of the scene, with the apostles and prophets occupying the lower part.[154]

---

149 Dionysius the Areopagite, 'Celestial Hierarchy I', 5.

150 Drpic, 'Art, Hesychasm', 217–233; Dionysius the Areopagite, 'Celestial Hierarchy 15', 2.

151 Such details were found in monuments throughout the centuries, such as: Church in Gračanica (1321) and the Church of God in Peribleptos, Mystra.

152 Chapter 13, f.16.

153 Cologne, second quarter of 11th century, Staatsbibliothek zu Berlin, Bibl. 94 (A.2.18) fol. 155.

154 This tendency was later heightened in the Paris illumination of the ninth century and Chludov Psalter illumination; Moscow Historical Museum, Cod. 129, f.88 Cf colour plates, figure 14a; Elsner, 'The Viewer and the Vision: The Case of the Sinai Apse', *Art History*, vol. 17, no. 1 (March 1994) 81–102.

The increasing gap between Christ and the apostles in the *Parisnus Graecus* miniature was a result of the spread of hesychast spirituality in Byzantium. The depiction of mountains and deserts in the iconography corresponds to the notion of mountains as traditional places for monastic asceticism and retreat, without which true hesychia was considered impossible.[155]

The acceptence of the doctrine of the vision of light as dogma provided the basis for the development of a more personalised and individualistic spirituality, a metaphorical cross that every Christian had to lift in imitation of Christ. This did not mean that individual spirituality was separated from the sacramental and inclusive *koinonia* (communion by intimate participation). On the contrary, only those transformed with the help of the Spirit, who is present in the sacraments, could receive the divine light and the grace of God.[156] Nevertheless, the light held significance for all. This is the beginning of transfiguration, a momentary foretaste of what will constitute the happiness of Paradise.[157] The process of Transfiguration, however, is individual and does not have the same effect on all belivers.

The miniaturist of *Parisinus Graecus* affirmed this fact by emphasising the distance between the transfigured Christ and the disciples, who stumble down precipitously, stunned by the supernatural light emanating from Christ. The powerlessness of the three disciples is palpable. Nevertheless, they are not just weak, but also 'fallen' human beings. The apostles are contained within the shape of the mountain and they lack the free movement of many previous Byzantine examples.

To understand this better, it is important to recognise that as Byzantine art developed, iconographers often varied the positioning and gesturing of the three disciples witnessing the Metamorphosis. Hence, in the so-called 'oriental type' rendering of the Transfiguration, the three apostles were depicted in the same position (standing, kneeling or sleeping on the ground).[158] There were few instances in which Peter was placed on the right, but in most extant images of the oriental type he was represented on the left side of the composition. James and John either kneeled or stood on either side of the composition. In some examples, James kneeled with his torso pointing upwards, or rarely, his body touched the ground, with his right hand covering his eyes. John, on the other hand, stood in the middle of the scene, his hands and knees towards the ground while his face opposed the light. Occasionally, he was shown in a state of deep

155 Gregory of Sinai, 'On Stillness: Fifteen Texts', in G.E.H. Palmer (ed.), *The Philokalia: Eastern Christian Spiritual Texts*, vol. 4 (Athens 1961) 264.

156 Palamas, *Triads*, III, 3.10, in Meyendorff (ed.), *Gregory Palamas: The Triad.*

157 M. Grace, 'Spirit-Centred Eastern Fathers: Symeon the New Theologian and Gregory Palamas', *Diakonia*, vol. 31, no. 2 (1998) 129–138.

158 Palamas, 'Pour la vénérable Transfiguration de notre Seigneur', 188.

sleep. From the 11th century on, however, changes occured in the positioning of apostles: John and James appeared closer to the ground and they covered their faces with their hands. Peter did not monopolise the upright position and his knees were often bent. The only exception to this rule is the fresco of the Transfiguration in the Church of Tokali Killise, in which the apostles are allo close to the ground, standing or prostrated. In most compositions of the Transfiguration, Peter takes primacy over John and James and is the only disciple to either face or gesture towards Christ.

Formal qualities of the *Transfiguration* miniature

Inscribed on a fine, creamy white parchment and enclosed in a frame painted in blue and grey tones, the *Parisinus Graecus* miniature of the *Transfiguration* is the product of careful planning by the scribe Ioasaph, the most outstanding calligrapher of later Byzantium.[159] The parchment has a distinctive, chalky surface that is characteristic of Ioasaph's works and the miniature has a retrospective, classic feel.[160] The placement of the inscriptions suggests that the painter did not uphold the authority of earlier Byzantine manuscripts while creating the illumination, but rather, he turned to contemporary manuscript examples.[161]

Elegantly executed in a luminous, painterly style, the miniature is essentially an icon in book format.[162] A varied combination of blue, green, grey and lavender appears across the miniature, while a shared colour scheme of electric royal blue illuminates the initials and unites the picture in a distinguished harmony with the ornament that surrounds the masterpiece. The overall background colour scheme, however, is expressed with shades of orange, yellow and black, and shows the interpretive nature of the Transfiguration. The light emitted from Jesus spreads a blue-green hue over the disciples.[163] The outer circle of the mandorla is a lighter blue, whereas the inner circle is deep blue. The beams of light appear transparent with their colour changing from light to dark. The mountain is

---

159 Voordeckers, 'Examen'; also Lazarev, *Storia Della Pittura Bizantina* (Torino 1967) 370, 379.

160 R.S. Nelson & J. Lowden, 'The Palaeologina Group: Additional Manuscripts and New Questions', *Dumbarton Oaks Papers*, vol. 45 (1991).

161 Buchthal, 'Toward a History'; H. Hunger, 'Herbert, Johannes Chortasmenos', *Wiener Byzantinische Studien*, vol. 7 (1969); D.D. Lixaceva, *Vizantitskaia Miniatiura* (Moscow 1977); Lixaceva, 'The Illuminations of the Greek Manuscript of the Akathistos Hymn (State Historical Museum Synodal Gr. 429)', *Dumbarton Oaks Papers*, vol. 26 (1972).

162 Buchthal, 'Notes on Some Early Palaeologan Miniatures', *Kunsthistorischen Forschungen Otto Piicht zu Seinem 70* (Salzburg 1972).

163 Guran, 'Jean VI Cantacuzène, l'Hésychasme et l'Empire: Les Miniatures du Codex Parisinus Graecus 1242', *Actes des Colloques Internationaux, L'Empereur Hagiograph: 13–14 Mars 2000 et 'Reliques et Miracles', 1–2 Novembre 2000 tenus au New Europe College* (Bucharest 2001) 73–121.

grey-brown with hints of dark green tinting the foliage. The five men are clothed in weaker pastel colours, ranging from greys to browns and blues. The repeated use of colour on the draperies creates a sense of interconnection. The kinship of the facial and figure type is clear and, by using reds and greens, the faces are made to appear loose and fresh. Highlights on the figures are angular; the use of a full brush creates a sense of fluid delineation.[164]

The figures of the apostles show compact body types, with stubby hips and long trunks. While James's flying drapery has a hollow, pointed form and his garments fall in tight folds from the hips, the overall modelling of the drapery folds is sharp.[165] The use of angular drapery is a Palaeologan convention and appears in the fresco-painting of several monuments from the 13th and 14th centuries. Frescoes of King Milutin's churches,[166] of the Church of Holy Apostles in Thessaloniki,[167] the Church of the Virgin Peribleptos at Mystra, as well as the mosaics of the Chora church,[168] affirm this trend.[169]

The *Parisinus Graecus* miniature has an elongated, tapering format which conveys a sense of upward movement.[170] The miniaturist shaped this narrow, trapezoid form from a wider rectangle that he scaled down. Auxiliary geometric figures appear at the centre of the miniature, such as a circle in the upper part and a pyramidal triangle in the lower part. In front of two concentric circles, a square and a rhombus create an octagonal mandorla (with Christ as the centre). Two triangles expand the compositional plan by arising on either side of, and behind, the third dominant triangle that forms in the middle. Across the diagonals, figures stand across one another, irrespective of whether they are in a group or separate.

Although Christ stands high on the mount, far from the viewer, and the apostles appear at the foot of the hill, considerably closer to the viewer, the figure of Christ is significantly larger than that of the apostles. Moreover, the miniature has two parts, representing both heaven and earth. The bodies of the three apostles fill the lower part of the miniature, their hands touching the lower edge of the icon. In contrast, Mt Tabor takes approximately one-third of the vertical

164 A.W. Carr, 'Two Manuscripts by Joasaph in the United States', *The Art Bulletin*, vol. 63, no. 2 (Jun., 1981).

165 R. Marcel, *Repertoiredes Biblioteques et des Cataloguesdes Manuscripts Grecs*, 2nd ed. (Paris 1958).

166 Millet, *La Peinture du Moyen-Age en Yougoslavie*, vol. 1 (Paris 1954) pl. 13, 2 (exonarthex of Hagia Sophia, Ohrid) and vol. 3, pl. 110, 2 (Staro Nagoriiino); R. Hamann-McLean & H. Hallensleben, *Die Monumen-Talmalerei in Serbien und Makedonien* (Giessen 1963) I, pl. 318.

167 A. Xyngopoulos, 'Les Fresques de l'Église des Saints-Apotres a Thessalonique', *Art et Societe a' Byzance sous les Paleologues: Bibliothkque de l'Institut Hellinique d'Etudes Byzantines et Postbyzantines de Venice*, vol. 4 (Venice 1971).

168 P. Underwood, *The Kariye Djami: Studies in the Art of Kariye Djami and its Intellectual Background* (Princeton1975) pl. 320.

169 Carr, 'Two Manuscripts'; Millet, *Monuments Byzantins de Mistra* (Paris 1910) pl. 117, 2.

170 Drpic, 'Art, Hesychasm', 223–240.

axis of the scene. The dominant feature of the middle section is two big caves under the two-sided mountain peaks. The cave entrances indicate an opening into the mountain which gives the mountain volume.

Riddled with big caves, the barren triangular mountain landscape fills the middle part of the figurative scene and serves as a prop against which the drama of divine revelation unfolds.[171] The feet of Christ rest on top of the rocky and arid mountain landscape. The lower part of the mountain does not extend to ground level and is, instead, obscured by gold paint ,which frames the lower section.

In contrast with the forceful diagonal gestures of the Old Testament dignitaries in the lower section, there is a sense of quiet in the top section of the miniature. The position of the apostles in the pyramidal triangle and their dramatic bodily postures, as well as the operative power of the three beams of light radiating from Christ, creates the sense of movement. Apostles move along a vertical axis (presented in the form of a mountain), seemingly engaged in a spiritual struggle, while the spiritual bodies of Moses and Elijah levitate next to Christ. In contrast, Peter, James and John plunge to the ground, gesticulate and crouch away from the blinding light.

The variations in the colour scheme also affirm the distinction between the upper and lower part of the miniature. Following the biblical narrative, Christ wears a white robe with light grey-blue shadows in the folds. The garments of Moses and Elijah are lighter in colour than those of the apostles, which signifies their advanced spiritual state, as well as their active participation in Christ's glory.[172]

While Christ is the main source of light in many earlier depictions of the Transfiguration, the immediate impression of luminosity in the *Parisinus Graecus* miniature comes from other sources.[173] The extensive use of gold and luminous colours intensifies the intense and harmonious experience of enlightenment. The three light beams that fall upon Peter, James and John reflect the source of their radiance, Christ. Moreover, a light source, which originates outside the pictorial plane and defies the conventional depiction of space within the miniature, conveys a sense of brightness.[174] The intentional use of highlights on draperies affirms the overall affinity of the miniaturist to represent the vision of

---

171 Similar landscape imagery can be found in Paris Psalter ca. 950–975 (Bibl. Nat. MS. GR. 139), L. Brubaker, *Vision and Meaning in Ninth Century Byzantium: Image as Exegesis in the Homilies of Gregory of Nazianzus* (Cambridge 1999) fig. 14, 18–19, 23, 26, 35, 44. Buchtal, *The Miniatures of the Paris Psalter: A Study in Middle Byzantine Painting* (London 1938) fig. 2, 10, 12.

172 Andreopoulos, 'The Vision of Light and the Icon of the Transfiguration in the Fourtheenth Century', in J. Goering et al. (eds), *Mystics, Visions and Miracles* (Leigas 2001).

173 Charalampidis, 'Representation of the Uncreated Light'.

174 Carr, 'Two Manuscripts'.

the uncreated light of God as reflected on the overall environment. The complex mandorla, on the other hand, is not a source of its own radiance, but rather a manifestation of the main source of light.[175]

Spatial analysis of the Transfiguration miniature reveals a dynamic relationship between the presentation of line and depth and displays two rather than three dimensions. The tendency to converge the parallel lines in reverse perspective serves as a way for the viewer to experience divine vision.[176] The octagonal mandorla provides a natural focus from which the other figures find their orientation, and it is the point where parallel lines intersect.[177] The use of the principle of simulating planes allows the objects and their parts to appear smaller the closer they are to the viewer. Therefore, the lower part of the mount appears smaller, whereas the upper part appears larger. The capricious distribution of light and shade that comes from inside and outside the pictorial plane creates the same illusion of depth. Moreover, although Elijah and Moses are the same size and operate within the same space, the fact that the three mountains overlap produces a sensation of depth. In other words, one perceives 3D despite the 2D image that is projected.

The *Transfiguration* miniature in the context of 14th- and 15th-century art

The *Parisinus Graecus* miniature is a complex and fascinating image, eloquently illustrating the vision of the uncreated light of God during the Metamorphosis.[178] The balance of mathematical harmony in line and shape, the master's use of an earth-toned palette and precious gold leaf, evokes a powerful spirituality and is a tribute to the genius of this relatively unknown miniaturist.[179] Three novelties characterise this miniature of the Transfiguration: the octagonal mandorla consisting of a concave square and a rhombus inside a circle, the tripartite representation of Mt Tabor, and the dramatic representation of the apostles in shock and disarray. These iconographical variations, however, were not exclusive to the *Parisinus Graecus* miniature. The angular-painted forms retaining the basic form of a hesychast mandorla also appeared in the churches of Thessaloniki, the main centre of the hesychast dispute.[180] Monuments from

175 M. Cheremeteff, 'The Uncreated Light: Hesychasm, Theophanes the Greek and Russian Iconostasis', *Zapiski Russkoi Akademicheskoi Gruppy v SShA*, Transactions of the Assoc. of Russian American Scholars of USA, vol. 21 (New York, 1988) 125–162.

176 V. Bychov, *The Aesthetic Face of Being: Art in the Theology of Pavel Florensky* (Crestwood 1993) 93, 7.1.

177 J. Spatharakis, *The Portrait in Byzantine Illuminated Manuscripts* (Leiden 1976) 129–137.

178 H. Caviness, 'Images of Divine Order and the Third Mode of Seeing', *Gesta*, vol. 11, no. 2 (1983).

179 Orange, 'Lux Aeterne'.

180 T. Velmans, 'Le Rôle de l'Hésychasme dans la Peinture Murale Byzantine du XIVe et XVe Siècles', in P. Armstrong (ed.), *Ritual and Art: Byzantine Essays for Christopher Walter* (London 2006) 218–219.

the complex of Mystra (Greece), namely, the Church of Hagia Sophia and the Virgin Peribleptos, contain paintings with geometric forms,[181] and octagonal mandorlas surround the images of the Virgin Orans with the inscription, 'Container of the Uncontainable.'[182] A square superimposed over a second square with its corners projecting beyond the four sides of the first square, creates an octagon.[183] Manuel Kantacuzenos, the son of John Kantacuzenos and a diligent hesychast adherent, was a patron of both churches.[184] This supports the idea that hesychasm informed the appearance of geometrically shaped mandorlas in both churches. Manuel Kantacuzenos shared the same predisposition as his father and it is not surprising, therefore, that the mandorla behind the Virgin Orans relates directly to that of the *Transfiguration* in the *Parisinus Graecus.*[185]

The mosaic decoration of the dome of the Holy Apostles church, Thessaloniki and the icon of the Monastery of Xenophon (Fig. 19), is one of the earliest depictions of the hesychast type of mandorla in a depiction of the Transfiguration as well as the composition of Despite the partial destruction of the image, the figure of Christ surrounded by Moses and Elijah is clear. The figures of Peter, John and James witnessing the divine splendour are also recognisable.[186] A circular mandorla, superimposed with an X-shaped star, surrounds the figure of Christ, which symbolises the three hypostases of the Trinity.[187] Nevertheless, the colour of this mandorla is much deeper and more sombre that of the *Parisinus Graecus* miniature. The four diagonal rays of light radiate from Christ and touch the apostles. Blinded by the divine light, Peter, James and John are hiding their faces with their hands while falling to the ground. Moreover, through the varied use of colour, animated gesticulation and fluttering drapery, the outer drama of the Transfiguration is represented. The shared stylistic and iconographic similarities between the mosaic of the Transfiguration and the miniature

181 Todorova, 'New Religion — New Symbolism: Adoption of Mandorla in Christian Iconography', Ninth Symposium Niš and Byzantium, 3–5 June 2010, *Collection of Scientific Works*, vol. 9 (Niš 2011).

182 S. Delvoye, 'Chronique Archaeologique', *Byzantion*, vol. 34 (1964) 160; T. Gouma-Peterson, 'Manuel and John Phokas and Artistic Personality in Late Byzantine Painting', *Gesta*, vol. 22, no. 2 (1983).

183 Millet, *Monuments*, pl. 140.

184 The use of this kind of mandorla in association with paintings of the Virgin Orans with a Child, the Pantokrator, and the Transfiguration reappears frequently in the 15th and 16th centuries in the churches and monasteries in Moldavia (Patterson, 'Hesychast Thought').

185 ibid., 665.

186 P. Serracino Inglott, 'La Trasfigurazione come Epiphania Monarchica', *Arta Christiana*, vol. 60 (1971).

187 M.L. Rautman, 'The Church of the Holy Apostles in Thessaloniki', PhD thesis, University of Indiana (1984). This unusual type of mandorla, which is supposed to represent the uncreated light on Mt Tabor, is depicted in three other monuments from the second half of 14th century: the rock monastery of St George in Potamies, Crete, the Transfiguration Church of Zrze, Macedonia (1384, 1385), and the Church of St Athanasius, Muzaki (1384–1385). A similar style is employed in several churches on Mt Athos (D. Kornakov, 'Манастирот Зрзе', *Културно — Моментиисториско Наследство Наследство во Ср. Македония*, vol. 11 (1972) 15–19). 'St Athanasius of Mouzakis' (in Greek), Kastoria City, http://www.kastoriacity.gr/index.php?option=com_content&task=view&id=135&Itemid=405&limit=&limitstart=4 M (accessed 17/07/10). M. Acheimastou-Potamianou, *Holy Image, Holy Space: Icons and Frescoes from Greece* (1988); Millet, *Recueil des Inscriptions Chrétiennes de l'Athos Paris* (Paris 1904) pl. 62.2; 123, 1.

indicate that iconographers of the same workshop created both compositions. In contrast with the dramatic narrative of the *Parisinus Graecus*, the mosaic of the Transfiguration gives a realistic and vivid expression of the event.[188]

Two images of the Transfiguration that share the same iconographical format as the miniature decorate the walls of the monasteries of Mt Athos. The Transfiguration from the Church of the Protaton, painted by Manuel Panselinos, is of importance. Specifically, the circumstantial evidence points to the Church of the Protaton being an important place for the hesychasts. Palamas produced and signed the first document opposing Barlaam at the hesychast assembly of Protaton around 1340–1341. Also, the monastery of Hodegon on Mt Athos held the theological writings of Kantacuzenos (the *Parisinus Graecus*) before it was sent to Bibliothèque nationale de France. Finally, both Palamas and Gregory of Sinai learned the practice of the Jesus Prayer while spending extended periods amongst the monastic brotherhood of Mt Athos — the centre of hesychast mystical practices. Although the influence of hesychasm on Panselinos's image of the Transfiguration is not certain, it cannot be excluded.

The paint on the lower part of the mandorla at Protaton is transparent, which allows the top of the mountain and the lower part of Christ's figure to be visible. The upper part of the fresco, however, which contains the two prophets and Christ inside a blue star-shaped mandorla, looks almost identical to the *Parisinus Graecus* miniature.[189]

Considering that iconographers often copied religious images, and thereby perpetuated certain types of illumination, it can be assumed that there was a causal connection between the *Parisinus Graecus* miniature and later images of the Transfiguration.[190] Panselinos painted another image of the Transfiguration in which he makes an unusual choice for the mandorla[191] of using an elliptical form, which radiates a rhomb with two acute edges,[192] instead of a circular doxa superimposed with a rhomboid and a rectangle as he did in the church of Protaton. Was the unusual choice of mandorla, perhaps, indicative of the need to represent the glory of God in the Transfiguration in a more intricate manner than in the earlier period, under the influence of hesychasm? It is difficult to prove or disprove this hypothesis; however, the introduction of an angular shape behind Christ demonstrates the need to change the shape of the traditional mandorla from oval to octagonal.

188 Underwood, *The Kariye* Djami, 109–159.

189 Makseliene, 'Glory of God', 5–9.

190 Borboudakis, 1991; S.M. Pelekanidis, *The Treasures of Mount Athos Illuminated Manuscripts Miniatures — Headpieces — Initial Letters* (n.d.) 2, 34.

191 Loerke, 'Observations'.

192 Daniilia et al., 'The Byzantine Wall Paintings from the Protaton Church on Mount Athos, Greece: Tradition and Science', *Journal of Archaeological Science*, vol. 34, no. 12 (December 2007).

The hesychast mandorla quickly became the dominant type for a couple of centuries, not just on Mt Athos (Fig. 20) but also in Bulgaria, Serbia and Macedonia and Russia (Fig. 21).[193]

The example from the Church of St George, Staro Nagoricane is the 14th-century composite scene of the Transfiguration (Fig. 22), characterised by an increased number of figures, a concentrated iconographical presence, and altered positions and gestures of the apostles. Following the hesychast interpretation of the Transfiguration, the iconographers dressed Christ in luminous white ceremonial dress decorated with gold ornaments. He stands in front of an oval mandorla with triangular projections, indicative of the transmission of divine light of the son of justice.[194] Although this is an unusual choice, it is consistent with the mandorla in the miniature. Nevertheless, more than 12 rays of light radiate from the four sides of the rhomb, illuminating the apostles and the landscape. This feature affirms the hesychast teaching about the unlimited splitting of the divine splendour of the inaccessible light. The hesychasts believed the uncreated light had no essence, and could not be contemplated as a hypostasis, that is as an independent reality. Having a personal focus, the only way one could consider the uncreated light is in a hypostasis. The divine energies reflecting this light are also 'enhypostatic'. Therefore, the light of the Holy Spirit that touches the whole creation in the Transfiguration at Nagoricane is the same light enlightening the eternity (the Godhead). It is also the light that reveals the second person of the Trinity (Christ).

The fresco of the Transfiguration at the Monastery of Lesnovo shows other variations (Fig. 23). The figurative scene has two parts: a shiny mandorla envelops the upper part of the composition, while the three apostles are depicted in the lower part of the Transfiguration.[195] This creates a sense of space and depth in the central motif. If the figures of Peter, John and James display feelings of wonderment and trepidation in the *Parisinus Graecus* miniature, the postures of the disciples at Lesnovo reflect both ecstatic tension and elevated calm. The overall stance of the three disciples testifies to the effect that the mystical vision has on them. Their facial expressions and gestures, however, are relatively controlled. This creates a contrast between the two parts of the icon: the upper part, where the Transfiguration of Christ occurs, and the lower part, where the apostles witness the miracle. On one hand, the Metamorphosis happens beyond the terrestrial plane, somewhere on the inner, invisible level where the energy emitted from Christ envelops and transforms everything. On the other,

193 B. Todic, *Staro Nagoricano* (Belgrade 1993) 27.

194 Andreopoulos, 'How Do We Represent the Glory of God? Theological and Iconological Connections between the Transfiguration and the Resurrection', *La Mort et la Résurrection dans la Tradition Orthodoxe* (University of Sherbrooke 2004).

195 I.M. Djordevic, 'The Dialogue Relationship between the Virgin and Christ in East Christian Art: Apropos of the Discovery of the Figures of the Virgin Mediatrix and Christ in Lesnovo', *Zograf*, vol. 38 (2000).

the great trembling and awe that seized the apostles on Mt Tabor, 'When a cloud overshadowed the apostles', depicts the transformation occurring in their hearts and minds at the moment of the Transfiguration. The Transfiguration at Lesnovo has parallels in other churches, such as the Monastery of Gračanica,[196] and the Church of Pec.[197] It has to be noted, however, that in the aforementioned monuments, the painter introduced a double mandorla into the Transfiguration. The internal mandorla represents the halo that surrounds Christ. The external mandorla, on the other hand, envelops the two Old Testament prophets who, by virtue of their holiness, acquired a certain level of vision. Variations in the development of the mandorla of the Transfiguration appear in the fresco decoration of churches in Macedonia and Serbia. Thus, at the Church of the Virgin Misericordiuse, Prespa, there is a star inside the mandorla behind Christ (of the Transfiguration).[198] At Leskoec, on the other hand, the mandorla includes Moses and Elijah. Moreover, at Leshani, one may observe a complex geometrical shape including two diamonds, a circle and two rays of light.[199] A star-shaped mandorla surrounds the image of Christ in the scene of the Dormition of the Virgin at Leshani.[200] A fresco of the Transfiguration in the Church of the Virgin Mary, Ivanovo (Fig. 24),[201] is similar in style to the *Parisinus Graecus* miniature, which testifies to the spread of iconographical influence from Thessaloniki and Mt Athos to neighbouring countries of Bulgaria, Macedonia and Serbia (Fig. 25).

In the Church of the Virgin Mary, Ivanovo, the obligatory scenes for the decoration of a liturgical space take four rows of three scenes each, starting from the north-east corner of the church. The middle scene of the Transfiguration is in good condition, and there is a marked dynamism in the representation of the figures, which is emphasised by the contrasting rocky landscape. The dark-green shadows under the pink rock on which Christ stands contributes to the overall feeling of the scene.[202] Christ holds a scroll in his left hand and blesses with his right. Inside an almond-shaped mandorla that has been painted in several bands from light grey to dark grey, a diamond is inscribed, whose edges go downwards, while behind Christ, the four pink-red beams cross on

196 Todic, *Gračanica: Slikarstvo* (Belgrade 1988) 116, 34.

197 S. Petkovic, *La Peinture Serbe du Moyen Age II*, vol. 2, pl. XCI ; Millet, *L'Iconographie de l'Evangelie*, 216–231; S. Gabelic, *Manastir Lesnovo: Istorija i Slikarstvo* (Biblioteka Monografije 1998) 70.

198 Subotic, *Ohridskata Slikarska Skola od XV Vek* (Ohrid 1980) note 78, fig. 16.

199 ibid., note 69, fig. 51.

200 The same arrangements are noted in the compositions of the Dormition of Virgin Mary, Gračanicaas, as well as in the Church of St George, Staro Nagoricane (Todic, Gračanica, note 60, fig. 37; Todic, *Staro* Nagoricane, fig. 26–27).

201 Mavrodinova, *Stenata Zivopis*, f. 85.

202 C. Cavarnos, 'Byzantine Churches of Thessaloniki, An Illustrated Account of the Architecture and Iconographic Decoration of Seven Byzantine Churches of Thessaloniki, Together with Important Historical Data', MA thesis, Institute for Byzantine and Modern Greek Studies (1995) 46–65; Metropolitan Tseemee, 'Βυζαντινή Θεσσαλονίκη', *Θεσσαλονίκη: ΡΕΚΟΣ, Γ έκδοση* (1996); G. Velnee, 'Οι Άγιοι Απόστολοι Θεσσαλονίκης και η Σχολή της Κωνσταντινοπούπολης', *Akten des XVI International Byzantinistenkongress*, vol. 2, no. 4 (Vienna 4–9 October), *Jahrbuch der Österreichischen Byzantinistik*, vol. 32, no. 4 (1981).

the diagonal.[203] The two beams of light that cross behind Christ radiate towards the corners of the chamber and flood it with light.[204] The apostles are frightened and confused. John falls upside down, the exploding light sweeps James away, and Peter collapses to his knees. With few exceptions, this composition resembles the mosaic decoration of the Transfiguration in the Church of the Holy Apostles, Thessaloniki (c. 1315). The apostle James lies on his back and a rhomb superimposed over a circle in the shape of the letter X forms the glow around Christ, symbolising the three hypostases of the Trinity.

The fresco of the Transfiguration at Ivanovo and the miniature of the *Parisinus Graecus* are analogous.[205] While the octagonal mandorla in the miniature is different to the rocket-shaped doxa at Ivanovo, the similarities between both testify to the changes occurring in the iconography of light in the 14th and 15th centuries under the impact of hesychasm.[206] Adherents to this spiritual movement inhabited the Monastery of Ivanovo in the 14th century and it is plausible that hesychasm influenced the fresco program in Ivanovo's complex. Regardless, it is important to note that Bulgarian fresco-painters used these complex types of mandorlas at least until the 17th century (Fig. 26).

The hesychastic iconography of the Transfiguration transferred to Russia with the help of travelling artists, such as Theophanes the Greek (Fig. 27). In Theophanes's portable icon of the Transfiguration, his fidelity to the theological teaching of Palamas is clear.[207] The technical challenge in both paintings was the influence that the uncreated light had on its surroundings, as opposed to the effect of the sunlight or another light source.[208] The miniature is luminous with the application of gold around the figures, and the use of harmonising colours of blue, grey and ochre giving the impression that the scene is immersed in serene blue light. In addition, the highlights on faces and clothes reflect the light source coming from different angles of the pictorial plane. A mixture of gold leaf and transparent egg tempera creates the impression of light permeating the matter, so that the landscape shines from within itself. The upper portion of the icon radiates with the light of Transfiguration, but at the same time an internal luminescence shines from all surfaces. The rendering of figures projects Hellenistic elegance in their correct proportions and plastic perfection, and the

203 Velmans, 'Les Fresques d'Ivanovo et la Peinture Byzantine à la Fin du Moyen Âge', *Journal des Savants*, no. 1 (1965).

204 Cheremeteff, 'The Uncreated Light'; Velmans, 'Les Fresques d'Ivanovo', 364–365.

205 B. Nikolova, *Православните Църкви през Българското Средновековие IX–XIV* (Sofia 2002) 79–82; Mavrodinova, *Stenata Zivopis*, 95.

206 ibid., 80.

207 Charalampidis, 'The Representation of the Uncreated Light'.

208 M. Cheremeteff, 'The Transformation of the Russian Sanctuary Barrier and the Role of Theophanes the Greek', PhD thesis, University of Oregon (1987).

illuminated slopes of the high mountain emphasise the specific iconographical detail of successive circles, as opposed to elliptical shapes, within the rhomboid formation.

Enriched with a corona of radiating beams, the star-shaped blue mandorla is an emblem of the uncreated light on Mt Tabor. The mandorla and the geometric (star-like) 'radiance' behind Jesus simultaneously emanate from him and from behind him. This mandorla surpasses any other doxa in the Byzantine art of Palaeologan period. Moreover, the iconographic element of three, blue, light beams, which become progressively lighter when approaching Christ, refers to the doctrine of Transfiguration. This iconographic element also asserts the essence–energies distinction, with the rays of light referring to 'the divine darkness' (essence of God) while reflecting the divine energies. The two darker insets of the disciples following Jesus up and down the mountain carry the same symbolism. In the same way, the angels who collect both Moses and Elijah from their heavenly abode are wrapped in grey colour tones.[209]

The brilliant and harmonious colouring, and a lively play of light, enriches the effect of the whole series. There is a general mood of calmness and concentration, which is enhanced by the use of soft layers of saturated colours. The application of highlights (above the eyebrows, and under the eyes) has a transformative effect on these colours.[210]

In contrast to Theophanes's Transfiguration icon, a strong central axis and symmetry pervade the illumination of the *Parisinus Graecus* miniature, which creates a geometrically balanced scheme. The square, the triangle, the circle and the semicircle are some of the forms used in this composition. Christ is the only figure facing the viewer and he is intrinsically balanced.[211] There are no converging lines to create a sense of depth and reverse perspective. Together with the interplay of light and shadows on the clothing, the overlapping mountains are the only elements that generate space in the composition. A sense of calmness prevails in the middle of the piece and movement is confined to the periphery. The ecstatic rapture of the disciples who, affected by their vision of the divine light, fall prostrate to the ground, alludes to a mystical

---

209 A. Tachioaos, 'Hesychasm as a Creative Force in the Fields of Art and Literature', *L'Art de Thessalonique et des Pays Balkaniques et les Courants Spirituels au XIVe Siècle,* (Belgrade 1987) 123. 1; Charlampides, 'The Representation of the Uncreated Light'.

210 A. Omont, *Miniatures des Plus Anciens Manuscripts Grecs de la Bibliotheque Nationale du VIe au XIVe Siecle* (Paris 1929); Voordeckers, 'Examen'.

211 S. Nes, *The Uncreated Light: An Iconographiocal Study of the Transfiguration In the Eastern Church* (Edinburgh 2007) 32–40.

text written by one of the main exponents of hesychasm, Symeon, in which he describes the mystical state of the hesychasts in the same manner as the apostles are positioned in the miniature.[212]

The icon of the Transfiguration by Andrei Rublev discards superficial detail and is limited to six essential figures (Fig. 28). The unusual arrangement of this icon depicts rays of light connecting the six figures who diverge into two groups of three. Moses and Elijah surround Christ, who sits on the mountain peak in the middle of the figurative scene. The three trembling disciples are in the lower part of the icon, and there is a significant gap between them and Christ. This space, which is repeated in the other iconographical features, represents the distance between the divine and the human world (in contrast to the Transfiguration at Sinai, where the apostles were close to each other, almost back to back). Rublev creates a feeling of awe before the mystery of the Transfiguration.[213] Comparing Rublev's icon of the Transfiguration with the *Parisinus Graecus* miniature, the difference between the two reflects the divergence in the styles of the Greek and Russian masters.[214] Traces of the Byzantine influence on Novgorodian iconography exist, however, and it seems that Russian artists adopted pecularities from Greek masters to create realistic works of art showing the balance between the human and the divine that reflect the spread of hesychasm from Byzantine to Slavic lands. The white lightning of the octagonal mandorla cut the space, 'piercing the flesh of the earth, and illuminating everything with light'.[215] A separate ray of light acting as a spear nails each of the apostles to the ground (Matthew 17:6). Rublev's *Transfiguration* icon, on the other hand, depicts the divine uncreated light as kind and gentle, the greatest mystery (a presence of dark mandorla marks this) and an ineffable grace. In addition, Rublev's icon reflects purity, luminosity, simplicity, and the richness of emotions that attract us to meditation.[216] The use of geometrically shaped mandorlas was a common feature of Russian interpretation for the Transfiguration, a tradition which persisted until after the 16th century (Fig. 29).

---

212 Cap 3, 21 in J. Darrouzes (ed.), *Symeon the Nouveau Theologien: Chapitres Théologiques Gnostiques et Pratiques*, vol. 51 (Paris 1951) 132.

213 M. Golubstov, 'Икона Живоначальной Троицы', *Журнал Московской Патриархии*, vol. 7 (Moscow 1972).

214 G. Every, *The Time of the Spirit: Readings through the Christian Year* (Oxford 1984) 220–222.

215 The aesthetic description of the light of Transfiguration is continued in the 14th century portable Russian icon from the Kirillo-Belozersky Monastery, Novgorod. The whiteness of the divine light has illuminated the clothes of the prophets and apostles (K. Dyadakova, *Science in Russia, Browsing Through a Book: Monasteries in Russia* (Moscow 2003) 89–96.

216 L. Hughes, 'Art and Liturgy in Russia: Rublev and his Successors', *The Cambridge History of Christianity*, vol. 5, *Eastern Christianity*, M. Angold (ed.) (Cambridge 2006) 291; N.V. Riasanovsky & M.D. Steinberg, *A History of Russia*, 7th ed. (New York 2005) 120.

Conclusion

The iconography of the Transfiguration in the 14th and 15th centuries underwent changes that were reflective of the renewed interest in the subject of uncreated light on Mt Tabor, the central doctrine of the hesychast controversy. The *Parisinus Graecus* miniature is a sublime attempt to capture this vision of the Taborian light in participial form, as well as an important example of the changes occurring in the iconography of the Transfiguration during the 14th century. The most dramatic change in the miniature is the introduction of the 'hesychast' mandorla consisting of two superimposed squares (rather a square and a rhomb) placed inside a circle consisting of three different layers of colour. The emergence of the star symbolism and the octagonal mandorla was a way of representing the hesychast concept of the vision and knowledge of God seen as light during Christ's Metamorphosis. The postures and gestures of the participants in this event reflect the dramatic elements of this vision. The varied use of colour and the animated gesticulation and fluttering drapery of the disciples reveals the drama of the Transfiguration. The agonising position of the apostles on the ground and their obvious avoidance of light are consistent with this. They fell to the ground headfirst, gesticulating and crouching away from the blinding light. In contrast, Christ stands calmly on the top of the mountain between the similarly calm figures of Moses and Elijah. Other iconographical features bear witness to the changes in the iconography of the Transfiguration. Mt Tabor has three parts joined at the base, with Christ, Moses and Elijah standing on separate peaks.[217] Overall, however, the miniature visually represents the intersection of God's transcendence and immanence as reflected in the Transfiguration. It also serves as a sign of hope for humankind, and as a reminder of the ultimate destiny of humanity, which is participation in the uncreated light of God.

217 Andreopoulos, *Metamorphosis*, 225.

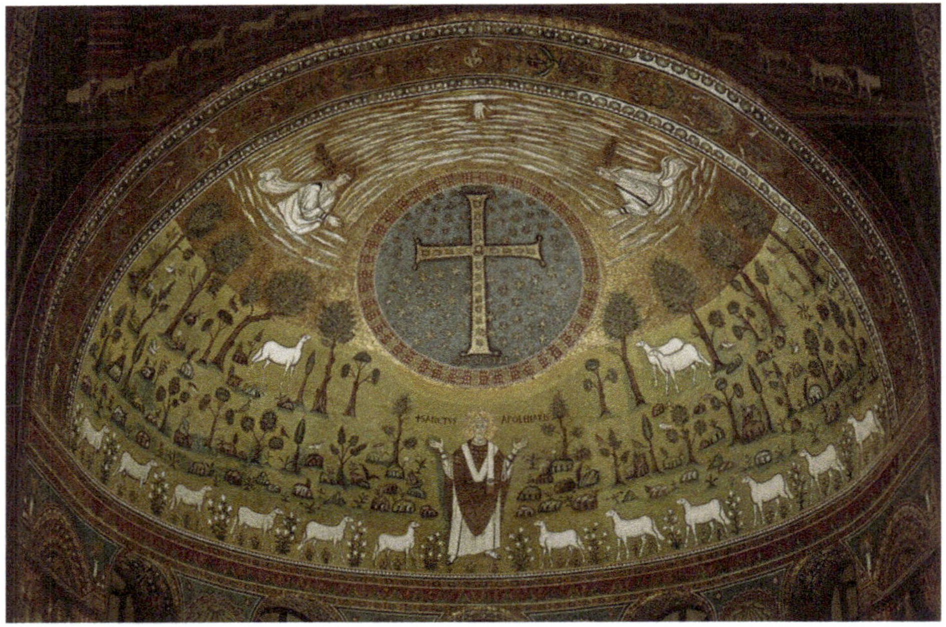

Figure 12. ***Saint Apollinaire amid Sheep*, c. 549, mosaic, apse, Basilica of St Apollinaire in Classe, Ravenna (Italy)**

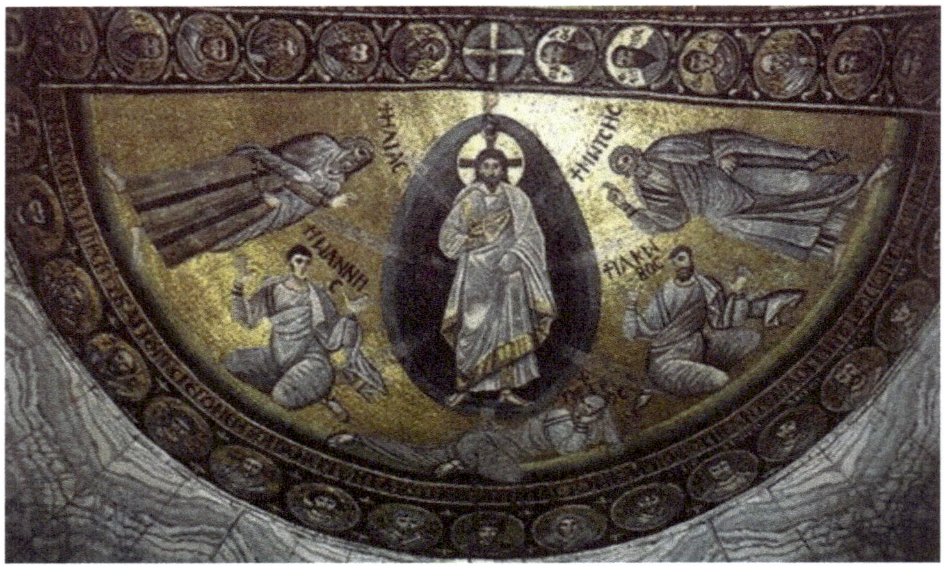

Figure 13. ***The Transfiguration of Christ*, c. 565, mosaic, apse, Church of the Virgin, Monastery of St Katherine, Mt Sinai (Egypt)**

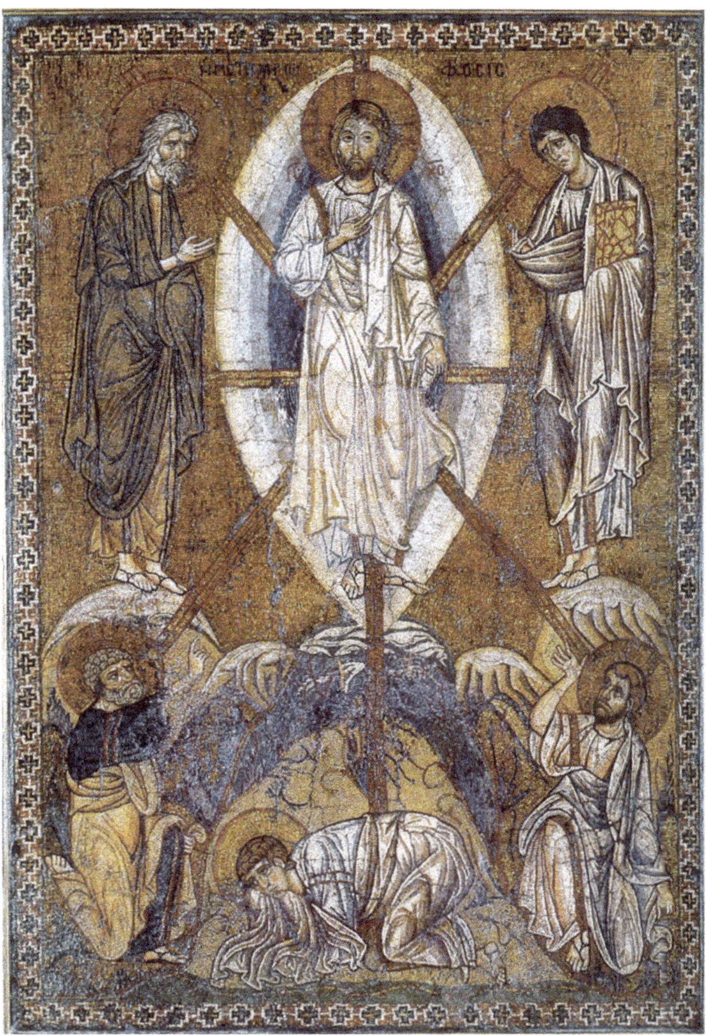

Figure 14. *The Transfiguration of Christ*, first half of the 12th century, tempera on wood, 52 × 35.3 cm, Musee du Louvre (France), inv. no. ML 145, 6591

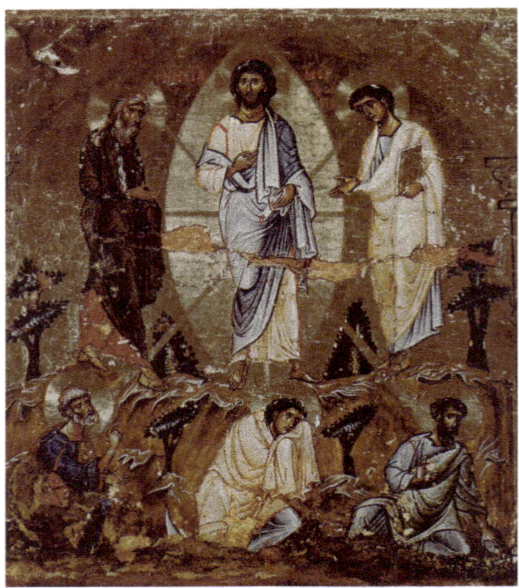

Figure 15. *The Transfiguration*, mid-12th century, tempera on wood, 41.5 x 159 cm, part of the iconostasis, Monastery of St Katherine, Sinai (Egypt)

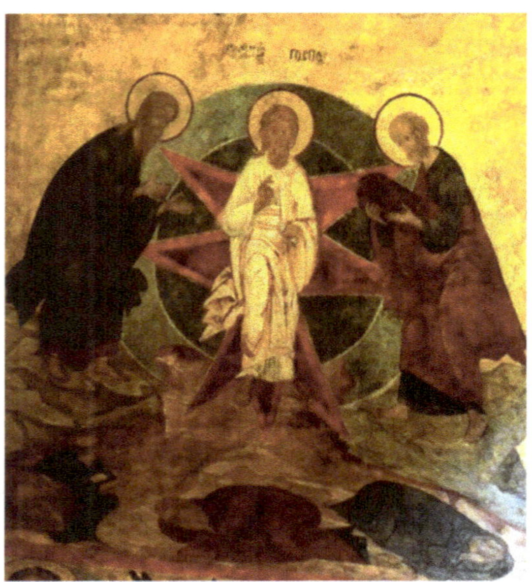

Figure 16. *Transfiguration of Christ*, 17th century, fresco, vault of the nave, right side, painters Sidor Pospeyev, Ivan Borisov and Semyon Abramov, Church of the Deposition of the Robe, Kremlin, Moscow (Russia)

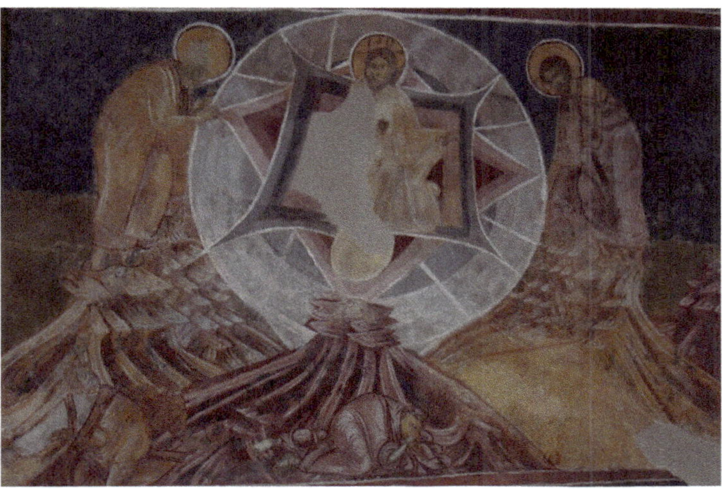

Figure 17. ***The Transfiguration of Christ*, 12th century, fresco, northern wall of the nave, Church of St George, Kurbinovo (Macedonia)**

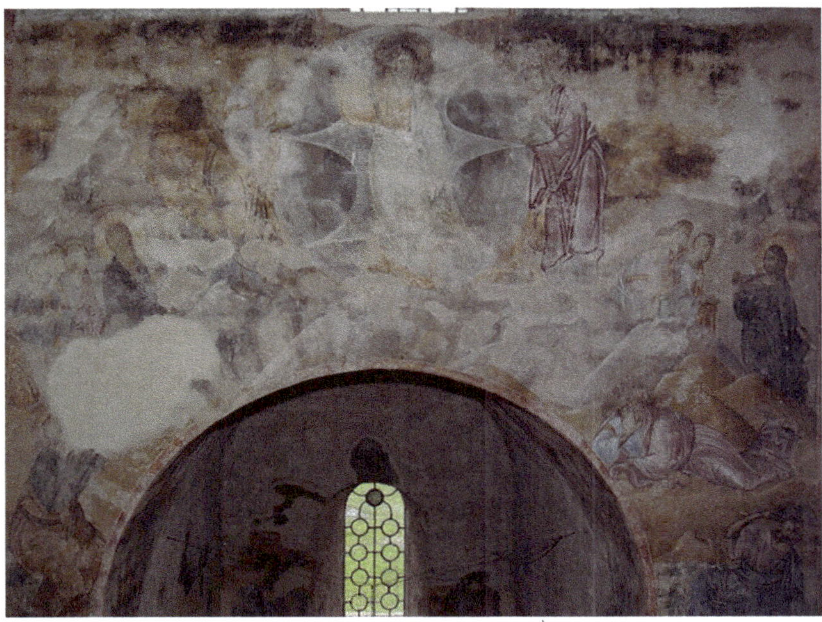

Figure 18. ***The Transfiguration of Christ*, 14th century, fresco, central zone of the nave, Monastery of Sopočani, Raška (Serbia)**

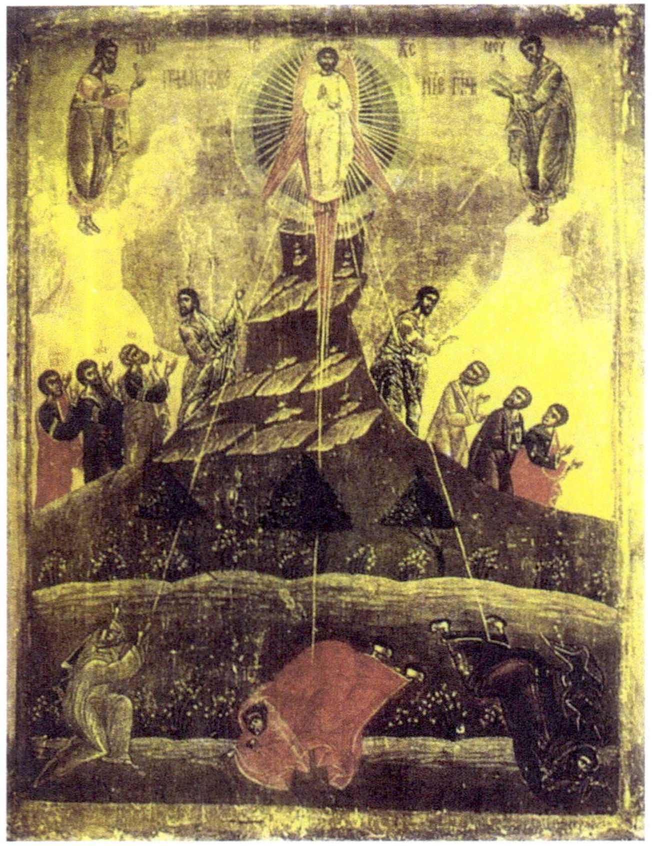

Figure 19. ***The Transfiguration of Christ*****, 13th century, tempera on wood, Monastery of Xenophon, Mt Athos (Greece)**

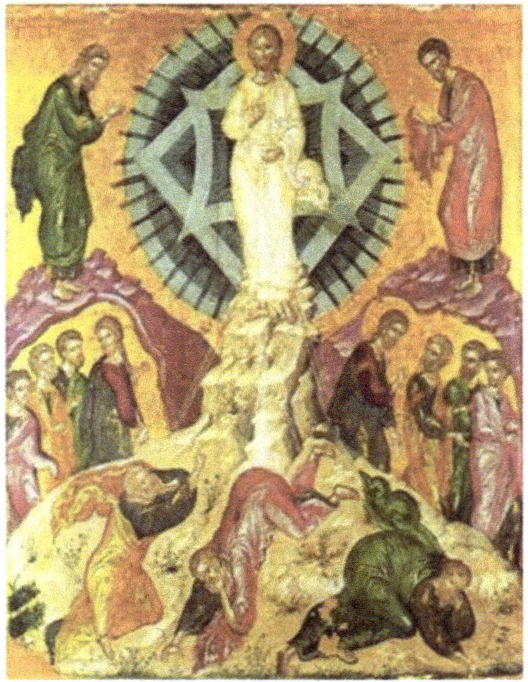

Figure 20. *The Transfiguration of Christ*, c.1535–1545, tempera on wood, 91 x 80 cm, att. Theophanes the Cretan, Monastery of the Pantokrator, Mt Athos (Greece)

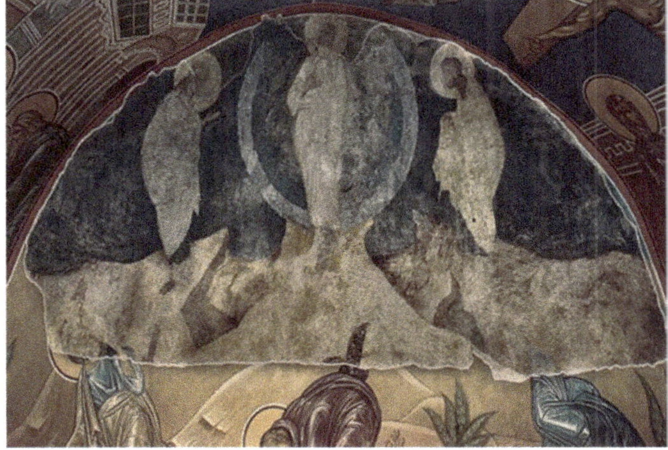

Figure 21. *The Transfiguration of Christ*, c. 1408, fresco, lunette walls in the northern arm of the cross, Dormition Cathedral of the Virgin, Vladimir (Russia)

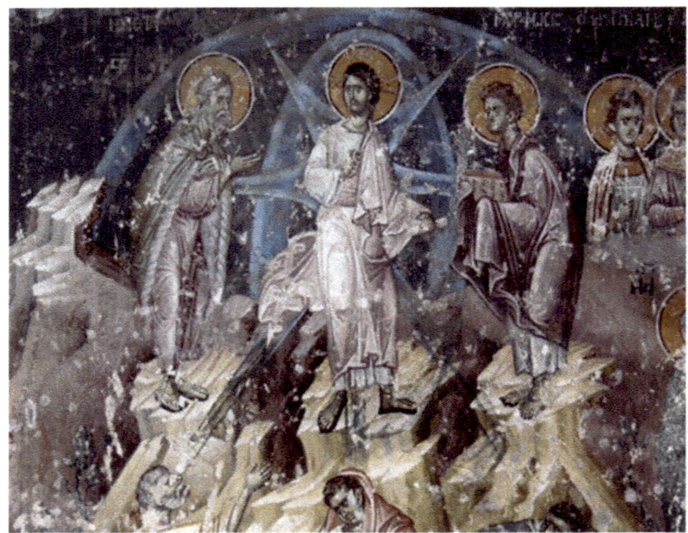

Figure 22. ***The Transfiguration of Christ*****, c. 1313–1320, fresco, west wall, painters Eutychios and Michael Astrapas, Church of St George, Staro Nagoricane, Skopje (Macedonia)**

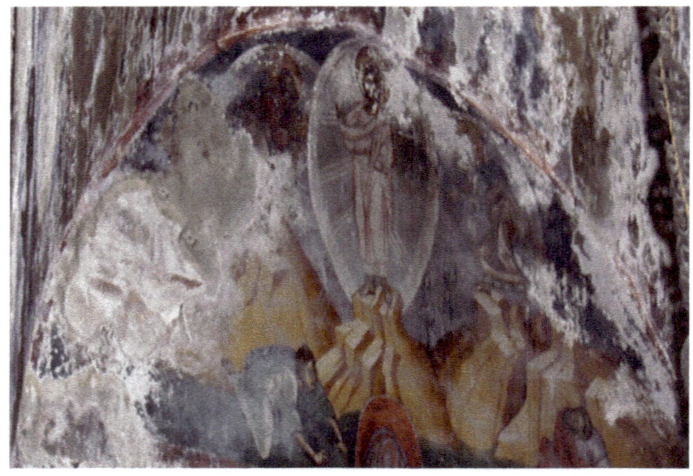

Figure 23. ***The Transfiguration of Christ*****, 14th century, fresco, narthex, Church of St Archangel Gabriel, Monastery of Lesnovo, Probistip (Macedonia)**

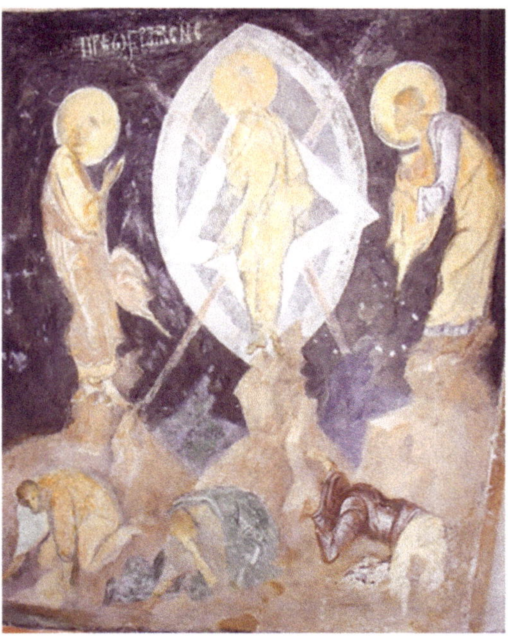

Figure 24. ***The Transfiguration of Christ*, 14th century, fresco, vaulted ceiling, Church of the Virgin Mary, Rock-hewn churches of Ivanovo, Rusenski Lom (Bulgaria)**

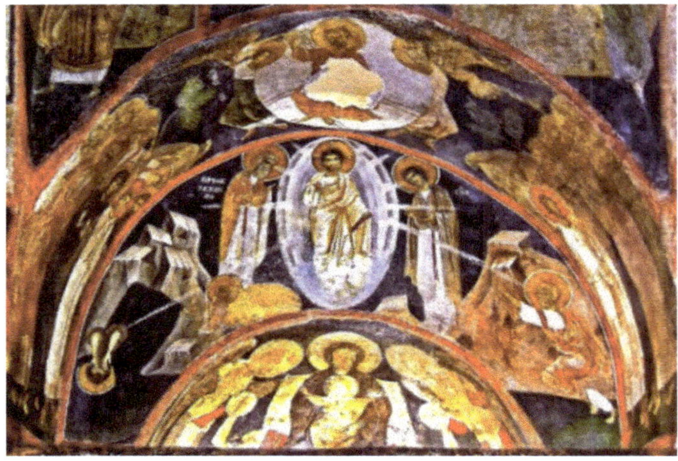

Figure 25. ***The Transfiguration of Christ*, c. 1259, fresco, sanctuary, Boyana Church of St Nicholas and St Panteleimon, Sofia (Bulgaria)**

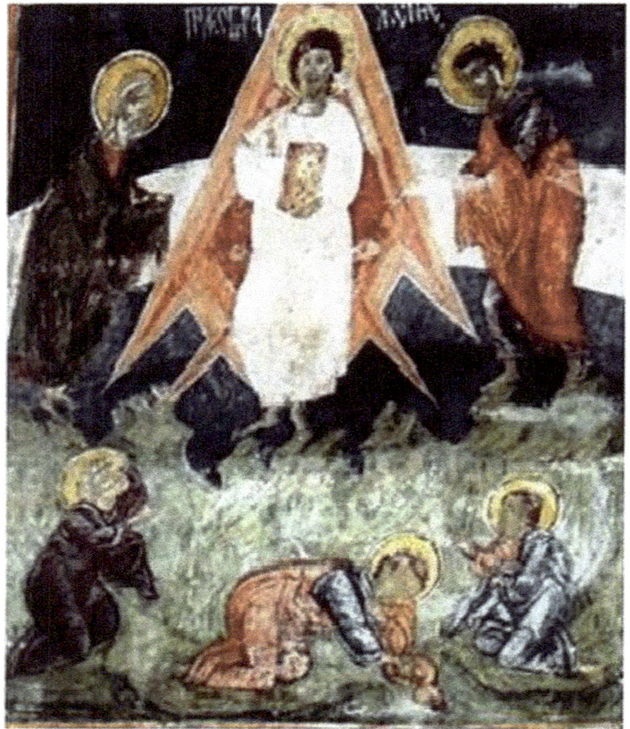

Figure 26. ***The Transfiguration of Christ*****, 17th century, fresco, northern wall of the nave, Church of Theodore Tyro and Theodore Stratelates, Dobarsko, Razlosko (Bulgaria)**

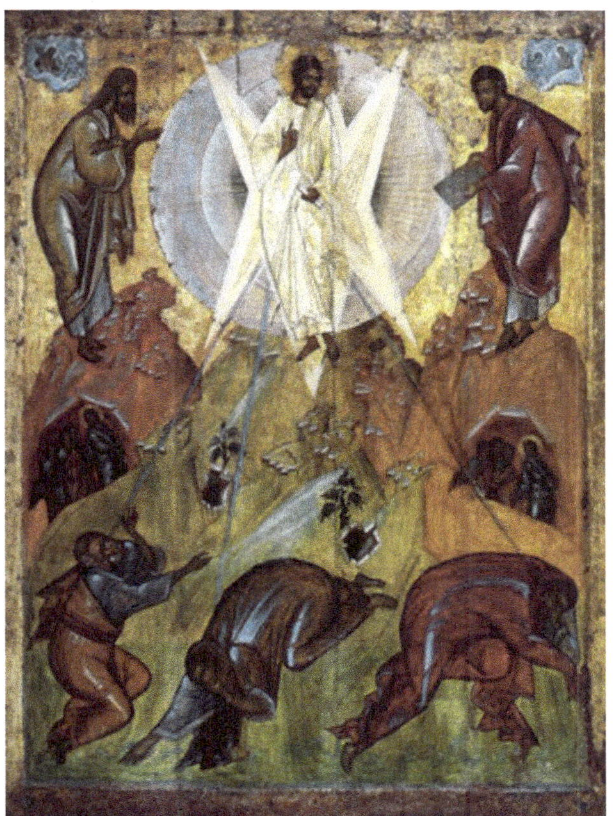

Figure 27. *The Transfiguration of Christ*, c. 1403, tempera on wood, 184 x 134 cm, painter Theophanes the Greek, Tretyakov Gallery, Moscow (Russia), inv. no. 12797

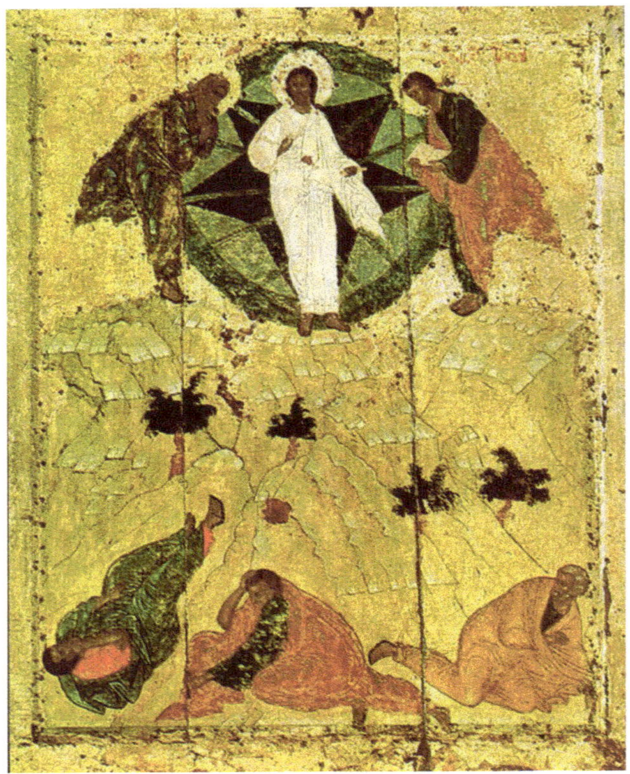

Figure 28. ***The Transfiguration of Christ*, 15th century, tempera on wood 80.5 x 61 cm, painter Andrei Rublev, Church of the Annunciation, Kremlin, Moscow (Russia), inv. no. 3248 СОБ/Ж–1401**

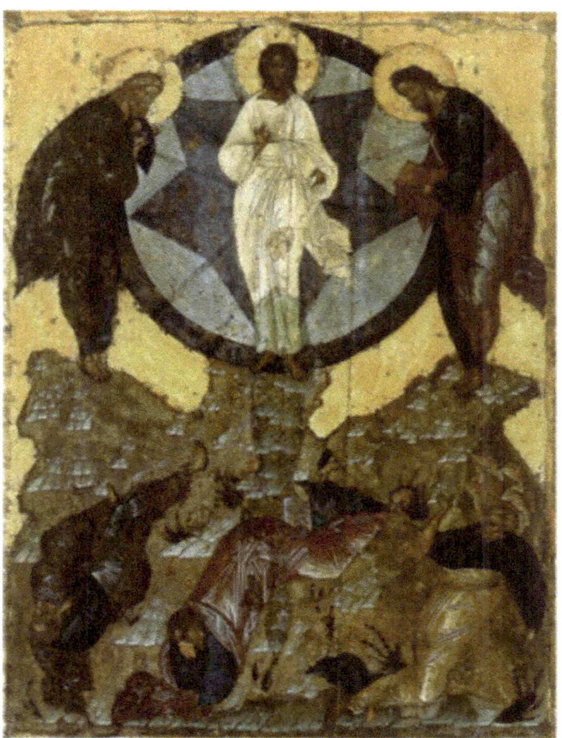

Figure 29. *The Transfiguration of Christ*, 15th century, tempera on wood, temple icon, Church of Our Savior in the Woods, Kremlin, Moscow (Russia)

4. The Fresco of the *Anastasis* in the Chora Church

The composition of the Transfiguration is the chief illustrative example of any vision of the uncreated light of the Godhead, which was the basis of hesychast theology. All the issues associated with the Transfiguration were, therefore, important for the hesychasts, such as the transfiguration of the body (by the divine light) equalling that of the Resurrection. The feast of the Transfiguration shares a common theological basis with the Anastasis, and both are a true expression of the divine nature of Christ and manifestation of the phenomenon of the supernatural light of glory. If the Transfiguration fulfills the Theophany on Mount Sinai, the Anastasis anticipates the *Parousia*. The Anastasis also expresses the well-known Eastern Christian doctrine of *theosis*; the mysterious relationship between God and his creatures according to energy or grace.[1] It also affirms the reality of the hypostatic union of two natures in Christ after his death and resurrection, as Christ remains perfect man and perfect God in heaven as well as on earth. Hesychasts believed that Christians can acquire deification only by participating in the corporeality of Christ, in the Eucharist, where the bread and wine become the circumscribed body and blood of Christ. Denial of the circumscription of the risen body of Christ, therefore, leads to denial of the salvific act of God.

The iconography of the Anastasis was consistent until the 14th century, when the conflict between humanism and hesychasm during the Palaeologan era resulted in the establishment of new artistic trends with new motifs and subjects. Variations in the scene of the Anastasis occurred in the circumscription of Christ in the state of resurrection as well as in the relation of Christ to Adam and Eve.[2] Although it is difficult to confirm that mystical movements were directly responsible for these iconographical changes, the fresco of the *Anastasis* in the Chora church (Fig. 30) illuminates the hesychast notion of *theosis* (union by grace).[3] It also expresses the central principle of Byzantine theology: the ability to acquire knowledge and experience of God through vision.

---

1 John of Damascus, *Oration*, III, 26, in P.B. Kotter (ed.), *Die Schriften des Johannes von Damaskos*, 5 vols, *Patristische Texte und Studien*, vol. 12 (Berlin 1973); Kotter 3, 134; Nikephoros, *Antirrhetici Tres Adversus Constantinum* III, 31, in *Patrologia Graeca*, 100, 375–534; 421D–424A.

2 J. Meyendorff , 'Spiritual Trends in Byzantium in the Late Thirteenth and Early Fourteenth Centuries', *Arte et Societé à Byzance sous les Paleologues: Acts du Colloque Organise par l'Association Internationale des Etudes Byzantines in Venice en Septembre 1968* (Venice 1971) 56.

3 D.M. Nicol, *The Last Centuries of Byzantium 1261–1453* (Cambridge 1972) 166.

The theological background of the Anastasis

The feast of the Anastasis in the Orthodox Church commonly celebrates the tripartite theme representing Christ's descent into Hades: his victory over Satan, death and darkness; his deliverance of the righteous from Hades; and his victorious resurrection on Easter morning. The Latin Church calls this event the Descent into Hell (Limbo), which, in fact, represents the first phase of the tripartite Anastasis, and neglects the most important aspect; that is, the rising of humankind through Christ's resurrection.[4] The Eastern Church's amalgamation of the two events of Christ's resurrection and his descent into hell into one feast, known as the Anastasis, illustrates the elaborate complexity of the historical reception of Biblical text.[5]

The 1st-century *Odes of Solomon* provide the earliest literary evidence for the description of the Anastasis.[6] Other significant literary sources are Hebrew and Christian scriptures, Syriac liturgical texts, and early Christian homilies and patristic manuscripts.[7] Nevertheless, the three synoptic Gospels are the most valuable sources in that they recount the event of resurrection of Christ. The canonical account of Mathew 27:45–54 relates specifically to the events during and after the Anastasis: 'and the graves opened; and many bodies of the saints which slept arose; and came out of the graves after his resurrection, and went into the holy city, and showed unto many'. Moreover, in Psalm 107:10–14, one finds an account of Christ's arrival in the realms of hell ('He brought them out of darkness and the shadow of death'). The underlying message in all written sources is the depiction of Jesus Christ as Alpha and Omega, the one who has a reign over Hades and who abolishes death (Revelation 1,:13). He breaks the gates of hell, extends his hand, and makes a sign of blessing over Adam, Eve and the saints: 'Christ takes hold of Adam's hand, He arises from Hell, and all of the saints follow Him' (Nicodemus VII, 24:1–2; 1 Peter 3:19).

Various other offices for public worship contain references to the feast of the Resurrection. The 'Liturgy of the Burial of Christ on Holy Saturday' reminds the faithful of Christ's Resurrection[8] with a Byzantine breviary and the three liturgies and propers of various offices.[9] The *Liturgy of the Blessing of the New*

4 J. Pierce, *From Abacus to Zeus: A Handbook of Art History* (Englewood Cliffs 1977) 100.

5 K.D. Kalokyris, *The Essence of Orthodox Iconography* (Brookline 1971) 34.

6 J. Baggley, Festival Icons for the Christian Year (Crestwood 2000) 120.

7 Irinaeus of Lyon, Adversus Haereses III, 20, 4; in *Patrologia* Graeca, 433–1225; 4; St Romanos the Melodist, 'Kontakia of Romanos', *Patrologia Graeca* 101–102, 775–785; Odes of Solomon, Ode 42; Ephrem the Syrian, *Des Heiligen Ephraem des Syrers Carmina Nisibena* 1–2, in E. Beck (ed. & trans) (Louvain 1961–1963); Carmina Nisibena 65; Acts 2:6 and 31–32 in E. Hennecke, *New Testament Apocrypha* (New York 1963, 1965).

8 H. Wybrew, *The Orthodox Liturgy: The Development of the Eucharistic Liturgy in the Byzantine Rite* (Creswood 1990) 157.

9 J. Raya & J. De Vinck, Byzantine Daily Worship: With Byzantine Breviary, the Three Liturgies, Propers of the Day and Various Offices (Allendale 1969) 835.

Light refers to Christ as the 'Light sent to the world', in the part devoted to the Resurrection of the protopsalts, coming after the 'Second Tome of the Expostulation'.[10] The *Eight Tome[s] of the Idiometa* (a part of the *Triodion of the Liturgy of Holy Week*) describes the destruction of the bronze gates of hell and alludes to the annihilation of Satan and his dissolutional powers over the souls in hell.[11] The liturgical service of Pentecost provides the same account. Finally, the hymn for Vespers affirms the universality of the event, indicating that 'Christ liberated those held captives for ages and He granted incorruptibility to all humankind'.[12]

Christian apologia against Gnostic teachings contains one of the accounts regarding the Resurrection of Christ. The followers of Gnosticism excluded the possibility of the resurrection of humankind from the outset; the destiny of the flesh or the substance of man was to perish after death.[13] Melito of Sardis in his *Homily on the Passion*, Tertullian in his *Treatise on the Soul* and Hippolytus in his *Treatise on Christ and Anti-Christ* refuted this doctrine. These ecclesiastical writers affirmed that the physical body of Christ placed in the tomb was raised immortal at the Resurrection. A noncircumscribable resurrection, they affirmed, has no verification. Many, however, saw Christ touching and sharing food after the Resurrection. The fact that Christ is no longer known according to the flesh, and now sits at the right hand of the Father, does not mean that Christ lost his human nature, which He received at the incarnation. Christ's death and Resurrection did not destroy the hypostatic union of his two natures. He remained perfect man and perfect God even after his Resurrection. Christ sits in glory at the right hand of the Father, and '*He will come again in glory* to judge the living and the dead, and his kingdom will have no end'.[14]

This apologetic approach to the subject of the Resurrection continued in the course of the anti-Origenistic controversy, when theologians such as Methodius of Olympus and Epiphanius of Salamis wrote theological treatises against Origen. Applying almost the same arguments as those used by the Gnostics, they asserted that Origen underestimated the physicality of the resurrection.[15] Methodius and Epiphanius attacked Origen's claim that the human body of Christ after the Resurrection was not the same body he possessed during his earthly life. They also challenged Origen's teaching on apocatastasis, or the state of restoration or re-establishment of all humanity at the end of time. Countering

10 ibid., 827.

11 ibid., 33.

12 Kalokyris, *Essence of Orthodox Iconography*, 34.

13 K. Rudolph, *Gnosis* (San Francisco 1985) 190.

14 John of Damascus, *De Fide Orthodoxa* IV, 1–2, in B. Kotter (ed.), *Schriften des Johannes von Damaskos*, vol. 2 (Berlin 1973). English trans F.H Chase, *St John of Damascus: Writings* (Washington 1958); Kot. 2, 172.

15 C.W. Bynum, *The Resurrection of the Body in Western Christianity, 200–1336* (New York 1995) 68; J.F. Dechow, *Dogma and Mysticism in Early Christianity: Epiphanius of Cyprus and the Legacy of Origen* (Marcon 1988).

Origen's position on the Resurrection, later writers such as Cyril of Alexandria, Ambrose of Milan and Athanasius of Alexandria claimed 'Christ put an end to corruption, by the grace of his resurrection'.[16]

Affirmation of the bodily resurrection was a frequent topic in the Christian apologia against Monophysites and Monothelites. Nowhere was it argued for more strongly than in the *Paschal Homily* of John Chrysostom, which is recited during the paschal vigil.[17] The homily provides an insight into the development of Christian understanding of the redemptive nature of the Resurrection and Chrysostom defends the sacrament of the Eucharist and invites all to partake of the paschal table.

The Latin fathers also emphasised the redemptive nature of the Anastasis. St Augustine, for example, affirmed the twofold nature of the feast.[18] Augustine proposed that there are two types of resurrection for Christians, the first begins with the experience of life in Christ, and the second, or bodily resurrection, will unfold in the *Parousia*.[19]

Similarly, later Byzantine theologians, such as Maximus the Confessor and John of Damascus provided elaborate teachings on the nature of the Resurrection. Maximus, for example, perceived Christ's incarnation and Resurrection as processes that reverse the effects of Adam's action in Paradise, which introduced sin and corruption.[20] John of Damascus, on the other hand, spoke about the state of grief, and the corruption of the body in the grave. He also, however, referred to the Resurrection as a 'vision of the unapproachable light' and a 'state of illumination', experienced by those who have passed from the state of death to incorruption (redeemed and resurrected in Christ).[21]

The iconography of the Resurrection of Christ in the East

It is difficult to establish the actual date when the first figurative scene of the Anastasis materialised. Its pictorialisation, however, was consistently circumvented, by the Christological difficulties inherent in the representation of

16 M. Young, Biblical Exegesis and the Formation of Christian culture (Cambridge 1997) 154; Athanasius of Alexandria, *On the Incarnation: De Incarnatione Verbi Dei*, C.S. Lewes (ed.) Chapter 5 (Crestwood 1996).

17 John Chrysostom, 'The Paschal Sermon of St John Chrysostom', http://oca.org/FSsermons-details.asp?SID=4&ID=10 (accessed 10/02/2012).

18 J.M. Rist, *Augustine: Ancient Thought Baptized* (Cambridge 1996) 110.

19 Augustine, *De Doctrina Christiana*, R.P.H. Green (ed.) (Oxford 1996) 115.

20 Maximus the Confessor, 'Epistulae 6', *Patrologia Graeca* 91, 362–650; 432A–B.

21 John of Damascus, *The Paschal Canon*, Archimandrite Ephrem (ed.), http://www.anastasis.org.uk/paschal_canon_with_notes.htm (accessed 2/02/2011).

the person of Christ in a state of resurrection. A few important doctrines radically altered the attitude of the painters. First, Christological cycles (including the Crucifixion and ending with the Resurrection) emerged, which reflected the orthodox position against the Monophysites and Monothelites, affirming that Christ has two wills (human and divine), which correspond to his two natures. Secondly, the Soteriological rather than Christological interpretation of Christ's death and resurrection during the iconoclastic controversy contributed to the birth of a new corresponding pictorial cycle.

Complementary to the Christological and the Soteriological aspects of the Anastasis, the ever-changing image of this event feast served as a pictorial echo for paschal themes, reinforcing their importance in the liturgy and typology of the church. Consequently, themes describing Christ's death and the Resurrection decorated many liturgical books and vestments. Finally, the birth of the new church rules such as canons 73, 82 and 100 affirmed the growing interest of the Church in the potential use of visual means to illustrate Christian dogmas.

Given the theological difficulties inherent in the subject of circumscription of Christ in the state of resurrection, there was an enduring absence of a standard way to depict the Anastasis.[22] Since there was no narrative to limit iconographers in the formation of the scene, the early Christian iconography of the Anastasis focused either on the representation of the theological significance of the Resurrection, or on using stylised symbolic language.[23] Hence, along with images of the Passion, iconographers used pictorial themes to symbolise the Anastasis including the image of sleeping soldiers around the church-rotunda of the Resurrection, the phenomenon of the myrrh-bearing women and the theme of the Bodily Rising of Christ from the tomb.[24]

The image of the Holy Sepulchre in the form of a temple provided a suitable Soteriological interpretation of Christ's death and Resurrection. The composition of the myrrh-bearing women, on the other hand, represented events that occurred after the Resurrection. Surviving evidence comes from a 5th-century carving on a plate that is currently held at the British Museum. It depicts both the myrrh-bearing women and the soldiers sleeping close to an open tomb. A plate from the 5th century, from the Museum of Castillo, Milan, represents the scene of the myrrh-bearing women as well as an angel sitting on a rock near the church with the door ajar. Another plate from the 5th century from the Bayerisches National Museum depicts Christ as a young boy entering a mountain. Finally, the lid of

22 Metropolitan Hierotheos of Naupaktos, Οἱ Δεσποτικες Εορτές: *The feasts of the Lord* (Lebadeia 1995) 262, 263.

23 A. Andreopoulos, 'How do we Represent the Glory of God? Theological and Iconological Connections between the Transfiguration and the Resurrection', *La Mort et la Résurrection dans la Tradition Orthodoxe* (Sherbrooke 2004).

24 J.F. Wilson, *The Story of Caesarea Philippi, Lost City of Pan* (London 2004) 93.

a 6th-century reliquary, held at the Vatican Museums, illustrates the myrrh-bearing women standing in the background of the rotunda with open doors, reminiscent of the royal doors of the altar.[25] Similarly, the Venetian mosaic of the Cathedral of San Marco depicts the *Descent into Hell, Christ appearing to Mary Magdalene*, and the *Assurance of Thomas*.[26] It appears, therefore, that by the 5th and 6th centuries these compositional types achieved wide distribution.[27]

By the later part of the 6th century, the pseudo-narrative character of the Resurrection of Christ, coupled with the story of the Descent into Hell dispensed with the need for a fully developed iconography, with exact reproduction of historical facts.[28] The legitimate portrayal of the Anastasis materialised in the 7th century.

A miniature of the Chludov Psalter is the earliest picture bearing the inscription 'Anastasis'. It provides a visual narrative of Psalm 68:1 ('Let God arise') and Psalm 82:8 ('Arise, O God, judge the earth; for You shall inherit all nations').[29] Other archaeological evidence for portrayals of the Ressurection narrative comes from the Cathedral of San Marco in Venice. Beyond that, the topic itself became a favourite subject at Sinai and Cappadocia in the 8th and 9th centuries, following the Iconoclastic controversy.[30] Subsequently, it became a part of a wider Christological cycle connected to the Passion of Christ.[31] Similar examples are found in the miniatures of the Gospel of John, the Iverian Gospel from Mount Athos and the Gospel of Trebizond, which are all held at the National Library of Russia.[32]

25 Rev. B.J. Lawrence et al., 'Anastasis: Icon, Text and Theological Vision', *Australian EJournal of Theology*, vol. 7 (2006), http://dlibrary.acu.edu.au/research/theology/ejournal/aejt_7/cross.htm.

26 Similar themes such as the appearance of Christ to the disciples, the assurance of Thomas, the miraculous catch of fish and the descent into hell, are reflected in the mural decoration found in the later churches, such as St Sophia in Trebizond (1238–1263); A. Eastmond, *Art and Identity in Thirteenth-Century Byzantium: Hagia Sophia and the Empire of Trebizond* (Oxford 2004) 98; D. Talbot Rice, *Byzantine Art and its Influences*, vol. 1 (1973) 126; O. Demus & H.L. Kessler, *The Mosaic Decoration of San Marco* (Venice 1988) 88–90.

27 J. Beckwith, *Early Christian and Byzantine Art* (Oxford 1993) 318.

28 The later abundance of variations may be attributed to the influence of new textual sources for the depiction of the Anastasis, for the thematic representation based on the action or position of Christ, the development of Christian dogma, as well as the enrichment of the composition through the addition of other participants, such as the figures of David and Solomon and other figures such as Abel, John the Baptist and Isaiah (C. Galavaris, *Studies in Manuscript Illumination* (Princeton 1969) 70).

29 N.P. Kondakov, 'Лицевой Иконописный Подлинник', *Иконография Господа Бога нашего и Спаса Иисуса Христа* (St Petersburg 1905) 12.

30 M. Quenot, *The Resurrection and the Icon* (Crestwood 1997) 73.

31 Among the known monuments illustrating the connection between both events are the Saviour Cathedral at Mirozhsky monastery (12th century) and the Church of the Ascension at Milesheva (13th century). Similar themes occur in other miniatures and icons, such as the miniature of the Trebizond Gospel. Also important are the frescoes of the 11th century Cathedral of St Sophia, Kiev, and those from the Church of St Theodore Stratilates on the Brook, Novgorod, from the last quarter of the 14th century; N. Necipoğlu, *Byzantine Constantinople* (Brill 2001) 149; S. Ćurčić, 'Medieval Royal Tombs in the Balkans: An Aspect of East, or West Question', *Greek Orthodox Theological Review*, vol. 29 (1984); E. de Muralt, *Catalogue des Manuscrits Grecs de la Bibliothèque Impériale Publique* (St Petersburg 1864) 40–41; I.R. Makaryk, *About the Harrowing of Hell* (Kiev 1989) 9.

32 de Muralt, *Catalogue*, 40–41.

By the 10th century the iconography of the Anastasis matured and became increasingly dramatic.[33] The narrative reflected in the surviving images of the Anastasis from the 10th onwards typically depicts Christ, surrounded by a blaze of glory, holding a cross in his left hand and descending into the dark cave of hell to bring Adam and Eve out of their sarcophagi. Many Old Testament figures stand in the foreground, led by King David and King Solomon. St John the Baptist guides a group of righteous and points with the scroll in his hand to Christ.[34] An excellent example of this trend is the *Anastasis* from the Church of the Karanlik Killise, Göreme, in Cappadocia (Fig. 31).

Beginning with the Macedonian churches at Kastoria during the 11th century, one may witness a new climate of experimentation marked by emotional tension.[35] The expressionist mannerism of the *Anastasis* at Kurbinovo (Fig. 32),[36] the simultaneous representation of Adam and Eve in Studenica, to the liturgical, benevolent representation of the *Anastasis* at the Church of Holy Apostle in Thessaloniki and the Church of the Protaton, Karyes, on Mount Athos (Fig. 33), reveals the emergence of a multiplicity of Palaeologan styles.

The Anastasis was a mandatory element in church murals, such as those from the 11th century at the Cathedral of the Monastery in Hosios Loukas (Greece) (Fig. 34). The composition of the Last Judgement often accompanied as asymmetrical type of Anastasis, which materialised during this time. In the asymmetric Anastasis, Christ stands in the middle of the piece with a cross in his hand. He pulls Adam out of his sarcophagus while Eve awaits her turn to be raised. The Cathedral of the Monastery of Nea Moni, Chios, (Fig. 35), the catholicon in the Monastery of Daphne (11th century) and the Cathedral of Santa Maria Assunta in Torcello (12th century) are examples of this trend.[37] Numerous other examples, which are identifiable in the miniatures of Byzantine Gospels, monuments of ancient Russia and other Orthodox countries, reveal that the basic outline of the scene remained unchanged throughout the centuries. It also spread outside Byzantine borders, mainly to Bulgaria and Serbia (Figs 36, 37, 38, 39); it persisted in some remote areas of Bulgaria until the 17th century, as can be seen in the Church of Theodore Tyro and Theodore Stratelates, Dobarsko, Razlosko (Fig. 40).

33 See also A.A. Kartsonis, *The Anastasis: The Making of an Image* (Princeton 1986) 9.

34 N.T. Wright, 'Jesus's Resurrection in the Early Christian Texts: An Engagement', *Journal for the Study of the Historical Jesus*, vol. 3, no. 2 (2005).

35 M.G. Parani, *Reconstructing the Reality of Images: Byzantine Material Culture* (2003) 178; G. Downey, 'The Tombs of the Byzantine Emperors at the Church of the Holy Apostles in Constantinople', *The Journal of Hellenic Studies* (The Society for the Promotion of Hellenic Studies, 1979).

36 L. Misguich, *Kurbinovo: Les Fresques de Saint-Georges et la Peinture Byzantine du XIIe Siècle* (Bruxelles 1975) fig. 45.

37 W.H. Hulme, *The Middle-English Harrowing of Hell and Gospel of Nicodemus*, vol. 100 (Montant 1907) 56.

At the onset of 12th century, the traditional scheme for the depiction of the Anastasis was changed, and the symmetrical placement of Eve on the right side of Christ transpired. In the earlier types of the Anastasis, Eve stood on the left side of Christ, directly behind Adam. She was positioned in the same sarcophagus as Adam, except in those instances in which Christ holds her by the hand.[38] From the 12th century onwards, however, Eve stood on the opposite side to Adam. A precedent for the symmetrical placement of Eve is found in the Sketchbook of Wolfenbuttel (1230–1240).[39]

The symmetrical Anastasis became popular during the Palaeologan period. The figurative scene of the *Anastasis* at the Monastery of Gračanica is a fine example of this trend, as is that at the Monastery of Marko, Markova Sušica in Macedonia (Fig. 41).[40] This model of the Anastasis also adorns the northern apses of monasteries on Mount Athos: the Great Lavra, the Monastery of Dionysius, the Monastery of Docchiariou, and the Holy Monastery of Chilandar.[41] The Church of the Holy Trinity, Sopočani (13th century) (Fig. 42),[42] and the Church of Christ, Veroia (14th century), contain similar images (Fig. 43).

The 14th century saw a new stage in the development of the Byzantine iconography of the Anastasis. The strict basis of the symmetrical Anastasis became emotionally rich, scenes were crowded with grouped figures of the just men, with their postures and gestures acquiring a natural, lively feel.[43] Sharp ledges and ridges grew to be mandatory details of the figurative scene, with the mandorla surrounding Christ acquiring a sharp-angled shape reminiscent of a rising star. The image of the cross, a common characteristic of the earlier samples of the Anastasis disappeared; the main emphasis was on the saving and

---

38 State Historical Museum, Moscow; A. Grabar, *Christian Iconography: A Study of its Origins* (Princeton 1986) 302. Other examples come from the 11th century Cod. Acc. No. 30.20 and Codex Gregory 550; fol. 5r, Bibliothèque Nationale de France, D.T. Rice, *Art of Byzantine Era* (London 1963) 331, pl. 174.

39 E.B. Schwartz, *The Wolfenbüttel Sketchbook* (New York 1973).

40 P. Underwood has done an extensive archological work on the Chora Church, which has been taken as a basis for my observations regarding this monument. See P. Underwood, *Kariye Dzami*, vol. 4: *Studies in the Art of the Kariye Dzami and its Intellectual Background, Program and Iconography of the Frescos of Parekklesion*, 321; 36–39.

41 O. Hjort, 'Oddities and Refinements: Aspects of Architecture, Space and Narrative in the Mosaics of Kariye Camii', in J.O. Rosenqvist (ed.) *Interaction and Isolation in Late Byzantine Culture, Papers Read at a Colloquium held at the Swedish Research Institute in Istanbul, 1–5 December, 1999* (Istanbul 2000) 27–44.

42 N.V. Kvlividze et al., 'Воскресение Иисуса Христа: Иконография', *Православная Энциклопедия*, vol. 9 (Moscow 2005).

43 Kartsonis recognised four compositional types of the Anastasis: Christ advances towards Adam and Eve and takes Adam by the hand in an effort to lift him from his grave, or He walks in the opposite direction from Adam and Eve while pulling Adam out of the tomb. Moreover, he either places the cross between himself and Adam, or he triumphantly sets up his cross upon Hades. In some later representations that are closely connected with the liturgy, Christ stands frontally with both hands extended sideways, and Adam and Eve flank him. Finally, in the 13th century, the fourth compositional type appeared, which is an amalgamation of all three types. The emphasis of this type is on Christ's effort to raise both Adam and Eve by the hand. He no longer bears the Cross, nor has marks on his hands. Kartsonis, *Anastasis*, 7.

transforming role of the Saviour's energy of light. A variant of this fourth type of the Anastasis shows Christ pulling both Adam and Eve out of hell. One of the finest examples is the fresco of the *Anastasis* at the Chora church.

Theodore Metochites and the parekklesion of the Church of the Saviour, Chora

When the emperor Andronicus II Paleologos succeeded to the throne in 1282, he appointed the polyhistor and author Theodore Metochites to be the Megas Logothetēs (the Grand Logette) and mesazōn (the chief minister and principal aide of the Byzantine emperor).[44] Faithful to the principles of Church dogma, Metochites also prided himself on his knowledge of Ancient Greek literature. Well-educated, an authority on classical authors, an admirer of Plutarch, Aristotle and Plato, and other talented statesmen, he was one of the greatest personalities of the Palaeologan era. His writings include rhetorical and astronomical treatises, several letters to contemporaries, philosophical and historical essays, and even autobiographical poems written in Homeric hexameters. In his main work, *Miscellanea Philosophica et Historica*, Metochites stressed the importance of the Byzantines being the descendants of the Hellenes, with whom they shared the Greek language.[45] His position in the royal court and the role that he played in the affairs of his day was so eminent that Andronicus II requested Methochites undertake the restoration and extension of the Chora church, a six-year project. His restoration campain, encompassing the rebuilding of Chora and its library, lasted from 1316–1321 and constitutes the fifth construction phase of the church.[46]

The name Chora has different connotations. The Greek words *choros* and *chorion* refer to such things as land, a landed estate, country, or a suburban area outside the city walls. It probably refers to the fact that the Church of the Saviour was built outside the walls of Constantinople. The name Chora also has mystical implications in relation to Christ and the Virgin. Applied to the Virgin Mary, the epithet refers to the popular *Akathistos Hymn*, and it means 'the Chora (the dwelling place) of the uncontainable God' (Ο Χώρα του Οί χώρητου, *hē Chōra tou Achōrētou*). When applied to Christ, the name Chora is most likely derived from Psalm 116, 'the land of living, the eternal reward for the faithful in heaven' (Χώρα των ζώντων, *hē Chōra tōn zōntōn*).[47]

44 I. Ševčenko, 'The Decline of Byzantium Seen Through the Eyes of Its Intellectuals', *Dumbarton Oaks Papers*, vol. 15 (1961).

45 R. Guilland, 'Les Poesies Inedites des Theodore Methocite', *Byzantion*, vol. 3 (1937) 265.

46 A. Karahan, 'The Palaeologan Iconography of the Chora Church and its Relation to Greek Antiquity', *Konsthistorisk Tidskrift: Journal of Art History*, vol. 2, no. 3 (1997) 89.

47 R. Ousterhout, 'Temporal Structuring in the Chora Parekklesion', *Gesta*. vol. 34 (1995) 63–76.

Metochites was the founder of the Church of the Saviour in 1315, before he was appointed a prime minister. The parekklesion was part of an extensive building and decorating program undertaken by the diplomat and it provided shelter and refuge for Metochites in difficult times of his career and served as a sepulchral monument for him and other important personages.[48] The fresco program of the parekklesion and the program of narthexes serve in many ways as the culmination of other cycles, which emphasise the past, present, and future as if occurring simultaneously. The complex program of the funerary chapel concludes in the apse, where the Anastasis is represented.

The *Anastasis* fresco

The fresco-cycle of the parekklesion at Chora establishes evocative links between the Old and New Testaments. At the same time, it reveals a close relationship between the fresco program and the purpose of the funeral chapel. The program of the parekklesion starts beneath the main dome, which is decorated with a fresco of the *Virgin Mary, the Queen of Heaven*. Underneath the dome, Metochites's body lies in one of the largest tomb arascolia. Immediately above the tomb is a fresco of *Jacob's Ladder*, and an image of the hymnographer, Theophanes of Crete, arranging a hymn dedicated to Metochites (to whom Theophanes points) is depicted in the pendentive. These works interrelate with the *Last Judgement* and the *Anastasis* by virtue of mimesis. Hence, in the fresco of the *Last Judgement*, which covers the upper walls of the bay and the entire dominical vault, Christ gestures with his hand towards the image of the soul of Metochites. In the majestic image of the *Anastasis*, the diagonals made by the sarcophagi of Adam and Eve direct the eyes of the viewer towards Metochites's tomb.[49] Several other images in the parekklesion at Chora also relate to each other. For example, the position of Adam and Eve ascending from their sarcophagi recalls the proskynesis of the angels flanking the Virgin Koimenis. The flowing red robe of Eve in the *Anastasis* mimics the form of the fiery stream of hell in the fresco of the *Last Judgment*.[50]

---

48 I. Ševčenko, 'Theodore Metochites, the Chora, and the Intellectual Trends of his Time', in Underwood (ed.) *The Kariye Djami*, 17–19; Ousterhout, 'Temporal Structuring', 67; P.L. Grotowski & S. Skrzyniarz, 'Towards rewriting? New Approaches to Byzantine Archaeology and Art', *Series Byzantina*, vol. 8 (2010).

49 The observations in this paragraph are largely based on Ousterhout's introductory remarks on the Church of Chora. See Ousterhout, 'The Kariye Camii: An Introduction', in D.S. Angelov (ed.), *Restoring Byzantium: The Kariye Camii in Istanbul and the Byzantine Institute Restoration*, (Columbia University 2004) 5–14.

50 J.M. Featherstone, *Theodore Methochites's Poems to Himself* (Vienna 2000) 118–120; S.E.J. Gerstel, 'The Chora Parekklesion, the Hope for a Peaceful Afterlife, and Monastic Devotional Practices', in H.A. Klein, R.G. Ousterhout, B. Pitarakis (eds), *The Kariye Camii Reconsidered*, Istanbul Research Institute Symposium Series 1 (Istanbul 2011) 107–145.

The images *Rising of the Widow's Son* and *Rising of the Daughter of Jairus* also flank the *Anastasis* in the parekklesion at Chora: these images complete the cycle of the ministry and miracles of Christ. In a similar way, the diagonals emphasise the drama of these scenes, which prefigures the resurrection.[51] At the eastern end of the chapel, the striking image of the Anastasis occupies the semi-dome of the apse.

Description

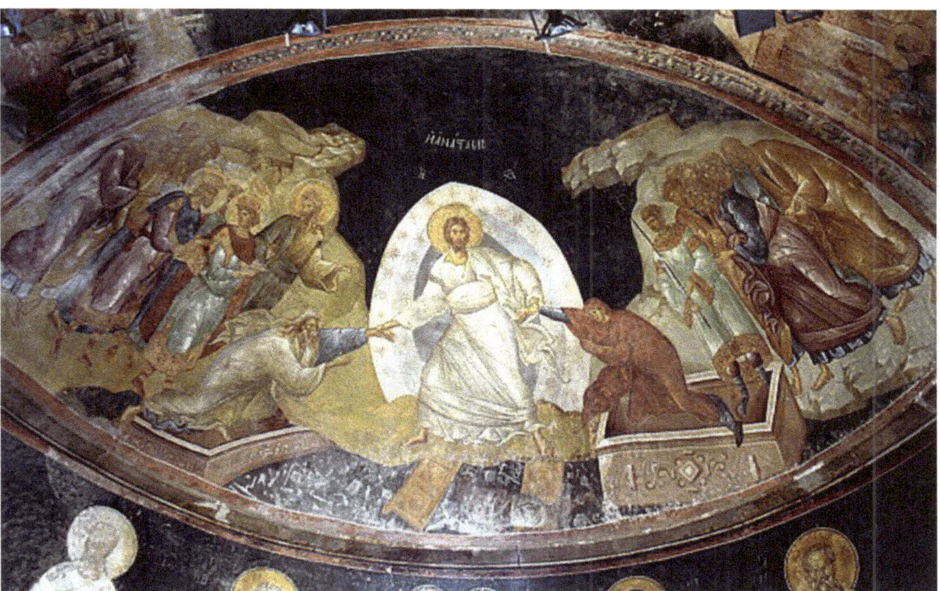

Figure 30. The Anastasis, c. 1315–1321, fresco, apse of the parekklesion, Church of the Saviour, Chora, Istanbul (Turkey)

Enclosed by a luminous oval mandorla decorated with stars, the dominant and glorious figure of the risen Christ, clad in a white luminous chiton (a draped garment held on the shoulders by a brooch) and himation vanquishes Satan and breaks down the gates of hell. With a vigorous motion, Christ grasps Adam by the wrist with his left hand, and Eve with his right. He seems to lift Adam with only a slight flexing of his arm, in contrast to the strength he uses to lift Eve out of her tomb. On the right hand of Christ (from the viewer's left side) are two groups of the righteous; each led by a single figure detached from the rest of his companions. John the Baptist stands behind Adam in his capacity as

51 S.H. Young, 'Relations between Byzantine Mosaic and Fresco Technique', *Jahrbuch der Osterreichischen Byzantinistik*, vol. 25 (1976).

forerunner. Solomon, David, and three other righteous kings accompany him.[52] Behind Eve, the young shepherd Abel leads a group of six other unidentifiable figures. Beneath Christ's feet, the entrance to Hades lies shattered, and the tiny, dark figure of Satan lies gagged and restrained. Various emblems of the broken powers of hell, such as chains, shackles, nails, and keys are in a circular cave of darkness. At the bottom of hell, Hades is tied with chains to a stake while, high in the sky, a group of angels is erecting a cross.[53]

Illuminated by a radiant light, the figure of Christ is the central point and energy field for the motif. It combines stability with movement and dynamic energy with power. Movement arises primarily from the dramatic positioning of the body in three different directions. Christ inclines his knees and posture slightly to the left while he places his feet firmly on the ground. He pulls Adam from the left and Eve from the right toward Him, up onto the vertical axis. The strong sense of upward movement indicates that Christ grants humanity and salvation from death, but also the possibility of participation in his true humanity and true divinity united in the single hypostasis.[54] It is an ascent of the body and soul towards God, attained through knowledge of the Scriptures and mediated by symbol and analogy. It alludes to the tripartite stage of the spiritual journey as affirmed by the hesychast: purification from passions (*praxis*), contemplation of nature as the work of God (*physike theoria*), and the vision of God (*theologia*) as light.[55]

The *Anastasis* at Chora affirms the theological interplay between the feast of the Transfiguration and the Resurrection, with the painters representing the resurrected body of Christ in the same way as the transfigured body of Christ was circumscribed in the Metamorphosis.[56] Christ's garments in the Transfiguration are more luminous than in the *Anastasis*. It is clear the white garments of Christ in the *Anastasis* represent his burial garments, but the feeling of this composition is anything but mournful. There is no explicit reason why Christ's garments are illuminated to such an extent in the *Anastasis*, other than that the same light emitted by the body of Christ on Mount Tabor during the Metamorphosis illuminated Christ during the Anastasis.[57] In other words, the colour of Christ's billowing garments shows the uncreated light that surrounded

52 Underwood, 'Notes on the Work of the Byzantine Institute in Istanbul: 1955–1956', *Dumbarton Oaks Papers*, vol. 12 (1958).

53 O. Demus & E. Diez, *Byzantine Mosaics in Greece, Hosios Lucas & Daphni* (Harvard 1931) fig. 104; M. Chatzidaki, *The Mosaics of Hosios Loukas* (Athens 1997) fig. 23.

54 Gregory Palamas, *Gregorie Palamas, Defense des Saints Hesychastes*, Meyendorff (ed. & trans) (Louvain 1959); Palamas, *Triads* II, 2: 4, and esp. II, 3: 35, in Meyendorff (ed.), *Gregory Palamas: The Triad*.

55 G. Maloney, *Pseudo-Macarius: The Fifty Spiritual Homilies and the Great Letter* (New York 1992).

56 B. Krivocheine, 'Аскетическое и Богословское Учение Святого Григория Паламы, *Seminarium Kondakovianum*, vol. 8 (Prague 1931).

57 Andreopoulos, *Metamorphosis: The Transfiguration in Byzantine Theology and Iconography* (Crestwood 2005) 165–166.

Christ at the Resurrection and the Transfiguration. This is the same light the Godhead shares with His Son and the Holy Spirit. The illuminated robes of Christ also serve as a witness to the beginning of an ascent that connects heaven to hell by a single beam of light. The choice of white garments, however, affirms that Christ maintained his human nature and the rational and spiritual soul was undiminished even after the Resurrection.[58] They also allude to the transformation of all creation. In fact, when Christ in his glory descended into hell, all dark places were enlightened and transformed in the same way as the event of the Transfiguration affected James, John and Peter. The figure of the Saviour surrounded by angels is transparent, subtle; it is like a melting image in contrast with the tight silhouettes of demons that swarm into the infernal abyss.

The fluttering end of Adam's robe billows from his shoulder and flows downward in jagged, pointed folds. The hem of his garment is equally ruffled and agitated. The lower edge of Eve's himation is rippled, terminating in a point at its tip, as do the robes of Adam and Christ. There is an inherent movement in the drapery of the figure representing Isaiah, who stands behind Abel and Eve. A piece of cloth cascades from his left arm. Dressed in garments of typological significance, the ancestors respond to the divine calling. They point to the New Adam (Christ) and the New Eve (the Virgin Mary) as well as to those mysteriously reconstructed and transformed in the realms of hell, not in any pantheistic sense of identification with the divine essence, but by grace, that is, 'empowered with divine energies'.[59] Christ's gestures towards Adam and Eve also affirm the hesychast view of grace and its relation to human salvation, embodied in the hesychast idea of co-operation (*synergia*).[60] Christ opens the way to paradise to Adam and Eve and calls them to salvation, but the response to Christ's call lies either in consent to follow Him or voluntary rejection of salvation.[61] In raising the ancestors who represent humanity's fall into degradation, Jesus acts out his role as the 'New Adam' who reversed the errors of the 'old Adam.'

Adam's strongly modelled figure is clad in alabaster clothes, but his robes are not as luminous as the garments of Christ, who is the source of light and an exemplar. Adam's features, his wavy locks of hair and beard are modelled with bold brushstrokes. His tunic of light blue symbolises the garments of glory, indicating the new life into which he has entered; in the same way the white robes of the newly baptised symbolise their new life in Christ.[62] Adam's sleeve

---

58 Nikephoros of Constantinople, *Antirrheticus* III, 38; *Patrologia Graeca* 100, 437BC.

59 John of Damascus, Oration I, 36; Kot. 3, 148.

60 Meyendorff, 'New Life in Christ: Salvation in Orthodox Theology', *Theological Studies*, vol. 50 (1989).

61 On the meaning of prayer see J.E. Bemberger, 'Evagrius Ponticus: The Praktikos and Chapters on Prayer', *Cistercian Studies Series* 4 (Spencer 1970); see also S. Tugwell, *Chapters on Prayer* (Oxford 1981); A. Guillaumont, *Les Six Centuries des 'Kephalia Gnostica' d'Evagre le Pontique*, *Patrologia Orientalis* 28 (Paris 1958).

62 Chatzidakis, 'Classicisme et Tendances Populaires au XIVe Siecle: Recherches sur l'Evolution du Style', *XIVe Congres International des Études Byzantines, Bucarest, Septembre 1971, Actes 1* (Bucharest 1971) 153, 88.

is of a much lighter colour than the rest of his clothing, serving as a proof that transfiguration or deification has taken place within him, filling him with the Holy Spirit. For the same reason, Moses and Elijah levitate around the corners of the hesychast mandorla in the Transfiguration. It affirms the concrete character of the vision of God in human form, the Christological vision adapted to the faculties of created beings. The long side of Adam's sarcophagus, which recedes into the abyss, is pinkish brown. The mouldings on the sarcophagus are in darker and lighter values of brown highlighted with white. The ornamental motifs are similarly coloured.[63] Beneath Adam, the interior face of the other two sides of the sarcophagus are visible. A considerably darker value of the same colour is applied on the far end and a slightly lighter shade is on the fourth side.

In the earlier models of the Anastasis, Adam and Eve stood in the same sarcophagus on one side of Christ, whereas, at the Chora church, they are on the opposite sides of him, emerging from their own sarcophagus. It is probable that the personal attachment felt by the all followers of hesychasm to the Virgin Mary influenced the development of the symmetrical type of the *Anastasis*.[64] It is by affirming the importance of the Virgin Mary for the salvation of humanity that the hesychast placed equal importance on the role of genders. Her role in human salvation was also much emphasised during the hesychast controversy. The Virgin Mary was a frontier between created and uncreated nature 'clearly announcing the divinity and the humanity of Christ in one hypostasis of the Word.'[65] Just as the original Eve fostered Adam's rebellion against His Creator, the Virgin Mary's acceptance of God's will fosters the reunification of God and man in the person of Jesus. She is the 'New Eve'.[66] In the Garden of Eden, Eve believed the lies of a fallen angel, disobeyed God, and so became the cause of Adam's transgression (Genesis 3:1–7). The Virgin Mary, however, trusted the words spoken by Archangel Gabriel, and she became Theotokos (the God bearer). The redemption brought through the Virgin Mary extends to Eve. Hence, while in previous models of the Anastasis Eve stood in the background, waiting her turn to be raised from death, in the symmetrical *Anastasis* Eve is on equal footing with Adam, but on the opposite side. She wears a red omophorion (a mantle with a hood) that covers most of her body, except for her right arm and her left foot, which are covered by a tight-sleeved blue tunic. Eve's red garment

---

63 R. Harries, *The Passion in Art* (Ashgate 2004) 81.

64 A. Kniazeff, 'La Theotokos dans le Offices du Temps Paschal', *Irenikon*, vol. 1 (1961) 30ff.

65 Palamas, 'Homily of Dormition' 37, in C. Veniamin (ed.), *The Homilies of St Gregory Palamas* (Waymart 2002) 430–431.

66 L.S.M. Gambero, *Mary and the Fathers of the Church: The Blessed Virgin Mary in Patristic Thought* (San Francisco 1999) 284–286.

alludes to the Virgin Mary's red robe. The highlights on Eve's drapery are not pure white, and it may be that the painter did this on purpose to accentuate the different stages of spiritual vision achieved by the two figures.[67]

John the Baptist, David and Solomon, ancestors and prophets, stand behind Adam, waiting their turn to be raised to life. The three kings on the left side of Jesus have haloes of various colours, whereas all of the figures on the right side of Jesus are without haloes. The presence of the kings on the left side crowds the anonymous group of righteous into a small space. In addition, the colours are muted. The imperial ideology is at play here, affirmed by the fact Christ's feet rest to the left side of hell, where imperial personages reside. In Byzantine art, secular and religious art combine references to the interconnection between Church and state and the cult of the Byzantine emperor provided a model for the general image cult.[68]

The emperor himself was a supreme ruler; his election was a gift of God, with the purpose of bringing peace and justice into the world.[69] The emperor had liturgical and administrative privileges which assigned him the role of guardian over the Church.[70] The halo of the Byzantine emperor indicated his executive and heavenly power.[71] Some formal elements can be traced to themes of classical mythologies, such as Hercules setting Cerberus free, by *pulling* him *out* of hell.

The hallowed figure of John the Baptist, whose has the accepted features of an ascetic, leads the group of righteous. A brownish-yellow tunic with black clavus covers his body. His face is turned three-quarters, and he makes the sign of supplication with his hands. He is the one who introduces Christ to the world during his lifetime, and he is the one that points to Resurrected Christ with his gestures. Most of the imperial personages on the left are dressed in a chlamys over a divitission. David's chlamys is dark blue, and Solomon's is red. In the hesychast context, affirming John the Baptist's link with Jesus is of uttermost importance. It is the element connecting the iconography of the Anastasis with that of the Transfiguration and, by extension, with the hesychast symbolism of light. In the same way, the Taboric light is more than an external phenomenon or an enhypostatic symbol. The light is both a symbol of the divinity and the divine,[72] a star preceded Christ who is the Light of the world; his forerunner

67 D. Balfour, 'Saint Gregory the Sinaite: Discourse on the Transfiguration', *Theologia*, vol. 52, no. 1 (1981–1983).
68 M.E. Kenna, 'Icons in Theory and Practice: An Orthodox Christian Example', *Harvard Review*, vol. 24, no. 4 (1985).
69 L.W. Barnard, 'The Emperor Cult and the Origins of the Iconoclastic Controversy', *Byzantion*, vol. 43 (1973) 13–29; see also H. Koester, *History, Culture And Religion of the Hellenistic Age*, vol. 1 (Philadelphia 1982) 32–36.
70 Barnard, 'Emperor Cult', 26.
71 E.H. Kantorowicz & W.C. Jordan, *The King's Two Bodies: A Study in Mediaeval Political Theology* (Princeton 1997) 80.
72 Gregory Palamas, *Triads* III, 1, 9, in Meyendorff (ed.), *Gregory Palamas: The Triad*.

to be, John the Baptist.[73] In other words, a 'ray of light' preceded the Light in the same way the divine energies precede (are reflections of) the essence of Godhead. The presence of John the Baptist in the Resurrection, on the other hand, affirms that he introduced a ritual effective for the forgiveness of sins that finds fulfilment with the Anastasis. 'Christ triumphed over infernos, releasing hell's captives, particularly Adam and Eve, and the righteous men and women of Old Testament times'.[74]

The youthful figure of Abel stands at the head of the group on the right. He wears a long greenish tunic that is adorned with rich gold embroidery and purple trousers. It is significant that Abel is standing in the same sarcophagus as his mother. In a series of complex contrasts, Abel and Christ are juxtaposed; the blood of the first human person sacrificed intercedes and the blood of Christ redeems. This symbolism also alludes to the theology of *oikonomia*, which is the eternal plan of God for the salvation, redemption and deification of humanity and the created world. This doctrine became an objective reality when the Virgin Mary conceived Christ.[75] Therefore, the mysterious creator of the *Anastasis* at Chora painted the picture of Eve as a symbol for the Theotokos and Abel as a symbol for the sacrifice made by Christ for humanity. Abel's companions wear chitons and himations in various colours. The chitons are blue and the himations are predominantly yellow, with two exceptions: the figure on the far right wears a reddish brown chiton, and the third person of the series in the second row has a green himation that is visible over his left shoulder. The highlights are usually white and there is much use of hatching in light yellow values. Both Abel and John the Baptist in this scene allude to Christ as the sacrificial lamb and recall the association of the image with the mystery of the Eucharist and Baptism. Did the painter have an awareness about the hesychast teaching concerning the uncreated light? It is plausible to think that this might have been the case. Hesychasts often stated that the active, unending, progressive movement of human beings begins with Baptism and continues in the Eucharist.[76] Consequently, they offer a genuinely theological anthropology, which perceives humanity as the unfinished creation of the Triune God. That is, having been created 'in the image' of the infinite God, humanity must transcend the limited boundaries of creation and become 'gods by grace'.[77] The means by which Christians attain deification (*theosis*) is through the sacraments of the church and through the act of *hesychia*, the mystical state of tranquility where

73 Abbot D.P. Guéranger, *The Liturgical Year*, vol. 12 (Powers Lake 1983) Book III; Luke 3:1.

74 L.E Ross, *Medieval Art: A Topical Dictionary* (Greenwood 1996) 10–11.

75 Nikephoros of Constantinople, *Logos*, 19; *Patrologia Graeca* 100, 584.

76 Meyendorff, *A Study of Gregory Palamas*, G. Lawrence (trans), (London 1964) 164; Nicholas Cabasilas, *The Life in Christ*, C.D. Catanzaro (trans), (Crestwood 1974) 50.

77 P. Nellas, *Deification in Christ: The Nature of Human Person*, N. Russell (trans), (Crestwood 1987) 28.

man can find his real being.[78] The painter of this fresco created a hierarchy illustrating the spiritual battle that rages in the spiritual world and in man's consciousness. Everyone strives to regain likenesses to God, but not everyone achieves the same level of perfection. Christ raises Adam first, then Eve, and later John the Baptist, David and Solomon with other imperial figures, and finally he delivers Abel and the rest of humankind. This fact can be taken as an indication of hesychast influence on the *Anastasis* at Chora. The hesychasts affirmed the diversity of degrees in spiritual perfection and the diversity of levels in spiritual life — the different stages for humanity to traverse. The image of *Jacob's Ladder* painted on the left side of the *Anastasis* in the Chora church reaffirms this hypothesis.

To accentuate the last stage in the kenotic act of God, as well as the salvation of the human race,[79] the painter of the *Anastasis* depicts the moment of Jesus' descent into hell as a sort of reverse transfiguration. This event is no longer played out on Mt Tabor, however, but at the centre of the earth and the cosmos, free from every geographical peculiarity. Thus, the step-like, cloven rocks of the Transfiguration become the barren, rocky plains of the Anastasis, which point towards the kataphatic aspect of human salvation from hell.[80] The rocky background on the right of Christ is a cool, greenish-grey with white highlights; the upper contour is reddish yellow, and facets of rock are in dark brown. The rocks on the left are warmer in colour and, at the centre, are green, with yellow and white highlights and brown shadows. They are slightly twisted towards Christ. The dividing of the rocks in the Anastasis icon recalls Moses' division of the waters of the Red Sea, when the chosen ones crossed from slavery in Egypt into the freedom of the Promised Land, as well as the splitting of the rocks after the Crucifixion.[81] The rocky landscape encompassing the background of hell is similar to the background of the dark cave depicted on the icon of the Nativity of Christ. In a homily attributed to Gregory of Nyssa, a parallel can be found between the birth of Christ in a cave and the spiritual light shining forth in the shadow of death that covers humankind when Christ descended into hell. The blackness at the centre of these two icons confesses this world's true state of darkness, torn from communion with God through the sin of man. Revealing himself in the heart of human suffering and struggle, Christ emerges triumphant within this very darkness:

---

78 Archimandrite Georgios, 'Theoretikos: The Neptic and Hesychastic Character of Orthodox Athonite Monasticism', http//www.greekorthodoxchurch.org/neptic_monasticism.html (accessed 11/03/2011).

79 S. Nes, *The Uncreated Light: An Iconographical Study of the Transfiguration in the Eastern Church* (Edinburgh 2007) 128.

80 The descent of God (kataphasis) represents a materialisation of the divine, while the ascent of men (anaphasis) represents deification of the material, Palamas, *Triads*, III, 1, 32; 37, in Meyendorff (ed.), *Gregory Palamas: The Triad*.

81 Baggley, *Festival Icons*, 122.

> The torch bearer, the flesh of God beneath the earth dissipates the gates of Hell. The birth of Christ was in a cave, and the jaws of Hades trembled. He rose from dead, and the bonds that could only be defeated by the triumph over death itself begin to feel the crushing weight of their overthrow.[82]

The pointed mandorla, which surrounds the figure of Christ, contains three concentric circles, each of a different shade of blue. The three zones within the mandorla have a Trinitarian connotation: they symbolise the intimate relationship of the Father, the Son and the Holy Spirit. Many Christian fathers and other authors described the Holy Trinity as one indivisible deity composed of separate hypostasis resembling three joined suns, which together emit one bright light. Furthermore, the use of a mandorla with three concentric circles is in keeping with the tenets of apophasis as expounded by Dionysius the Areopagite.[83] It describes the three stages of the soul's journey to God as a movement from the light through the cloud into the darkness.[84] As holiness increases, there is no way to depict the one who is above all, that cannot be an object of knowledge, except by 'darkness'. It also shows that, although the essence of God is beyond human comprehension and understanding, God manifests in one *ousia* or essence and three hypostases.

The inner zone of the mandorla is the same shade of blue as some of the garments; the second zone is lighter blue and the outer zone pale blue-gray. Eight-pointed stars are visible all over the mandorla, formed by sharply tapered strokes that radiate from a central dot. Originally, the star-shaped rays of light were painted by using a gold leaf over a mordant, but when the fresco was restored, the stars were repainted in dull red.[85] There is varied interpretation of the symbolism of the eight rays of light. In the context of the Anastasis, however, it has four interrelated meanings. Firstly, the Greek and Latin fathers, as well as non-Christian authors, often perceived the holy number eight in connection with the Resurrection and the Second Coming of Christ or *Parousia*. Second, influenced by the Christian eschatological tradition, many Byzantine painters adopted the eight rays of light as figurative means of representing the uncreated light of God.[86] Third, in the context of Dionysius the Areopagite's teaching on the 'light-giving

---

82 M.C. Steenberg, 'The Nativity of the Paschal Christ', http://www.monachos.net/content/liturgics/liturgical-reflections/434-nativity-of (accessed on 15/02/2012).

83 F.S. Carter, 'Celestial Dance: A Search for Perfection, Dance Research', *The Journal of the Society for Dance Research*, vol. 5, no. 2 (Autumn 1987).

84 ibid., 53.

85 Underwood, 'First Preliminary Report on the Restoration of the Frescoes in the Kariye Camii at Istanbul by the Byzantine Institute 1952–54', *Dumbarton Oaks Papers*, vol. 9 (1956) 265.

86 J. Miziołek, 'Transfiguratio Domini in the Apse at Mount Sinai and the Symbolism of Light', *Journal of the Warburg and Courtauld Institutes*, vol. 53 (1990) 43.

illuminations' (*photodosia*), the rays of light are carriers of the spiritual vision.[87] Dionysius the Areopagite saw the entire universe (material as well as spiritual) as a system of images, symbols and signs, which point to God and uplift us to Him. This is a key principle and indicates several important aspects. It affirms the possibility of access to the Father through Jesus (the Father is the principle of light and the Son reflects the light of the Father). Additionally, it affirms the light-giving (*photodosia*) of the Father, which proceeds from the Godhead, revealing the hierarchies of the heavenly minds, and then returns to the Father by uplifting the human mind. Finally, it shows that the rays of *photodosia* are real. They manifested during the Transfiguration and the Anastasis.[88]

The symbol of a circle with eight rays represented the sun in early Christian art, the *Sol Domini Imperii Romani*.[89] In addition, the image of the sun as a circle of eight rays or an octagon became a symbol of Christ in the artistic tradition. The examples found in the *Joshua Roll*, the Gerona *Beatus*, the Florence *Cosmas*, the *Sacra Parallela* and the Smyrna *Physiologus* all testify to this trend.[90] Moreover, many Christian ecclesiastical writers used this general analogy to describe the antinomical nature of the Triune God, who is visible and invisible at the same time.[91] Gregory Palamas, in particular, used this parallel to illustrate the distinction between essence and energies within God.[92] His teaching states we can experience the energies of God, but to acqure knowledge of his essence would be impossible.[93] The importance of this point has to do with deification — union with God.[94] Palamas established that humanity can participate in the divine energies in the same way we share in the rays of the sun, although we cannot participate in the essence of the sun.[95] Therefore, to be in communion with God means to be united with him fully, though one may never know the divine essence or the three hypostases.[96]

---

87 This term occurs 12 times in Corpus Dionysiacum: Divine Names 115, 1 [592c], Celestial Hierarchy 8, 2 [121b], 9, 2 [121d]; Corpus Dionysiacum (1990–1) 2:299; in *Dionysius the Areopagite: The Complete Works*, C. Luibheid & P. Rorem (trans), Classics of Western Spirituality Series (New York 1987).

88 B. Schomaker, *Pseudo-Dionysius de Areopagiet: Over Mystieke Theologie* (Kampen 1990); Dionysius the Areopagite, 'De Divinis Nominibus', *Patrologia Graeca* 3, 586–997; Dionysius the Areopagite, *Divine Names and Mystical Theology*, C.E. Rolt (ed.) (London 1957); Dionysius the Areopagite, 'Mystical Theology 1', *Patrologia Graeca* 3; Dionysius the Areopagite, О Небесной Иерархии (St Petersburg 1997).

89 Miziołek, 'Transfiguration Domini'.

90 T. Mathews, *Byzantine Aesthetics* (New York 1971) 31.

91 In some sources the star-shaped mandorla was taken as a symbol of wisdom, theophany and divinity. The eight-pointed star is used in a miniature of Beatus to symbolise the women of the apocalypse; H. Rahner, *Griechische Mythen in Christlicher Deutung. Greek Myths and Christian Mystery*, B. Battershaw (trans), (London 1963) 154ff.

92 D. Papanikolaou,'Divine Energies or Divine Personhood: Vladimir Lossky and John Zizioulas on Conceiving the Transcendent and Immanent God', *Modern Theology*, vol. 19, no. 3 (July 2003) 359.

93 Palamas, *Triads*, 95, in Meyendorff (ed.), *Gregory Palamas: The Triad*.

94 Papanikolaou, 'Divine Energies'.

95 A. Louth, *Denys the Areopagite* (London 1989) 90.

96 Meyendorff, *Gregory Palamas*, 293ff.

The depiction of three concentric circles within the mandorla could be interpreted in the same context. The circles mark out the three levels of union within or with God as discussed by the hesychasts.[97] First is the union in essence between the three divine hypostases of the Triune God, each of whom is *homoousios* — 'one in essence' or 'consubstantial' with other two. Secondly, there exists a hypostatic union of the divine nature and the human nature in Christ. Finally, there is a union according to energy or grace, between God and the saints.[98] According to Palamas, the vision of light and the state of deification and union with God offer humanity an existential knowledge of God. The deifying gift of the Holy Spirit, which is a mysterious light, transforms those who have attained the grace of God not only filling them with eternal light, 'but also granting them knowledge and divine participation'. This is a stage of vision of God through ignorance (*ignoratio*).[99]

The use of an azurite colour for the sky affirms the symbolism of light in the *Anastasis* at Chora. Originally, the background of the *Anastasis* was azurite over charcoal black. Owing to humid conditions, however, the thin washes of azurite oxidised and the background turned an unpleasant green. Conservators removed the background when they restored the fresco. Tiny patches of greenish colour are still visible under the inscription. The azurite was a symbol of 'irreducible otherness', to affirm the presence of the 'radiant opacity'. One might audaciously suggest this 'participle of glory' is, in fact, 'the eternal glory of God', as Palamas and Gregory the Theologian claimed, while separating such light from the 'imparticiple essence of God'.[100] This light illuminates humankind and transforms the whole cosmos.[101] By virtue of sharing in the light of its prototype, the painting of the *Anastasis* 'contains within itself the divine power'.[102]

Another iconographical feature reflects the supremacy of God in the *Anastasis* at Chora. Having descended into Hades with authority, the Lord takes a magnificent stance upon the gates of hell. However, these gates are no longer depicted as the symmetrical lids of coffins in the form of a cross. Instead, they are orange-yellow painted coffered panels. The grotesque figure of Hades, painted in monochrome

---

97 Divine essence is represented by the three cycles of the mandorla. The divine energies are represented through the eight rays of light within the mandorla. Palamas, *Triads*, I, 3, 43, in Meyendorff (ed.), *Gregory Palamas: The Triad*; K. Ware, 'God Hidden and Revealed: The Apophatic Way and the Essence–Energies Distinction', *Eastern Churches Review*, vol. 7, no. 2 (1975).

98 John of Damascus, Oration, III, 26; Kotter 3, 134; Nikephoros of Constantinople, *Antirrheticus* III, 31; PG 100, 421D–424A.

99 Metropolitan Hierotheos of Nafpaktos & E.E. Cunningham-Williams, *Orthodox Psychoterapy* (Athens 2005) 89.

100 C. A. Beeley, *Gregory of Nazianzus on the Trinity and the Knowledge of God: In your Light we see Light* (Oxford 2008) 10.

101 M.H Abrams, *The Mirror and the Lamp: Romantic Theory and the Critical Tradition* (Oxford 1971) 154.

102 S.K. Ware & J.M. Dillon, *Dionysius the Areopagite and the Neoplatonist Tradition: Despoiling the Hellenes* (Crestwood 2007) 65–68.

umber tones, lies beneath Christ's feet; his arms and wrists are tightly fettered. Hades is neither capable of any meaningful resistance to the power of Christ, nor is he called into salvation by God. His presence in the the *Anastasis* alludes to the state of human darkness brought about by transgressions and sin. By disobeying the divine commandment, Adam turned away from God, who is 'immortality and love, and brought upon himself and the world ugliness and corruption'.[103] His mind and willpower could no longer have communion and unity with God and he could no longer hope to attain the likeness of God. God's benevolence, however, was employed after the Fall when Christ adopted a corruptible body.[104] Christ entered Hades and delivered humanity from death. He reunited heaven and earth, and closed the ontological gap between the creator and his creatures, thus making possible man's eventual deification.[105] Even the human body was no longer perceived as being 'unclean'; rather, it has been transformed by grace.[106] Christ reformed not only the ancient Adam, renewing and bringing human nature back to the original state of happiness, but he restored humanity's physical environment.[107] The painter of the *Anastasis* conveyed this fact artistically by accentuating the vision of light that occurred when Christ approached Hades. Significantly, in the fresco of the *Anastasis* at Chora, Christ bears no wounds of his passion. The wooden cross that Christ holds in most earlier representations of the Anastasis, such as those at Hosios Loukas and Nea Moni, is also missing.[108] The meaning behind the creation of the earlier images of the Anastasis was, however, primarily Soteriological. At Chora, on the other hand, the painter focused on the eschatological meaning of the event of the Resurrection.[109]

Formal qualities of the *Anastasis* fresco

In many respects, the style employed by the painter at Chora represents a summa in the development of the iconography of the image of the Anastasis. It reveals a well-defined canon of taste, 'slightly prettified, mannered as well as overcharged with conscious classical reminiscence'.[110] Little is known of

---

103 Ware, 'The Value of the Material Creation', *Symbolae: Osloenses: Norwegian Journal of Greek and Latin Studies*, vol. 6, no. 3 (Summer 1971).

104 Nikephoros of Constantinople, Antirrheticus III, 37–38; PG 100, 441.

105 K. Parry, 'Theodore Studites and Patriarch Nicephoros', *Byzantion*, vol. 59 (1989) 178.

106 John of Damascus, Oration II, 10; III, 9; Kotter, 3, 100; 105–15.

107 J.A. MacCulloch, *The Harrowing of Hell: A Comparative Study of an Early Christian Doctrine* (Edinburgh 1930) 248–500.

108 See Appendix, figures 1 and 2 in G. Vikan, *Illuminated Greek Manuscripts from American Collections* (Princeton 1973) fig. 53.

109 Beckwith, *Christian and Byzantine* Art, 253–254; H. Maguire, 'The Mosaics of Nea Moni: An Imperial Reading', *Dumbarton Oaks Papers*, vol. 46, *Homo Byzantinus: Papers in Honor of Alexander Kazhdan* (1992).

110 Hjort, 'Oddities and Refinements'. Also E. Kitzinger, 'The Byzantine Contribution to Western Art of the Twelfth and Thirteenth Centuries', *Dumbarton Oaks Papers*, vol. 20 (1966) 25–47.

the painter, yet it is clear that curious refinements and oddities concerned him. In part, the elegantly mannered style parallels the complex architectural framework.[111] The architecture and the landscape take predominance and are integral to the scene.[112] Both play a complex role in the narrative; they give space and time, and space and movement a more explicit significance. It is possibile that the peculiarities in style in the Chora church are due to the patronage of Theodore Metochites, a published author who was self-conscious about his originality. There are significant parallels between the artistic style of the Chora church and the mannered and obsessive literary style of Methochites. Emergence of new iconographic trends in the *Anastasis* at Chora also testifies to the spiritual movement of hesychasm affecting the humanistic phase of the Palaeologan revival.

In the Anastasis, complexity is more important than monumentality, and each unit has a defined meaning. All figures have distorted, elongated and voluminous bodies. The absence of naturalism is most evident in the hands and feet, which lack anatomical precision. It is an obvious sign of avoiding naturalism while reverting to abstraction. The facial types are classical, with linear and decorative modelling of hair and beard. Painted in a mixture of yellow ochre, the faces project Hellenic elegance, but their expressions show unspecified concern or distrust, with eyes half averted, or pointed at their object obliquely. Facial highlights are not intense; terra verte and white are used for highlights. Another trait is the use of a linear connection, which weaves through the singular form into a continuous pattern. The arms and the hands are in a garland, beginning with the crossed arms of the long-bearded old man in the front row of the *Anastasis*, and continuing to the hands of the third figure from the right in the middle row. Their position regarding the vertical and horizontal axes varies to a high degree; the raised or lowered heads of the figures create different effects. Three-quarter and full-faced views are the most frequent projection of the turning heads; there are one or two portrait types.[113] The *Anastasis* at Chora brings a new depth of feeling, a human quality going beyond the dignified Byzantine formula; it introduces a new style informed by hesychasm.

Garments and draperies serve to suggest attitudes, movements, and action of the bodies. A fluid delineation replaces the jagged abstraction of drapery which characterised the Commnenian art. The drapery is of various colours; blue shades outline the folds while brighter hues highlight them. All surface differentials consist of broken and splintery forms. The same holds true for the hatchlings, formed by alternating rows of dark and light colours.

111 Ousterhout, 'Temporal Structuring', 67.

112 S. Yadim, 'The Italo-Cretan Religious Painting and the Byzantine-Palaeologan Legacy', *Edebiyat Fakültesi Dergisi, Journal of Faculty of Letters*, vol. 25, no. 1 (June 2008) 269.

113 Demus, 'The Style of Kariye Djami and its Place in the Development of Palaeologan Art', in Underwood (ed.), *The Kariye Djami*.

The bodily movement is psychologically intense; the expressiveness of postures and attitudes takes predominance. The dramatic action, however, is presented by an extraordinary sense of physical movement and force. The three central figures move dramatically on the vertical axis and bodily postures, as well as the superimposing of geometrical shapes, create a sense of diagonal and horizontal movement.

The scene centres on the three chief protagonists who are placed in a triangular space: Christ, Adam and Eve. The two ends by the two opening sarcophagi create the base of the triangle while the point of the mandorla, which frames the figure of Christ, forms the apex of the triangle. John the Baptist and Abel stand at the edges of the triangle. The pictorial space and the room taken by the observer are the same. The sense of depth is obtained by varying figure sizes and the placement of one row of figures directly above the other. The power of reverse perspective does not create a sense of three-dimensionality, as was the case with most images of the Anastasis; rather, the painter has created tridimensional representations that appear to the viewer on interacting with the image. Although the central figure of Christ is larger than the rest of the figures, the arrangements of the objects in space gives a sense of good proportion to the composition. The sides of the central axis are not fully symmetrical; yet they have the same visual weight.[114] A marked equilibrium connects different parts of the image, while its design is forceful. The right side of the fresco manifests the painter's ardent interest in experimenting with perspective. Aside from the obvious attention to detail regarding Abel's garments, there is a strange and experimental spatial projection of his figure and his robe. His body is presented in two perspectives. Eve's abruptly tipped sarcophagus and the shallower tipped sarcophagus of Adam are part of an intentional figural distortion. Indeed, the lack of perfect plastic corporeality, the expressionist use of light and shadow and interest in spiritual ideals succeed in giving work its transcendent quality.

The painting has a stylised sketchiness or rigidity in its execution; it is free enough to show the brushstrokes, which are especially visible where highlights emerge. The colours in the scene are delicate and the subtle hues[115] are warm on the left to allow objects to appear closer to the viewer. Cool shades on the right push the image away from the viewer. Brilliant white is seemingly detached from the dark blue background. The decorative folds on drapery, as well as its shades and shadows are in warm grey. The highlights in Christ's garments are pure white; and there is much use of hatching in light values of yellow. The strong modelling of features, the wavy locks of hair and beard are depicted with bold

114 P. Treadwell, *The Resurrection of Eve: A Study of the Anastasis in the Kariye Camii* (London 1988) 42–60; Demus, 'Kariye Djami', 145–50.

115 R. Lange, *The Resurrection* (London 1967) 50.

brushstrokes. Blue is the colour for the garments of glory, indicating the new life into which Christ has entered.[116] It also refers to the state of transfiguration or deification, effected by Christ and filled with the Holy Spirit.

The essence of the light of redemption and victory takes predominance in the *Anastasis* at Chora. The aura of heavenly light pervades the Saviour's body, which extends to his mandorla. Following the principle of mirror symmetry, Adam and Eve stand on either side of Christ. There is a sharp contrast between the upper and lower part of the composition, with Christ as the centre of the column. The different positions of the characters within the hierarchical structure of the cosmos dictate this contrast. The light on the figures is broken into small abstract parts and discontinuous strips. The bold and sharp streaks of highlighted areas are a characteristic feature of art in Palaeologan era. These explosive splatters of light are reminiscent of the bursting fireworks of monumental frescoes, manuscript illumination and icons informed by hesychasm. For example, the bold and sharp streaks of highlights remind the viewer of the white lead highlights and crosshatching that Manuel Panselinos used to obtain bold expressive effects in the Church of Protaton.[117] Even though the central portion of this fresco of the Anastasis is approximately symmetrical; the realms of hell, below, have an interesting asymmetry.[118]

The immaterial uncreated light of the mandorla mingles with the blue through a merging of white, light blue and darker blue. The semiotics of the mandorla affirms that God is human and divine, and the unity of the material world and the world of ideas. The use of dark blue produces an effect of depth and tranquillity and gives an illusion of an unreal world, one that is without weight. The use of white has an impressive psychological effect in the *Anastasis* at Chora: the figure of Christ dressed in luminous white clothes is like lightning which starts in the East and blazes across the sky. He descends like lightning in hell, pulling the Old Testament righteous from their tombs. In this fresco, white is made brilliant through movement, which detaches it from the dark blue background. The colour of the central triangle (in which Christ stands with Adam and Eve), symbolises the Trinity; just as Plato, in an abstract way, represented the world of ideas as a basic axiom for the supreme knowledge of God.[119]

Figures and objects are uniformly lighted, rather than being illuminated by a single source. The light effect heightens the illusionist, immaterial feel of the

---

116 M. Alpatov, 'Die Fresken der Kachrie Djami in Konstantinopel', *Mimchner Jahrbuch der Budenden Kuntt*, vol. 6 (Munich 1929).

117 Lange, *Resurrection*, 65–85; N. Teteriatnikov, 'New Artistic and Spiritual Trends in the Proskinetaria Fresco Icons of Manuel Panselinos, the Protaton', in L. Mavromates (ed.), *Manuel Panselinos and his Age* (Athens 1999).

118 B. Cvetković, 'Intentional Asymmetry in Byzantine Imagery: The Cvetkovićthe Apostles in St Sophia of Ohrid and later Instances', *Byzantion*, vol. 76 (2006).

119 Karahan, 'Palaeologan Iconography'.

image. As a crucial part of hesychast philosophy, it is fitting that light plays an important part in this scene. Christ turns his hallowed head to the left, although his eyes glance to his right. His luminous robes and the radiant mandorla which surrounds him make the divine light apparent.

The *Anastasis* fresco in the context 14th- and 15th-century art

The fresco of the *Anastasis* at Chora replaced the more heroic, monumental and dramatic type which characterised Byzantine art in the late 13th century.[120] Among the most interesting paintings heralding these changes are the frescoes of St Nikita near Cucer, those of St George at Staro Nagoričane, and the paintings at the Church of the Virgin Mary, Gračanica.[121]

The period of this evolution of the Byzantine painting of the Anastasis is a matter of dispute, but it is plausible that it began to emerge some time after the middle of the 12th century. The fresco of the *Anastasis* at the Church of St George, Kurbinovo (Fig. 32), reflects this style, which is transitional, and heralds the changes that occurred in the iconography of the *Anastasis* as seen in Chora. The work is characterised by a new stylisation and use of angular lines, which affect not just the forms of the bodies but also the details of costumes. The facial muscles are severely exaggerated, and the draperies are twisted as if blown by a violent wind.[122] This fresco, however, is perhaps best known for the imposing mandorla by which it is dominated. The glimmering white mandorla is articulated by a bold white corona, different to that of the *Anastasis* at Chora. Circular in shape, the mandorla contrasts with the turquoise-blue background of the sky. Within this mandorla, the figure of Christ floats over the gates of hell. Christ's luminous clothes, which are highlighted by streaks of ochre, combine with the lilac of Adams's robes, to reflect a unified vision of light. Adam's arm is the only other entity included within the space of the mandorla, symbolising his state of redemption.

The most interesting element in this fresco, however, is the dynamic diagonal of 45 degrees created by Christ, who strides aggressively forward. In fact, his

120 C. Grozdanov, 'On the Conceptual and Thematic Foundations of the Fresco Paintings in the Diaconicon of the Church of Virgin Peribleptos in Ohrid', *Zograf*, vol. 33 (2009) fig. 24.

121 G. Millet & A. Frolow, *La Peinture du Moyen Age en Yougoslavie*, vol. 3 (Paris 1962) fig. 31–53 (St Nikita, Cucer); N.L. Okunev, 'Црква Св. Ђорђе у Старом Нагорићану', *Гласник Скопског Научног Друштво*, vol. 5 (1919) 87; B. Petkovic, *La Peinture Serbe du Moyen Age* (Belgrade 1930) fig. 67.

122 D.T. Rice, *Art of Byzantine Era* (London 1963)194–195; Misguich, *Kurbinovo*, 130, 166, 516, fig. 55; C. Grozdanov & L. Misguich, *Kurbinovo* (Belgrade 1992) fig. 38–41, 43–44, 55.

figure forms the upright part of an inscribed cross, as well as a part of the Greek letter Rho. His outstretched arms, the bottom line of His himation, and the angle of his upper left thigh, as well as the radiating rays of light, form the Greek letter Chi. This creates the impression of a gale-force wind issuing from hell. Christ carries the cross, attached to a crown of thorns, on his shoulders.[123] The so-called tongues of fire appear in the Anastasis for the first time. There is no doubt that the turmoil of movement and linear convolutions in the *Anastasis* of Kurbinovo personify dynamism, especially in comparison to that of Chora. This *Anastasis*, however, contains elements that depart from convention, and even present what might be termed an anti-classical interpretation of the subject, which is a characteristic of the *Anastasis* at Chora. The difference between both frescoes is due to the possible Slav patronage and training of the painter at Kurbinovo.[124] This departure from convention continued in the later centuries, especially in the frescoes found in King Milutin's churches, as well as in the monuments of Thessaloniki. In the *Anastasis* at Kurbinovo, the dominant feature is the painter's contribution to the development of a new Christocentric humanism in Byzantine and Slavic art. The painting is imbued with the contrast between the doctrine of hesychasm, which emphasises synergy and the psychosomatic knowledge of God as *theosis*, and scholastic humanism, which postulates a dualism of body and soul.

The three compositions of Anastasis in the Church of St Nikolas Orphanos, Thessaloniki (1310–1320), the Church of Joachim and Anne, Studenica (1313–1314), and the Church of the Holy Saviour, Chora show the same stylistic trend, which lacks the intensity of expression found in the earlier monument at Kurbinovo. Even though there are certain differences between these three variations of the Anastasis, the similarities between them show that members of the same workshop worked in these churches. A growing interest in the use of a graphic element and a plastic modelling of figures characterises the *Anastasis* in King Milutin's Church, Studenica (Fig. 44). At Studenica, Christ briskly raises the protopsalts; his bold and statuesque figure accentuates the dynamic flow. Parts of his drapery, parts of the trailing garments of Eve, and a portion of Adam's robe have a crisp and modeled definition, and also a clear–cut, brittle quality. The tilted heads of the prophets and of John the Baptist project angularity. Two sources of tension present in the image: one is the figure of Christ crashing the gates of hell, and the other is His victory over Satan. Even though the landscape is in accordance with the architecture, the peaks of the two mountains above the lateral group of figures are not as exaggerated as they are at Chora.[125] The strict basis of the symmetrical Anastasis remains the

123 E.C. Dodd, *Medieval Painting in the Lebanon* (Reichert 2004) 32.

124 Rice, *Byzantine Painting: The Last Phase* (London 1968) 11.

125 Cvetković, 'Intentional Asymmetry', 76.

same, but it is emotionally enriched. Scenes are crowded;[126] the figures of the just men are grouped and their postures and gestures have a natural, lively feel. Sharp ledges and ridges are common and, with the star-shaped mandorla, they become compulsory. The cross, which was a central detail in earlier Anastasis, is not depicted and the main emphasis is on the saving and transforming role of the Saviour's light.

While the *Anastasis* at Chora contains only the indispensable protagonists, the fresco of the *Anastasis* at Sopočani (Fig. 42) has a number of additional figures, who orchestrate a Soteriological panorama of universal significance. Through the avoidance of dramatic elements, such as a sudden or unexpected action by the protagonists, the *Anastasis* at Sopočani radiates a majestic atmosphere of calmness. Even the emotions of awe and love are subtly expressed. The palette varies, and a range of colours brings out the modelling of figures.[127] The background is partially gold, and cross-hatched lines suggest mosaics, but in general, the colours in the image are naturalistic. Unity is created by the close-knit interweaving of horizontal and diagonal lines. The upward and downward movement of the figures interchanges and mountains create an ascending path of movement towards Christ. The rhythmic pattern of repetition from the lower part creates an apophatic directional path.[128] A triangular shape surrounds the angels; John the Baptist, the shrouded female figures, and Christ are surrounded by a mandorla, which gives the figurative scene a sense of universality.[129] Adam's position is peculiar, for he kneels on the ground, instead of the lid of his sarcophagus (as shown in the earlier representations of the Anastasis). A sense of reverence, warmth and personal humanity permeates the piece. The tearful, pleading face of Eve, emphasised by the abrupt angle of her outstretched arms, evokes raw emotion, in the same way as the subtle gestures of the just men who surround the Protopsalts do. This new anecdotal style became the accepted mode, at least among prestigious patrons. While this image did not mark a break with the earlier Palaeologan traditions, it showed more elaboration, expansion and toning down of the them.

It is possible that the patronage of King Milutin, who initiated a project to translate important philosophical and theological texts, resulted in their being a hesychast influence on the art of these monuments. An exceptional and important feature of this project was the rendition of powerful hesychast texts. The work of the Serbian translation school, which embraced a strict, iconographically correct rendition of texts, approached this project with enthusiasm. The selected examples in Studenica and Sopočani show that the translation of these texts was

126 Kartsonis, *Anastasis*, 7.
127 C. Jolivet-Lévy, *Etudes Cappadociennes* (London 2002) 251.
128 V.J. Djurić, *Sopočani* (Belgrade 1991) 19; fig. 9.
129 M. Reste, *Byzantine Wall Painting in Asia Minor*, vol. 1 (New York 1984) 86–87; Djuric, *Sopočani*, 141.

a part of a comprehensive scholarly and iconographical reform undertaken by Serbian authors.[130] A similar iconographic trend can be seen in Macedonian and Serbian monuments, such as the Monastery of Marko, Markova Sušica, Macedonia (Fig. 41), as well as at the Monastery of Decani, Kosovo (Fig. 45). Variations of it continued to run through most of the painting of the 14th and the first half of the 15th century. Stylistic and iconographical transformations from the heroic Anastasis of Kurbinovo to the late anecdotal Anastasis of the early 14th century are also present in the mosaics of the Church of Holy Apostles, Thessaloniki, which were created by the same workshop as that of Chora. The figures of Adam and Abel at the Church of Holy Apostles show a striking similarity to those at Chora. In addition, the general treatment of the hands, heads and beards is the same in both churches. Moreover, the palette is similar, although the colours are lighter at Chora.[131] There are some discrepancies, however, in the modelling of figures in the two churches. The style of the Anastasis in the Church of the Apostles is more rigid than that at Chora, and embodies the classical renaissance spirit of the 13th century.[132] Bodies have plasticity in representation; their draperies are bold and curved. In contrast, the style of the *Anastasis* at Chora is more mannered, and the composition has centralised broken lines.

The preserved fresco of the *Anastasis* from the Church of St Nicholas Orphanos dates from the same period as the *Anastasis* at Chora and Studenica, which would support its connection with Milutin's artistic patronage in the city. In both churches, Christ wears a mannerist flying drapery. Whereas the robes of Christ at Chora radiate light, which illuminates the fresco from within, the garments of Christ at Nicholas Orphanos are in a medium value of ochre. They contrast with the light of the cavern's ceiling and the black chasm of hell.[133] The optical blending of the carefully gauged linear strokes of alternate tints and shades of colour, which are highlights in blue, create a surface plasticity. At the Church of Nicholas Orphanos, whereas Christ pulls Adam in a swift motion, Eve is presented in a three-quarter view. Her face is grave, penitent and cautious as she glances at Christ, who turns his body toward her, even though he turns his face away. An unusual participant in the *Anastasis* at Nicholas Orphanos is Prophet Samuel; no narrative of the Anastasis mentions him and this is the only extant representation of him in the Anastasis.[134]

---

130 B. Milosavljević, 'Basic Philosophical Texts in Medieval Serbia', http://www.doiserbia.nb.rs/ft.aspx?id=0350-76530839079M (accessed on 11/01/2012).

131 A. Xyngopoulos, *The Mosaic Decoration of the Church of the Holy Apostles in Thessaloniki* (Thessaloniki 1953) fig. 28.

132 Demus, 'Kariye Djami'.

133 Xyngopoulos, *The Wall Paintings of St Nicholas Orphanos in Thessaloniki* (Athens 1964) 13.

134 T. Velmans, 'Les Fresques de Saint-Nicolas Orphanos à Salonique et la Decoration Monumentale au XIVe Siècle', *Cahiers Archéologiques*, vol. 16 (1966).

The symmetrical Anastasis, which grew directly out of the Palaeologan tradition spread to Russia, while the asymmetrical type was still at use in Pskov (Figs 46, 47). The Rostov school, on the other hand, preferred the symmetrical model (Figs 48, 49). The asymmetrical icon of the *Anastasis* from Rostov is from the first half of the 14th century,[135] and its style differs from its later or symmetrical Anastasis in several ways. In the asymmetric model, Christ is turned to his side and has no mandorla. Christ grasps only Adam with his hand and raises him from the dead; Eve merely kneels at His side. In addition, the figure of Christ is no longer depicted as weightless or floating, as it is in the Anastasis from the 12th and 13th centuries. Rather, he is depicted as strong and sure.[136] This figurative scene of the *Anastasis* reflects the spirit of the early 14th century, showing the strong movement of Christ as well as emphasising the emotional relationships of the characters. The contours of the figures and drapery are traced with white highlights, with an appreciation of graphic delineation. Olive-yellow hues and dense blue shades replace the common delicate milky-blue colour.[137]

In the later or symmetrical Anastasis, which is highlighted by a red halo, the figure of Christ stands at the centre of the composition. Outlines of the other figures are simple and schematic, their gestures sharp and expressive, and colours pure and bright. Reflecting upon the nature of the event, all figures show reverence and contemplation. Combinations of reds, blues, light yellow, and subtle of colour comparisons, for instance, a gentle milky-blue tint, enhance the prayerful, contemplative mood of all figures in the composition.

The stylistic and iconographical differences between the *Anastasis* of Rostov and that of Pskov bear witness to the interplay of two diverging trends in religious art of the 14th and 15th centuries. These variations, however, testify to the development of new iconography of the Anastasis in these areas, which were created in response to the Trinitarian and Christological heresies in Russia in the second half of the 14th century. Moreover, the adoption of the symmetrical Anastasis reflects the influence of the spiritual trend of hesychasm, which was felt strongly in these areas, in the 14th and 15th centuries.

The icon of the *Anastasis* at Tikhvin (14th century) preserves the older iconographical tradition of the Resurrection. Relating closely to the *Anastasis* at Chora, the only difference is the placement of a black cross on the vertical axis of the iconic plane. Christ breaks the symmetry of the scene by making a three-quarter turn to Adam. Adam and Eve's position on each side of Christ,

135 E.S. Smirnova, 'Иконографический Вариант Сошествия во Ад Ростов, Москва, Север', *Иконы Русского Севера. Двинская Земля, Онега, Каргополье, Поморье, Статьи Материалы* (Moscow 2005).
136 Smirnova, 'Иконы XIV-Начала XVI века', http://rus-icons.ru/publication/detail.php?ID=256] (accessed 4/08/2011).
137 O.S. Popova, *Особенности Искусства Пскова. Из кн. Отблески Христианского Востока на Руси* (Moscow 1993) 20; Lazarev, *Живопись Пскова', История Русского Искусства*, vol. 2 (Moscow 1954) 370.

however, restores the harmony of the composition. The bright red figure of Eve on the right side mirrors the figure of Adam on the left side of Christ in both posture and gesture. The number of people depicted increases with groups of the righteous being easily identified. The images of King David and Solomon, and of Moses and John the Baptist, correlate with each other, symbolically. They stand on the bright firmament, in opposition to the black abyss of hell.[138] This icon testifies to the use by Russian artists of the first half of the 14th century of features from the earlier Byzantine representation of the Anastasis. The creator of the Tikhvin *Anastasis* seems unconcerned with the psychological subtleties of the image. Rather, he emphasises the decorative colour and brightness of the image by giving it a more impressive form.

The painter of the 16th-century *Anastasis* at Pskov (currently held at the Pskov State United Historical, Architectural and Fine Arts Museum) incorporated the same symmetrical arrangement of the kneeling figures of Adam and Eve, as did the painter of the *Anastasis* at Chora. Similarly, both models show the simultaneous pulling of Adam and Eve into Christ's mandorla, in concert, which conveys a sense of leading, guiding and protection.[139] A sense of fullness in the play of episodes, a spatial freedom, and a restless rhythm shape both compositions. In contrast to Christ's white garments in the *Anastasis* at Chora, which are reminiscent of his Transfiguration, the vermillion dress of Christ at Pskov refers to the paschal sacrifice and his redemption of humankind (Fig. 49).[140] Another important feature of the *Anastasis* from Pskov is the absence of haloes, which is rare in the Byzantine iconographic tradition. The presence of a halo is a sign of holiness, indicating the redemptive nature of Christ.[141] Other features bear witness to changing Russian attitudes towards the iconography of the Anastasis, For instance, the Pskov's model introduced an ascending type of Anastasis in which Christ steps upwards from hell. Also, while turning his head to Adam, he makes an S-shaped bend.[142] The postures of Adam and Eve, who arise on each side of Christ, enhance this effect. Christ reaches out his hands to the ancestor Adam on the left and to the ancestor Eve on the right and lifts them both out of the sarcophagi at the same time. The tension in the figures of Adam and Eve and the Protopsalts is evident, which is in contrast to the active, determined gestures of the Saviour. The body of Christ, extended

---

138 O.A.Vasileva, *Иконы Пскова* (Moscow 2006) 145–150.

139 I. Nicoletta, 'Chorós: Dancing into Sacred Space of Chora', *Byzantion*, vol. 75 (2005).

140 K. Polyvios, 'From the Resurrection to the Ascension: Christ's Post Resurrection Appearances in Byzantine Art', PhD thesis, University of Birmingham (2010) fig. 12, 54.

141 V. Kesich, 'Resurrection, Ascension, and the Giving of the Spirit', *Greek Orthodox Theological Review*, vol. 25 (1980) 253; Meyendorff, *St Gregory Palamas and Orthodox Spirituality* (Crestwood 1974) 71.

142 Vasileva, *Иконы*, 84–180.

and expanded in the lower part of the image, creates a spatial allusion to the celestial sphere. His body gives the impression of having a convex spherical surface that is emphasised by the tonal variation in the mandorla.[143]

The icon of the *Anastasis* from the Church of the Nativity of Virgin Mary, the Monastery of Ferapontov,[144] was painted by Dionysius, a contemporary of Andrei Rublev (Fig. 50). It shows a slight shift from the artistic tradition of Constantinople, as seen in the fresco of the *Anastasis* at Chora. The main iconographic details are the same as those at Chora, but Dionysius broke the scene into smaller parts and arranged it semantically in different zones, with added images of women as foremothers, as well as personifications of the virtues and vices. The narrative is enhance by original elements including two bright angel figures binding Satan in the abyss of hell. On each side of the angels, the figures of the saints wear white robes and raise their hands. The bright silhouettes of the angels are luminous and triumphant against the blackness of the underworld, which brings a new festive note into the atmosphere of this celebration. The red expresses the merger of the beginning and the end of human history and represents the emotional intensity of the meeting between Christ and the Protopsalts. The red also compensates for the absence of traditional attributes of the Passion of Christ, such as the image of the cross and the stigmata.[145] The eschatological texts of the Easter service may have inspired this use of red, which refers to the uncreated light of God as an 'eternal flame that transforms and leaves imperishable those chosen by God'.[146] The pictorial surface has the quality of a portal, opening the doors between the physical world and the exquisite terrestrial spheres. Likhachev's ideas about the Eastern Предвозрожденииа (the Second Slavic influence) described a collision of cultures that met a need inherent in the domestic culture and which led to the development of a specific Russian literature and art. This is relevant to Dionysian art, which was influenced by the work of Nil Sorsky, who promoted the practices of hesychasm and eremitism in early modern Russia and was the spiritual father of Dionysius.[147]

---

143 *Государственныї Русскиї Музеї, Санкт-Петербург: Живопис ХИИ — Начала XX Века* (St Petersburg 1993) 8.

144 N.K. Goleizovskii, 'Факты, События, Люди: Живописец Дионисий и его Школы', *Вопросы Истории*, no. 3 (March 1968).

145 L.P. Plamondon, 'Divine Illumination: Light as Mystical Imagery in Transfiguration and Anastasis Scenes of Byzantine Iconography', MA thesis, Northern Illinois University (1998) 74; K.M. Barnard, 'Anastasis (The Anastasis): A Study of the Iconographical Development of the Anastasis in Monumental Mosaic and Fresco Decoration during the Macedonian, Comnenian, and Palaeologian dynasties', MA thesis, Northern Illinois University (1982) 190.

146 Nicol, *The Last Centuries of Byzantium*, 166.

147 V.N. Lazarev, *Дионисий и его Школа* (Moscow 1955) 524–526; Alpatov Всеобщая История Искусств, vol. 3 (Moscow 1955) 242–244; I.E. Danilova, 'Иконографический Состав Фресок РождестВенской Церкви Ферапонтова Монастыря', *Истории Русского и Западноевропейского Скусства: Материалы и Исследования* (Moscow, 1960) 128–129.

Conclusion

While it provides an eschatological vision, the magnificent fresco of the *Anastasis* at Chora also reveals nuanced symbolism that is closely connected to the mystical tenets of Byzantine spirituality in the 14th century. Overcharged with classical reminiscences, mannerisms and oddities, the portrayal of the *Anastasis* at Chora is indeed revolutionary.

Adding diverse and unexpected features to the fully evolved Palaeologan style, the *Anastasis* at Chora shows the contrast between the humanistic and the theocentric view of God and man, which became apparent during the hesychast controversy. It also expresses the hesychast concept of *theosis*, the union of grace (by adoption) between human beings and Christ. It is as though, through the supernatural grace of God, the painter of the *Anastasis* had transcended his creatureliness, his human intellect, and had become transcendent even to his own self-knowledge. The symbolism of light within this fresco is crucial as it enhances the illusionist, immaterial feel of the image. The fresco is illuminated by the mystical light of God.

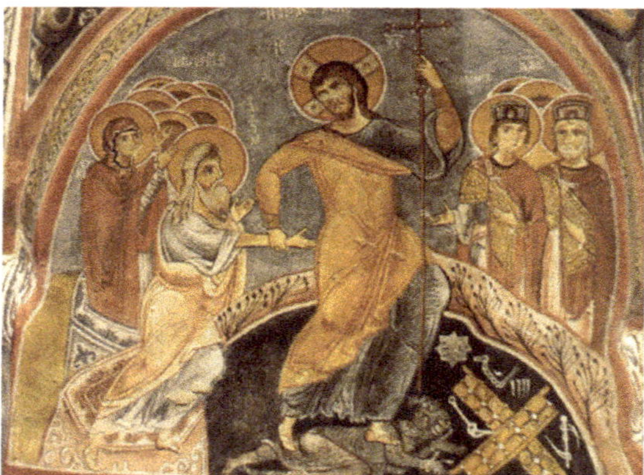

Figure 31. *The Anastasis*, c. 1060s – 1070s, fresco, right wall of the smaller apse, Karanlik Killise, Göreme (Cappadocia)

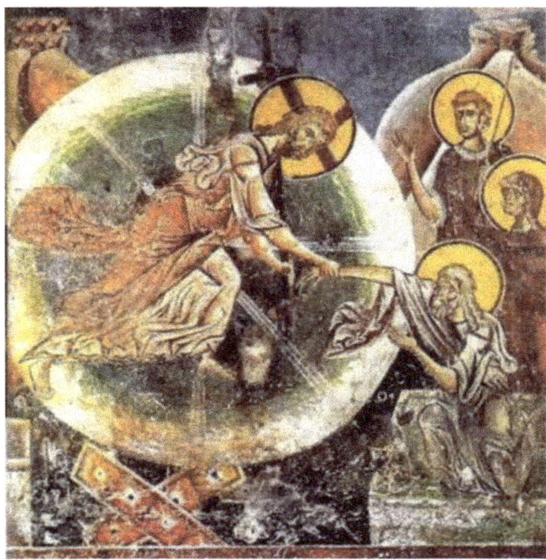

Figure 32. ***The Anastasis*****, c. 1191, fresco, western wall of the nave, Church of St George, Kurbinovo (Macedonia)**

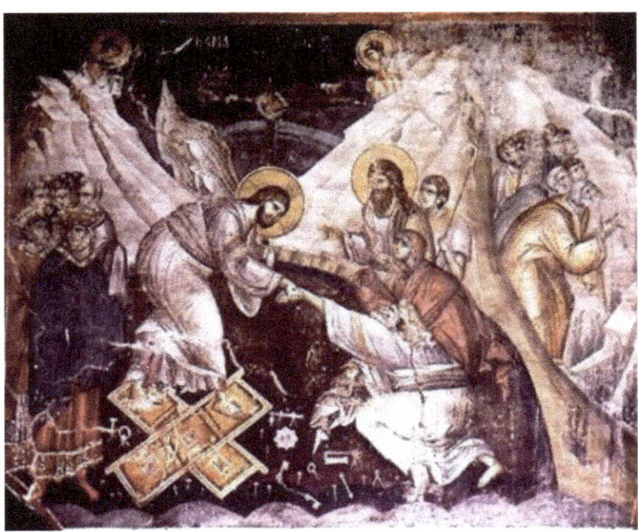

Figure 33. ***The Anastasis*****, 14th century, fresco, northern wall of the nave, Church of the Protaton, Karyes (Greece)**

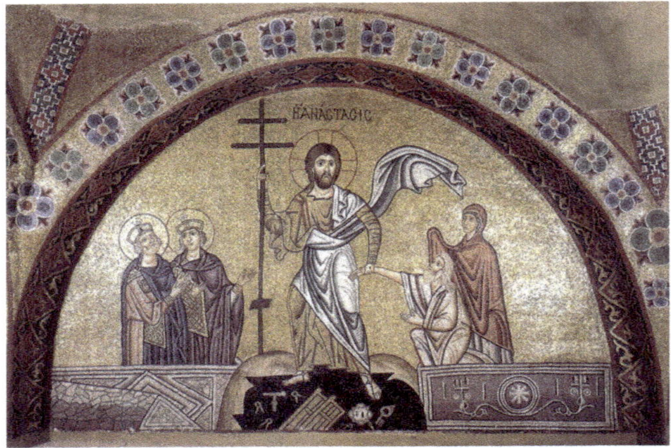

Figure 34. ***The Anastasis*, first half of the 11th century, mosaic, narthex, Church of Hosios Loukas, Phocis (Greece)**

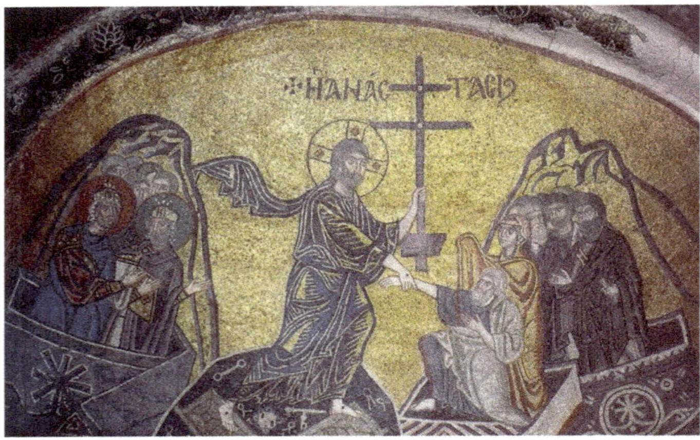

Figure 35. ***The Anastasis*, mid-11th century, mosaic, naos, north apse, Church of Nea Moni, Chios (Greece)**

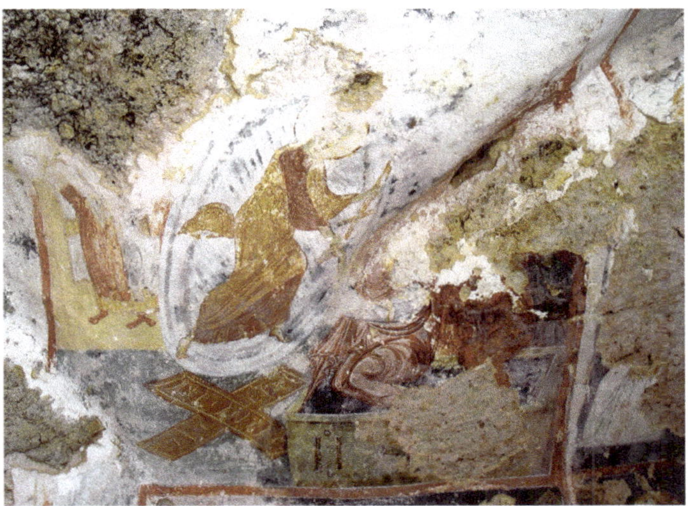

Figure 36. ***The Anastasis*, 14th century, fresco, vaulted ceiling, Church of Archangel Michael, Rock-hewn churches of Ivanovo, Rusenski Lom (Bulgaria)**

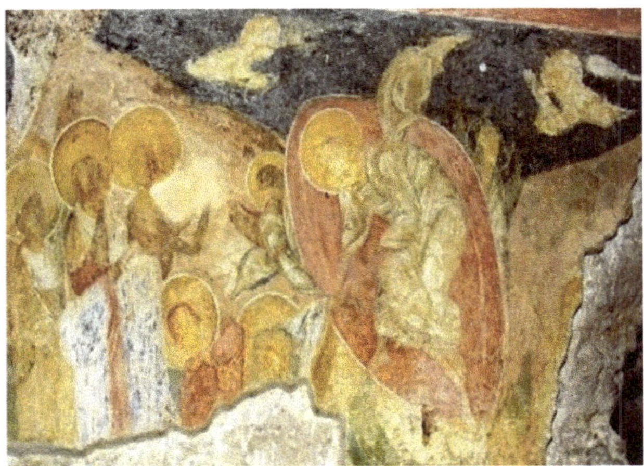

Figure 37. ***The Anastasis*, 14th century, fresco, vaulted ceiling of the nave, Church of the Virgin Mary, Rock-hewn churches of Ivanovo, Rusenski Lom (Bulgaria)**

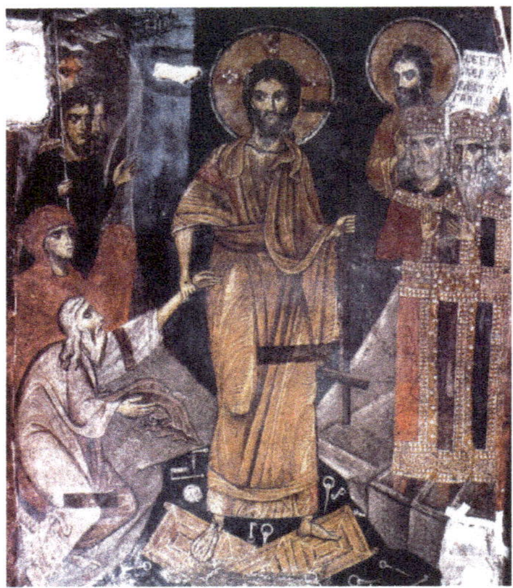

Figure 38. ***The Anastasis*, c. 1259, fresco, sanctuary niche, Boyana Church of St Nicholas and St Panteleimon, Sofia (Bulgaria)**

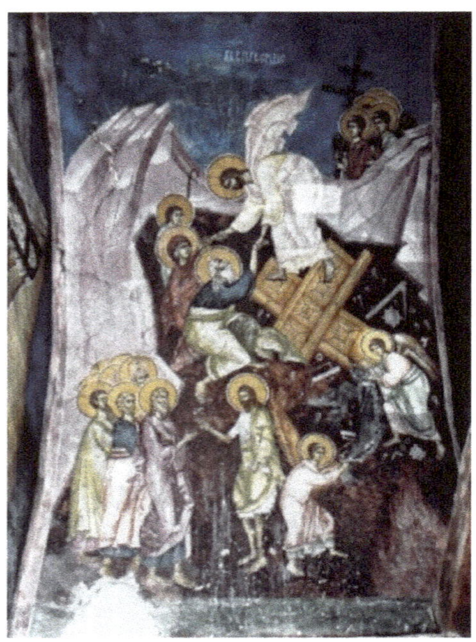

Figure 39. ***The Anastasis*, 14th century, fresco, south wall, Church of the Virgin Hodegetria, Peć (Serbia)**

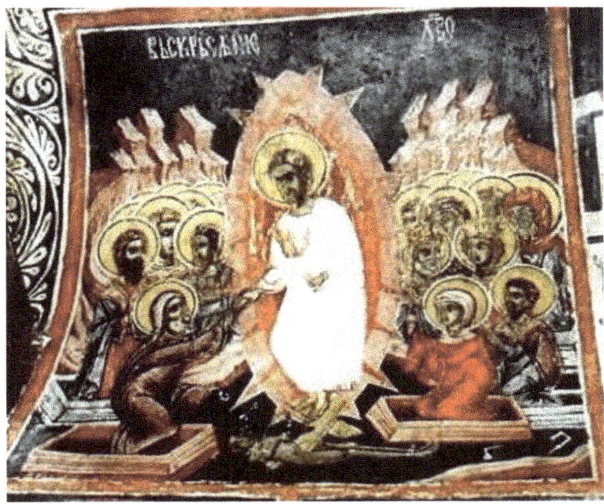

Figure 40. ***The Anastasis*, 17th century, fresco, west wall, Church of Theodore Tyro and Theodore Stratelates, Dobarsko, Razlosko (Bulgaria)**

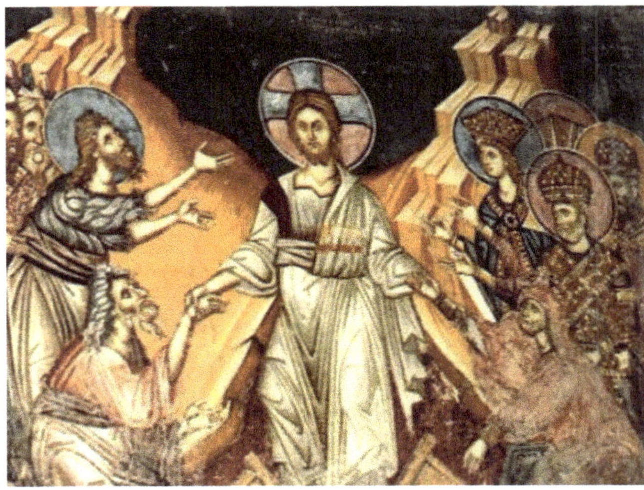

Figure 41. ***The Anastasis*, 14th century, fresco, north wall of the naos, Monastery of Marko, Markova Sušica, Skopje (Macedonia)**

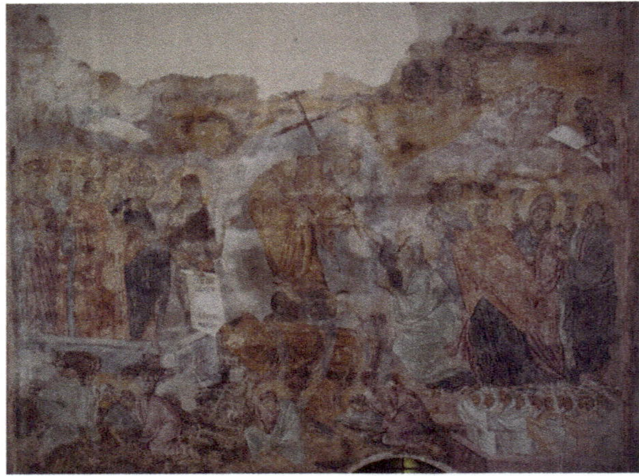

Figure 42. *The Anastasis*, 14th century, fresco, north wall of the nave, Monastery of Sopočani, Raška (Serbia)

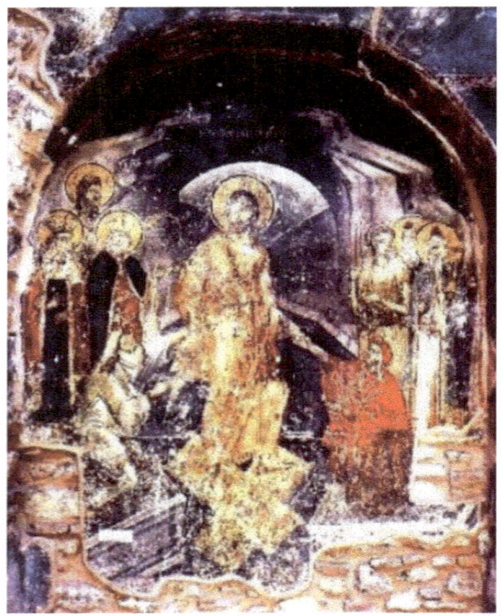

Figure 43. *The Anastasis*, 14th century, fresco, painter Georgios Kalliergis, Church of the Resurrection of Christ, Veroia (Greece)

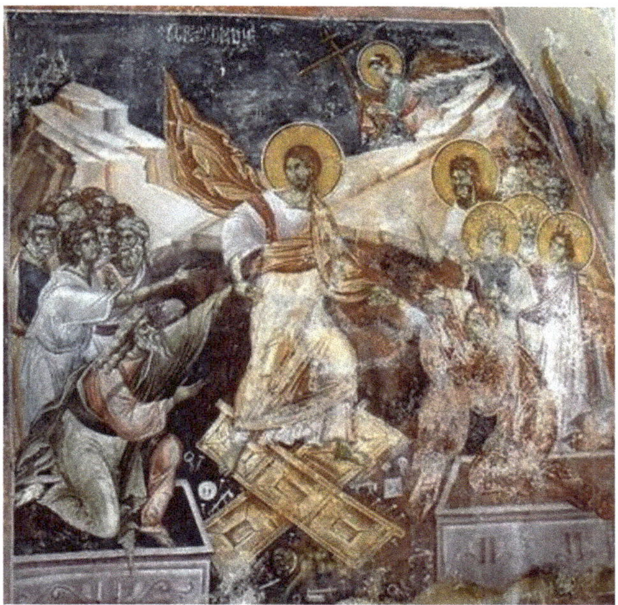

Figure 44. *The Anastasis*, 14th century, fresco, west wall of the nave, King Milutin's Church, Monastery of Studenica, Studenica, (Serbia)

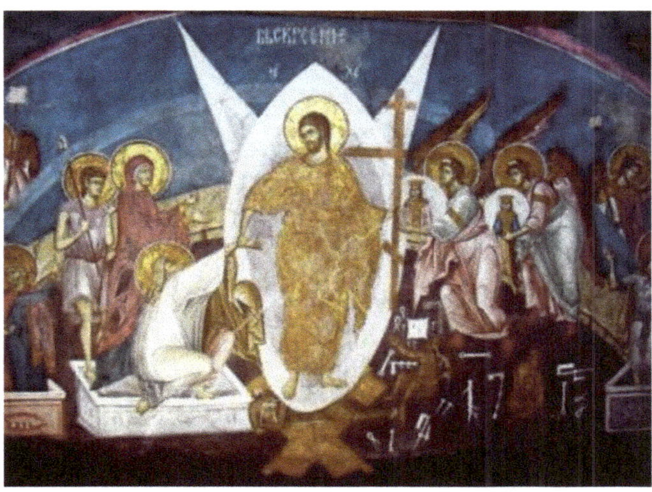

Figure 45. *The Anastasis*, 14th century, fresco, east wall of the narthex, Monastery of Dećani, Dećani, (Kosovo)

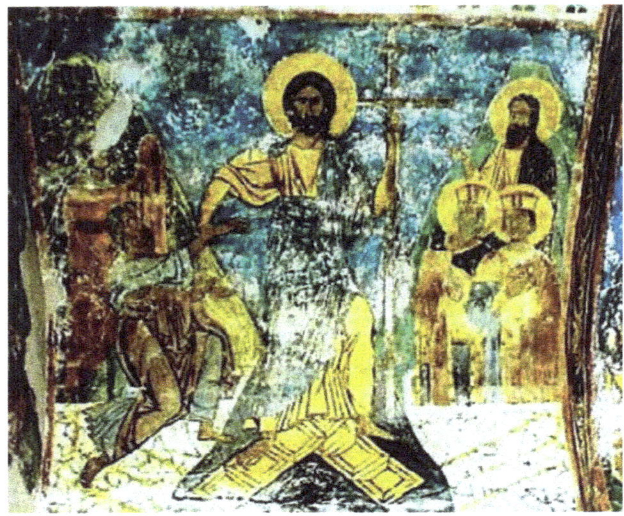

Figure 46. ***The Anastasis*****, c. 1130–1140, fresco, north vault of the narthex, Cathedral of the Transfiguration, Mirozhsky Monastery, Pskov (Russia)**

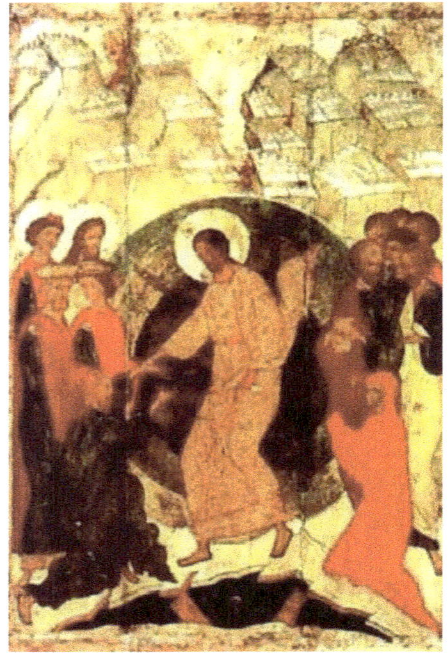

Figure 47. ***The Anastasis*****, late-15th century, tempera on wood, 91 x 63 cm, Tretyakov Gallery, Moscow (Russia), inv. no. 14316**

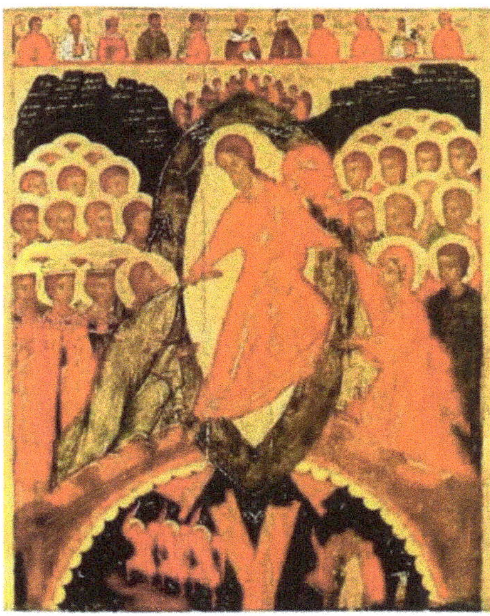

Figure 48. *The Anastasis*, 15th–16th century, tempera on wood, 20 x 99 cm, Pskov State United Historical, Architectural and Fine Arts Museum-Reserve, Pskov (Russia), inv. no. 2731

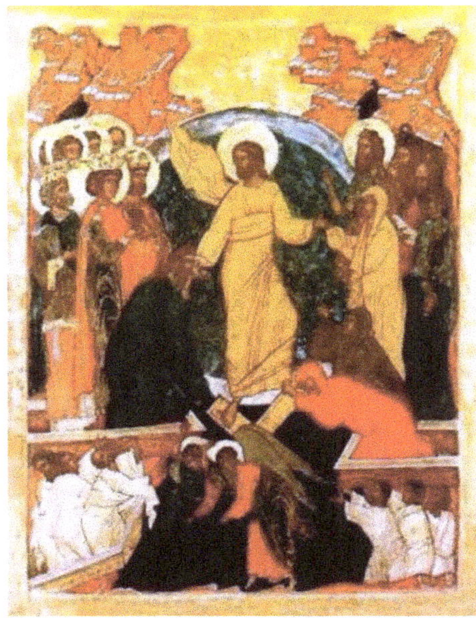

Figure 49. *The Anastasis*, first half of the 16th century, tempera on wood, 76 x 55 cm, Pskov State United Historical, Architectural and Fine Arts Museum-Reserve, Pskov (Russia), inv. no. 1616

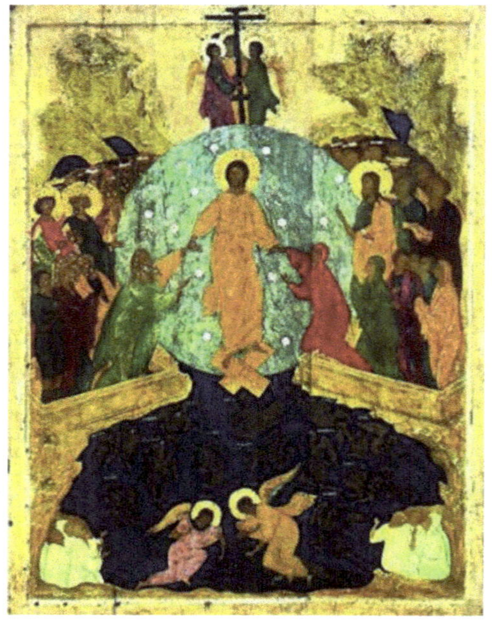

Figure 50. ***The Anastasis*****, c. 1502 , tempera on wood, 137.5 x 99.5 cm, painter Dionysius, Russian Museum, St Petersburg (Russia), inv. no. ДРЖ–3094**

5. The Icon of the *Trinity* by Andrei Rublev

While the compositions of the Anastasis and the Transfiguration represent the realm of *oikonomia* (all the works by which God reveals himself and communicates his life), the figurative representation of the Trinity circumscribes the domain of *theologia* (the mystery of God's inmost life within the Blessed Trinity).[1] Prior to the hesychast controversy, Latin fathers introduced the *filioque* clause as an addition to the Nicene Creed, but the hesychasts condemned and refuted this dogma. In their endeavour to defend the Christological and Trinitarian dogma, the hesychasts affirmed the ontological distinction within the Triune God. They accepted the difference between the hypostases of the Father, the Son and the Holy Spirit and, at the same time, acknowledged the unity of nature in the Trinity. Palamists also developed an elaborate teaching concerning the Soteriological role of divine grace. These theological presuppositions were founded in the steadfast parameters of *theophania* (the Epiphany) and *theoptia* (the vision of the Triune God). The art of the Palaeologan era reflected the theological dogma of the hesychast, with the iconography of the Hospitality of Abraham acquiring a Trinitarian rather than Christological connotation.[2] Rublev's version of the *Hospitality of Abraham* (Old Testament Trinity) is the best example of this iconographical trend (Fig. 51).

The Old Testament Trinity in theology

Images of the Trinity in the form of three angels represent Chapter 18 of the Book of Genesis. Abraham treats the visit of the three angels as a revelation of God (contrast Judges 13), but what he sees is not God alone but 'three men standing nearby' (Genesis 18:2). Abraham meets the men and greets them with low bows; initially he addressed his fulsome words of welcome to one of the men only (18:3), but he subsequently addressed all three (18:4–5a) who respond. The shift from one to three (18:1–3) matches the corresponding shifts that occur in Abraham's speech (18:3–5). In the follow-up, however, the reverse happens, and the focus shifts from the three to the one. The three men dine together

1 A. Strezova, 'Relations of Image to its Prototype in Byzantine Iconophile Theology', *Byzantinoslavica*, vol. 66, no. 1–2 (2008). In using the term theology, the Byzantine fathers understood it to be about God as he is in himself; this is Trinitarian theology. The term *oikonomia* (divine dispensation), on the other hand, also presupposed a Trinitarian basis, and focused on two facts: the work of Christ (Christology–Soteriology), and divine and continuous work through the Spirit (Pneumatology and Ecclesiology).

2 In the earlier representations of the Trinity the main emphasis was on the figure of the middle angel–Christ (Christological connotation), whereas in later centuries the painters aimed to represent the unity of the Trinity (Trinitarian connotation).

under a tree and they invite Abraham's wife Sarah to join them, but it is one of them (God) who proclaims to Abraham that Sarah 'will give birth to a son'. He also expresses his displeasure at Sarah's incredulity (18: 8–15). When they finish the meal, however; 'the three visitors' depart for Sodom together with Abraham. God decides to inform Abraham about the purpose of their journey (18:17–19); although the declaration that follows seems atypical in this situation (18:20–21) and it is not clearly addressed to Abraham, but it is communicated in the first person rather than in plural ('I will go down to see …' in contrast to 'come, let Us go down and there confuse their language' (Genesis 11:7–8). 'The two men' now continue their journey to Sodom, but Abraham questions God about his plans for the town (18:22).

God is shown as one of the 'three visitors', and not, for example, as speaking and acting through all three of them. A clear difference exists between God, who leaves once he finishes the dialogue with Abraham, and the 'two travellers' (18:33), who 'came to Sodom in the evening' (19:1, cf. 18:1). The 'three men' (18:2) thus consist of God himself and 'two angels', even if the narrator does not, surprisingly, affirm this difference, or dismiss the likelihood of three divine beings, two of them unknown to Abraham, visiting his home. The two visitors are identified as 'angels' (19:1–15), but their relationship to God is puzzling. The men take Lot and members of Lot's family and lead them safely out of town. However, it is only one God who states, 'Flee for your lives! Do not look back, and do not stop anywhere in the plain!' (18:17). The reference to one God raises the question of whether God has met the two angels outside the gates of Sodom, after they escorted Lot out of the city? It is not clear that such a meeting ever took place as the narrator tried to preserve God's essential mystery. However, the Septuagint's plural reading brings this statement into an agreement with Lot's response: And 'Lot said to them. "No my Lords please!"' (18:18). In spite of this, Lot discusses a possible shelter for himself with a particular partner (18:18–20) who openly identifies himself as the Lord, the cause of the forthcoming destruction of Sodom and Gomorrah (18:21–24). There is no further information about the angels. The angel who said 'I cannot do anything until you reach it' is obviously identical to God who 'rained down burning sulphur on Sodom and Gomorrah' (18:22, 24). Does this denote that God reverted to heaven after conversing with Lot, in order to begin the destruction from there? Or, does the odd repetition of Yahweh's name indicate that he exists simultaneously in heaven and on earth? If the Lord is indeed almighty, as Abraham points out (18:25), one would not expect him to leave his heavenly throne vacant.

There are three distinct but interrelated problems in the narrative of Genesis 18–19. First, the affiliation between the Lord and the 'three angels' is uncertain in Genesis 18. Secondly, while Adam identifies two of the visitors as 'angels' (19:1–15), their function is puzzling, especially the one who acts as authority.

Thirdly, there is the difficulty of accepting the presence of God in heaven and on earth at the same time. The first and the second issues describe the dogma of *perichoresis* (the interactions among the three). The third deals with the issue of the hypostatic union in Christ, which affects the liaison between the visible God and the Godhead.

Interpretation

Philo was one of the earliest writers to provide an allegorical interpretation of Genesis 18.[3] He supposed that it was a mystical vision of God in which the three angels are the self-existent, beneficent, and sovereign powers of God.[4] Hence, Abraham's vision of three travellers was only a sighting of three men because he could not perceive their divine nature.[5] Flavius Josephus avoided the ambiguity, which is present in the Holy Scriptures, the Septuagint and Philo's writings, and claimed that angels can and did assume human form and even eat men's food.[6] Origen affirmed that the revelation of the uncreated light of God given to Abraham was a prerequisite for his vision of God and the two 'angels'.[7] The appearance of the angels, on the other hand, signifies the mystery of the Trinity.[8] Origen considered Abraham a model of a spiritual person who could see the ultimate mysteries of God.[9] Western fathers, such as Ambrose of Milan from the 4th century, Peter Chrysologus from the 5th century, and Caesarius of Arles from the early 6th century, affirm Origen's interpretation.[10] The Origenist tradition continued in the theological tradition of the Eastern fathers, in particularly in the writings of the 5th-century Cyril of Alexandria, and Procopius of Gaza from the 6th century.[11]

Justin the Philosopher discussed God's apparition to Moses and to Abraham and other Old Testament prophets, but did not perceive those visions as revelations

---

3 S. Sandmel, *Philos's Place in Judaism : A Study of Conceptions of Abraham in Jewish Literature* (Jersey City N.J. 1972) 119.

4 Philo, 'De Abraham', 119–132 in L. Cohn (ed.), *Philonis Alexandrini Opera Quae Supersunt*, vol. 4 (Berlin 1902) 1–60.

5 A. Arterbury, 'Abraham's Hospitality Among Jewish and Early Christian Writters', *Perspectives in Religious Studies* (2003) 359–376.

6 L.H. Feldman, *Judaean Antiquities 1–4: Translation and Commentary* (Leiden 2000) 74.

7 R.E. Heine, 'Introduction', in R. Heine, (trans), *Origen: Homilies on Genesis and Exodus*, vol. 17, *Fathers of the Church* (Washington D.C. 1982) 21.

8 Origen, *Commentarium in Canticum Canticorum* 2; in N.P. Lawson (trans), *Song of Songs: Commentary and Homilies* (Washington D.C. 1957).

9 Origen, *Commentarium in Evangelium Johannis* 20, 10, 67, in C. Blanc, (ed.), *Commentarii in Evangelium Johannis*, 5 vols., Sources Chrétiennes 120, 157, 222, 290, 385 (Paris 1964–1992).

10 Ambrose of Milan, 'De Excessu Fratris sui Satyri 2.96'; *Patrologia Graeca* 16, 1401AB; Peter Chrysologus,'Sermo 99', *Patrologia Latina* 52, 478C; Caesarius of Arles, 'Sermo 5', 2–5, in Caesarius of Arles, *Sermons , M.M. Mueller (trans), (Washington D.C. 1964); also Patrologia Latina* 39, 1747–1748.

11 Cyril of Alexandria, 'Adversus Julianum Libri Decem'1', *Patrologia Graeca* 76, 489–1058; 29C, 532D. Procopius of Gaza, 'Commentarius in Genesin 18', 1–3; *Patrologia Graeca* 88, 19–511; 363AC.

of the Godhead, who cannot be a subject of vision.[12] Abraham, Isaac and Jacob did not see the Father and the ineffable Lord of all (even of Christ); rather, they saw the invisible God becoming flesh. The Logos conducted the providential and creative work of the Father. God did reveal himself in the form of angels; he also took a human body and appeared to Abraham. Tertullian also claimed that Abraham received a vision of the Son, but this revelation was not about the Trinitarian exegesis.[13]

Eusebius of Caesarea argued that the Hospitality of Abraham was a theophany. Abraham saw one 'man' whom he worshipped as a deity, he fell down immediately and addressed one of them as Godhead. John Chrysostom upheld that the righteous Abraham referred to the three strangers as 'my Lord', but he gave precedence to one of them. Chrysostom elaborated further by stating the two angels went to destroy the town while the Lord continued the conversation with the righteous.[14] He further read this story as a revelation of Christ to Abraham. The two angels shared in his redemptive work and divine mysteries. Cyril of Alexandria established the episode at Mamre was a revelation of the Holy Trinity because, although Abraham saw three people, he addressed them as one.[15]

The tradition that affirmed this episode as a revelation of the Holy Trinity continued in the later Eastern exegetic tradition. The author of the *Anonymous Dialogue with Jews*,[16] as well as Maximus the Confessor, wrote extensively about this aspect. Maximus perceived the spiritual world as mystically imprinted on the sensible world in symbolic forms. This reciprocity allowed any material image, like Abraham's three angelic forms, to serve as signs manifesting the invisible and unknowable Trinity to those prepared to see it properly with their spiritual sight. For Abraham, it was a true contemplative, transcending matter through the recognition of the *imago Trinities* (image of the Trinity) in his soul. The Hospitality of Abraham affirms the fusion of antinomical nature of God, both the Monad (unity of the Trinity) and the Triad (the three hypostases of God).[17]

Gregory the Theologian claimed that Abraham received a vision of God, not in his role as deity, but as a man.[18] Augustine of Hippo affirmed Abraham's

---

12 Justin's Dialogue with Trypho, 127, in P. Schaff & H. Wace, 'Justin Martyr: Second Apology (Dialogue with Trypho)', *Ante-Nicene Fathers*, vol. I, (Grand Rapids 1955) 188–270.

13 Tertullian, 'Adv. Marc. iii. 9', in E. Evans (ed.), *Tertullian Adversus Marcionem*, (Oxford 1972).

14 Maximus Confessor, *Избранные Творения: Пер. и Комментарии*, vol. 4, chap. 1 (Moscow 2004) 449.

15 R.M. Grant, 'Greek Literature in the Treatise the Trinitate and Cyril Contra Julianum', *Journal of Theological Study*, vol. 15 (1964) 265–299.

16 E. Grypeou & H. Spurling, *The Exegetical Encounter between Jews and Christians in Late Antiquity* (Leiden 2009) 196.

17 L. Thundberg, *Microcosm and Mediator: The Theological Anthropology of Maximus the Confessor* (Chicago 1965) 137–139.

18 J. Børtnes & T. Häggws, *Gregory of Nazianzus: Images And Reflections* (Copenhagen 2006) 45.

understanding of the Unity of the Trinity:[19] 'while greeting the three strangers Abraham confessed to one God in three hypostases.[20] This event was, therefore, a symbolic prefiguration of the Trinitarian nature of God.[21] In his later writings, Augustine of Hippo refrained from any visual representation of the doctrine of the Trinity.[22]

Athanasius of Sinai and Ambrose of Milan noted the event to be a Trinitarian revelation.[23] Procopius of Gaza summarised the Christian view about the identity of Abraham's three guests as follows: the three men were either three angels, or possibly one of them was God while the other two were angels. Most probably the three men addressed by Abraham in the singular served as a type for the holy and consubstantial Trinity. Finally, the great defender of icons, John of Damascus, wrote that Abraham did not see the divine nature. 'For no one has ever seen God, but he saw an image of God to whom he made a sign of supplication'.[24]

The *General Vigil Service of the Holy Fathers* describes the event as a revelation of the triune hypostatic God to Abraham (song 5). In addition, the Canon of Joseph the Psalt reads 'you saw the Trinity as was possible for humans and provided them with hospitality, the righteous Abraham' (song 5). Similar statements are found in the *Canon of the Metropolitan of Smyrna* (from the middle of the 9th century).

The iconography of the Trinity

The desire to represent the ineffable mystery of the Trinity goes back to the early stages of Christian iconography. Any iconographic evidence of the Western composition of the Trinity is sparse, however, perhaps reflecting the weight of Augustinian authority.[25] Also, due to the iconoclastic controversy, only limited examples remain from the Christian first millennium in the East.[26]

---

19 Since three men appeared, and no one was said to be greater than the others, either in form, age, or power, why should we not understand, as visibly intimated by the visible creature, the equality of the Trinity, and one and the same substance in three persons? Augustine of Hippo, De Trin. ii. 20, in F. Meiner (ed.), *De Trinitate: (Bucher VIII–XI, XIV–XV, Anhang Buch V)* (San Francisco 2001).

20 Bishop Sylvester, *Опыт Православного Догматического Богословия* (Kiev 1892) 213–217.

21 S. McKenna, 'Saint Augustine: The Trinity', *The Fathers of the Church*, vol. 46 (Washington DC 1963) 7.

22 B. McGinn, 'Trinity Higher than any Being! Imagining the Invisible Trinity', *Aesthetic des Unsichtbaren* (Erschienen 2004) 77–93.

23 A. Lebedev, 'Ветхозаветное Вероучение во Времена Патриархов I' (St Petersburg 1886) 118.

24 John of Damascus, *John Damascus: On Holy Images*, M.H. Allies (ed.), part 3, chpt. 4 (London 1898).

25 F. Boespflug & Y. Zaluska, 'Le Dogme Trinitarie et l'Essor de son Iconographie en Occident de l'Epoque Carolingienne au IVe Concile du Latran 1215', *Cahiers de Civilisation Medievale*, vol. 37 (1994) 181–240. From beginning of the Christian era, simple geometric shapes were used in the West to symbolise the Trinity.

26 T. de Régnon, *Etudes sur la Sainte Trinité*, vol. 1 (Paris 1892) 167–215.

Analysis of Western images of the Trinity shows that, until the 13th century, the Western tendency to emphasise one substance (*ousia*) of the Trinity, rather than affirming the characteristics of the three hypostases of God, was reflected in art. In fact, the image of a single Godhead as a symbol for the grandeur of the Holy Trinity was common in Western art. Occasionally, however, the image of Christ symbolised all three hypostases of the Trinity.[27] Panofsky stated that it was essential to use a single image to represent the Trinity in the West, and for that purpose the painters in the Western tradition introduced the image of glorified Christ (Majestas Domini).[28] This evolution passed through the stages of polymorphic images of Christ, such as compositions of the Paternitas, the Synthronoi and the Throne of Mercy as seen in Carolingian examples of the 9th and 10th centuries.[29]

Because of the complexity of the hypostatic relationships of the Trinity, the search for an acceptable representation of the Holy Trinity in the Eastern tradition started from a different perspective than in the West.[30] The use of anthropomorphic iconographic variants for circumscription of the Trinity proved unpopular in the East. The first stage in this direction dates from the time of Photius; however, after the schism of 1054, new iconographic models of Christ Emmanuel and the Ancient of Days arose, as well as anthropomorphic images of the Holy Trinity, especially the Paternitas images.[31] Despite the spread of archaic images of the Trinity, only one iconic type; e.g., the Hospitality of Abraham (the Old Testament Trinity), was in accordance with the doctrines of the Church.[32]

The earliest evidence of the Hospitality of Abraham (Genesis 18) comes from the catacombs of the Via Latina, Rome; the paintings in these catacombs date to about 320–350. This composition represents only the first phase of the biblical story —Abraham's meeting with the angels. A bearded Abraham sits at his midday meal under the oak of Mamre with three youths in white garments standing before him on the right, on a raised circular platform. Abraham greets the approaching youths with his raised right hand, and they respond with the same gesture.[33] To his right, a calf symbolises hospitality. The treatment of this subject in the following two centuries came in the form of magnificent

27 A.M. Di Achille, 'Sur Iconographia Trinitaria Medievale: La Trinita del Santuario sul Monte Autore Presso Valapietra', *Art Medievale*, vol. 2, no. 5 (1991) 49–73.

28 M. Alpatov, 'La Trinité dans le Art Byzantine et l'Icone de Roublev', *Echoes de Orient*, vol. 30 (1927) 151–186; E. Panofsky, *Studies in Iconology: Humanistic Themes in the Art of the Renaissance* (Oxford 1939) 433.

29 M. Kuyumdzieva, 'The Face of God's Divinity: Some Remarks on the Origin, Models and Content of the Trinity Images of Synthronoi Type in Post-Byzantine Painting', *Scripta & e-Scripta*, no. 5 (2007) 161–182.

30 A.C. Moore, *Iconography of Religions: An Introduction* (Minneapolis 1977) 250–260.

31 C. Galavaris, 'Στη μνήμη του Ανδρέα Γρηγ, Ξυγγόπουλου (1891–1979)', *Δελτίον ΧΑΕ*, vol. 10 (1980–1981) 85–94.

32 S. Papadopoulos, 'Essai d'Interprétation du Thème Iconographique de la Paternité dans l'Art Byzantin', *Cahiers Archéologiques*, vol. 17 (1968) 132–136.

33 N. Malickii, 'К Истории Композиций Ветхозаветной Троицы', *Seminarium Kondakovianum*, vol. 2 (Prague 1928) 33–45.

mosaics, which combined several scenes in a single picture; the 6th-century representation from San Vitale, Ravenna,and the 5th-century mosaics of Santa Maria Maggiore, Rome, are good examples (Figs 52, 53).[34] In these monuments, the regular scheme of the Hospitality of Abraham takes on a dogmatic character. The three beardless youths are notable in being depicted with halos; a mandorla encloses the central figure. The clothes of the three angels are the same; with slight variations in the gestures. The youth on the right points his finger at the bread, whereas the youth on the left holds up his hand in blessing; he slightly turns towards the figure of the middle youth, who points at the calf. Clearly, the focus is on the sacrificial meal, which suggests the artist had an interest in the symbolic meaning of the event. Similary in the San Vitale *Hospitality of Abraham* in which the three youths are almost identical to each other, even as far as gestures. The central angel and the angel on the right make a sign of benediction with their right hands. The left- and right-hand of the figures point to three disc-shaped loaves each marked with an X. Besides the figures of angels in the iconographic scheme, Abraham, Sarah and the servants are represented. Symbolic images of Abraham's hamber and the oak at Mamre fill the landscape surrounding the figures.[35]

At the beginning of the 11th century, the iconography of the Hospitality of Abraham gained new momentum, presenting its characteristic components and roles in a direct and distinct way. The central angel is in the guise of the historical Jesus, wearing characteristic costume and depicted with symbolic adjuncts. The middle angel is larger than the two flanking angels, who move to the corners of the table and are turned to the side.[36] The meaning of this composition is Christological, the middle angel (Christ) serves as a prototype for the Trinity. Infrequently, the flanking angels also had a cruciform halo as well, as in the icon of the 14th-century *Paternitas* composition from Tretyakov Gallery.[37] The setting differs as guests sit around a semi-circular, as opposed to square, table. These representations are regularly labelled as images of the 'Holy Trinity'. A miniature found in the Greek Psalter of the 9th century is a good example of this trend. The central characteristic of this image is the fact that the three figures have no wings. The middle angel has a nimbus decorated with a cross.[38] The *Armenian Gospel of Vehap'ar* (unknown in the West until 2000), is of importance, presenting the Biblical narrative of Genesis

34 A. Grabar, *A Christian Iconography: A Study of its Origins* (Princeton 1936) 113f.

35 V.N. Lazarav, *История Византийской Живописи* (Moscow 1986) 117–118, pl. 384.

36 A. Heimann, 'L'Iconographie de la Trinite: L'Art Chretien', *Revue Mensuelle*, vol. 1 (September 1934) 37–54.

37 S. Bigham, 'Image of God the Father in Orthodox Theology and Iconography', *Studies in Orthodox Iconography* (Crestwood 1995) 45–57.

38 'Codex Vaticanus Barberinianus Graecus 372', in G. Bunge, *The Rublev Trinity: The Icon of the Trinity by the Monk–Painter Andrei Rublev*, f. 85, pl. 8.

18 in a theological context.[39] This was a gradual process culminating in the 14th-century manuscript of Kantacuzenos.[40] Although Abraham and Sarah are visible in this scene (Rublev removed them), the manuscript illumination of the Trinity was decisive for Rublev.

It is important to note the positioning of the figures in the previous two examples. Their arrangement was not consistent with the principle of *isocephalia* (the heads of the figures in the composition brought to the same level), but in a semi-circle. The table has a semi-circular shape. The middle angel is slightly higher in the pictorial plane with the two other angels standing on both sides of the horizontal plane. This is the so-called Syriac model of the Trinity, commonly used in the Eastern provinces,[41] and later spreading to the Western world.[42] In its fundamental conception, this iconographic type remained almost unchanged during the 12th century. Slight variations are evident in the Cappella Palatina at Norman Place, Palermo (12th century), where the three men have wings and messengers' staves; one of the angels has a nimbus with a red outline, and above the scene is the inscription 'Holy Trinity'.[43] During the Comneanian era, the moment of greeting and the reception of the three personages at the table became separate compositions, for example, in the Cathedral of Monreale (end of the 12th century).[44] A tendency to unify all three angels, by slightly bending the heads of the side angels towards the middle angel, was initiated in the late Byzantine artistic tradition.[45]

The 'medieval' model of the Trinity continued in the late Comnenian and Palaeologan periods. An arduous contrapposto substituted the frontal position of the central angel;[46] who turns his head towards the left angel. As a result, the affective relations between the three angels are elicited, creating a revived sense of movement and spatial depth. Churches of the Forty Martyrs, Turnovo; St Sophia, Kiev; St Sophia, Ohrid; are excellent representations of the Trinity.[47]

---

39 The Armenian Gospel of Vehap'ar was shown for the first time in the *Treasures from the Ark* exhibition at the British Library. M. Golubtsov, 'Икона Живоначальной Троицы', *Журнал Московской Патриархии*, vol. 7 (Moscow 1972) 69–76.

40 C. Lock. 'The Space of Hospitality: On the Icon of the Trinity Ascribed to Andrei Rublev', *Sobornost: Incorporating Eastern Churches Review*, vol. 30, no. 1 (2008) 21–53.

41 Malickii, 'К Истории Композиций Ветхозаветной Троицы', 34.

42 Alpatov, 'La Trinite, dans l'Art Byzantine er l'Icone de Roublev', 6.

43 ibid., 7–9.

44 Bunge, *The Rublev Trinity*, 65–67.

45 ibid., 10.

46 *Encyclopedia Brittanica*, online version, http://www.britannica.com/EBchecked/topic/135385/contrapposto (accessed 10/11/2011).

47 M. Conceva, 'За Търновската Живописна Школа', *Търновска Кнuйовна Школа* 1371–1971 (Sofia 1974) 343; Detailed information about the Church of Forty Martyrs, Turnovo, can be found online at http://www.st40martyrs.org/ (accessed 03/02/2012); A. Комес, 'Роль Княжеского Заказа в Построении Софийского собора в Киеве', *Древнерусское Искусство: Художественная Культура Домонгольской Руси* (Moscow 1972) 50–64; C. Grozdanov, *Saint Sophia of Ohrid* (Zagreb 1991) 25–34.

In the late Palaeologan period, depictions had an indefinite architectural coulisse (background), serving to abstract the figures from their historical context. Moreover, Abraham and Sarah abandon their original post and all other elements and superfluous objects were removed from the pictorial plane. The figures of the three angels were no longer depicted in semi-circle, with a special position given to the middle angel, as in previous times. Rather, the three angels are equal and represented in a full circle. The table changes shape from circular to square.[48]

The *Trinity* of San Marco,Venice (13th century), heralds the beginning of a new type in the West, which aims to reflect the history of Hospitality of Abraham, rather than portraying the Trinity. There is a tendency to unify the three angels by inclining their heads toward the centre. The figures are positioned according to the standard of *isocephalia*; they resemble a frieze.[49] Unfortunately, no similar icon of high artistic value can be found from 13th-century Constantinople except, possibly, a small circular icon bearing the title of the Holy Trinity. Greek in origin, this example goes back to the same prototype as that of Rublev.[50] The knees of the central angel rise and the shape of the chalice and the gold lines of the table are reminiscent of Rublev's *Trinity*. This detail, the semicircular shape of the table, around which the angels sit, comes from the Oriental model of the previous century. It is not repeated in the Palaeologan iconography. Whereas the purpose of this icon was to highlight the central angel, Rublev aimed to present the three angels as equals.[51]

A 13th-century Italian miniature in the British Museum (Ad. 15, 268) resembles a Byzantine example from the 12th century (in particular, the figure of Abraham resembles that of Amos from the 12th-century Vatican manuscript), with the proportions of the drapery almost reproducing that of Vat. Gr. 1153, fol. 20. A singular angelic form is subordinate to the figurative scene (in the curve of the body), and the central angel is slightly shifted, resembling the middle angel of Rublev. The motion of the oak repeats the movement of the body of Christ, as is the case in Rublev. This iconographic novelty contributed to the development of a new composition of the Trinity.

In Russia, this innovative development in iconography surfaced before Rublev. Some of the finest artworks of this period include a mural in St Sophia Cathedral, Kiev (11th century), and the bronze south door of the Church of Nativity of the Virgin, Suzdal (13th century).[52] Two famous frescoes from the Church in

48 V.N. Lazarev, *Feofan Grek i Ego Shkola* (Moscow 1961) 18.

49 A. Robertson, *The Bible of St Mark, St Mark's Church the Altar and Throne of Venice* (Venice 1898) 109.

50 Alpatov, 'La Trinité dans le Art Byzantine et l'Icone de Roublev'.

51 R. Arnheim, 'Inverted Perspective in Art: Display', *Leonardo*, vol. 5, no. 2 (Spring 1972) 125–135.

52 L.W. Mitrovic & N. Okunev, 'La Dormition de la Sainte Vierge dans la Peinture Orthodoxe', *Byzatlinoslavica*, vol. 3 (1931) 134–174.

Alexandrovo near Moscow, and the Church of the Transfiguration, Novgorod (14th century), are also good illustrations.[53] In all three models of the Trinity, the central angel alone has a cross nimbus and holds a scroll in his left hand, while the other two angels hold messenger staves. Three breads and three chalices are placed on the table, with a large chalice being in the middle of the table. The most significant details are the gestures of the three angels; the one on the left points to the chalice, the one on the right blesses one of three loaves, and the one in the middle blesses the table.[54]

The advent of the Anaphora Troparion (of the third hour) and the liturgical reforms brought by Metropolitan Cyprian and patriarch Philotheus brought out new elements into the figurative scene of the Trinity. The fundamental importance of the anaphora predetermined significant changes in the structure of the iconostasis in Russia, with a new iconography of the 'Trinity' arising for the first time as part of the Feast cycles.[55] The image of the Old Testament Trinity gained popularity after hesychasm's spread into Russia. It was no longer overloaded with details of the Biblical narrative of Genesis 18 and, instead, an allegorical reading of the narrative occurred, and the story itself took on a more rudimentary character in art. The best example of this trend is Rublev's Old Testament icon of the Trinity.

Andrei Rublev and his art

Little is known about the life of Andrei Rublev, the famous painter of the Trinity. Many scholars agree that he was born between 1360 and 1370. For a short period, he lived in the Trinity Lavra of St Sergius near Moscow. He was under the spiritual guidance of monk Nikon, a hegumen of the monastery after the passing of Sergius of Radonezh (1392).[56] Afterwards, Rublev lived in Zvenigorod, in Vladimir Suzdal and at the Spaso-Andronikov monastery near Moscow.[57]

The first mention of Rublev comes from the chronicles which testify that in 1405 the Grand Prince Vasily Dmitrievich, commissioned three iconographers,

53 M. Cheremeteff, 'The Transformation of the Russian Sanctuary Barrier and the Role of Theophanes the Greek', in A. Leong (ed.), *Millennium: Christianity and Russia, A.D. 988–1988* (Crestwood 1990) 107–121; M.E. Frazer, 'Church Doors and the Gates of Paradise: Byzantine Bronze Doors in Italy', *Dumbarton Oaks Papers*, vol. 27 (1973) 145–162.

54 A.A. Saltykov, Иконография Троицы Андрея Рублева, *Древнерусское Искусство XIV–XV* (Moscow 1984) 80.

55 O.G. Uliyanov, *О месте Иконы Живоначальной Троицы в Праздничном Ряду Русского Иконостаса Троицкие Чтения 2003–2004 гг. Большие Вяземы* (Moscow 2004) 153–154.

56 L. Hughes, 'Inventing Andrei: Sovet and Post-Soviet Views of Andrei Rublev and his Trinity Icon', *Slavonica*, vol. 9, no. 2 (Nov. 2003) 84–85.

57 V. Kopylov, 'Hesychasm and Creative Activity of Andrei Rublev', paper given to the 16th International Patristic Byzantine Symposium in Thessaloniki 26th May 1999, *Patristic and Byzantine Review*, vol. 18–19 (1999) 41–47.

Theophanes the Greek, Prokhorov of Gorodets and Rublev to work on the Annunciation Cathedral in Moscow's Kremlin. Rublev's name, with the designation 'the monk', is last on the list of masters, which suggests that he was the youngest.[58] Researchers assert that seven icons of the festival cycle in this cathedral, including *Baptism, Birth of Christ, Presentation of the Lord, Transfiguration, Annunciation, Resurrection of Lazarus* and *Entry into Jerusalem* belong to Rublev. These works are in a Byzantine style and demonstrate Rublev's exceptional talent. Rublev created another work of art during this period, a book illumination of Khitrovo Gospel. This wonderful miniature contains an image of an angel, which as Alpatov claimed, symbolises Evangelist Matthew.[59] The chronicles also mention that Rublev and Daniil Chernii (another famous Russian iconographer) worked on the Assumption Cathedral, Vladimir in 1408. The frescoes painted by Rublev exist in fragments and occupy the western wall of the church. The fragments depict images of the trumpeting angel, of Apostle Peter as well as of the Last Judgment.[60]

Extensive research has revealed that in 1410 Rublev painted one of the Zvenigorod churches. The icons *Saviour, Archangel Michael* and *St Paul* from Zvenigorod are attributed to Rublev and they feature a new stage in Rublev's painting, expressing the beginning of the Golden Age — the flourishing of icon painting in Russia. About the same time, Rublev created another outstanding work, a version of the famous Byzantine image of *Our Lady of Vladimir.* The image indicates that Rublev created this icon as an experienced master, who had his own school of painting.[61]

From 1425–1427 Rublev worked together with Chernii on the new stone cathedral of the Holy Trinity. It is probably during this time Rublev painted the main feature of the monastery — the icon of the Holy Trinity. Epiphanius the Wise claimed that Rublev helped with the decoration and construction of the church. Rublev painted his last works at the Cathedral of the Saviour at Andronikov Monastery, Moscow, where he passed away in 1430. He was buried in the altar vaults near his close friend Chernii. Rublev was canonised a saint in 1988 by the Russian Orthodox Church and his feast day is celebrated on 29 January and 4 July.[62]

---

58 Uliyanov, 'The Deesis Painted by Andrey Rublev from the Annunciation Church of the Moscow Kremlin (on the 575th year of the demise of the reverend icon-painter)', *Hierarchy in Aancient Russia*, M. Mozhaisk-Terra (trans), (Moscow 2005) 172–223.

59 O. Popova, *Russian Illuminated Manuscripts* (London 1984) 36–39.

60 L. Bourdeau & S. Chassé, 'Actes du Colloque Sites du Patrimoine et Tourisme, 2–4 Juin 2010, Québec, Canada', *Conference Proceedings World Heritage and Tourism: Managing the Global and the Local, June 2–4, 2010* (Quebec City 2011) 621–622.

61 L.A. Aleksandrovic Fyeoktistov, *Города Россuu* (Moscow 2007) 13–15.

62 'Moscow Patriarchate Glorifies Saints', *Orthodox America* IX (82), August 1988, http://www.roca.org/OA/82/82e.htm (accessed 16/03/2008).

Rublev's biography raises questions as to the possible influences on his art, particularly on his icons. The Byzantine canon of icon-painting, which spread to Russia under the influence of Theophanes, as well as the legacy of the older Russian school of art, are often mentioned in connection with the development of Rublev's style. Also, the Novgorodian school of painting, as well as Rublev's spiritual beliefs and monastic life, were important influences on him. Sergius of Radonezh's affinity to the hesychast dogma and the cult of the Trinity, as well as Theophanes's artistic style, penetrated by a mystical spirit, affected the development of Rublev's style of painting.

Sergius of Radonezh and the cult of the Trinity

Sergius of Radonezh was a crucial influence on Rublev who lived and worked under his auspices. In fact, Rublev painted his famous icon of the Trinity to serve as a memorial to Sergius of Radonezh.

Sergius was a Russian ascetic who exercised significant influence on domestic spirituality as well as on Rublev's personality. In fact, the life of St Sergius, the hegumen of the Holy Trinity Lavra, was often taken as a model of ascetic existence by contemporaries of Rublev. The Monastery of the Holy Trinity, in turn, was a place where notions of love of God, calm and self-discipline, and mystical union with God were propagated.

Sergius was a prayer enthusiast; he revived monasticism in Russia in the 14th century and brought the tradition of *bezmolvie* (*hesychia*) to Russia, both in theory and practice (his disciples were on Athos at the height of the hesychast controversy). In the *Vitae of St Sergius*, Epiphanius stated that the saint had frequent visions of the uncreated light during prayer and other beatific revelations.[63] The most important of them is the the icon of Theotokos, when the Virgin Mary promised to Sergius the protection of Russian people. The particulars of the epiphany are reminiscent of Abraham's vision of the three angels in the Old Testament (Genesis 18). Apparitions of the Virgin Mary were uncommon in the 14th and 15th centuries and Russian monks took it as a divine sign that the Lord granted Russia a special protection.

Sergius apparently had other spiritual visions during prayer, which were also witnessed by his followers, whose testimony asserts the frequency of his visions of the divine light. Some aspects of these visions are reminiscent of those experienced by Byzantine practitioners of hesychasm, such as Symeon

63 Епифанием Премудрым, 'Житие и Чудеса Преподобного Сергия', Chpt 31, online version http://www.stsl.ru/lib/book2/index.htm (accessed 10/07/2012).

the New Theologian.[64] For instance, one of Sergius's disciples, Simeon, stated that when Sergius conducted the liturgy, the 'divine light' was often seen at the altar situated around the Eucharist. On one occasion, when Sergius wanted to receive communion, 'the divine fire moved up from the altar, curled up as a kind of cloth, and entering the holy chalice'. Simeon claimed that this insight gave Sergius his wonderful mystical knowledge, and many other gifts such as healing the sick, casting out demons, and even resurrecting the dead.[65]

Apart from the fact that Sergius was a recipient of visions and a miracle worker, the most significant feature of his spirituality was his special affinity with the Holy Trinity.[66] In the *Vitae of St Sergius*, Epiphanius recorded Sergius's founding of the Monastery of the Trinity and aspects of his devotion to this cult.[67] To give sound support to this claim, Epiphanisu referred to the hymns written by Sergius in praise of the Trinity.

Sergius was the first Russian religious to give a sound idea of the Holy Trinity. He transformed it into a symbol of the Christian dogma of unity, the accord to which all must strive to live on earth. In the religious and philosophical sense, this image of the Trinity, as the ideal of life on earth, opened the way for the removal of the dilemma — national or universal. Consequently, the cult of the Holy Trinity, in whose honour Sergius dedicated a monastery, became a symbol of the unity of Russia. As a result of this dogma, images of the Holy Trinity appeared throughout Russia as a possible way to save the real state.[68] Interestingly, before Sergius accepted the dogma of the Holy Trinity, the cult of the Trinity was not seen as a necessary part of orthodox life in Russia. For example, pictorial cycles were usually devoted to Christ, the mother of God, St Nicholas, the holy warriors and the fathers of the Church. Only in the Kiev-Pechersk Monastery was the cult of the Trinity followed in the early 12th century.

It is possible that Sergius was familiar with the cult of the Holy Trinity established by the monks of the Kiev-Pechersk and that he used it as an example. The cult of the Trinity in the 14th and 15th centuries spread to such extent that Serius of Radonezh was activly followed by a constellation of students and belivers. Some of them testified to receiving visions of the Trinity themselves. St Alexander Svirsky (1433) spoke about his vision of the Triune God, showing in the form of three men. St Macarius Zheltovodsky (1444) also experienced a similar kind

64 H. Alfeyev, *Saint Symeon, the New Theologian, and Orthodox tradition* (Oxford 2000) 226.

65 J.L. Opie, 'The Trinity in Andrei Rublev's Icon of the Holy Trinity', *Il Mondo e il Sovramondo del'Icona* (Florence 1998) 197–209.

66 R. Dulskis, 'Hesychast Ideas in the Oeuvre of St Andrei Rublev', *Logos-Vilnius* (2007) 126–142.

67 D. Likhachyov, *Культура Руси Времени Андрея Рублева и Епифания Премудрого Конец XIV–Начало XV в* (St Petersburg 1962) 52–63.

68 K. Ware, *The Orthodox Way* (Crestwood 1995) 39.

of vision in 1435, after which he founded the monastery of the Holy Trinity.[69] Joseph of Volokolamsk described such exalted mystical experiences in his writings. The *Acts* of the Church Council headed by St Macarius of Moscow mention visions of light experienced by the monk, as well as the Council of Hundred Chapters (Stoglav) in 1551 and the councils of 1553–1554, which further affirmed the possibility and necessity for sacred images of the Holy Trinity.[70] Sergius called the Russian people to brotherly love, unity and spiritual creation. He embodied the image of the Trinity as a symbol of Russian unity, which was sought so eagerly in the 13th and 14th centuries. Shortly after his death in 1392, he was canonised and later honoured as the patron and defender of Moscow.

Sergius's devotion to the Holy Trinity was later reflected in Rublev's icon of the Trinity. The creation of this icon had a personal meaning for Rublev: it was a gift to his mentors from the Trinity Sergius's Lavra, who enriched his moral values. This scene represented the significance of Sergius's spirituality for Russian people; a symbol of immersion in the mystery of the divine being, God's unity and indivisibility.[71]

Theophanes the Greek and Andrei Rublev

Rublev's art has arguably diverse influences, the most prominent of which is Byzantine, and Greek Christian art, particularly of Theophanes the Greek, the famous iconographer who came to Russia at the end of 14th century.

Theophanes was born around 1330, and died sometime between 1405 and 1409. During his short-lived residency in Novgorod, Theophanes painted the famous murals of the Church of the Transfiguration. He also decorated the Church on Volotovo-Field and the Cathedral of St Theodore Stratelates. After finishing work in Kostroma in 1390, Theophanes relocated to Moscow in 1395. The production of miniatures for the illuminated *Khitrovo Gospel* was the first of Theophanes's Muscovite work.[72] He also prepared the design of well-known manuscripts, such as the *Psalter of Ivan VI Grozny* (Ivan IV the Terrible, from the last quarter of 14th century) and the *Pogodin's Manuscript* (second half of the 15th century). Moreover, he is credited as the painter of the famous icon *Our Lady of the Don* (c. 1395).[73] While Theophanes probably produced many art works during the

69 A.V. Motorin, 'Образы Пресвятой Троицы в Русском Государственном Самосознании', http://spbda.ru/news/a-1856.htm (accessed 12/05/2010).

70 E.B. Kravyets & L.P. Medvedeva, Иосиф Волоцкий (Moscow 1993) 89, 142, 144; C. Bartolo-Abela, *The Icon of the Divine Heart of God the Father* (Apostolate-The Divine Heart 2012) 18–19.

71 Alpatov, 'О Значении Троицы Рублева', *Этюды по Истории Русского Искусства* (Moscow 1967) 119–122.

72 J. Lawler, *Encyclopedia of the Byzantine Empire* (2004) 284.

73 'Prominent Russians: Theophanes the Greek', online paper http://russiapedia.rt.com/prominent-russians/art/theophanes-the-greek/ (accessed 07/06/2011).

course of his life, scholars accept the following nine paintings as his: *Dormition of the Virgin, Virgin of the Don, St Paul, Saviour in Glory, St John Chrysostom, St John the Evangelist, St Basil* and the *Archangel Gabriel*. He created these icons in 1405 for the iconostasis of Moscow's Cathedral of the Annunciation. The utilisation of complex drawing techniques and the mystical qualities of these representations suggest that Theophanes was a master painter.[74]

Epiphanius described the discipline and austerity characteristic of Theophanes's art:

> while he [Theophanes] sketched and painted, no one saw him glancing at models as some of other painters do, staring at forms with amazement, looking here and there, doing less of the actual painting than observing. In his spirit, he encompassed distant and intellectual realities. With his spiritual eyes, he contemplated spiritual beauty.[75]

The relationship between Theophanes and his pupil Rublev was enigmatic, but he invited Rublev and Prokhorov of Gorodets to work with him on the Annunciation Cathedral. In the process, he advanced Rublev's genius.[76] Rublev later refrained from the dramatic expression, which characterised the style of Theophanes and instigated his own style of painting. Theophanes's use of monochrome colours and his use of pure forms, however, testify that he was an extraordinary master who played a great part in development of the mature Moscow icon painting.

A single hesychast dogma influenced both Theophanes and Rublev, but their differences in artistic style are the result of the humanist debate, a poignant part of the hesychast controversy within Byzantium, but not in the Slavic lands.[77] Certain tension between the humanist and hesychast trend existed in Byzantine culture from its beginnings. Russian people, however, who felt no loyalty to the classical Hellenic tradition, experienced no conflict between humanist and hesychast thought. Liturgical practices, monastic obedience and icon painting were the main spiritual practices in Russia before the 14th century. Hesychast components were integrated in Russian consciousness without the humanist thought which affected the hesychast movement in Byzantium.[78] It is on this basis that the art of Rublev was created. On the other hand, Theophanes's affinity with Byzantine hesychast tradition presented through his adoption of

74 D. Talbot Rice & T. Talbot Rice, *Icons and their History* (Overlook Press 1974) 102.

75 Alpatov, Феофан Грек (Moscow 1990) 113.

76 P.D. Steeves, *The Modern Encyclopedia of Religions in Russia and the Soviet Union*, vol. 2 (Accademic International Press 1988) 5.

77 Alpatov, 'Искусство Феофана Грека и Учение Исихастов', *Византийский Временник*, vol. 33 (1972) 190–202.

78 I. Ekonomtsyev, 'Исихазм и Возрождение: Исихазм и Проблема Творчества', *Златоуст*, vol. 1 (Moscow 1992) 139–170.

an energetic style of painting and the creation of vivid and memorable images. The frescoes of the Church of the Transfiguration, Novgorod, testify to his spiritual insight, knowledge of the mystical contemplative experience, as well as his sympathy with the ancient past.

Although the frescoes of the Church of the Transfiguration, Novgorod, are preserved in small fragments, such incomplete forms show the skill, depth and exceptional qualities of Theophanes's creative genius. Most notable is the adoption of a monochrome technique of painting, in ochre and white. Theophanes's unusual colour palette has been the subject of substantial research, with some scholars suggesting that a fire bleached the frescoes of the Church of the Transfiguration. Extensive archaeological investigation, however, has not discovered traces of fire and restorers have confirmed that the layer of painting is preserved in its original form. The colours of the original monochrome black and white installation are an analogy to the hesychast method of prayer where monks recite only few words ('Lord Jesus Christ, Son of God, have mercy on me, a sinner') during meditation. The aim of this meditative practice was to reach the final stage of mystical contemplation and acquire unity with God (by grace).[79] The affirmation of the Palamist dogma of the 14th century shaped to an extent Theophanes's unsurpassed painting style. Even greater, however, was the influence of the mystical spirituality of St Macarius of Egypt and St Ephraim the Syrian (in the 4th and 5th centuries) on Theophanes's personal style of Byzantine art.[80] His most famous frescoes, in the Church of the Transfiguration, Novgorod, depict saints Macarius and Ephraim.

The fresco of St Macarius has a striking quality, reflecting all stages of the spiritual journey of the saint and his mystical ascent to God. It illustrates the state of transformation of St Macarius and his participation in the uncreated light.[81] The heavenly light, in the form of a white flame, envelops his long ascetic figure. A bleaching flare burst shows the face of Macarius, but his eyes are not defined. This unusual depiction is a deliberate statement that the saint does not need sight because he could see God through his inner (spiritual) eye. The face and the hands of the saint point against the light, with the subtle shape of the saint's body being transformed into an image of exceptional strength. St Macarius plunges into the light, into the divine reality, but he does not dissolve like salt in water. On the contrary, he retains his identity. St Macarius lives in the light, and he is the light. This is a classic illustration of the hesychast mystical experience.

There are other important images in the ensemble of the Transfiguration Church, Novgorod. Frescoes painted by Theophanes, which can be found in the Chapel

---

79 T.A. Subbotin, *Отражение Идей Исихазма в Творчестве Феофана Грека* (Moscow 2011) 6–10.

80 ibid., 114.

81 V.S. Pribitkov, 'Сквозь Жар Души: О трех Древнерус', *Живописцах: А. Рублеве, Дионисии, С. Ушакове* (Moscow 1968) 22–25.

of the Trinity are, however, the most important, at least in relation to Rublev's icon of the Trinity.[82] These relatively well-preserved murals in the small chapel are designed for individual prayer. The program of the paintings is dedicated to the contemplation of the ascetics of the Holy Trinity. In particular, the Old Testament Trinity largely defines the style and personality of Theophanes.

Rublev's icon of the *Trinity*

Rublev's icon of the *Trinity* is the best known of all his paintings and the only one that is fully authenticated. He painted it in honour of Sergius and at the request of Nikon, the new abbot of the Lavra. Rublev was commissioned by Nikon to paint an icon that would represent Sergius's devotion to, and understanding of, the Holy Trinity. Rublev painted the icon between 1392 and 1427 when Nikon became abbot of the Holy Trinity Monastery. During those 30 years, two churches were dedicated to the Holy Trinity: the wooden church (1411–1412) and the stone cathedral (1422–1424). The 15th-century *Life of St Nikon* by Pachomius the Serb reports that Rublev and Daniil Chernii went to the Holy Trinity Monastery for adornment of the stone church of there. It is probable, therefore, that Rublev painted his icon for one of these two churches.

For more then 170 years after its creation, Rublev's icon of the *Trinity* was hidden under darkened oils and covered with surrounds of silver, gold and precious gemstones.[83] It was then repainted with fresh colours. The modern restoration began with the cleaning of the icon in 1904–1906, a landmark in the rediscovery of the icon and elevation of Rublev into the artistic canon. Restoration of Rublev's *Trinity* in 1918, by the team of Grabar and Anisimov, which involved cleaning three layers of paint, revealed not the dark olive colours that are typical of Rublev's style, but rather, bright translucent colours.[84] Rublev's icon was exhibited at the State Tretyakov Gallery in Moscow.[85]

Stories abound the unusual origin of this icon, such as that it was a part of the iconostasis of the wooden church of the Trinity from the 15th century until archaeologists discovered it in the early 20th century.[86] Plugin upholds the view that the only written text associating Rublev's *Trinity* with the Monastery of the Holy Trinity was the 17th century *Narrative of the Holy Icon Painters*. This treatise contains praise for the work, although Nikon's *Vita of St Sergius* does

82 G. I. Vzdornov, *The Frescoes of Theophanes the Greek in the Church of the Transfiguration in Novgorod* (Moscow 1976).

83 E.A. Skorobogaceva, *Троице-Сергиева Лавра и Иконография 'Троица Ветхозаветная' в Северных Письмах XVII'*, Троице-Сергиева Лавра в Истории, Культуре и Духовной Жизни России: Материалы IV Международной Конференции 20 Сентября – 1 Октября 2004 Года (Moscow 2007) 228–243.

84 A. Nikitin, 'Кто Написал Троицу Рублева?', *Наука и Религия*, no. 10 (1988) 44–48.

85 Hughes, 'Inventing Andrei'.

86 Nikitin, 'Кто Написал Троицу Рублева?', 46.

not have such references.[87] While it is difficult to establish the exact date of production, it is certain Rublev painted his *Trinity* during the despoilation of Russia by Tartar and Mongol invaders.[88]

Description

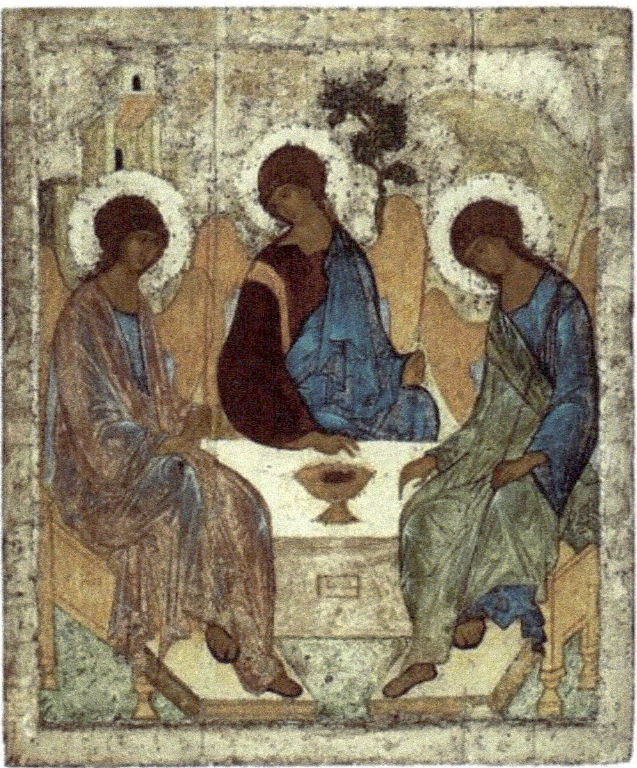

Figure 51. *The Trinity*, 15th century, tempera on wood, 142 x 114 cm, painter Andrei Rublev, Tretyakov Gallery, Moscow (Russia), inv. no. 12924

87 V.A. Plugin, О Происхождении Троицы Рублева, *История СССР*, vol. 2 (Moscow 1987) 68.

88 L. Hughes, 'Inventing Andrei', 88.

On the light (originally gold) background, three angels sit around a table on which a bowl is placed. The middle angel stands above the rest; behind his back is a tree, a mountain is depicted behind the angel on the right and behind the left angel is a building. The heads of all three angels incline in silent conversation. Their facial expressions are calm, and their facial types correspond to each other, as though they are three versions of the same face. A system of concentric cyrcles envelopes the composition. The haloes, the contours of the wings and the angels's hand movements create circles which converge at the chalice in the epicentre of the icon. The shape of a lamb's head is inside the chalice, or, if the chalice is turned clockwise, this is the visage of the dead Christ.[89] The lamb symbolises the sacrificial offering of the Old Testament, and it is also a metaphor for Christ, the sacrificial Lamb of God (cf. 1 Peter 1:9; John 1:29). The middle angel blesses the chalice; the angel sitting at his right hand accepts the blessing, and the angel to the left offers the chalice to the observer.

The meaning of Rublev's icon is transparent — in the heart of the *Trinity* icon, a council for the redemption of humanity is in proceeding. The Eucharistic meal is served — the section of the New Covenant and the blood of Christ (cf. Luke 22:20). Salvation comes, however, universally. The three angels discuss the restoration of the lost likeness (to God) of those redeemed and recreated by Christ (Genesis 1:27).[90] Thus, through love and the sacraments, and especially through Baptism and the Eucharist, the faithful unite with Christ and through him with God (John 4:15; 3:5; 6: 32; 17:1).

On the front of the table, a small rectangle alludes to the cosmos. As God is greater than all creation, and the cosmos is in the will of God and, what is more important, is the plan of salvation of everything created. the true subject of the icon is the eternal plan of God for redemption of humanity.

Behind the middle angel, the oak of Mamre takes the form of a tree with leaves arranged in a spiralling fashion, ascending to the right or to the left. The use of a spiral motif goes back to the ancient tradition and refers to the rising aspects of the soul's journey to the divine.[91] It also points to the symbolism of a ladder, wonderfully depicted in the composition of the *Ladder of Divine Ascent*. The oak itself is a metaphor of the 'tree of knowledge of good and evil' (Genesis 2:17), by which both sin and death were introduced into the world. The oak also symbolises the tree of the Crucifixion by standing right behind the central angelic figure.[92]

89 In the Roman ritual of the Mass, the priest uses the same sentence to invite worshippers to communion: 'behold the Lamb of God who takes away the sin of the world; P. Turner & K. Coffey, *Understanding the Revised Mass Texts* (Chicago 2010) 59.

90 K. Barth, 'The Christian Life', *Church Dogmatics*, vol. 4 (Grand Rapids 1982) 28.

91 D. Mackenzie, *Migration of Symbols* (Whitefish 2003) 175.

92 Dionysius the Areopagite, On the Divine Names, 5, 5–8 and 11, 2, in J.D. Jones (trans), *The Divine Names and Mystical Theology* (Wisconsin 1980).

The mount above the angel on the right has several meanings; one of them being the emblem of the rock that Moses struck to extract water for his people in the desert during the Exodus (Exodus 17:8). It is also reminiscent of Old Testament passages (the Psalms in particular) referring to God as the 'rock and the fortress'; that is, the unshakable, unchangeable and eternal creator (Psalm 70:3). The rock is also the cave of Bethlehem, in which the Virgin Mary gave birth to Christ. Moreover, it represents the tomb of the Resurrection from which Jesus rose (Matthew 27:60). Most importantly, the rock refers to the mountain of spiritual ascent, the point of the revelation of the Triune God.[93] The left angel sits before a building, which may be the home of Abraham, father of the people of Israel. It is also an allusion to the dwelling place of the Godhead. On the other hand, the presence of the colour green, which runs from the church's temple to the green outer garment of the right-hand angel, and through the dark greenish-blue outer garment of the central angel, points to the renewal of creation. Overall, however, the icon reflects the Greek idea of *hesychia* that affirmed the unity of the One, instead of the multiplicity of many.[94]

What does Rublev's *Trinity* portray if production of images of the Father and the Holy Spirit was considered to be a breach of the second commandment? To answer this question, one has to refer to the doctrine of metaphysical antinomy of the absolute who is, at the same time, both visible and invisible (essence–energies distinction).[95] The Cappadocian fathers explored the esoteric nature of this antinomy in an attempt to defend the paradoxical nature of the Christian God. Dionysius the Areopagite, however, also spoke about this dogma when identifying 'unions' and 'distinctions' in the Godhead. Unions represent the hidden essence of God, and distinctions are manifestations and powers, making God known to humanity.[96] In a similar fashion, Maximus affirmed the doctrine of essence–energies, claiming God is knowable in what he imparts to us, but he is not knowable in the incommunicability of his essence.[97]

During the hesychast controversy Gregory Palamas advanced the difference between the divine nature (essence) and the divine energies. Palamists understood the divine nature of God as forever inaccessible (like the centre of the Sun) while the divine energies penetrate the universe (like the sunlight).[98]

93 P. Hunt, 'Andrei Rublev's Old Testament Trinity Icon in Cultural Context', in V. Tsurikov (ed.), *The Trinity-Sergius Lavr in Russian History and Culture: Readings in Russian Religious Culture*, vol. 3, (Jordanville 2006) 118; Plugin, 'Мастер Святой Троицы', *Труды и Дни Андрея Рублева* (Moscow 2001) 295.

94 D. Balfour, *St Gregory the Sinaite, Discourse on the Transfiguration* (St Bernardino 1986) 8, 29–30.

95 Gregory of Nyssa, 'De Beatitudinibus', *Patrologia Graeca* 44, 1269A; also Otis, Gregory of Nyssa and the Cappadocian Conception of Time, *Studia Patristica*, 117 (1976) 339–241.

96 Dionysius, *De Divinis Nominibus*, 2, 24; *Patrologia Graeca* 3, 640.

97 F. Lauritzen, 'Pagan Energies in Maximus the Confessor: The Influence of Proclus on the Ad Thomam 5, *Greek Roman and Byzantine Studies*, vol. 52, no. 2 (2012), http://grbs.library.duke.edu/article/view/13971/277 (accessed 20/10/2013).

98 P. Evdokimov, *The Art of Icon: A Theology of Beauty* (Crestwood 1992) 207.

The essence of God is beyond knowledge, contemplation, or participation.[99] The divine energies, on the other hand, could be obtained and participated in as ineffable, supersensible light — God's glory.[100] The divine energies act through the deified subject, 'energies to energies', making it, by adoption, all that God is by nature.[101] The divine energies radiate to the created order 'from the Father as a source, through the Son as a form or definition, and in the Spirit as activator and perfector'.[102] The work is dependant on the relation each hypostasis 'inheres in the other two hypostases' (*perichoresis* or *communicatio idiomatum*).[103] The relationship between the three hypostasis is determined by the origins of the Son and the procession of the Spirit from the unoriginate Father.[104] Because the divine essence is not a subject of knowledge that is, 'uncreated, indivisible, incomprehensible and uncircumscribable', the difference between the generation of the Son, and procession of the Spirit cannot be understood in any other way except by using negations.[105]

The implication of the doctrine of unknowability of the Trinity, which also concerns the portrayal of the Father, the Son and the Holy Spirit, becomes clearer in relation to Dionysius's teaching on the role of symbols adopted by Palamists. Dionysius believed that visible symbols fill the earthly hierarchy, which being dissimilar to God, are superior forms of representation of his essence.[106] Symbols, signs and images have an important role in the hierarchical system of the spiritual ascent or 'uplifting' of man to God, according to Dionysius. The visual elements are furthermore valuable

in the graded system of descent or *kataphasis*, or transmission of mystical knowledge from God to man through the terrestrial and celestial realms. This is the process of 'illuminations' or advanced 'light-giving' *photodosia* received through the faculty of sight.[107] Certainly, Dionysius did not concern himself with pieces of art, such as icons, but rather with the fundamental question of knowledge of God.[108]

---

99 A. Louth, *Denys the Areopagite* (London 1989) 90.

100 Gregory Palamas, *Triads, Patrologia Graeca* 151, 723C, in Meyendorff (ed.), *Gregory Palamas: The Triad*, 160–162.

101 ibid., 3, 1, 33.

102 C. Tsirpanlis, 'Epistemology, Theognosis, the Trinity and Grace in St Gregory Palamas', *Patristic and Byzantine Review*, vol. 13, no. 1 (1994) 5–27.

103 Theodore the Studite, Refutation III, 7CD, in 'Antirrhetici Tres Adversus Iconomachos', *Patrologia Graeca* 99, 327–436; 432.

104 Gregory the Theologian, Oratio 31, 41, *Patrologia Graeca* 36, 149A, in Gregory the Theologian, 'Orationes' 27–45, *Patrologia Graeca* 36, 9–623.

105 Germanos I of Constantinople, 'Letter to Thomas of Claudiopolis', *Patrologia Graeca* 98, 147–222; 192B.

106 Dionysius, 'De Caelesti Hierarchia', 140D, in C. Luibheid & P. Rorem (trans.), *Dionysius the Areopagite: The Complete Works*, Classics of Western Spirituality Series (New York 1987) 149.

107 Louth, *Denys the Areopagite*, 38–40.

108 B. Teitelbaum, 'The Knowledge of God', *Eirenikon*, vol. 3, 1 (Fall 1982) 40–47.

Maximus upheld the 'theandric' understanding of reality based on the notion of unity (by grace) between humanity and God.[109] This ontological statement is influenced by the assumption that the created order is an expression of the Logos, who, by becoming man, introduced a new relationship between creator and creatures. In this context, the assumption of early Christians regarding the so-called *logoi* of creation should not be overlooked, mainly within the framework of natural knowledge of God (*phisiki* theory). This concept refers to the mystical contemplation of the *logoi* of creation, leading to knowledge of the Logos and ultimately the Holy Trinity.[110] The importance of this doctrinal assumption is the fact that human beings, on account of their 'logical constitutions', are able, through contemplation of things in their *logoi*, to keep the created universe together and to refer it to its primary cause.[111] Hence, according to Maximus, the revelations of God given to the saints, as well as the Old Testament visions of him, are perceivable signs of his divine presence, yet never revealing his essence. Maximus thought that the true contemplatives, like Abraham, are able to perceive the three angelic forms as a symbolic representation of the Trinity.[112] In the same way, the iconographers who attempt to portray the Trinity seek to accentuate God's transcendence and, at the same time, show their ability to perceive him according to their level of perfection.[113] Rublev followed the same principle in his icon of the Trinity. The three angels are identified by their attitudes and meaningful gestures as the three hypostases (the Father, the Son and the Holy Spirit); they are dissimilar while being almost identical.[114]

Although many contemporary scholars agree that Rublev's icon does not represent the narrative of Genesis 18 in historical terms, but instead shows the divine council of the Trinity, there is a discrepancy in their views over the designation of the three angels. Ouspensky[115] and Lazarev[116] understood the middle angel to be Christ and the left angel to be God the Father. Golubstov,[117]

---

109 J. Pelikan, 'Council of Father or Scripture: The Concept of Authority in the Theology of St Maximus the Confessor', in D. Neiman & M. Schatkin (eds), *The Heritage of the Early Church*, Orientalia Christiana Analecta 195 (Roma 1973) 227–288.

110 This doctrine was introduced by Origen and developed by Evagrius Ponticus, Pseudo-Dionysius, and later, Maximus; see L. Thundberg, 'The Human Person as an Image of God', *Christian Spirituality*, vol. 16 (1985) 303; see also Maximus the Confessor, 'Ambiguorum Liber 7', in *Patrologia Graeca* 91, 1031–1418; 1081BC.

111 J. Rossum, 'The Logoi of Creation and the Divine Energies in Maximus the Confessor and Gregory Palamas', *Studia Patristica*, vol. 27 (1993) 212–217.

112 Maximus the Confessor, 'Epistula 2', *Patrologia Graeca* 91, 400CD, in L. Thundberg, *Microcosm and Mediator*, 137–139.

113 L.M. Evseeva, 'Две Символические Композиции в Росписи XIV века Монастыря Зарзма', *Византийский Временник*, vol. 43 (1982) 134–140.

114 N.A. Demina, *Троица Андрея Рублева* (Moscow 1963) 52, 105.

115 L. Voronov, 'Андрей Рублев-Великий Художник Древней Руси', *Богословские труды*, no. 14 (1975) 83–86.

116 Lazarev, *Андрей Рублев и его Школа* (Moscow 1966) 61–62.

117 Golubtsov, 'Воплощение Богословских Идей в Творчестве Преподобного Андрея Рублева', *Богословские Труды*, no 22 (1983) 3–67.

Demina and Vetelev were in favour of taking the middle angel to be God the Father while Christ was the angel on the left. Ainalov believed the middle angel represented God the Father, the left one was Christ, and the right one was the Holy Spirit.[118] Lebedev offered three options for reading the Old Testament Trinity of Rublev.[119] First, the three angels represent the three hypostases of the Father, the Son and the Holy Spirit. Secondly, Genesis 18 was a vision of Jesus Christ as God accompanied by two angels. Finally, the three angels represent the 'image and likeness' of the Holy Trinity. This interpretation was based on the inscription found in the so-called Zyrian 'Trinity' (Fig. 54) from Vologda's Cathedral (1395), commonly credited to Stephen of Perm, a disciple of Sergius of Radonezh. This model is often used to help with identifying each of three angels in Rublev's icon of the Trinity. Although researchers claim Stephen of Perm provided an inscription on each of the three angels in the Zyrian Trinity, a closer examination reveals the inscription, located in the centre of the composition, refers to the Trinity at large.

The issue regarding the designation of the three angels was resolved during the Council of Stoglav in 1551. The canons of this council state that the hypostasis of the Father is on the left, and the house behind him symbolises the house of creation. His hand points to the chalice, calling the Son to take upon himself the work of salvation. Christ is the central angel, and the tree behind him represents the cross and the redemptive work of God the Son. His head is bowed gently to the Father, indicating total and faithful obedience. To see God the Father is impossible (John 1:18), 'because people cannot see Him and live' (Exodus 33:20). Only the Son gives this opportunity: 'No one comes to the Father except through me' (John 14:6). The Holy Spirit is on the right side. He is the comforter, the Paraclete, witnessing the holy act of divine self-dedication.

Whether any of these hypotheses can be taken as valid is difficult to ascertain; however, the various definitions reflect the failure of the Eastern and Western church to resolve their diverging views on Trinitarian theology during the hesychast controversy. Palamists condemned the *filioque* clause and affirmed the Holy Spirit proceeds from the Father alone.[120] Palamists believed *filioquism* invalidated the appropriate antinomy between Monad and Triad. Moreover, it stripped the three hypostases of their concrete properties and turned God into abstract essence. The Western church underscored the consubstantiality of God, leading to a neglect of inter-hypostatic differences. The followers of hesychasm,

---

118 A. Glebova et al., 'Древнерусское Искусство в Собрании Вологодского Музея-Заповедника: Путеводитель по Экспозиции', *Северный Паломник*, vol. 11 (2004) 20–22; Uliyanov, *О Месте Иконы Живоначальной Троицы в Праздничном Ряду Русского Иконостаса Троицкие Чтения 2003–2004 гг. Большие Вяземы* (Moscow 2004) 44–47.

119 L.L. Lebedev, 'Кто Изображен на Иконе 'Троица' Андрея Рублева?, *Наука и Религия*, vol. 10 (Moscow 1988) 60–64.

120 Gregory Palamas, *Dialogue between an Orthodox and a Barlaamite* (Oxford 1999) 3.

on the other hand, accentuated the differences between the three hypostases of the Trinity. The Chalcedonian and post-Chalcedonian Christological doctrine grounded on the doctrine of the hypostatic union of two natures in Christ served as a conceptual basis for the hesychast refutation of the Western concept of the Trinity.[121] In turn, the dogma of hypostatic union of divine and human natures in Christ, as well as the patristic doctrine of *hoomousios* gave support to hesychast teaching, implying that the divine life is accessible only through deification of the body of Christ and participation in the sacraments. To support their claim, the hesychasts referred to Gregory the Theologian and John of Damascus,[122] both of whom defended the conceptual difference between the three hypostases in the Trinity.[123] The hesychastic focus on the hypostatic difference of the Father, the Son and the Holy Spirit informed the iconography of the Old Testament's Trinity as clearly indicated in Rublev's icon.[124]

Guided by a conviction of the need for and benefit of love, Rublev emphasised the unity of the Godhead and reaffirmed the hypostatic difference of the Father, the Son and the Holy Spirit. He adorns the three angels with iconographic characteristics to point their different functions within the Trinity.[125]

The first angel, shown at the left, is vested in a blue undergarment. His light-purple outer garment attests to his unfathomable nature and royal dignity and his demeanour reflects this fatherly authority. The expression on his face and the position of his head and hands, his gaze aimed at the two other angels and the way he is sitting, point to the hypostasis of the Father.

The eyes of the two other angels are turned attentively toward the first angel, as though conversing with him about the salvation of humanity. The central angel wears blue outer robes signifying his divinity and celestial nature. His dark-crimson undergarment symbolises the incarnation.[126] The second angel is Christ, the Son of God.[127] The light blue undergarment and the smoky-green outer garment, representing heaven and earth, suggest the angel on the right is the Holy Spirit. By him, every soul that lives ascends in purity. The mountain above the third angel indicates this advancement, assisted by the power of the divine grace.

---

121 Dulskis, 'Hesychast Ideas'.

122 John of Damascus, 'Homily of the Transfiguration', in H. Weatherby (trans.), *Greek Orthodox Theological Review*, vol. 32 (1987) 10.

123 Palamas, *The Triads* iii, I, 22, in J. Meyendorff (ed. & trans.), 2nd edn (Louvain 1973) 596–569.

124 Gregory the Theologian, 'Oratio 29', 16, in *Patrologia Graeca* 36, 9–623; 96.

125 N. Malitskii, 'К Истолкованию Композиции Троицы,' *Seminarium Kondakovianum* (Moscow 1928) 30.

126 Saltykov, 'Иконография Троицы Андрея Рублева', 77–85.

127 J. Reimer, 'The Spirituality of Andrei Rublev's Icon of the Holy Trinity', *Acta Theologica Supplementum*, vol. 11 (2008) 167–169.

Apart from Rublev having adorned his three angels with individual characteristics[128] he also placed them in a circle to allude to the doctrine of the mutual relations of the three hypostases in the Trinity.[129]

Both the models of Rublev's Trinity and the conversational relationship of the three angels express the notion of unity and divine oneness of the Trinity.[130] As a qualitative category, the unity of the Trinity is expressed in various ways. For example, Rublev eliminates the concept of time from this icon, showing the essence of time—eternity. The differentiation between the images of the three angels affirms the notion of Trinitarian unity.[131] The three angels differ in postures and gestures, but a circular rotation embraces their bodies in a dance, which if sped up will blur the distinctions between them. Finally, the placement of Christ at the centre of the icon also creates the sense of unity and allows the observer to meditate on the nature of the Trinity. Without the participation of the Father and the Holy Spirit, Christ would have been unable to fulfil his salvific act of humanity.

Formal qualities of Rublev's icon of the *Trinity*

The movement in Rublev's *Trinity* is described with attention to the icon's properties of quietness, gentleness, anxiety, and sorrow; or the mood permeating the icon, which is often described as detached, meditative, contemplative, intimate, gentle and direct. The image of the middle angel, however, from whom all movement proceeds is invested with a note of sovereignty, independence and strength. Thus, Rublev's *Trinity* produces a lyrical aura of harmony and quietness while simultaneously it conveys the rhythmic movement of an unstoppable power.[132]

The figures of the three angels are almost symmetrical, and seem frozen in deep spiritual peace, a holy calm assuming an inward movement.[133] The mirror symmetry on the opposing sides of the icon reflects stability and equilibrium.[134] The outlines on the back of the left and right angels coincide exactly, although

128 Gregory the Theologian, Oratio 29, 16; *Patrologia Graeca* 36, 96.

129 Nikephoros, 'Logos' 18, 19, in *Patrologia Graeca* 100, 584–790; 580–581; Nikephoros, 'Epistula ad Leonem III Papam', in *Patrologia Graeca* 100, 170–206; 181–184.

130 C. Chaillot, 'Contemplating Rublev's Icon: The Authority of the Trinity and the Community of Man and Women in the Church', *The Ecumenical Review*, vol. 60, no. 1–2 (Jan.–Apr. 2008) 137–144.

131 Evdokimov, 'The Icon of the Holy Trinity', *Lutheran World*, vol. 23, no. 3 (1976) 166–170.

132 L. Teholiz, 'Religious Mysticism and Socialist Realism: The Soviet Union Pays Homage to the Icon Painter', *Art Journal*, vol. 21, no. 2 (Winter 1961–1962) 72–78.

133 A. Titz, 'Some General Features of the Compositions of the Icons of Rublyov and His School', *Ancient Russian Art of the Fifteenth and Early Sixteenth Centuries* (Moscow 1963) 22–53.

134 A.V. Voloshinov, 'The Old Testament Trinity of Andrey Rublyov: Geometry and Philosophy', *Leonardo*, vol. 32, no. 2, (1999) 103–112.

their faces and haloes are shifted slightly. The mountain and the building are also symmetrically positioned. Parallel lines emerge, vanishing and re-emerging at different points, but in the same direction, drawing all elements of the icon, including buildings, the three angels and the rock into the flow of forms.[135]

Against the symmetry and equilibrium of the group, a movement starts from the Father, with two counter movements bringing the second and the third person back to the first. A movement proceeds from the back of the Father's shoulders, which is directed towards the middle angel and the angel on the left. This motion is strengthened by the location of the emblematic house. A counter movement starts from the foot of the Father and gains momentum as it passes through the posterior of the Spirit, lingers over the hands of the central angel and the angel on the right and finally comes to rest in the Father.[136] The Son and the Holy Spirit carry within them, by implication, the entire creation, including the onlooker, in return to the Father. Hence, though Rublev concentrated on the inverted perspective and expressed eternity by excluding earthly movement, the three figures create the perfect movement of love.[137]

While the Father places one of his hands atop the other, the hands of the Son and the Holy Spirit are apart. It confirms the traditional viewpoint that the Son and the Holy Spirit represent the two modes of operation of the Father. The Son responds to the Fathers' calling by consenting to perform the assigned act of incarnation, so the action of his movement expresses love and obedience.[138] He bows his head to the right, in the direction of the first angel. Alpatov noted the elevation of the left knee of the middle angel, whereas his right knee remains in place. Clearly, the middle angel gets up and follows the guidance of the first angel.[139] Moreover, the rising stance of this angel portrays his descent into the world and his commitment to the redemptive work of sacrifice. The act of salvation of humanity commences from the Father, it is followed by the Son, continues in the Holy Spirit before returning to the Father. The circular movement reaches a degree of climax in the middle angel. The two angels conceal signs of firmness under the all-pervading beauty of the image, and the icon reflects their free will and consistent and full implementation of their decisions. The fact the three angels epitomise one other alludes to the hesychast theology of *synergia*, as well the doctrinal concept of *perichoresis* (mutual indwelling of each person of the Trinity within the Godhead).[140]

---

135 D. Snyman, 'In the Gaze of God: Aspects of the Spiritual Significance of Rublev's Holy Trinity', MA thesis, Rhodes University (2001) 68–84.

136 N. Nikeforov, 'Икона Святой Троицы Преподобного Андрея Рублева', *Источник: Православная Жизнь*, vol. 51, no. 5 (1955) 616.

137 Dionysius, *De Divinis Nominibus* II, 7.

138 Opie, 'The Trinity in Andrei Rublev's Icon', 202.

139 Alpatov, 'La Valeur Classique de Rublev', *Commentari*, vol. 1 (1958) 25–37.

140 Perichoresis is a Greek term used to describe the Triune relationship between each person of the Godhead. It can be defined as co-indwelling, co-inhering, and mutual interpenetration; Golubstov, 'Пресвятая Троица и Домостроительство', *Журнал Московской Патриархии*, vol. 7 (1960) 37.

The first angel sits more front-on than the rest. In addition to the gesture of his blessing, the rod of the first angel is pushed forward, while the rods of the second and the third angel are bent.[141] His hands are also close to each other, which reflects self-discipline and focus. The image of God the Father is powerful, not just relative to the Son, but also in regards to the Holy Spirit. The Father aims his gesture of blessing at the second, and the third angel. The posture of the third angel on the right reflects the greatest peace and concentration, even a certain looseness and softness. His rod rests on his shoulder, and its lower part rests against the outside of his right thigh, not between the knees. This position conveys thoughtful, leisurely reflection.[142]

In contrast to the general peace coming from the third angel, the position of his wings is dynamic. If the wings of the first and the second angel are smooth, the wings of the third angel suggest movement in varying degrees. The rise of the left wing transfers the viewer's eye to the mountain to express a spiritual uplift that complements the symbolism of spiritual rest.[143] The states of motion and rest in the third angel show predominantly through symbols. On the contrary, the motion in the central angel is expressed by discrete forms, such as the form of his wings which are almost flattened in opposition.[144] The Father's wings overlap those of the Son and the wings of the Spirit and the Son touch each other without overlapping. Thus, the Father generates the Son and causes the Spirit to proceed while the Spirit reposes in the Son but proceeds from the Father alone.

The three viewpoints of the icon are represented by the left angel to the right, the right angel to the left and the middle to the front. The two angels on the side present opposite points of view, which leads to an inverted perspective of the communion table. Since the size of this table is inadequate to the space, Rublev placed its sides behind the knees of angels.[145] The background is larger than the foreground, and the chalice pushes to the outer end of the traprezoid table, a feature that is repeated in the podium. The trapezoid form is the result of the unfolding of the surfaces of a regular square form, of which only the rear parts are lost in the representation. The process of unfolding is visible in the chairs and further denotes recession. The use of the reverse perspective takes the observer inside the icon, allowing him to experience a vision of the Trinity outside historical parameters. The icon provides the viewer with a visual representation of the otherwise hidden Holy Secret.[146]

---

141 Opie, 'The Trinity in Andrei Rublev's Icon', 202–209.

142 Demina, Андрей Рублев и Художники его Круга (Moscow 1963) 48.

143 Titz, 'Some General Features'.

144 Observations on geometry are based on Voloshinov, 'The Old Testament Trinity'.

145 A. Uspenskiĭ, *Semiotics of the Russian Icon* (Philadelphia 1976) 64–65.

146 C. Antonova, *Space, Time, and Presence in the Icon: Seeing the World With the Eyes of God* (Ashgate 2010) 162.

The composition of the Trinity also contains two centres of gravity, one above the middle angel and the other above the left angel. In the two-dimensional perspective, positioning the second angel represents the natural centre, in respect of the assured symmetry of the first and third angels. Following the laws of three-dimensional perspective, however, the fact that the image of the middle angel is higher on the pictorial plane corresponds to the equal position of angels in real space.[147] Nevertheless, Rublev shifts the centre of gravity close to the angel on the left by turning the head of the middle angel in the direction of the left angel.

The diagonals of the icon are, at the same time, diagonals of the arc. As a result, there is no difference if the proportions of the composition of the figurative scene are calculated on the inner outline (the outline of the arc) or on the outer, that is, the contour of the whole icon. There is an unlimited scale of golden proportions relative to the centre of Rublev's icon.[148] For any point inside the circle, a parallel point on the opposite side is found, that is to say, in golden proportion to the given point.[149] The icon has a harmonious proportion, expressed in the silhouettes of the three figures on the surface of the board.[150] This ideal ratio of angels can be likened to the equality of angles in a triangle.[151]

Rublev's placement of the three angels onto an implicit circle is a key innovation, as is the placement of the chalice at the centre of the composition.[152] The aesthetic of the circle, with a higher degree of perfection, led Pythagoras to develop the hypothesis of the circular trajectory of planetary orbits. Different cultures have used the circle as a symbol for the sky and everything lofty, eternal and close to God. The cycle was always viewed as an expression of eternity and everlasting love, as noted by Dionysius.[153] The circular movement signifies that God remains identical with himself and that he envelops (creation) in synthesis and recalls to himself all that has gone forth from him.[154] The hesychast meditation technique is also circular: God flows out to humanity and gives knowledge of him, and humanity responds, through the mind and body, to his call.[155]

---

147 P. Florensky, 'Reverse Perspective', in N. Misler (ed.), W. Salmond (trans.), *Beyond Vision: Essays on the Perception of Art* (London 2002) 201.

148 V. Petrov & N. Pryanishnicov, 'The Formulas of Beautiful Proportions', *Number and Thought*, vol. 2 (Moscow 1979) 72–92.

149 C. Ungureanu, 'Dialogue between Sphere and Cube: The Secrete Geometry of Byzantine Icons', *Cultura: International Journal of Philosophy of Culture and Axiology*, vol. 6 (2006) 88.

150 B. Ioganson, 'Великий Русский Художник', Правда (14 Sept. 1960) 6.

151 O. Boonpitak et al., 'Aspects of Symmetry', 15–18; www.uic.edu/honors/learning/hc_aspects_4.pdf (accessed 02/02/2011).

152 Hunt, 'Andrei Rublev's Old Testament Trinity Icon', 3.

153 E. Wilberding, 'A *Defense* of Dionysius the Areopagite by Rubens', *Journal of the History of Ideas*, vol. 52, no. 1 (Jan.–Mar., 1991) 19–34.

154 G.M. Prokhorov, *Dionisii Aeropagit* (St Petersburg 1995) 291.

155 Meyendorff, 'Le Theme du Retour en Soi dans le Doctrine Palamite du XIV siecle', *Byzantine Hesychasm: Historical, Theological and Social Problems* (London 1972) 204–206.

Rublev's icon is inscribed in three circles: the circle of the faces, the arms and wings of the angels on the side, and the arms of the angel in the middle and the central chalice.[156] Interestingly, not one but three manifestations of a chalice emerge. The first chalice is the sacrificial faith offering of Abraham to the three angels who visited his house. The second is God's sacrifice in Christ for humanity (the Eucharist). The third is the chalice of the Trinity, in which the whole Trinity participates in the salvation of humanity.[157]

Most art historians locate circles at the centre of the icon using the golden rectangle. These circles form concentric rings connecting the face of the left angel with the hand of right one, and the face of the angel in the middle with the chalice. When looking at the middle angel within the circle, it becomes clear the he neither suppresses nor dominates the other angels, although he appears to be placed higher than they are. Ungureanu's description of the composition's three circles is different.[158] He interprets the circle inscribed in the rectangle that corresponds to the painted surface of the Holy Trinity icon as the circle of the Son. The green circle, inscribed between the horizontals obtained by connecting the small sides of the square, is the circle of the Holy Spirit. When the circle of the Holy Spirit doubles with the light of his radius, the circle of the Father is obtained. The chord obtained from the intercession of the circles is the side of an equilateral triangle inscribed in the circle of the Holy Spirit. The circle in this triangle is the circle of the Father. The grace circle that inscribes the square within the icon is the one which gives form and dimension to the representation of the Holy Trinity.[159] The position of the sceptres in the hands of the three angels, however, determines the problem of geometrical space.[160]

The circular movement alludes to the doctrine of *perichoresis*. It is precisely because the Father, the Son and the Holy Spirit unite in the Trinity[161] that Rublev gives the same characteristics to each of them, distinguishing them by postures, the colours of their robes and spatial positions. A dynamic pattern of rotational symmetry connects the three angels.[162] Their round dance is charmingly depicted in Rublev's icon where the dogma of *perichoresis* involves 'making room', at the centre of the Hospitality. The artist has created a space that enfolds, yet permits discernment. Hence, this icon makes a room for the observer, and offers hospitality to him as a fourth guest. The Trinity is like the centre of the cosmos, and the centre of the Trinity is the chalice featured in the centre of the table.

156 Snyman, 'In the Gaze of God', 35–57, 20–22.

157 Alpatov, 'La Valeur Classique de Rublev', 30–37.

158 Ungureanu, 'Dialogue between Sphere and Cube', 83–90.

159 Voloshinov, 'The Old Testament Trinity'.

160 D. Pedoe, *Geometry and the Liberal Arts* (Harmondsworth 1976).

161 K. Ware, 'The Human Person as an Icon of the Trinity', *Sobornost*, vol. 8, no. 2 (1986) 18.

162 E.P. Buschevitch, 'The Limits of Hesychasm: Some Notes on the Monastic Spirituality in Russia 1350–1500', *Forsch sur Osteurop Gesc*, vol. 38 (1986) 97–109.

Rublev's use of blue also manifests the Trinitarian ontological power, that is, the outpouring of divine energies and the angels' relation with one another (*perichoresis*).[163] The blue outer garment of the central angel faces us and flows downward over his left shoulder, as his tunic flows down over the chalice. This feature alludes to the sacrificial act of God in history. The inside of the second angel's garment is blue on the shoulder and reappears under the table, at the third angel's feet.[164] This alludes to the Spirit continuing the work of Christ. The blue of the third angel is visible at his centre and shines through within, as whitish and bluish highlights, and also suffuses his other garments. Used in this manner, azure and blue summarise the outer and inner action of two other angels, giving the icon a serene, shimmering and unearthly beauty.[165] It also signifies Christ's historical manifestation of the uncreated light that he shares with the Father.[166] This corresponds to the ontological position of the three hypostases of the Trinity, which are *hoomousios* (of the same substance) with each other.[167] The chalice is also a symbol of providence, by which God realises all in all and embodies his essential self-sameness and immovability.[168]

Just like the circles, three octagons emerge when a circumference touches the horizontal sides of the arc of the icon. The smallest octagon includes the focal point of the composition, that is, the chalice and the arms stretching towards it. The middle octagon involves the central elements of the scene — the angels and the sacrificial chalice and finally, the largest octagon embraces all elements of the figurative scene with mathematical precision. It mirrors the slopes of the angels' thrones and pedestals, the axonometric axis of the left building, and even the tangent of the right mountain.[169] The octagon reflects a hesychast concept of the eighth day or Parousia as affirmed by the 12th-century mystic, Symeon the New Theologian. He held the cosmic week of seven millennia culminates in the age of Christ. He has already, in time, mystically inaugurated the eighth day of the new creation beyond time. According to Symeon, the coming of the Lord has already taken place, and the revelation of divinity became, in fact, a judgment for those to whom it is revealed.[170]

The abundant use of gold, golden-yellow and golden-greenish for the background and fields, for the angel's wings, low seats and foot rests, for the walls and ceiling and the chalice, imparts to the icon a serene, shimmering, unearthly

---

163 Hunt, 'Andrei Rublev's Old Testament Trinity Icon: Problems of Meaning, Intertextuality, and Transmission', *A Journal of Russian (Religious) Thought*, vol. 7–12 (2002–2007) 15–46.

164 Ungureanu, 'Dialogue between Sphere and Cube', 82–96.

165 Alpatov, 'On the Global Significance of Andrey Rublyov's Art', *Khudozhnik*, vol. 12 (1980) 48–57.

166 V.G. Briusova, *Бруисова Андрея Рублева и Московскои Школы Иконописи* (Moscow 1998) 351.

167 Strezova, 'Knowledge and Vision of God in Cappadocian Fathers', online paper, http://www.oodegr.com/english/filosofia/gnwsi_8ewria_kappadokes.htm (accessed 10/09/2011).

168 Hunt, 'Andrei Rublev's Old Testament Trinity Icon', 112.

169 Voloshinov, 'The Old Testament Trinity', 106–108.

170 E.S. Smirnova, *Litsevye Rukopisi Velikogo Novgorod a XV vek* (Moscow 1994) 189–190.

beauty of the 'age to come'. Rublev also used the technique of scumbling; that is softening the outlines or colour by applying thin coats of opaque colour. The result is the three heavenly visitors are transfigured like a luminous cloud. Rublev's contemporaries called it *dymon pisano*; e.g., transparent like smoke.[171] The clothing of the left angel reveals Rublev's mastery of the scumbling technique; shining through the delicate pink-purplish tone of the himation, the reflection of light on the edges on the folds enlightens the blue of his tunic.[172]

Rublev offered other puzzles in the form of recessed colour, light and shadows. The two most intense areas in the image are the black doorways of the house above the angel on the left. These are much darker than the cloak of the central figure or the chalice, which is the focal point of the composition.[173] The two optical mysteries match one another in the foreground: the absence of shadow in the recess made in the table below the chalice.[174] As the shadows change according to position, to be in all positions at once is to see no shadow. 'The lack of the contrast of shadow and light in the depiction of icon figures refers to individuals who are psychologically fully integrated'.[175] As many other 14th- and 15th-century Russian painters did before him, Rublev made the rare appearance of shadows an expression of the uncreated light, the light that does not come from a particular place but rather comes from the Godhead who resides in all places at once. The light of celestial objects, such as the sun or other stars, is subject to variation, whereas the uncreated light of God has no variations.[176] This feature represents the uncreated light manifested to the apostles at the Transfiguration on Mt Tabor. The saints perceive this light during prayer. The iconographers represented it in the shape of a halo or mandorla in art. The light seen at the Transfiguration is also the 'light of the *Parousia*'.[177]

Rublev's icon of the *Trinity* in the context of 15th- and 16th-century art

Rublev's *Trinity* is amongst the greatest achievements of Russian art. Crowning the extensive artistic career of a master, it was also the epitome of the ingenious thought of numerous authors.[178] Like any other medieval artist, Rublev

171 Golunstov, 'Икона Живоначальной Троицы'.

172 Chaillot, 'Contemplating Rublev's Icon'.

173 S. Brooks (ed.), *Byzantium: Faith and Power 1261–1557 Perspectives of Late Byzantine Art and Culture* (New York 2007) 188.

174 D. Mouriki, 'Αφηγηματική Σκηνή ή Εικονιστική Παράσταση', *Δελτίον της Χριστιανικης 'Αρχαιολογικης Εταιρείας*, vol. 4, no. 3 (Athens 1962–1963) 87–114.

175 D. Milivojevic, 'Semiotics of Russian and Serbian Icons' http://nesusvet.narod.ru/ico/books/mlvjvch/ (accessed 10/03/2012).

176 M. Casey, *The Trinity of Rublev* (London 1981) 93.

177 Gregory Palamas, *Triads*, I, 3, 43, in K. Ware, 'God Hidden and Revealed: The Apophatic Way and the Essence–Energies Distinction', *Eastern Churches Review*, vol. 7, no. 2 (1975) 132–145.

178 Lazarev, 'Андрей Рублев и его Школа, 37–40; M.A. Ilin, *Искусство Московской Руси Эпохи Феофана Грека и Андрея Рублева: Проблемы, Хипотезы, Исследования* (Moscow 1976) 51–54.

esteemed tradition and collective effort. A method of theoretical generalisation, outwardly abstract, but with a remarkably tangible content, an aptitude to affirm through symbolic images the domestic character, as well as the creative expertise attaining to the zenith of world art combined in Rublev's icon. So pronounced was Rublev's reputation that the 1551 Church council, held in Moscow,[179] recommended that all icon painters must follow Rublev's canon of painting, and use ancient images painted by Greek iconographers and Rublev as models.[180]

Rublev abandoned many features that made explicit reference to the text of Genesis 18: Abraham and Sarah are missing, and there are no utensils on the table. In Rublev's innovative reinterpretation of the Biblical text, there is no praise of Abraham's hospitality; rather, the purpose of the icon is to express the psychological idea of unity as well as the undivided nature of the Father, the Son and the Holy Spirit.[181]

Such dogmatical issues were often explored by Rublev's spiritual teacher Sergius, who brought the tradition of the hesychast-style of contemplation to Russia. He took the veneration of the Trinity as a sign of the unity of celestial and terrestrial realms, and the unity of heavenly and earthly hierarchy and of the Church. The unity of the Trinity was a symbol of the unity of both Testaments, enshrined in the Russian national consciousness.

Sergius adhered to the mystical tradition of hesychasm.[182] He received visions of the Trinity, of the divine light and of the Theotokos and these revelations inspired works praising the cult of the Trinity. An important composition is the *Apparition of the Virgin to Sergius of Radonezh* (Fig. 55) which depicts the vision of the mother of God, accompanied by the apostles Peter and John, promising to watch over the monastery. An extant example, from the Trinity Lavra of St Sergius, is kept at the Museum of Art at the University of Oregon.[183] That Sergius's vision matches Abraham's vision of the three angels in the Old Testament is important for three reasons: the artwork affirms the special affinity that the saint had with the Trinity, it asserts the importance of the Virgin Mary in the economy of salvation,[184] and it attests to the iconographer's preoccupation with the uncreated light of God.[185]

---

179 E.B. Emchenko, *Стоглав: Исследование и Текст* (Moscow 2000) 304.

180 C. Lock, 'The Space of Hospitality'; After Rublevs's death his icon was copied by Nichephorus Grablenij. The prototype became a trademark of Trinity Sergius Lavra monastery. Rublev's *Trinity* also influenced narrative cycles in the history of Abraham, such as the Novgorod Bible of 1477 (Moscow Museum of History).

181 Hunt, 'Andrei Rublev's Old Testament Trinity Icon: Problems of Meaning, Intertextuality, and Transmission', 38.

182 ibid., 105.

183 P. Buschkevich, 'The Limits of Hesychasm'.

184 Alpatov, *Russian Impact on Art* (Moscow 1950) 41.

185 Plugin, 'Сергий Радонежский , Дмитрий Донской, Андрей Рублев', *История СССР* (Moscow 1989) 71–88.

In the later versions of this icon, the image of the Hospitality of Abraham is placed above the figure of the Virgin (Genesis 18). This feature is evidence of the connection between this image and Rublev's icon. In turn, the likenesses between Rublev's *Trinity* and the *Apparition of the Virgin* point to the influence of Sergius's spiritual teaching on Rublev. Clearly, there are iconographic differences in both models that are reflected in the positions assumed by the righteous welcoming their celestial visitors in the icon of the *Apparition*,[186] as well as the number of chalices depicted. Instead of one chalice, as found in Rublev's *Trinity*, three chalices are placed on the table. The three chalices evoke God's transcendence as a self-identity, which paradoxically exceeds its limits in interaction with another being. As a result, one knows its ontological nature, its inner being in God.[187] Furthermore, the combination of stillness and motion communicates the essential oneness of the Trinity, the centre of the hesychast response to Barlaam's definition: that God's transcendence is unknowable by definition.[188] The shape of the circle represents a communion of angels united in *hesychia*, the ideal monastic community which Sergius wished to establish.

A new icon of the *Trinity* from the Trinity Sergius's Lavra (Fig. 56), created about the same time as Rublev's *Trinity*, affirms the doctrines of Sergius, paralleling Palamas's teachings on the Uncreated Light[189] as well as with Iosif Volotsky's tradition of безмолвие.[190] As this icon belongs to Sergiev's Posad, it is possible its creator and Rublev were in the same monastic community, working together on the decoration of the stone church of the Trinity.[191] Providing a vision of the Old Testament Trinity, both icons are almost identical. Rublev, however, overcome the inherent difficulties artists faced when depicting the consubstantial and indivisible nature of the Trinity.[192] The unknown painter of the *Trinity* icon from the Trinity Sergius's Lavra, on the other hand, reflects a patristic-liturgical interpretation of Genesis 18, which perceives all Old Testament theophanies as manifestations of the Word.[193] In the earlier depiction of the Trinity, the central angel has a note of sovereignty, independence and strength, whereas the ontological distinction between other two hypostases of the Trinity is not clearly affirmed. The left and the right angel are distinguished with features such as drapery and the colour of the clothes. Subtle changes undercut the

---

186 While Abraham and Sarah are not represented in Rublev, they assume an almost liturgical function in the icon of the apparition.

187 Plugin, 'Мастер Святой Троицы', 325.

188 Hunt, 'Andrei Rublev's Old Testament Trinity Icon', 103.

189 D.M. Goldfrank, *The Monastic Rule of Iosif Volotsky* (Kalamazoo 2000).

190 L. Muller, 'Epiphanius, Die Legenden des Heiligen Sergij von Radonez', *Slavische Propylaen*, vol. 17 (Munich 1967) 40–49.

191 M.N. Tikhomirov, *Андрей Рублев и его Эпоха* (Moscow 1967) 3–15.

192 E.I. Ostashenko, 'Троица Ветхозаветная', *Сергиево-Посадского Музея-Заповедника и Проблема Стиля Живописи Первой Трети* (St Petersburg 2002) 324.

193 Louth, 'The Oak of Mamre, the Fathers and St Andrei Rublev: Patristic Interpretation of the Hospitality of Abraham and Rublev's Icon of the Trinity', *The Trinity Sergius Lavra in Russian History and Culture*, ed. V. Tsurikov (London 2005) 3, 91–96.

rhythm and link Christ to the messengers, such as the angles shared by the central the angel and right-hand angel, which are not symmetrical with one another and do not express a shared relationship with the left-hand angel, as is the case in Rublev's icon. The landscape features in the icon of the *Trinity* from the Monastery of Sergius of Radonezh are large and define the structure of the piece on the high–low axis.

The peripheral mountain and the church form the point of two spirals, beginning with the side angels and continuing with the cross shared between the central angel and the bowl (on the central axis) in the foreground, and the tree in the background.[194] The spirals point to the profound and beautiful interconnection between creator and creatures. The form of a spiral symbolises the process of moving outward and remaining still, thus yielding a curve so that 'created nature may return to God once again' (916D, 119).[195] The spiral on the left moves through the red colour of the middle angel's garment continuing to Sarah and finishes on the tilted axis formed by the central angel's head. The other spiral starts with the blue garments of the angel on the right continues to Abraham and then goes back around the church (with blue balustrades and a blue roof). The interlocking peaks of the spirals make the path of the cross join the chalice with Christ.[196] Instead of an inward movement towards greater fullness and inclusion, which symbolises the Trinitarian unity, the upward-facing bowls delineate the ascetic path.[197] The crossing paths of two spirals also create a circle that frames the torso of the Christ–angel and mirrors the circle of the central bowl. A larger circle enclosing the five figures mirrors the smaller circle and embodies a broader revolution of the same spiral.[198] To reveal the power of the Eucharist, the circles are taken upwards, which is evidence of the Resurrection.[199] This unique expression of God fully captures the imagination of the worshipper, in bringing the mind into a deeper sense of God. It is in this way that the minds of the worshippers, of the many, are brought back towards the understanding of the 'one', as suggested in Neoplatonic philosophy. The sign of the number seven in two sets of filigree circles as well as in the placement of seven fluted partitions in the cupola symbolises the divine energies and the Trinity revealing the Monad in the Triad.[200] Through the interaction of the Spirit with the other two persons,

---

194 I am indebted to P. Hunt who, in pointing to the appearance of spirals in this icon, inspired me to look beneath the suface; Hunt, 'Andrei Rublev's Old Testament Trinity Icon: Problems of Meaning, Intertextuality, and Transmission', 20–26.

195 T. Velmans, 'Le Rôle de l'Hésychasme dans la Peinture Murale Byzantine du XIVe et XVe Siècles', in P. Armstrong (ed.), *Ritual and Art: Byzantine Essays for Christopher Walter* (London 2006) 187–190; D.S. Lixačev, *Некоторые Задачи Изучения Второго Югославянского Влияния в России: Исследования по Славянскому Литературоведению и Фольклористик* (Moscow 1960) 128–139.

196 Hunt, 'Andrei Rublev's Old Testament Trinity Icon: Problems of Meaning, Intertextuality, and Transmission', 23.

197 Plugin, 'О Происхождении Троицы Рублева'.

198 D. Balfour, *Gregory the Sinaite, Discourse on the Transfiguration* (Princeton 1986) Section 8, 29–30.

199 Briusova, *Андрей Рублев и Московская Школа Иконописи*, 6–8.

200 R.E. Sinkewicz, *Saint Gregory Palamas: The One Hundred and Fifty Chapters* (Toronto 1988) 165, 167.

the Father and the Son, the Trinity exists and dominates Christian theology. It is with the reinterpretation of the Dionysius's neoplatonic triadic manifestations of God, however, that there was a deeper understanding of the Christian Trinity in the early Church.[201] The three angels having the same proportions, size and the same unmarked halo, proves the interaction of the Father, the Son and the Holy Spirit. Their circular interrelation, symbolising an inward attachment and communion reflects the gestures and postures of the three angels. This circular pattern differs from the spiral because it is not placed directly between the worshipper and icon. The circular motion of the soul moves in on itself, then outwards, towards the rest of the members.[202]

The mixture of red and gold dominates this icon, making the image a different visual experience for the viewer than Rublev's *Trinity*. The *Trinity* from the Monastery of St Sergius emphasises the symbolism of love, blood and the fire of martyrdom, confirmed by the use of red. The symbolism of the number seven presents the completeness and perfection achieved through participation in the spiritual fire of Christ (Proverbs 6:16–1; 9:1). This, in turn, alludes to the work of the Holy Spirit that began after the Pentecost.[203] The association of this icon with the Pentecost verifies the hesychast stand against *filioquism*: it shows the presence and manifestation of the Holy Spirit within the Church, inspiring unity, worship and service. It also places the feast of the Pentecost in eternal rather than temporal parameters, announcing ontological truths that would be fully accessible in the 'age to come'. This new iconography of the Holy Trinity, which appeared in Byzantium in the 14th century, and was later reflected in Rublev's *Trinity*, became widespread in Russia, where the Church already celebrated the feast of the Trinity.[204]

Other causes, which were at work simultaneously with the increase of hesychasm on Russian soil, affected the spread of Rublev's model of the Trinity in Russia. The anti-Trinitarian currents, which began to grow and spread in Russia during the 14th and 15th centuries, are worth noting.[205] The heretical sects in Russia, notably those of the 14th century, which are a direct continuation Bogomil and Cathar doctrines, rejected Trinitarian and Christological dogma.[206] Moreover, the sect of Strigolniki and of the Judaizers, which appeared in Pskov and Novgorod in the 14th century and were indirectly connected to Bogomilism, renounced

201 Luibheid & Rorem, *Dionysius the Areopagite*, 149.

202 J.K.N Hedrick, 'Visual Constructions in the Reign of Justinian: A Neo-Platonic Influence', *Journal of History and Social Science* (Spring 2010) 5–19.

203 Hunt, 'Andrei Rublev's Old Testament Trinity Icon: Problems of Meaning, Intertextuality, and Transmission', 20.

204 ibid., 21.

205 N.A. Kazakova & Ia. S. Lur'e, *Антифеодальные Еретические Движения на Руси Xiv-Начала Xvi века* (Moscow 1955) 34–71.

206 D.M. Goldfrank, 'Burn, Baby, Burn: Popular Culture and Heresy in Late Medieval Russia', *The Journal of Popular Culture* 31, no. 4 (1998) 17–32.

the Holy Trinity and the divine status of Jesus. Substantiating this point, these heretical sects came, finally, to a denial of the possibility of the image of the Trinity.[207] The spread of anti-Trinitarian currents generated a response from visual artists of this period. The increased production of Trinitarian *Paternitas* compositions, as well as images of the Old Testament Trinity (of Rublev's type) in the 14th and 15th centuries, demonstrates this fact. The anti-sectarian sentiment reflected in the spread of the cult of the Trinity in Russia during this period. A church feast was dedicated to the Trinity and was prominent in the provinces of Novgorod and Pskov.[208] In the religious and philosophical sense, these images as well as architectural objects aimed to represent the Christian ideal of life on earth, opened the way for the removal of dilemma — national or universal.[209]

A significant example of the *Trinity* from Rostov is representative of the way in which many artists from this region used Rublev's *Trinity* as a model for their paintings. In comparison to the hesychast type of Trinity exemplified by Rublev's icon, however, the new version of the Trinity emerging in Rostov and Pskov was created as a response to the acute anti-Trinitarian controversies in Russia. The Rostov type of Trinity has its own characteristics and aim, showing the hypostatic equality of the three hypostases of the Trinity and their unity in the single image of the Trinity. Hence, the new version of the Trinity surfaces with three angels seated in one row of a rectangular table; their heads placed strictly on the same level (Fig. 57). The anti-heretical role of the image is further affirmed by the use of two other iconographical features; the gesture of blessing of the three angels is the same and they all have crucifixes on haloes inscribed with a monogram of Christ.[210] This testifies to the probability that Pskov's school of painting fought against heresy by incorporating the characteristics of the Greek iconographic tradition of the 'Hospitality of Abraham' and combining them with those of the Russian tradition for representation of the Trinity. The use of the horizontal axis of the image of the angels, pillows on the seats, and the representation of rounded vessels points to Greek influence.[211] The model of Pskov incorporates many elements of symmetry from Russian artists. The three angels sit in the same position and the Eucharistic meal on the table forms a strong horizontal line. Simple details, such as the uneven texture and the abundance of gold decorations, suggest the painting is from the start of the 15th century. Other archaic features, such as the rectangular table, point to the iconographic tradition from the last quarter of the 14th century.

---

207 ibid., 20.

208 N.K. Gavryooshin, *Философия Русского Религиозного Искусства XVI–XX вв* (Moscow 1993) 200–201; Malickii, 'К Истории Композиций Ветхозаветной Троицы'.

209 J. Baggley, *Festival Icons for the Christian Year* (New York 2000) 152.

210 According to J. Shakarabei, in the Old Testament Abraham served God, who was accompanied by two angels; see Ilin, *Искусство Московской Руси Эпохи Феофана Грека и Андрея Рублева*, 50–58; Heimann, 'L'Iconographie de la Trinite: L'Art Chretien'.

211 Lazarev, 'Русская Иконопись от Истоков до Начала XVI века,' *Искусство*, no. 83 (2000) 79–80, 325.

The placement of the angels around the square table repeats the oriental type[212] of the *Trinity* icon of Novgorod (15th century), which is currently held at the Museum of History of Moscow (Музей истории Москвы) (Fig. 58).[213] The wings of the central angel are fully opened to produce movement beyond the composition. Implements on the table, large background features, and the figures of Abraham and Sarah, allude semantically to the historical presence of God. Three chalices are on the elongated table, with no shroud on it. The rhomboid shape of the bowl has no precedent.[214]

The central angel is Christ the Logos (he has a crucifix on his halo), but the main feature of Rublev's *Trinity* is not lost, as neither the Father nor the Spirit bear separate characteristics. Placed within a circle, the three angels refer to the Trinity as a whole, affirming the mutual indwelling of the Father, the Son and the Holy Spirit. Colours are restrained and warm and not as bright and transparent as in Rublev's *Trinity*. The composition is closer to the pictorial plane due to the emphatic treatment of the background. In comparison to the mystical meaning of Rublev's icon of the *Trinity*, the Trinitarian image from the Museum of History, Novgorod, affirms the realistic dimension of human salvation.

While the hesychast influence on Russia narrowed after 1504, and outward ritualistic monasticism replaced the teachings of Sergius and Nil Sorsky,[215] the movement's importance for Russian spirituality should not be underestimated (Figs 59, 60, 61).

The spread of hesychasm and the interchange between the Byzantine and Russian traditions reflected in the art of Mt Athos, resulted in paintings reflecting an intermingling of Russian and Byzantine style. Rublev painted his icon under the direct influence of Byzantine icons from Athos, where the cult of the Trinity existed before the 15th century. The icon of the *Trinity* from the Monastery of Vatopedi on Mt Athos (Fig. 62) and from the Byzantine Museum, Athens, attests to this fact. It is possible that the Vatopedi icon served as a prototype, due to the close associations between the monastic communities of the Trinity Sergeus's, Lavra, and those of Mt Athos, beginning in the time of Sergius and Metropolitan Cyprian.[216] The icon of the *Trinity* from the Monastery of Vatopedi, painted at the end of the 14th century, also attests to the widespread representation of the new hesychast iconography of the Holy Trinity, which first appeared in the miniature manuscript of *Parisinus Graecus* 1242 from 1375. Moreover, this variant alludes to the divine presence within history. It elaborates the Biblical

212 Malickii, 'Панагия Русского Музея с Изображением Троицы', *Материалы по Русскому Искусству*, vol. 1 (St Petersburg 1928) 34.

213 V.N. Lazarev, *Страницы Истории Новгородской Живописи* (Moscow 1977) 16, 19.

214 Evseeva, *Эсхатология 7000 года и Возникновение Высокого Иконостаса* (Moscow 2000) 411–430.

215 L.V. Betin, 'Митрополит Киприан к Феофан Грек', *Etudes Balkaniques*, vol. 1 (Sofia 1977) 109–115.

216 Florensky, 'Троице-Сергиевой Лавры: Сергиева Монастыря и в России', *Троице-Сергиевой Лавры Сергиева Монастыря* (Moscow 1919) 19–20.

narrative of the Hospitality of Abraham. The table and larger background features allude to Abraham's dwelling, the Oak of Mamre and Abraham and Sarah.[217] The *Trinity* of Vatopedi also emphasises Christ with his two messengers; which is a good expression of the sacramental mystery of the sacrifice of the Mass, for which Christ's incarnation is a precondition.[218] Moreover, the icon's exegesis affirms the power of the Eucharist in offering communion in the resurrection and descent of the Spirit. Finally, this icon also alludes to the Pentecost, while observing Christological parameters. The middle angel exhibits the traditional attributes of Christ the Logos. His figure and his wings are larger than the wings of the two other angels, his clothing shines, and he wears a cruciform nimbus. The middle angel is flanked by two other, smaller, angels.[219] The central angel serves as a centre to the symmetrical background features. While his right arm gestures at a large central bowl, his two messengers on either side of the table gesture towards two smaller bowls. Sarah and Abraham incline in an attitude of reverence and prayer towards the middle angel. They co-participate with the side angels who are blessing their respective bowls.[220] Abraham and Sarah take the priestly role by conversing with the angels (who are inserted between them). In response, the central angel turns to the side; he no longer raises his hand in blessing, but rather indicates with a benedictory gesture the chalice in front of him. The side angels are active participants; while the one on the right reaches out for the piece of bread or the vessel, the one on the left blesses the table. The architectural setting behind the angels is richly decorated. A unique feature is the portrayal of Abraham's tent as a cupola-like structure with seven divisions. This shows possible influence on the Vatopedi icon by the composition *Wisdom has Built her House*.[221]

The symbolism of the seven pillars of Wisdom's house asserts the energy of the Spirit and the gifts of grace, such as knowledge, prudence, sound judgement, counsel, understanding and power. The Vatopedi icon upholds the symbolism of the number seven as the sign of the completion of God's initial creative act. While Rublev's *Trinity* shows God's manifestation in the Church, the Vatopedi icon offers a cogent *analogia relationis* between the creator and the creatures. The new iconography of the Holy Trinity created during the hesychast controversy was entrenched in the tradition of Athos, preserving the same iconographic qualities after several centuries (Fig. 63). The placement of the feet of the left angel (the Father) are always deployed along the entire edge of the

217 Hunt, 'Andrei Rublev's Old Testament Trinity Icon: Problems of Meaning, Intertextuality, and Transmission', 30–37.

218 Louth, 'The Oak of Mamre'.

219 A.A. Karaktasanis, *Treasures of Mount Athos* (Thessaloniki 1997) 2, 17–21; Hunt, 'Andrei Rublev's Old Testament Trinity Icon: Problems of Meaning, Intertextuality, and Transmission', 33–37.

220 Titz, 'Some General Features'.

221 R. Percival, *The Seven Ecumenical Councils, Nicene and Post-Nicene Fathers*, vol 14; online version on http://www.ccel.org/ccel/schaff/npnf214.txt (accessed 20/02/2012).

throne. The middle angel (the Son) has his hands in a gesture of blessing. On the other hand, the hands of the right angel (the Holy Spirit) are in a sign of action. In his *Trinity*, Rublev embodies many elements of the Vatopedi icon.

The frequent encounters between monks and travellers from Constantinople allowed the ideas and patterns of Byzantine civilization to pour into Russia.[222] The patriarchate of Constantinople used its executive authority in vast territories, but the elitist character of Byzantine humanism precluded any transmission of secular Greek culture to the Slavs.[223] Therefore, the great mass of translated literature was religious (chiefly hesychastic) and ecclesiastical. It was not uncommon to see Byzantine artists moving to Russian municipalities, especially during times of conflict. When the hesychast controversy raged through the Byzantine state, many Greek painters moved to Russian territories. Theophanes, whose style was tense, expressive and full of mystical contemplation, was one of them.

The fresco of the *Trinity* by Theophanes is on the walls of the small chapel dedicated to the Trinity, which forms a part of the Church of the Transfiguration, Novgorod (Fig. 64). The composition was created in 1378 and reflects the oriental type (Fig. 65) to which Theophanes was exposed during his frequent trips to the East, especially to Capaddocia.[224]

At the bottom of the mural, Abraham and Sarah prepare the meal. At the top of the fresco, the three angels are gathered around a semi-circular table on which the sacrificial meal is placed. The depiction of angels is unusual, with the figure of the central angel being expressive and higher on the pictorial plane than the other two; he raises his right hand in blessing while holding a scroll in his left. He has large outstretched wings that overshadow and embrace the two other angels, dominating the painted scene. The central angel also bears a cross nimbus and carries a scroll in his left hand; both symbols are commonly used in reference to Christ.[225] The central angel sits closer to the angel on the right than to the one on the left; this was a common feature in the iconographic tradition of the 11th and 12th centuries.[226] The masters of that time made use of a full circle, arranging the other angels around the central angel representing the Son.

---

222 The Serbian and Bulgarian influence upon cultural, religious, literary and artistic development in Russia was also immense. The transmission of liturgical and disciplinary reforms, pilgrims journeying to Constantinople, and artists, diplomats and ecclesiasts travelling to and from Byzantium, constitute various channels through which ideas and patterns of Byzantine civilization poured into Russia. Meyendorff, *Byzantium and the Rise of Russia: A Study of Byzantino-Russian Relations in the Fourteenth Century* (Crestwood 1989) 120.

223 ibid., 121.

224 Ilin, Искусство Московской Руси Эпохи Феофана Грека и Андрея Рублева, 54–58.

225 Ulyanov, 'В Филоксения Авраама: Библейская Святыня и Догматический Образ', *Богословские Труды*, vol. 35 (1999) 225–229.

226 Malickii, К Истории Композиций Ветхозаветной Троицы, 35–37.

In contrast, Theophanes used the half-circle as a starting point. Accordingly, the haloes of the angels keep equal distance from the line of the frame from top left to right.[227]

The overall background of the fresco of the *Trinity*, as well as the outline of the halo, the glare on the wings, the recesses in the hair and shapes of the eyes of the three angels are in monochrome, with bright highlights to create depth and contour.[228] The three angels have no pupils; instead, their retinas are expressed with bright white strokes, which light their eyes like flames of fire. This recalls the account of the Biblical story following the event of the Hospitality of Abraham, that is, the destruction of Sodom and Gomorrah (Genesis 19:23).

Rublev was a pupil of Theophanes, from whom he learned the technique of iconography. Rublev, already a mature master, conducted an internal dialogue with his predecessor and teacher. Nevertheless, the personality and the demeanour of the pupil (Rublev) were unlike those of his master (Theophanes) and their artistic interpretation of Genesis 18 reflects. Theophanes painted the Old Testament story and included all the features of the Biblical text. Rublev, on the other hand, embodies the image of the divine Trinity. Theophanes's vision of the Trinity is to be experienced as a poignant revelation. Rublev offered a clear and terse vision of the Trinity belonging to the realm of divine wisdom and contemplation.[229]

Theophanes created his works of art by following Byzantine models, even though Epiphanius claimed that Theophanes did not look at any iconographical manuals.[230] As an educated philosopher and iconographer, however, he must have known the works of contemporary theologians and artists from Byzantium and Russia. They must have inspired him to produce brilliant paintings, such as the fresco of the *Trinity*. Of particular importance for understanding the impact of hesychasm on art, and on the development of Rublev's *Trinity*, is the double portrait miniature of John Kantacuzenos as a monk and emperor from the theological works of Kantacuzenos (*Parisinus Graecus* 1242). This complex and captivating image eloquently illustrates the life of Kantacuzenos, as well as his theology.[231] The interpretation of this image finds its full theological revelation in the text of Kantacuzenos, namely his *First Apology against Islam*,

227 Popova, 'Medieval Russian Painting and Byzantium', in R. Grierson (ed.), *Gates of Mystery: The Art of Holy Russia* (Fort Worth 1992) 55.

228 N.I. Sokolova, *Selected Works of Russian Art: Architecture, Sculpture, Painting, Graphic Art: 11th – Early 20th Century* (St Petersburg 1976) 4.

229 K. Ware, *The Inner Kingdom: The Collected Works* (Crestwood 2000) 108–110.

230 ibid., 111.

231 V.J. Djurič, 'Les Miniatures du Manuscript Parisinus Graecus 1242 et le Hesihasme', *L'Art de Théssaloniques et de Pays Balcaniques et les Courants Spirituals au XIVe Siecle: Recueil des Rapports du IVe Colloque Serbo-Grec* (Belgrade 1987) 89–94; Uliyanov, *Воплощение Тринитарного Догмата в Иконе 'Архангел Михаил с Деяниями', Из Собрания Музеев Московского Кремля, Троицкие Чтения 2003–2004 гг* (Moscow 2004) 141–142.

written somewhere between September 1369 and June 1370. Kantacuzenos was the principal propagator and supporter of hesychasm during the 14th-century controversy, and he visited Mt Athos after the victory of the hesychasts in 1375. In a letter from 1371 to Bishop John on Cyprus, Kantacuzenos refers to Mt Athos as a place where hesychasts reside.[232] The theological works of Kantacuzenos were popular on Mt Athos. The library of the Monastery of Hodegon, Mt Athos, holds the original manuscript. A translation into Serbian existed in the Monastery of Chilandar, Mt Athos.[233] St Sava distributed this version in Russia and Slavic lands.[234]

The miniature accompanying the tract against Islam is peculiar. It contains a double portrait of Kantacuzenos in his imperial garb and in a monastic *schema*. As a monk, Ioasaph Kantacuzenos holds a scroll with an inscription while his raised right hand points to the three angels from the *Philoxenia of Abraham*. This image belongs to Rublev's variant of the *Trinity*.[235]

This indicates that Rublev knew this model of the Trinity and borrowed some aspects of it. Hence, the three angels in the *Parisinus Graecus* 1242 match those presented in Rublev's *Trinity*. They sit around a rectangular table covered with a green cloth. Each of the three angels wears a blue himation covered by a blue-grey chiton. The three persons of the Trinity are distinguished from each other by individual characteristics; the central angel has cruciform halo, and the right angel carries in his left hand a red unidentified object.[236] Iconographical novelties are the inclusion of this image of the Trinity above the double portrait of Kantacuzenos, and the inscription found on his scroll, which reads 'this is a picture of the Christian God'. These features engage the image of the Trinity in a visual polemic, providing further métier to the thesis expanded in the dogmatic text accompanying the miniature.[237] In Rublev's *Trinity*, the three angels are equals, in the *Parisinus Graecus* miniature, the middle angel is identified as Christ and the Father at the same time, which has a dual significance. It refers to Kantacuzenos's statement that, although the Father did not appear in human

232 J. Darrouzes, 'Lettre Inedite de Jean Cantacuzene Relative a la Controverse Palamite', *Revue Biblique*, vol. 7 (1959) 7–12, 50.

233 Венская Королевская Библиотека, no. 34; J. Prolovic, 'Списки Рукописи XIII и XIV Века у Бечу и Монастир Хиландар', *Хиландарски Сборник* (Beograd 1986) 213–215.

234 John Kantacuzenos, 'Беседа с Папским Легатом: Против Иудеев и Другие Сочинения', in G.M. Prohorov (ed. & trans), *Издательство Олега Абышко, Серия Библиотека Христианской Мысли Источники* (Moscow 2008), vol. 41. (1988) 331–346; vol. 42 (1989) Cc. 200–227; vol. 43 (1990) Cc. 305–323; vol. 44 (1990) Cc. 226–245; vol. 45 (1992) Cc. 390–398; vol. 46 (1993) Cc. 270–286; vol. 47 (1993) Cc. 164–200; vol. 48 (1993) Cc. 151–186; vol. 49 (1996) Cc. 339–355.

235 H.A. Omont, *Miniatures des Plus Anciens Manuscripts Grecs de la Bibliotheque Nationale du VIe au XIVe Siecle* (Paris 1929) 58–59, pl. 126.

236 P. Guran, 'Jean VI Cantacuzène, l'Hésychasme et l'Empire: Les Miniatures du Codex Parisinus Graecus 1242', *L'Empereur Hagiographe, Culte des Saints et Monarchie Byzantine et Post-Byzantine* (Bucarest 2001) 73–121.

237 Djurič, 'Les Miniatures du Manuscript Parisinus Graecus 1242'.

form, Christ manifested him. Therefore, the halo of the Father bears the cross in the *Parisinus Graecus* miniature.[238] Also, the insistence on the value of this Christological revelation meets another topic addressed by Kantacuzenos in his *Four Words against the Jews*. Through his dual nature (divine and human), Christ simultaneously revealed the hypostases of the Father and of the Holy Spirit.[239] Kantacuzenos stated that Christ deified the flesh and sanctified it by means of the incarnation.[240] Hence, the circumscription of God's nature manifested in Christ throughout his *sub specie incarnationis* (his earthly life). This affirmation certainly bears a connection to the hesychast theology of the Trinity, as expressed by Palamas.[241] The appeal of this miniature lies precisely in its ambiguity. The composition combines elements of the biblical narrative of Genesis 18, the official imperial canon of portraiture, and the semi-private *Double Portrait of Emperor John Kantacuzenos* (Fig. 66). Confronted by the portrayal of the same individual, as it were, in two incarnations and surmounted by the canonical representation of the Holy Trinity, 'the viewer contemplates the paradox of divine and human natures, hypostatically united in one person of Christ'.[242]

Hesychastic spirituality transferred to Serbia after 1350 and it transpired through various channels. First, the mystical movement of hesychasm emerged in Serbia under the direction of Gregory of Sinai, as well as the multiplying of translated patristic sources in Slavic languages. Second, the settlement of immigrant monks from Bulgaria as well as the influence exercised by the Chilandar Monastery on Mt Athos affected the spread of hesychasm to monasteries in Serbia.[243] In terms of the production of manuscripts, this monastery superseded Zographou, its Bulgarian counterpart.[244] Third, fostered by Athos, St Sava, a Serbian prince, Orthodox monk and the first Archbishop of the Serbian Church, brought the practice of hesychasm to Serbia.[245] His two writings *Karyes* and *Chilandar*

---

238 John Kantakuzenos, 'Contra Secam Mahometicam', *Patrologia Graeca* 154, 371–692.

239 V.J. Djurič, 'Les Miniatures du Manuscrit *Parisinus Graecus* 1242 et le Hésychasme', *L'Art de Essalonique et es Pays Balqaniques et les Courants Spiritueles au XIVe Siecle, Recueil des Rapports du IVe Colloque Serbo-Grec Belgrade 1985* (Belgrade 1987) 90.

240 John Kantacuzenos, *Беседа с Папским Легатом: Диалог с Иудеем и Другие сочинения* (St Petersburg 1997) 145; G. M.Prohorov, 'John Kantacuzenos, Диалог с Иудеем', Труды Отдела Древнерусской Литературы, vol. 41 (1988) 331–346; vol. 42 (1989) 200–227; vol. 43 (1990) 305–323; the style seen in the image of John Cantakouzenos in the Paris mniniature is similar to the style of frescoes executed in 1371 in the monastery of Vatopedi; this is is especially noticeable in assessing the composition of St Gregory Palamas in Vatopedi. This apparent similarity suggests that the manuscript was created in Vatopedi, online paper, http://drevn2005.narod.ru/ill4StGrogorijPalamaVatoped1371.jpg (accessed 12/01/2011).

241 Florensky, 'Троице-Сергиева Лавра и Россия', 21.

242 Djurič, 'Les Miniatures du Manuscript Parisinus Graecus 1242', 93–94.

243 V.A. Moshin, 'O Периодизации Русско-Южнославянских Литературных Связей X-XV в'в', *Труды Отдела Древнерусской Литературы* (St Petersburg 1963) 28–106.

244 ibid., 94.

245 В. Žikić, 'Културни Херој као Морални Трикстер': Свети Сава у Усменом Преда у Срба из БиХ', *Bulletin of the Ethnographical Institute SASA* , vol. 46 (1997) 122–128.

Typikon became a reference for the hesychastic monastic lifestyle.[246] Forth, the involvement of Stefan Dušan in Byzantine internal affairs during the period 1341–1354 was crucial to the spread of hesychasm. Finally, Prince Lazar's transfer of the spiritual centre of the state to Moravia, with clusters rising in Ljubostina, Resava, Lazarica, affected the promulgation of the hesychasm in Serbia.[247] This style of representing the Trinity also spread to neighbouring countries, such as Macedonia, as reflected in the example from the Church of St Nikita, Banjani, Macedonia (Fig. 67).

Hagiographical literature in Serbia flourished during the Palaeologan period, when in-depth translations of the liturgical texts, as well as development of new works of art, materialised.

The Moravian school of painting was a creative and contemporary example of the changes occurring in Serbian art of this period, reflecting a style informed by hesychasm. The image of the Old Testament Trinity changed, bearing elements of artistic trends of Mt Athos (Fig. 62), Cappadocia (Fig. 65) and Novgorod (Fig. 68).

A mural painting of the Old Testament Trinity from the Monastery of Gračanica (Fig. 69) reflects the style that arose in Byzantium at the beginning of 14th century and testifies to the possible development of new artistic trends informed by hesychasm in Serbia. The painters from Gračanica used new iconographic and stylistic devices, as later Byzantine and Russian iconographers did, but they gave them a different interpretation.[248] The prominent feature is the circumscription of the faces of the bema (raised platform); they are modelled in a rough fashion and not anatomical. While the facial structure is strong, the nose, cheeks and, sometimes, the bones of the forehead are bypassed. Details are modelled by the play of light and shadow, and the use of colours of varying intensity, as seen in the early Byzantine churches.[249] In addition, the position of the three angels varies from those seen in the earlier iconographic prototypes, and also from the later versions of the Trinity, such as that of Rublev. The forms of angels in the fresco of the *Trinity* at Gračanica are generous and affect the volume of the composition. In contrast to this, in Rublev's *Trinity*, the volume is less apparent and the creases of the garments are rigid (in keeping in with the style of the 12th century).[250] At Gračanica, the figures of the angels tilt in three different directions, whereas in Rublev they point to the same direction (the chalice). This affirms their different roles in the economy of salvation, rather than

246 N. Velimirović, *The Life of St Sava* (Platina 1989) 41–49.

247 A. Jevtic, *The Heavenly Kingdom in Serbia's Historic Destiny*, B. Dorich & B.W.R. Jenkins (ed.) (Pec 1992) 63–69.

248 Alpatov, 'La Trinité dans le Art Byzantine et l'Icone de Roublev'.

249 B. Todic, *Serbian Medieval Painting: The Age of King Milutin* (Belgrade 1999) 331.

250 J. Radovanovic, *Ikonografska Istrazivanja Srpskog Slikarstva XIII i XIV Veka* (Belgrade 1988) 89–102.

reflecting the Trinitarian intercommunication that Rublev was eager to affirm.[251] The peripheral movement of the three angels at Gračanica represents the endpoint of two spirals that begin with the side angels and cross the Christ figure on the central axis. Furthermore, their crossing paths form an oval shape that frames the upper torso of Christ and mirrors the circle of the central bowl. These spirals take the circle associated with the bowl upward and reveal the power of the Eucharist; assuring that the icon's allusion to the Trinity is not merely typological.

Both models of the Trinity (from Gračanica and of Rublev) employ inverted perspective and polycentrism, but Rublev's depth and rhythm of colours contribute to the quality of his *Trinity*. Nevertheless, the main focus of the *Trinity* fresco at Gračanica is the Christological doctrine of the hypostatic union of two natures in Christ. Furthermore, the distinction between the divine essence and energies — the basis of the hesychast controversy, served as a conceptual framework for the *Trinity* in Gračanica. The triadological issue concerning the unjustifiability of the *filioque*, in turn,[252] introduced the notion of the wisdom of God as a manifestation of God's energies that are accessible to humans, though the *ousia* of God remains hidden.

The notion of wisdom was central to the hesychast controversy, which motivated the development of symbolic images of Christ as the wisdom of God in the guise of the Angel of Great Council (Isaiah 9:6). He is seated in front of the temple with seven columns, which represent the 'home' of wisdom and convey the inseparable and indivisible union between the Father, the Son and the Holy Spirit.[253]

The dual meaning of wisdom as the energy of the divine and Christ, the power and wisdom of God, as argued by patriarch Philotheus, makes a clear connection between the two images.[254] If the image emphasised the motif of the Godhead, wisdom was the energy of the divine, and if the angel had a crucifix on the halo, it represented the incarnate word of God. The altar frescoes, the *Hospitality of Abraham* and *Wisdom has Built her House* in the Assumption Church of the Monastery of Gračanica, are placed on the sides of the composition of the *Communion of the Apostles*. Both paintings are likened to each other frontally and symmetrically, in the dominant motif of the Trinity. Rublev also merged these concepts in his *Trinity*.[255] His *Trinity* is a place where contemplation and action

---

251 Vzdornov, 'Новооткрытая Икона 'Троицы' из Троице-Сергиевой Лавры', *Троица Андрея Рублева: Антология* (Moscow 1970) 6.

252 ibid., 28.

253 Meyendorff, 'Spiritual Trends in Byzantium in the Late Thirteenth and Early Fourteenth Centuries', in P. Underwood (ed.), *Kariye Dzami* (Princeton 1975) 103–106.

254 Meyendorff, 'L'Iconographie de la Sagesse Divine dans la Tradition Byzantine', *Cahiers Archeologiques*, no. 10 (Paris 1959) 259–277.

255 F. Winkelmann, 'Adrei's Icon of the Old Testament Trinity: Observation on its Interpretation', *Byzantinoslavica*, vol. 50, no. 2 (1989) 197–202.

merge, and the creation and salvation of the world is inseparable.[256] The two frescoes at Gračanica single out the central angel as Christ–Wisdom. They share a common hesychast idea about the manifest nature of the divine transcendence through the hypostasis of the Logos. In the fresco of the *Sophia* at Gračanica, however, the middle figure is the Angel of Great Council, officiating behind an altar table, offering Wisdom's feast of knowledge of the hidden Father through communion in his Eucharistic mystical body. Depicted this way, the middle angel represents Christ, which communicates the transcendence of the Father. On either side of Christ, two servants make the symmetrical arrangement of the three. The numerical symbolism of the three marks the divine completeness or perfection, and it alludes to the triad or the Trinity. The composition reaches fulfilment with the representation of the seven columns on the temple behind Wisdom, which symbolise the seven gifts of the Spirit. It also refers to the New Testament church built on Christ, which stands against 'the house of the harlot' (Proverbs 7:8).

In the *Trinity* at Gračanica, conversely, the tent of Abraham is a cupola, like structure with three divisions, which represent the different roles of the Father, the Son and the Holy Spirit. The middle column is the largest, which suggests that the middle angel has sovereignty. This in turn, is a figurative transmission of the text of Proverbs 9:1–7 (Wisdom created her house) referring to Christ as the wisdom of God who reveals the Godhead in history.[257] While assessing the influence of Rublev's *Trinity* on the art of the 15th and 16th centuries, it is important to note another work, from Serbia, which shares some of the features commonly found in Rublev's *Trinity*. The fresco, from the Monastery of Kalenić, depicts the biblical narrative of the Wedding at Cana (Fig. 70).[258] The original drawing style of master Radoslav, the mastery of colour and chromatic effects, the bald approach in the composition of the masses and retouching of the old iconographic schemes make this fresco one of the highest Serbian artistic achievements.

Rublev's *Trinity* and the fresco of the *Wedding of Cana* circumscribe two different subjects, yet they share some common elements. The *Trinity* is predominantly abstract, and it contains only the essential features of the biblical narrative of the Hospitality of Abraham. The *Wedding at Cana* is an elaborate description of the Gospel's story of the miracle embodied in *realia*.[259] While in Rublev's *Trinity* there is only a select group of participants, chiefly, the three angels sitting around a table on which the chalice is placed, at Kalenić there is a

---

256 R. Williams, *The Dwelling of the Light: Praying with Icons of Jesus* (Norwich 2003) 57.

257 Meyendorff, 'L'Iconographie de la Sagesse Divine', 259–277.

258 O. Upadhya, *The Art of Ajanta and Sopoćani: A Comparative Study: An Enquiry in Prāna Aesthetics* (1994) 55–57.

259 S. Radojčić, *The Frescoes at Kalenic* http://www.monumentaserbica.com/mushushu/story.php?id=26&t=THE%20FRESCOES%20OF%20KALENI%C4%86 (accessed 23/04/2011).

multitude of guests, such as the marriage celebrant, the wedded couple, Christ and Theotokos, an elderly male, and three child-like servants. At the far corner of the table, two elders taste the miraculous wine while the wedding celebrant and his cohorts pay attention to Christ's speech. An unusual feature is the groom pricking his bride's finger to mix her blood with his wine in token of his fidelity (certainly a pagan component). An interesting feature is the guests dining with forks, a practice almost unknown outside Venice during the 15th century. The overall atmosphere in this fresco is of lyrical melancholy, tranquility and joyful celebration.

The strict equilibrium of those seated at the table is presented as in Rublev's example by sums: two, three, and two. The *Wedding at Cana* does not have the same austere numerical symmetry as Rublev's *Trinity*. Vessels in which the water becomes wine are emphasised in composition at Kalenić.[260] The table, the water vessels and the uneven masses, which disturb the balance, interlink with the murky exteriors of the robes of the invitees, the Virgin's, Christ's, the husband-to-be, and the two helpers. The central figure of Christ inclines and turns his head slightly to the side.[261] The ingenious arrangement of dark-clothed figures creates a new symmetry that envelopes the whole composition. The contours of the wings, the movement of the hands of the angels, and the merging of background features converge at the epicentre of the icon, which shows the chalice in which the sign of sacrifice is depicted.[262]

Against the obvious stylistic similarities and differences between both pieces, Rublev painted his concept of the Trinity in the sphere of ideas, whereas the painter at Kalenić aimed to represent the incomprehensible mystery of the Eucharist in earthly terms. The artists at Kalenić depicted a wedding of angelic youths. Accordingly, the postures and gestures of the three figures reflect supplication and *apotheosis* of earthly happiness. Rublev's *Trinity*, on the other hand, represented a vision of the Trinity as perceived in the Old Testament. It reveals the heavenly *agape* given by God to humanity and also expresses the hesychast spirituality. Needless to say, a rare icon of the *Wedding at Cana* painted in the Ferapontov Monastery, Russia, at the beginning of 16th century repeats the patterns of the Serbian fresco, and even includes its poetical components.[263] These similar models, made in two different areas and without communication, could have only one common denominator, a Byzantine centre, as the starting point of this diffusion.[264] From this survey of several frescoes

260 ibid.

261 In the fresco at Kalenic, the middle angel's hand is no longer raised in blessing, and he makes a gesture towards the vessel in front of him. The two angels on the side are making clear gestures in both paintings.

262 Compare the Wedding of Cana with that of the Trinity in the Monastery of Dećani, Kosovo; See fig. 72.

263 G.V. Popov, *Živopis i Minijatjura Moskvi Seredini XV Načala XVI veka* (Moscow 1975) fig. 147.

264 D. Simić-Lazar, 'Observations Sur le Rapport Entre les Décors de Kalenić, de Kahrié Djami et de Curtea de Argeş', *Cahiers Archéologiques*, no. 34 (1986) 143–160; Simić-Lazar, *Kalenić et la Dernière Période de la Peinture Byzantine* (Paris 1995) 151–169.

and icons of the Old Testament Trinity, it is clear that Rublev's *Trinity* is a pure expression of the hesychast experience that he learned under the guidance of Sergius. It also reflects a new style of art informed by hesychasm, which Rublev learned from Theophanes, who combined the Byzantine artistic canon with the Russian mentality.

Conclusion

The analysis of Rublev's Old Testament *Trinity* reveals that specific symbolism associated with hesychasm inspired and informed Rublev's innovative composition. Rublev combined the asceticism which characterised Russian monasticism with the classic harmony of Byzantine iconography, and thus maximised the proximity of the divine and the mortal.[265] Among the feuds and hostilities, Tartar raids and savagery of contemporary Russia, Rublev revealed the indivisible, eternal, ineffable peace of the heavenly kingdom.[266]

Rublev's *Trinity* offers a view into the spiritual state of *hesychia*, tranquillity and stillness. It represents the union of God and man in *theosis,* when all movement ceases.[267] Reflecting a subtle hesychast worldview, Rublev's *Trinity* depicts the incarnation of the Son of God. The wondrous icon also affirms the role of the Holy Spirit, and his mysterious, inspiring and spiritual development of humankind. Rublev created a vision that was suitable for divine meditation, allowing the observer to enter the uncreated light of God and experience divine transformation. The icon became a window to the divine light as well materialisation of God's presence.

---

265 A. Zotov, 'Народность Искусства Андрея Рублева', *Искусство*, vol. 9 (1960) 60, 83.

266 Kopylov, 'Hesychasm and Creative Work of Andrei Rublev', *Patristic and Byzantine Review*, vol. 18–19 (2000).

267 Some researchers praised Rublev's hesychasm as coming from the supposed Russian variety: the wonderful colours of the Trinity icon absorbed the light bluish-green of the young rye, the dark azure of the field cornflower, the lilac-yellows of the mass of the flowery carpet of heart's-ease, and the gold of the autumn forest (N. Kuz'min, Андрея Рублева, *Новый Мир*, vol. 10 (Moscow 1960) 204–210).

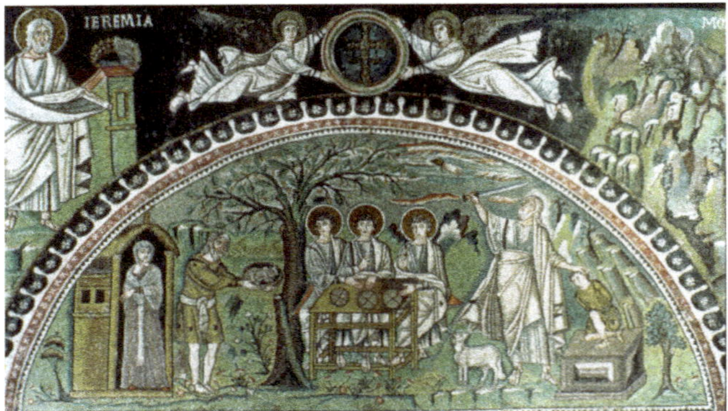

Figure 52. *The Hospitality of Abraham*, c. 532–547, mosaic, nave, Church of San Vitale, Ravenna (Italy)

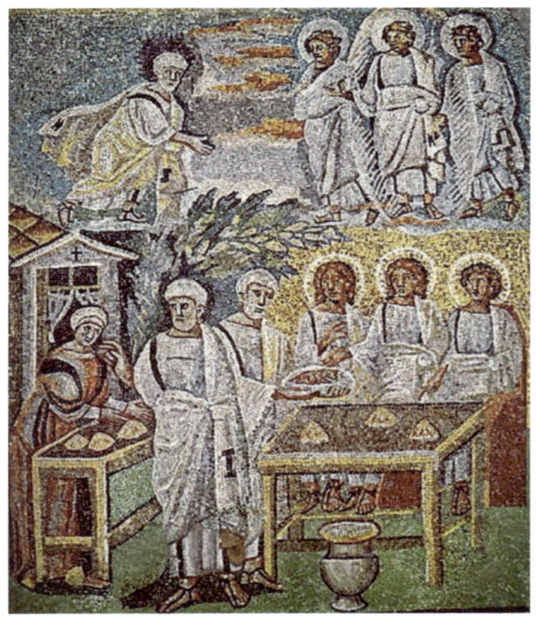

Figure 53. The Hospitality of Abraham, c. 432–440, mosaic, sanctuary, Church of Santa Maria Maggiore, Rome (Italy)

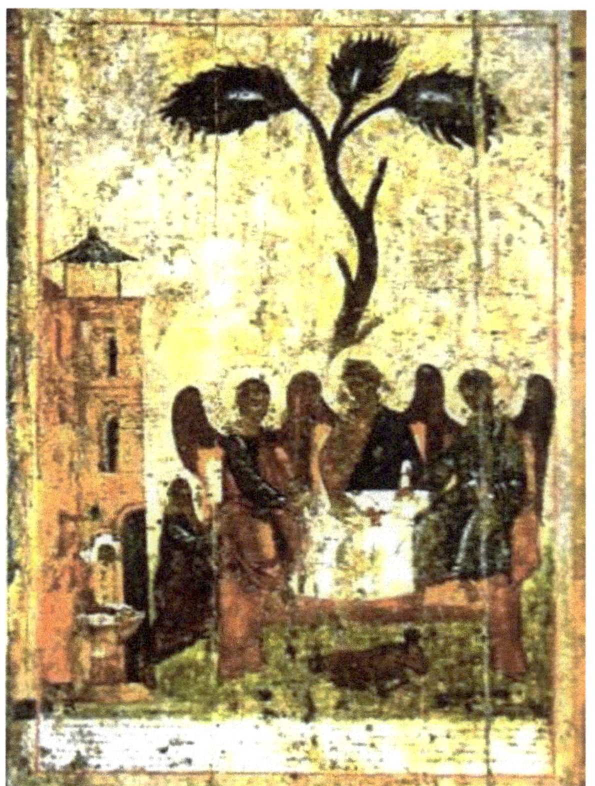

Figure 54. The Zyrian Trinity, 14th century, tempera on wood, 119 x 75 cm, painter Stephan of Perm, Vologda State Historical and Architectural Museum, Vologda (Russia), inv. no. 2780/6466Д

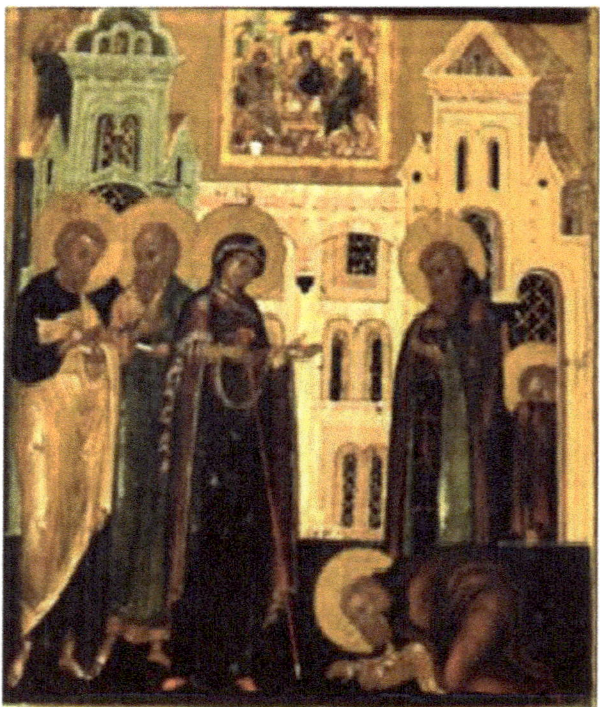

Figure 55. The Apparition of the Virgin to Sergius of Radonezh, late-16th century, tempera on wood, 30 x 25 cm, Trinity Lavra of St Sergius, Novgorod (Russia), currently at Murray Warner Collection of Oriental Art, University of Oregon (USA), inv. no. MWRU 34/15

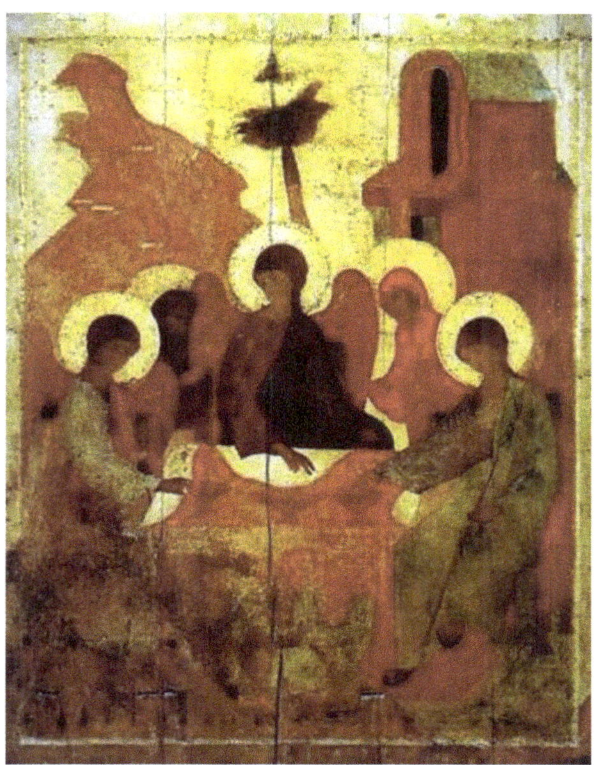

Figure 56. The Trinity, 15th century, tempera on wood, 161 x 122 cm, Trinity Sergius's Lavra, Sergius's Posad State History and Art Museum–Reserve, Moscow (Russia), inv. no. 2966

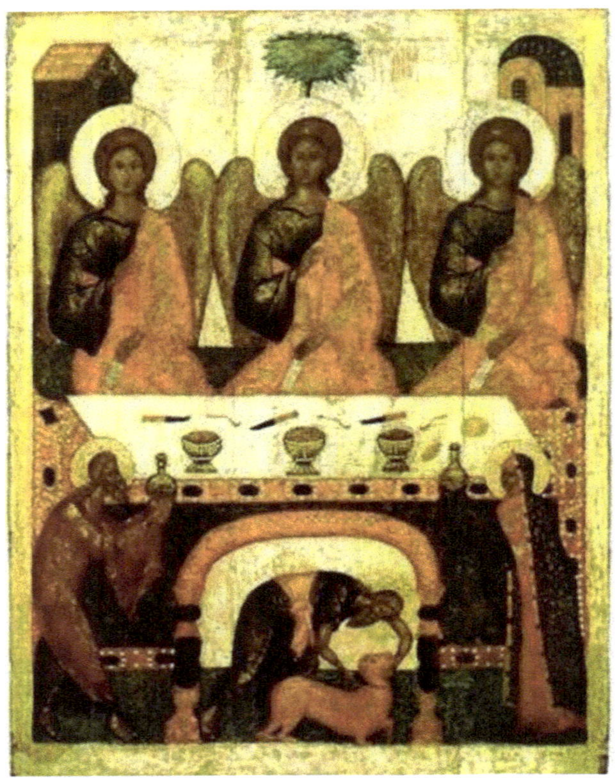

Figure 57. The Trinity, late-15th – early 16th century, tempera on wood, 145 x 108 cm, Pskov School, Tretyakov Gallery, Moscow (Russia), inv. no. 28597

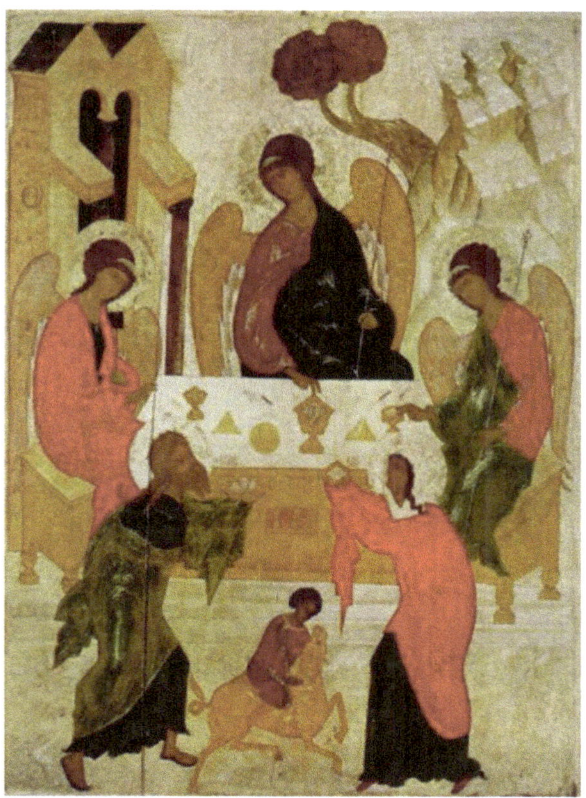

Figure 58. The Trinity, 15th century, tempera on canvas, 23.5 x 17.3 cm, Museum of History of Moscow, Novgorod (Russia), inv. no. 93096

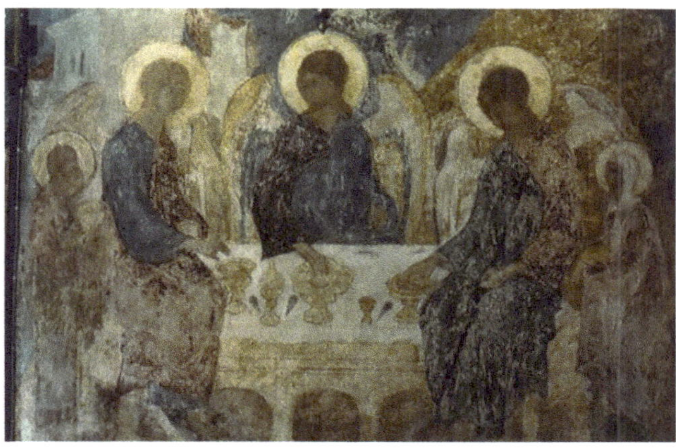

Figure 59. The Trinity, c. 1508, fresco, western wall of the gallery, painter Theodosius, Annunciation Cathedral, Kremlin, Moscow (Russia)

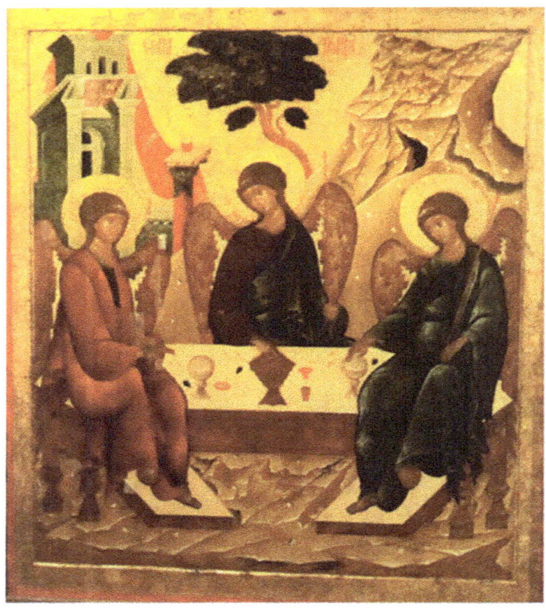

Figure 60. The Trinity, 15th century, tempera on wood, in front of the iconostasis (soleas), lower tier, painter Sidor Osipov or Ivan Borisov, Church of the Deposition of the Robe, Kremlin, Moscow (Russia)

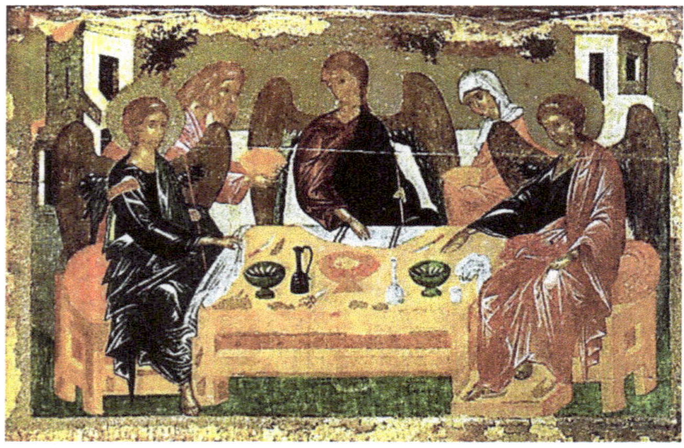

Figure 61. The Trinity, late-14th – early 15th century, tempera on wood, 36 x 54.2 cm, State Hermitage Museum, St Petersburg (Russia), inv. no. I–1/Лих.II–165 (1806)

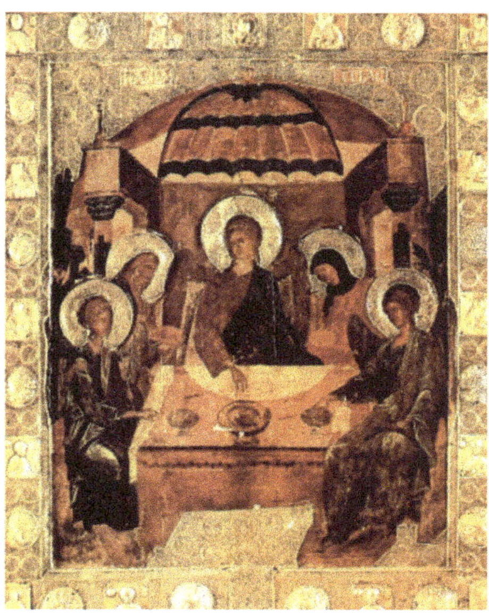

Figure 62. The Trinity, late-14th century, tempera on wood, 117 x 92 cm, Monastery of Vatopedi, Mt Athos (Greece), exclusive photograph of O.G. Uliyanov, Head of Department of Church Archaeology, Andrei Rublev Museum of Early Russian Culture and Art, Moscow (Russia), 2005

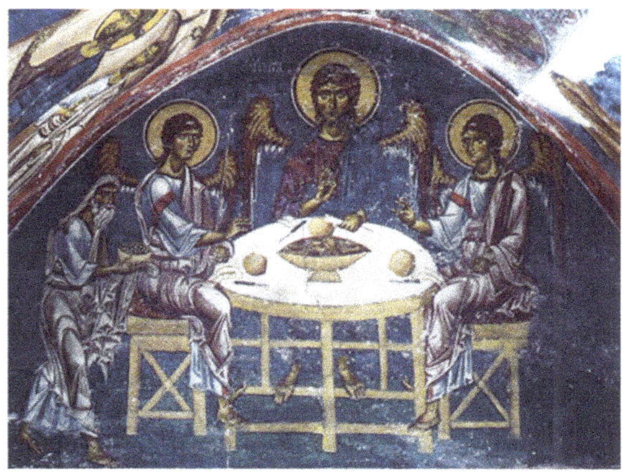

Figure 63. The Trinity, c. 1176–1180, fresco, left wall of the nave, Chapel of the Virgin Mary, Monastery of St John the Theologian, Patmos (Greece)

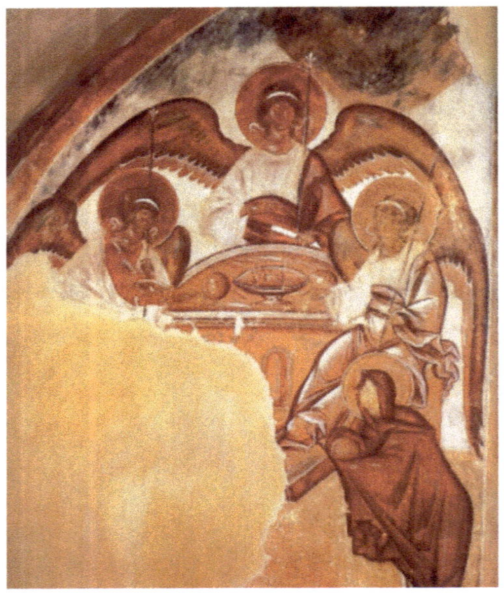

Figure 64. The Trinity, c. 1378, fresco, eastern wall of the western vestry, painter Theophanes the Greek, Church of the Transfiguration, Novgorod (Russia)

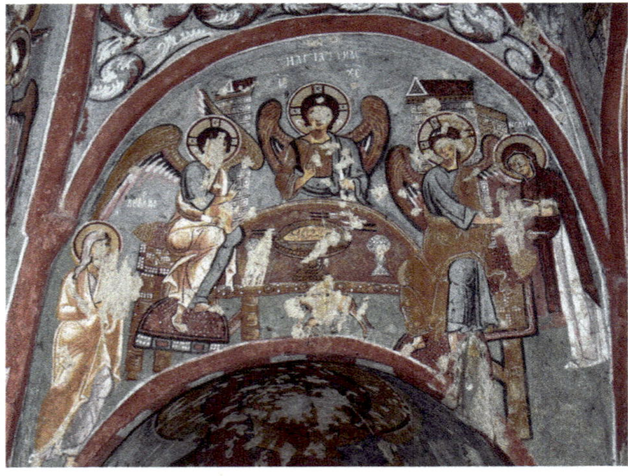

Figure 65. The Trinity, c. 1060s–1070s, fresco, western wall of the narthex, Church of Karanlik Killise, Göreme, Cappadocia (Turkey)

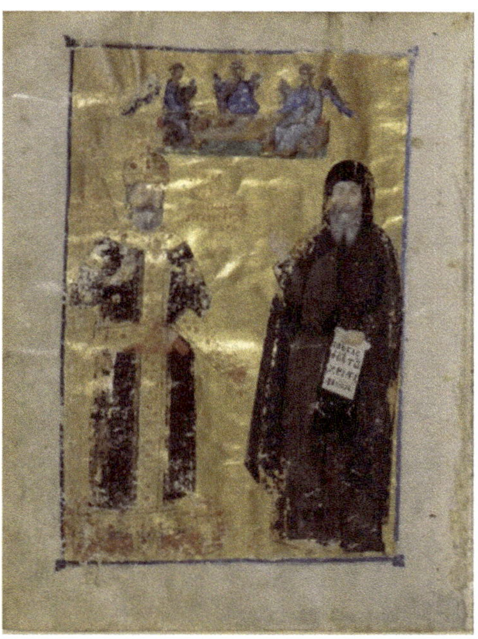

Figure 66. The Double Portrait of Emperor John Kantacuzenos, c. 1375, book illumination, scribe Ioasaph, in J. Kantacuzenos, Disputatio cum Paulo Patriarcha Latino, Bibliothèque nationale de France, (Parisinus Graecus 1242), fol. 5V

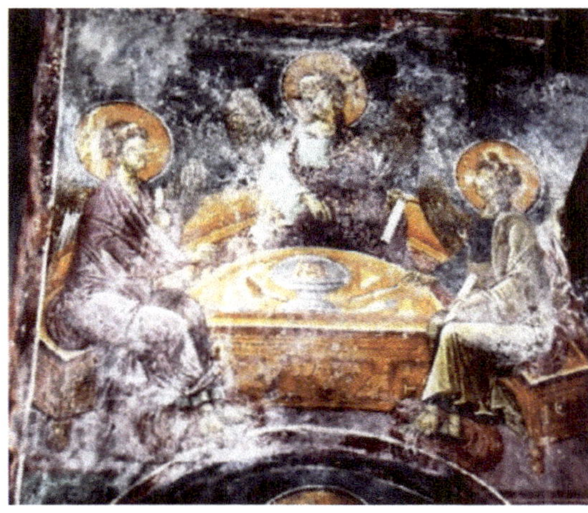

Figure 67. The Trinity, early 14th century, fresco, left part of the narthex, Church of St Nikita, Banjani (Macedonia)

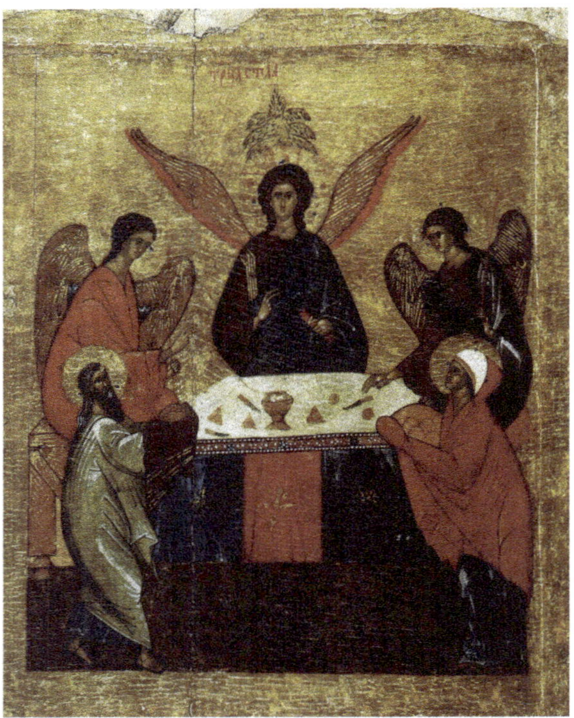

Figure 68. The Trinity, late-15th – early 16th century, tempera on wood, 23.5 × 17.3 cm, Museum of History and Architecture, Novgorod (Russia), cat. no. 35367

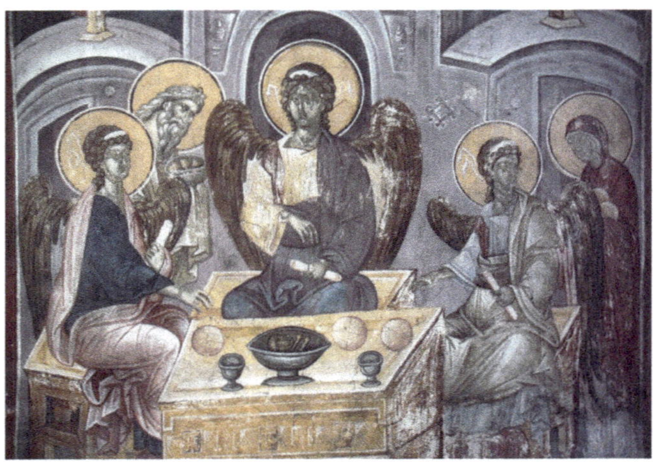

Figure 69. The Trinity, 14th century, fresco, east wall of the sanctuary, Monastery of Gračanica, Gračanica (Kosovo)

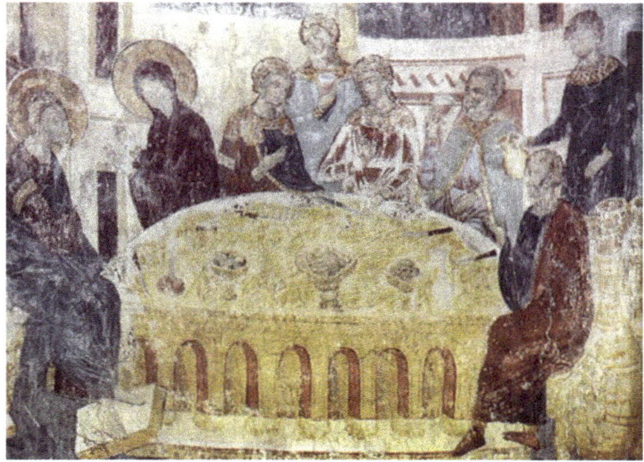

Figure 70. The Wedding at Cana, 15th century, fresco, southern apse, painter Radoslav, Monastery of Kalenić (Serbia)

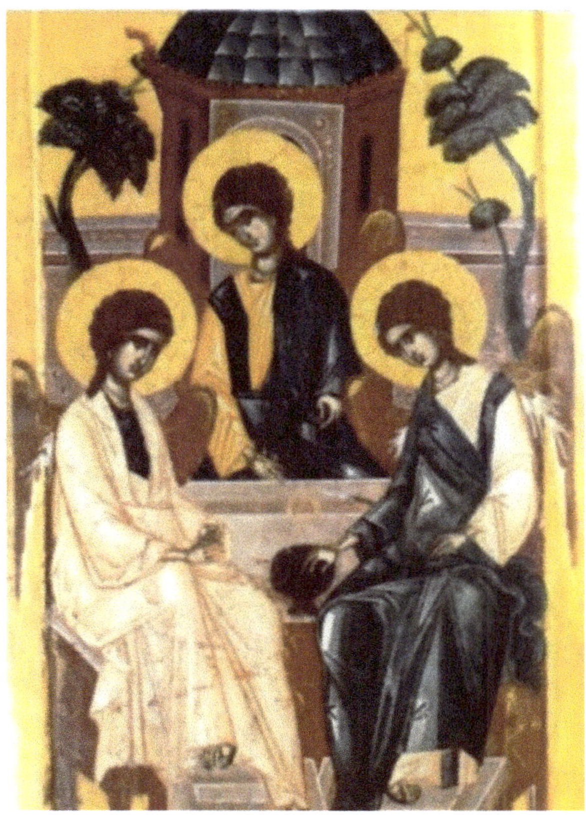

Figure 71. The Trinity, 16th century, tempera on wood, 101 x 61 cm, attached to the iconostasis, Monastery of Dećani

Conclusion

The dominant subject of this book is the impact of hesychasm on the development of new artistic trends during the Palaeologan era.

A brief overview of the origins of the term hesychasm explored four distinct, but interrelated, meanings of the word. Primarily, the phrases hesychasm and *hesychia* distinguish the 'solitary life' from that of living in a *coenobium* or monastic community. Hesychasm also refers to the psychosomatic technique of meditation that involves bodily ascesis and recitation of the Jesus Prayer. Moreover, the expression 'hesychasm' signifies the synthesis between the early Christian spiritual tradition of the desert fathers and the mysticism of the middle Byzantine period, putting an emphasis on knowledge of God through the work of the Holy Spirit. In the contemporary usage of the word, however, hesychasm is a synonym for the theological exposition of Gregory Palamas and his spiritual followers.

As a spiritual movement, hesychasm became a part of Byzantine theological tradition from the beginning of 9th century onwards. In the 14th century, however, the leader of the humanist movement, Barlaam of Calabria, took exception to the hesychast doctrine of the nature of uncreated light and refuted it as heretical and blasphemous. Palamas defended hesychast teaching and the conflict between Barlaam and Palamas escalated into the so-called hesychast controversy.

Palamas was not the only propagator of hesychasm in the 14th century. The attractive personality of Gregory of Sinai, whose dogmatic system was a theological fusion of the speculative and intellectual mysticism of Evagrius Ponticus and Symeon the Theologian, also proposed hesychastic principles. His doctrine was predominantly practical, with an emphasis on outward exercises, manual labour and ascetic prayer. Gregory of Sinai instigated a new hesychastic model for the perfection of humanity, reflecting the recreation of the lost likeness to God.

Moreover, he affirmed the cosmological event of Christ's incarnation and emphasised the deification of man. In such a framework, intellectual knowledge was a point of transition, either descending to a lower realm — the wisdom of the world, or ascending to the supernatural wisdom of grace. Gregory of Sinai introduced a tripartite system of spiritual ascent, where the struggle against passions culminated in supernatural union with God. The three steps of spiritual advance were: *ethike* or *praktike*, *physike* and *theologike*.

It is difficult to ascertain the true cause of the hesychastic controversy, however, many scholars represent the hesychast quarrel as a conflict between two philosophical schools: the Aristotelian, whose doctrines were accepted by the Eastern Church, and the Platonic school whose teachings the Church rejected.[1] Lossky sought the cause of this quarrel in the contrast between mystical theology and religious philosophy — the God of revelation and mystical experience confronted the God of the philosophers on the battlefield of mysticism.[2] Finally, Ostrogorsky and Meyendorff claim that the triumph of mysticism in late-Byzantine society was the reason behind the deepening religious and cultural gulf between East and West, not only in Byzantium proper, but also between Eastern Europe and the West.[3] Archbishop Chrysostom claimed that the tracts against the *filioque* clause, which Barlaam wrote at the time of union debates between Byzantines and Latins in Constantinople in 1333 and 1334, sparked the hesychast controversy.[4]

The followers of the hesychast tenet in Byzantine society supported the doctrines of the incarnation. They shared the eschatological notion of the Resurrection and the Second Coming of Christ and refused the neoplatonic dualistic view of the soul in opposition with the body. First, the dominant issue was the contribution made by the hesychasts to the development of a new Christocentric humanism, which emphasised synergy and the psychosomatic knowledge of God as *theosis*. This is in contrast to scholastic humanism, marked by intellectual rationalism and the dualism of the body and soul. Second, an important novelty in Palamite theology is the distinction (not division) between essence and energies in the uncreated God. This constituted an *antinomy* where God was knowable (*kataphasis*) and unknowable *(apophasis*) at the same time. Third, the Palamite doctrine of immanent energies also implies a vision of the relationship between God and the world, and hesychasts experienced God's energies in the form of uncreated light. This light manifested to the apostles during the Metamorphosis, the saints receive it through spiritual contemplation, and in art it is often represented by various symbols and artistic methods (the use of halo, gold, and highlights on painted areas). The uncreated light is also a symbol of the 'Light in the Age to come' (*Parousia*). Fourth, hesychast teaching on *theosis* offered a genuinely theological anthropology, which considered human beings as the unfinished creation of God, who are called to transcend the

1 H.W. Haussig, *A History of Byzantine Civilization*, J.M. Hussey (trans), (London 1971) 364–365.

2 V. Lossky, *The Mystical Theology of the Eastern Church* (Crestwood 1976) 220–221.

3 B. Krivocheine, *St. Symeon the New Theologian* (Crestwood 1986), G.A. Ostrogorsky, 'Афонские Исихасты и их Противники', Записки Русского Научного Института Велграде (Belgrade 1931); Arhimandrite Cyprian, Антропология Св. Григория Паламы (Cambridge 1996); Lossky, Мистическое Богословие (Kiev 1991); J. Meyendorff, 'О Византийском Исихазме и его Роли в Культурном Историческом Развитии Восточной Европы', История Церкви и Восточно-Христианская Мистика (Moscow 2003).

4 R.E. Sinkewicz, 'The Doctrine of the Knowledge of God in the Early Writings of Barlaam the Calabrian', *Mediaeval Studies*, vol. 48 (1982).

limited boundaries of their creation and to become infinite. This transcendent dimension of salvation was/is achieved by two means: the sacramental and liturgical life of the Church, and the hesychast practice of the invocation of the name of Jesus.

Neither hesychasts nor humanists left writings dedicated to art, and no document bears witness to a connection between religious movements in Byzantium during the Palaeologan period and the development of new iconographic trends in Byzantine and Slavic religious art. A polarisation of the ascending (mystical, hesychastic) and descending (antique, humanistic) characterised the art of this period. They, in turn, corresponded to two dichotomous paths in the Byzantine culture (hesychasm/humanism, Christianity/Hellenism), which influenced the formation of artistic styles and canons in the 14th and 15th centuries. Hence, the religious paintings of the Palaeologan era expressed the essential foundations of Byzantine and Old Greek culture, revealing at the same time the spiritual ideals of contemplation and transfiguration of humanity and Hellenistic ideals of perfection and beauty. These iconographic trends did not exclude a plethora of private, complicated and interwoven trends (hesychasm and humanism). When hesychasm became a universally accepted doctrine, not only in monastic life but also in the Byzantine Church, transformations in iconography occurred that affected the overall form and meaning of the compositions. The aim of this art also changed; its purpose was to show the contemplation of transfigured flesh and matter, shading divine light, the fullness of ascending to ethereal heights where everything is perfect. No work of art represents the possible reciprocal influence of hesychasm on art more than paintings representing the oeuvre of Palamas. Another influential image for the hesychasts was the composition of Barlaam and Iosaphat.

Along with illustrations of the liturgy, new images appeared whose main task was to reveal the meaning of the sacrament by abstract symbolic images, such as the Image of Sofia and the Communion of the Apostles. Other iconographic changes occurred in the late-14th century, and many compositions were either reintroduced or redeveloped, such as the Akathist Hymn, Barlaam and Iosaphat, the Prayer of John Chrysostom, Pachomios and an Angel, the Heavenly Ladder, and Symeon the New Theologian's vision of light. Moreover, there was an increase in images representing monks, hermits and stylites, and known hesychasts. New subjects emerged, such as the images of John Chrysostom, Basil the Great, Gregory the Theologian, and Athanasius the Great as seen in the Church of the Archangel Gabriel, in Lesnovo. The Theotokos of the Life-Giving Spring emerged in the 14th century, due to changes in the liturgy and the introduction of a new liturgical office in honour of the Virgin Mary in 1335.

Other important changes occurred in Christian art of the 14th and 15th centuries. The emergence of the complex mandorla, the eight rays of light, the OWN monogram, three-dimensional rainbows, zigzag patterns on murals consisting of red and blue bands within a circular band, and fanlike highlights on figures, all are hesychast innovations. There is a use of monochrome colours (red, ochre and dark shades of blue). White strokes — the rays of divine light — illuminate painted surfaces (as white patches on the face, neck and hands). Iconographical changes occurring in the Transfiguration, the Anastasis and the Trinity allude to the possible development of artistic trends informed by hesychasm. The revisionary semantics emphasising the light of Tabor and its symbolism clearly materialised in the miniature of the Transfiguration, accompanying the theological writings of John Kantacuzenos, *Parisinus Graecus* 1242. This reflected the impact of the conflict, and it provides a visual representation of the uncreated light of God — the underlying doctrine defended by the hesychasts.

The illumination of *Parisinus Graecus* includes references to doctrines advanced by Palamas. The use of black and blue for the mandorla, as well as the introduction of geometrical shapes to represent the glory of Christ, are important. The hesychast type of mandorla was formed by superimposing two squares (a square and a rhomb) over a circle. The manuscript of Kantacuzenos contains the most prominent composition containing this symbol. Kantacuzenos was a known supporter of Palamas and a chief protagonist of the hesychast controversy. Moreover, the hesychast mandorla was a favourite amongst painters on Mt Athos in the late Byzantine and post-Byzantine periods. The monastic circles at Mystra promoted this mandorla during the 14th and 15th centuries. From the doctrinal point of view, the hesychasts adopted the eight-pointed mandorla as the principle means of expressing their belief in the concept of divine light. The shapes of a star or an octagon were symbols for rebirth and resurrection, frequently decorating baptismal fonts in churches large and small. For the hesychasts, however, eight symbolised not just the transcendence of created order but also the eighth day and eschatological perfection. Another interpretation suggests that the three geometrical forms (the square, the rhombus and the circle) crossed by rays of light, signified the three hypostases of the Trinity.

Not only was the shape of the mandorla changed, Mt Tabor became a mountain of spiritual ascent while the theological memory of Sinai was still present. The most prominent difference was the introduction of a three-fold mountain, instead of one angular and rocky landscape. It stresses the upward movement of the soul towards God. The appearance of Moses and Elijah alongside Christ at the Transfiguration provide further evidence, which strengthens this assertion. Both Moses and Elijah are specifically connected to Mt Sinai. Both were hesychast models of ascetic monasticism, rather than Old Testament archetypal visionaries. Moses is a prototype mystic who rejected worldly beliefs and entered the divine darkness. Prophet Elijah, on the other hand, 'embodied the hagiographical topos of the solitary hesychast', receiving the experience of God in the desert of Mt Horeb by practising the noetic prayer of the heart. Principally, however, the hesychastic way of life as presented through Christ's Transfiguration on Mt Tabor was a full manifestation of the divine nature of Jesus Christ and the eschatological 'glory of God's presence'.

The Transfiguration miniature of *Parisinus Graecus*, in turn, can be taken as a sublime attempt to capture the effects of the Taboric light on humanity (in participle form). In particular, the miniaturist gave special emphasis to the emotional effect of what the disciples saw and how this vision affected their spiritual states. To be precise, the three disciples fell headfirst to the ground, gesticulated, and crouched away from the blinding light. In contrast, Christ stood calmly on the top of the mountain between the figures of Moses and Elijah.

The symmetrical position of Adam and Eve on both sides of Christ was of particular importance. Christ pulled both Adam and Eve simultaneously into his mandorla in a choral movement that conveys a sense of leading, guiding and protection. God envisaged deification as the final destiny of all material creation. Also, Christ's gestures affirmed the hesychast view of grace and its relation to human salvation, embodied in the idea of cooperation (*synergia*). Christ opened the way to paradise for Adam and Eve, and he called humanity to salvation. The response to Christ's calling, however, lies in the voluntary consent of humanity to either accept or reject his salvation.

The moment of Christ's descent into hell is, in a way, a reverse Transfiguration, accentuating the last stage in the kenotic act of God, and the salvation of humanity. This event was no longer played on Mt Tabor, however, but at the centre of the earth and the cosmos, free from every geographic peculiarity. Thus, the step-like, cloven rocks of the Transfiguration changed into the barren rocky plains of the Anastasis, which pointed towards the kataphatic aspect of the human salvation from hell. The white garments of Christ have a twofold significance in the Anastasis scene. They affirm that Christ maintained his human nature, the rational and the spiritual soul undiminished even after the Resurrection and they allude to the transformation of all creation.

The bearer of light, the flesh of God beneath the earth dissipated the gates of Hades. The Virgin Mary gave birth to Christ in a cave, and the jaws of Hades trembled. He rose from the dead, and the bonds of hell begin to feel the crushing weight of their overthrow. The world was enlightened and rebuilt from the burdens of sinful existence. The event of the Anastasis did not aim to fulfil the act of salvation, but offered a path; it was not a quiet acceptance of the divine, but a complex spiritual work in progress aspiring to a higher purpose.

The fresco of the *Anastasis* at the Chora church added distinctive and unexpected features to the fully evolved Palaeologan style. Overcharged with classical reminiscences, mannerism and oddities, the portrayal of this scene in the Church of the Holy Saviour was revolutionary. Coming in the 14th century, the adoption of this style showed that, 800 years after Justinian, when the subject first appeared, Byzantine art still had all its creative powers. Although it is difficult to confirm hesychasm influenced these changes, it is almost certain that the fresco of the *Anastasis* at Chora illuminates the concept of *theosis* (the union of grace) between human beings and Christ.

The significant installation of Christian art informed by hesychasm in the Slavic lands is remarkable. This art was characterised by a continued ability to apply the formulae of its great past. It shares common iconographic schemes and details, not just in regard to compositions created in the very beginnings of Christianity, but in subjects dealing with Trinitarian dogma. This issue was the central topic behind the development of the hesychast controversy. A detailed analysis of Andrei Rublev's *Trinity* shows how his art was dependent on, or rather informed by, hesychasm. Whereas, in the Transfiguration, changes occurred in iconography, in the Anastasis the changes are of style and, in the Trinity, there are differences in form and perspective. Rublev created the icon of the *Trinity* in memory of Sergius of Radonezh, a known hesychast and expounder of the doctrine of the Trinity. Rublev followed the life of solitude and *hesychia*, and he never referred to the *podilniki* (iconographical guides) to create a work of art, but received visions of the images depicted in his paintings.

Under the influence of hesychasm, Rublev made significant changes to the composition of the 'Hospitality of Abraham' (Old Testament Trinity). He applied an allegorical reading of the narrative, and the story took on a more rudimentary character. Abraham and Sarah are missing from the composition. Rublev placed the three angels in a full circle and he depicted them as equals. There is a little house over the left angel, a mountain over the head of the right and a tree over the central angel. There is not, however, a full description of the Biblical text. Overall, in Rublev's interpretation, the Hospitality of Abraham acquired Trinitarian rather than Christological connotation.

Rublev's *Trinity* was rooted in the theology of hesychasm, in its essential doctrinal foundation of unity and power, harmony and peace, and the divine presence of God within history. Rublev also sought, however, to depict the salvation of the individual, a theotic transformation in God's image driven by the idea of the possible *theosis* of humankind. In other words, *kenosis* precedes *theosis*. The presence of the Trinity and the salvific act of God were to be experienced in the Eucharistic community, where the faithful received the uncreated light of *theosis*. Finally, the three hypostases engage in a common action of Trinity in the *oikonomia*, as in the case of Eucharistic consecration.

The contours of the building in this composition are reminiscent of graphics used in the emblem for Christ, whereas the palace itself is reminiscent of yet another iconographic component — the tablet placed the Cross with the inscription 'Jesus of Nazareth, King of Judaea'.

Rublev sought to emphasise the Trinitarian communication of the Father's transcendence, and the ability to receive this communication and know God. Moreover, Rublev affirmed the same principal of antinomy as invented by the hesychasts in his depiction of the angels's attitudes, gestures and their inclinations. While being almost identical, these characteristics have some differences. The use of blue summarises the outer and inner action of the three angels, and alludes to the hesychast understanding of the Trinity's ontological outpouring of the uncreated energies that are common to hypostases of the Father, the Son and the Holy Spirit. It also signifies Christ's historical manifestation of the uncreated light, which the Son shares with the Father. Hesychast theologians tried to define how the hidden, divine person of God the Father realises his transcendence by exceeding himself through the action of the Son and the Holy Spirit. The action reveals the hidden nature shared by the three hypostases outside the essence of the Father. Rublev structured his *Trinity* to present a sophisticated theological understanding of transcendence made manifest, and to relate it to the Trinity's creative interaction.

The relation between the three hypostases of the Trinity remains unique, immovable, and distinct for each hypostasis, in particular the hypostasis of the Father. The angels mirror each other, which alludes to hesychast theology; the use of blue refers to the hesychast understanding of the Trinity's ontological power, which came from the uncreated energies of God. Rublev's *Trinity* produces a lyrical aura of harmony and quietness while, at the same time, inviting a rhythmic movement of unstoppable power. Rublev's *Trinity* represents the state of *hesychia*, a condition of tranquility, interrupted by a movement from God, and by the idea of Trinitarian unity. The sense of movement in Rublev's *Trinity* has usually been described as quiet, gentle, anxious, and sorrowful, or as detached, meditative, contemplative, intimate, gentle and direct. The middle angel's action of bending the knee, and the movement of the wings of the third angel (the Holy Spirit), express the spiritual uplift that complements the symbolism of spiritual rest. The movement of the middle angel bears a note of sovereignty, independence and strength; while the discrete forms express the motion of the third angel.

Rublev used circles and many other geometric shapes. Three octagons emerge when the arc of the horizontal sides of the icon construct a border. The smallest octagon includes the focal point of the piece — the chalice and the arms stretching towards it. The middle octagon involves the central elements of the scene — the angels and the sacrificial chalice, and the largest embraces all elements of the figurative scene with mathematical precision. It mirrors the slopes of the thrones and pedestals of the angels, the axonometric axis of the left building, and even the tangent of the right mountain. Rublev used the mixture of deep blue and dark red to create an impression of light shining out of the icon. This created a place for a divine meditation, allowing the observer to enter the uncreated light of God and experience divine transformation. Although the divine essence is beyond human comprehension, humanity participates in the divine energy and hence, in a way, comprehends the manifested hypostases of the Father (Nous), the Son (Logos) and the Holy Spirit (Pneuma). Maximum similitude between the creator and creatures is achieved through unity of the mind, the heart and body. The first step is harmony between body and soul, and the domination of the latter over the former. It is by concentrating all his physical and spiritual efforts that one acquires a state of communion (*koinonia*).

The appearance of circles in Rublev's *Trinity* evokes God's transcendence as a self-identity which exceeds its limits through interaction with another. The circle itself signifies the dual action of the outflowing and return of God: he flows out to humanity through *kataphasis* and humanity returns inwardly to him by a circular movement of *ascesis* (*apophasis*). Moreover, the circular shape of the chalice alludes to two different doctrines. First, it reflects the process of actualising the divine outpouring, which occurs through the Eucharist, and secondly, to the inner movement of return of faithful souls during communion with God. This also reflects on the landscape. The rock behind the angel symbolises the mountain of ascent, while the symbolism of three landscape features behind the angels' heads represents the redeeming power of Christ's condescension. The spiral structure of foliage is Rublev's innovation and alludes to the teaching of Dionysius the Areopagite on divine names, where the soul which turns inwards from external things to God, takes an inverse motion to that of the body. Rublev discarded the unnecessary elements from his composition so the observer can feel the divine aura emanating from the angels. This leads to a sense of communion with the heavenly world. This unique solution to the challenge of symbolising the divine transcendence of God discards experimental human knowledge of God.

A survey of the religious art in Byzantine and Slavic lands during the 14th and 15th centuries shows that, in all epochs dominated by an ideological or a spiritual orientation, one may find texts or works of art reflecting the particulars of the given period. During the Palaeologan era, the rise of Byzantine hesychasm informed new iconographic trends in religious art of Byzantine and Slavic lands. The miniature of the Transfiguration from *Parisinus Graecus* 1242 confirms the introduction of complex iconographic symbolism under the impact of the Byzantine hesychasm (octagon mandorla, tripartite representation of Mt Tabor and positioning of the apostles). In the fresco of the *Anastasis*, the Chora church, variations transpire in terms of symmetrical positioning of protopsalts, dynamic movement of Christ (presented without the cross) and architectural design of the landscape (the Anastasis appears as a reverse Transfiguration). Finally, in Rublev's *Trinity*, the variations that are present in the use of form, proportion, perspective and the overall aim of the figurative scene, present the trinitarian nature of God (a figurative scene inscribed within circles and octagons as well as the removal of unnecessary elements from the composition).

Bibliography

Primary Sources

Akindynos, 'Report to the Patriarch', *Синодик в Неделю—Православия*, Известия Русского Археологического Института в Константинополе, F. Uspenskii (ed.), (Odessa 1893) 86–92.

——, *Letters of Gregory Akindynos*, A.C. Hero (ed.), (Washington D.C. 1983).

——, *Gregorii Acindyni Refutationes Duae Operis Gregorii Palamae cui Titulus Dialogus Inter-Orthodoxum et Barlaamitam*, in C.J. Nadal (ed.), *Corpus Christianorum Series Graeca*, 31 (Louvain 1995).

Ambrose of Milan, 'De Excessu Fratris sui Satyri', *Patrologia Latina* 16 (Paris 1980).

Anastasius of Sinai, 'Sermon on the Transfiguration 6–10', *Melanges d'Archeologie et d'Histoire*, vol. 67 (1955) 241–244.

Antonov, V., *Classics Of Spiritual Philosophy And The Present* (Santa Fe, N.M. 2008).

Antonova, C., *Space, Time, and Presence in the Icon: Seeing the World With the Eyes of God* (Ashgate 2010).

'Apophthegmata Patrum', *The Catholic Encyclopedia*, online version, http://www.newadvent.org/cathen/01623c.htm (accessed 18/05/2012).

Archimandrite Georgios, 'Theoretikos: The Neptic and Hesychastic Character of Orthodox Athonite Monasticism', http//www.greekorthodoxchurch.org/neptic_monasticism.html (accessed 11/03/2011).

Athanasius of Alexandria, *On the Incarnation: De Incarnatione Verbi Dei*, C.S. Lewis (ed.), (Crestwood 1996).

Augustine, *De Doctrina Christiana*, R.P.H. Green (ed.), (Oxford 1996).

De Trinitate: (Bucher VIII–XI, XIV–XV, Anhang Buch V), F. Meiner (ed.), (San Francisco 2001).

Barlaam of Calabria, 'First Letter to Palamas', *Barlaam Calabro Epistole Greche i Primordi Episodici e Dottrinari delle Lotte Esicaste*, G. Schiro (ed.), vol. 1, Instituto Siciliano di Studi Byzantini e Neogreci (Palermo 1954).

Basil the Great, 'Basilii Opera Omnia', *Patrologia Graeca* 29 (Paris 1886).

——, Epistulae, *Patrologia Graeca* 32, 67–113 (Paris 1886).

Caesarius of Arles, *Sermons*, M.M. Mueller (trans), (Washington, D.C. 1964).

Clement of Alexandria, 'Stromates', Clemens Alexandrinus; Band II: Stromateis I–VI, O. Stählin (ed.), (Berlin 1960); Band III: Stromateis VII–VIII, O. Stählin (ed.), GCS, vol. 17 (Berlin 1970) S. 3–102.

Cyril of Alexandria, 'Adversus Julianum Libri Decem', *Patrologia Graeca* 76, 489–1058 (Paris 1863).

Diadochos of Photiki, 'On Spiritual Knowledge', *The Philokalia: The Eastern Christian Spiritual Texts*, G.E.H. Palmer (ed.), vol. 1 (London 1983).

Dionysius the Areopagite, 'De Divinis Nominibus', *Patrologia Graeca* 3, 586–997 (Paris 1857).

——, 'Mystical Theology ', *Patrologia Graeca* 3, 997–1065 (Paris 1857).

——, *Divine Names and Mystical Theology*, C.E. Rolt (ed.), (London 1957).

——, *Dionysius the Areopagite: The Complete Works*, C. Luibheid & P. Rorem (trans), Classics of Western Spirituality Series (New York 1987).

——, *О Небесной Иерархии* (St Petersburg 1997).

Evagrius of Pontikus, *The Praktikos: Chapters on Prayer*, J.E. Bemberger (trans), (Spencer 1970).

——, *Chapters on Prayer*, S. Tugwell (ed.), (Oxford 1981).

Encyclopedia Brittanica, online version, http://www.britannica.com/EBchecked/topic/135385/contrapposto (accessed 10/11/2011).

Germanos I of Constantinople, Epistulae, *Patrologia Graeca* 98, 147–222 (Paris 1887).

Gouillard, J., *Petite Philocalie* (Seuil 1978).

Gregory of Sinai, 'Opera', *Patrologia Graeca* 150, 1240–1345 (Paris 1865).

——, 'Praecepta ad Hesychastas', *Patrologia Graeca* 150, 1330–1346 (Paris 1865).

——, 'On Prayer: Seven Texts', *The Philokalia: The Eastern Christian Spiritual Texts*, G.E.H. Palmer (ed.), vol. 4 (Athens 1961) 207–285.

——, 'On the Transfiguration', in D. Balfour (ed.), *St Gregory the Sinaite, Discourse on the Transfiguration, Theologia*, vol. 52, no. 4 (1981) 647–651.

——, *St Gregory the Sinaite: Discourse on the Transfiguration*, D. Balouf (ed.), (Athens 1985).

Gregory of Nyssa, 'De Beatitudinibus', *Patrologia Graeca* 44, 1303–1327 (Paris 1863).

——, 'In Psalmos', *Patrologia Graeca* 44, 298–434 (Paris 1863).

——, 'Quod non Sunt Tres Dii', *Patrologia Graeca* 45, 11–30 (Paris 1863).

Gregory Palamas, 'De Hesychasti', *Patrologia Graeca*, 150, 1101–1118 (Paris 1905).

——, 'Hagieriteos Tomos pro Hesychastis', *Patrologia Graeca* 150, 1225–1237 (Paris 1905).

——, 'Homily on the Transfiguration', *Patrologia Graeca* 151, 424–436; 436–449 (Paris 1905).

——, 'Operum coninuatio', *Patrologia Graeca* 151, 9–551 (Paris 1905).

——, 'Pour la Vénérable Transfiguration de Notre Seigneur, Dieu, et Sauveur Jésus-Christ; Où il est Démontré que la Lumière qui y est Apparueest Incréée', Homélie 36, *Patrologia Graeca* 151, 9–551 (Paris 1905).

——, 'Tomus Contra Barlaam et Acyndinum', *Patrologia Graeca* 151, 679–693 (Paris 1905); 717–763 (Paris 1905).

——, 'Tomi Synodici Tres in Causa Palamitarum', *Patrologia Graeca* 151, 655–671 (Paris 1905).

——, *Gregorie Palamas, Defense des Saints Hesychastes*, J. Meyendorff (ed. & trans), (Louvain 1959).

——, *Gregory Palamas: Works*, P. Chrestou (ed.), vol. 3 (1962–1972).

——, *Gregory Palamas: Works*, P. Chrestou (ed.), vol. 4 (Thessaloniki 1962, 1966, 1970).

——, *Gregory Palamas: The Triads*, J. Meyendorff (ed.), (New Jersey 1983).

——, *Douze Homélies pour les Fêtes*, Jérôme Cler (trans.), (Paris 1987).

——, *Dialogue between an Orthodox and a Barlaamite* (Oxford 1999).

——, *The Homilies of St Gregory Palamas*, C. Veniamin (ed.), (Waymart 2002).

——, *Che Cos'e L'Ortodossia: Capitoli, Scritti Ascetici, Lettere, Omelie Testo Greco a Fronte*, E. Perella (ed.), (Rome 2006).

Gregory the Theologian, *Discourse* 32–37, C. Moreschini (ed.), SC 318 (Paris 1985).

——, *Discourse* 38–41, C. Moreschini (ed.), P. Gallay (trans), (Paris 1990).

——, 'Orationes' 27–45, *Patrologia Graeca* 36, 9–623 (Paris 1886).

Irinaeus of Lyon, 'Adversus Haereses', *Patrologia Graeca* 7, 433–1225 (Paris 1857).

John Chrysostom 'Spuria Contra Theatra', *Patrologia Graeca* 56, 517–564 (Paris 1862).

——, *On the Incomprehensible Nature of God*, in P.W. Harkins (trans), vol. 72 (Washington D.C. 1984).

——, *The Paschal Canon*, Archimandrite Ephrem (ed.), http://www.anastasis.org.uk/paschal_canon_with_notes.htm.

John Climacus, Ladder of Divine Ascent, *Patrologia Graeca* 88, 1095–1130 (Paris 1884).

John Kantacuzenos, *Johannis Cantacuzini Imperatoris Historiarum Libri IV*, L. Schopen (ed.), vol. 2 (Bonn 1830) 438–439.

——, 'Refutationes duae Prochori Cydonii et Disputatio cum Paulo Patriarcha Latino Epistulis Septem Tradita Nunc Primum Editae Curantibus', *Iohannis Cantacuzeni Opera*, E. Voordeckers & F. Tinnefeld (eds), Corpus Christianorum. Ser. Graeca, vol. 16 (Belgium 1987) 3–105.

——, 'Беседа с Папским Легатом: Против Иудеев и Другие Сочинения', in G.M. Prohorov (ed. & trans), *Издательство Олега Абышко, Серия Библиотека Христианской Мысли Источники* (Moscow 2008).

——, *Historiarum Libri IV* (Nabu Press 2010).

——, 'Contra Secam Mahometicam', *Patrologia Graeca* 154, 371–692 (Paris 1866).

John Kyparissiotes, 'Palamicarium Transgressionu', *Patrologia Graeca* 152, 734D–736A (Paris 1866).

John of Damascus, 'Homilae on the Transfiguration', *Patrologia Graeca* 96, 848–856 (Paris 1864).

——, *John Damascus: On Holy Images*, A.H. Allies (ed.), (London 1898).

——, *Die Schriften des Johannes von Damaskos*, 5 vols, *Patristische Texte und Studien*, P.B. Kotter (ed.), vol. 12 (Berlin 1973).

——, 'Homily of the Transfiguration', H. Weatherby (trans), *Greek Orthodox Theological Review*, vol. 32 (1987) 4–12.

Leo the Great, 'Homily Delivered on the Saturday before the Second Sunday in Lent: On the Transfiguration: Matthew 17:1–13', http://www.newadvent.org/fathers/360351.htm (accessed 05/08/2010).

Macarius the Great, *Die 50 geistlichen Homilien des Macarius*, in H.Dorries & E. Klostermann (ed.), (Berlin 1964).

Mark the Hermit, Sermons, *Patrologia Graeca* 65, 893–1140 (Paris 1864).

Maximus the Confessor, 'Ambiguorum Liber 10', *Patrologia Graeca* 91, 1031–1418 (Paris 1865).

——, 'Epistulae 6', *Patrologia Graeca* 91, 362–650 (Paris 1865).

——, 'Quaestiones ad Thalassium 28', *Exegesis and Spiritual Pedagogy in Maximus the Confessor: An Investigation of the Quaestiones ad Thalassium*, P. Blowers (ed.), (Notre Dame 1991).

——, *Избранные Творения: Пер. и Комментарии*, vol. 4 (Moscow 2004).

Migne, J.P. (ed.), *Patrologia Graeca (electronic version)* (Stone Mountain, Ga. 2003).

Nicephorus the Italian, 'Tractatus de Sobrietate et Cordis Custodia', *Patrologia Graeca* 147, 945–967 (Paris 1865).

Nicholas Cabasilas, *The Life in Christ*, C.D. Catanzaro (trans), (Crestwood 1974).

Nikephoros Gregoras, *Romaike Historia*, L. Schopen & L Bekker (ed.), (Bonn 1829–1830).

——, 'Byzantinae Historiae 37', *Patrologia Graeca* 148, 115–119; 149, 1–503 (Paris 1865).

——, *Antirrhetika*, B.H. Veit (ed.), (Vienna 1999).

Nikephoros of Constantinople, 'Antirrhetici Tres Adversus Constantinum Copronymus', *Patrologia Graeca* 100, 206–574 (Antirrheticus I, 205–328; Antirrheticus II, 329–74; Antirrheticus III, 375–534) (Paris 1863).

——, 'Epistula ad Leonem III Papam', *Patrologia Graeca* 100, 170–206 (Paris 1863).

——, *Logos, Patrologia Graeca* 100, 584–790 (Paris 1863).

Nikiphoros the Monk, 'On Watchfulness and the Guarding of the Heart', *The Philokalia: The Eastern Christian Spiritual Texts*, G.E.H. Palmer (ed.), vol. 1 (London 1983).

Nil Sorskij, 'The Tradition to the Disciples', in G.A. Maloney (ed. & trans), *Nil Sorsky: The Complete Writings* (Mahwah 2003).

Origen, 'Commentaria in Evangelium Secundum Matthaeum, *Patrologia Graeca* 14, 829–1801 (Paris 1862).

——, *Commentarium in Canticum Canticorum*, in N.P. Lawson (trans.), *Song of Songs: Commentary and Homilies* (Washington D.C. 1957).

——, *Origen, Song of Songs: Commentary and Homilies*, N.P. Lawson (trans), (Washington D.C. 1957).

——, *Origen: Homilies on Genesis and Exodus*, vol. 17, *Fathers of the Church*, R. Heine (trans), (Washington DC 1982).

Commentarii in Evangelium Johannis, C. Blanc (ed.), 5 vols., Sources Chrétiennes 120, 157, 222, 290, 385 (Paris 1964–1992).

Patriarch Philotheos, 'Enkomion', *Patrologia Graeca* 151, 558–717 (Paris 1905).

——, 'Synodical Tome of 1368', *Patrologia Graeca* 151, 693–715 (Paris 1905).

Philo, *Philonis Alexandrini Opera Quae Supersunt*, L. Cohn (ed.), vol. 4 (Berlin 1902).

Procopius of Gaza, 'Commentarius in Genesin', *Patrologia Graeca* 87A, 19–511 (Paris 1865).

Pseudo-Macarius, *Patrologia Graeca* 4, 1857–1866 (Paris 1889).

——, *Pseudo-Macarius: The Fifty Spiritual Homilies and the Great Letter*, G.A. Maloney (trans) (New York 1992).

Symeon the New Theologian, *Symeon le Nouveau Theologien*, B. Krivocheine (ed.), vol. 96 (Paris 1964).

——, *The Discourses*, C.J. de Catanzaro (ed. & trans), (Toronto 1980).

Tertullian, *Tertullian Adversus Marcionem*, E. Evans (ed.), (Oxford 1972).

Theodore the Studite, 'Theodori Praepositi Studitarum Antirrhetici Adversus Iconomachos', *Patrologia Graeca* 99, 327B–436A (Paris 1903).

Theophanes of Nicae, 'Refutation' I, 6 (9–10); 'Refutation' II, 1 (109–112); *Ioannis Cantacuzeni Refutationes Duae,* E. Voordeckers & F. Tinnefeld (eds), (Turnhout 1987).

Secondary Sources

Abrams, M.H., *The Mirror and the Lamp: Romantic Theory and the Critical Tradition* (Oxford 1958).

Acheimastou-Potamianou, M., *Holy Image, Holy Space: Icons and Frescoes from Greece* (1988).

Alfeyev, H., *Saint Symeon, the New Theologian, and Orthodox Tradition* (Oxford 2000).

Aghiorgoussis, M., 'Christian Existentialism of the Greek Fathers: Persons, Essence, and Energies in God', *The Greek Orthodox Theological Review,* vol. 23, no. 1 (Spring 1978) 15–42.

——, 'Orthodox Soteriology', in J. Meyendorff (trans) & R. Tobias (ed.), *Salvation in Christ: A Lutheran Orthodox Dialogue* (Augsburg 1992).

Allchin, A.M., 'The Appeal to Experience in the Triads of St Gregory Palamas', in F.L. Cross (ed.), *Studia Patristica,* vol. 8 (Berlin 1966) 323–328.

Allendale, N.J., *Byzantine Daily Worship: With Byzantine Breviary, the Three Liturgies, Propers of the Day and Various Offices* (Alleluia Press 1969).

Alpatov, M.V., 'La Trinité dans le Art Byzantine et l'Icone de Roublev', *Echoes de Orient,* vol. 30 (1927) 150–186.

——, 'Die Fresken der Kachrie Djami in Konstantinopel', *Mimchner Jahrbuch der Budenden Kuntt,* vol. 6 (Munich 1929) 345–364.

——, *Russian Impact on Art* (Moscow 1950).

——, *Всеобщая История Искусств,* vol. 3 (Moscow 1955).

——, 'La Valeur Classique de Rublev', *Commentari,* vol. 1 (1958) 25–37.

——, 'О Значении Троицы Рублева', *Этюды по Истории Русского Искусства* (Moscow 1967) 119–122.

——, 'Искусство Феофана Грека и Учение Исихастов', *Византийский Временник*, vol. 33 (1972) 190–202.

——, 'On the Global Significance of Andrey Rublyov's Art', *Khudozhnik*, vol. 12 (1980) 48–57.

——, *Феофан Грек* (Moscow 1990).

Anastos, T.L., 'Gregory Palaamas's Radicalization of the Essence, Energies and Hypostasis Model of God', *The Greek Orthodox Theological Review*, vol. 38, no. 4 (1993) 335–339.

Andreev, A., *Bdinski Sbornik: Literaturna Antologiia 'Stoletie', Vidin, 1900–1999* (Bulgaria 1999).

Andreopoulos, A., 'The Vision of Light and the Icon of the Transfiguration in the Fourteenth Century', in J. Goering et al. (eds), *Mystics, Visions and Miracles*, (Leigas 2001) 103–111.

——, 'The Mosaic of the Transfiguration in St Catherine's Monastery on Mount Sinai: A Discussion of its Origins', *Byzantion*, vol. 72, no. 1 (June 2002) 9–42.

——, 'How Do We Represent the Glory of God? Theological and Iconological Connections between the Transfiguration and the Resurrection', *La Mort et la Résurrection dans la Tradition Orthodoxe* (University of Sherbrooke 2004) 47–59.

——, *Metamorphosis: The Transfiguration in Byzantine Theology and Iconography* (Crestwood 2005).

Angelov, D., 'Към Историята на Религиозно-Философската Мисъл в Средновековна България: Исихазьм и Варлаамитство', *Известия на Българското Историческо Дружество*, vol. 25 (1976) 73–92.

——, 'Hesychasm in Medieval Bulgaria', *Bulgarian Historical Review*, vol. 14, no. 3 (1989) 41–61.

Angold, M., 'Eastern Christianity', *The Cambridge History of Christianity*, vol. 5 (Cambridge 2006).

Anthonopulos, A. & Therezis, C., 'Aspects of the Relation between Faith and Knowledge according to Gregory Palamas', *Byzantinische Zeitschrift*, vol. 101, no. 1 (September 2008) 1–20.

Archbishop Alexis (Dorodnitsyna), *Vizantiiskie Cerkovnьe Mistiki 14go Veka: Grigorii Palama, Nikolaii Kavasila, i Gregorii Sinait* (Kazan 1906).

Archbishop Chrysostomos & Hieromonk Patapios, 'Comments on the Transformation of Hellenistic Philosophic Nomenclature in the Byzantine Patristic Tradition', *Glossa: An Ambilingual Interdisciplinary Journal*, vol. 2, no. 1 (December 2006) 12.

Archbishop S., 'Воплощение Богословских Идей в Творчестве Преподобного Андрея Рублева', *Богословские Труды*, vol. 1, no. 22 (Moscow 1981) 3–67.

Arguelles, J. & Arguelles, M., *Mandala* (London 1972).

Arhimandrite Cyprian, *Антропология Св. Григория Паламы* (Moscow 1996).

Arnheim, R., 'Inverted Perspective in Art: Display', *Leonardo*, vol. 5, no. 2 (Spring 1972) 125–135.

Arterbury, A., 'Abraham's Hospitality among Jewish and Early Christian Writters', *Perspectives in Religious Studies* (2003) 359–376.

Avinoff, A., 'A Loan Exhibition of Russian Icons', *Art Bulletin of the Metropolitan Museum of Art*, new series, vol. 2, no. 8 (Apr., 1944) 227–232.

Babic, G., 'Le Iconographie Constantinopolitane de l'Acatiste de la Vierge i Valachie', *Zbornik Radova Vizantiskago Institute* (Belgrade 1973) 14–15.

——, *Kraljeva Crkva u Studenici* (Belgrade 1987).

Babić. J., 'Портрет Данила ли Изнад Улаза у Богородичину Цркву у Портрет Данила II изнад Улаза у Богородичину Цркву у Пеħи', *Данило II и Негово Доба* (Belgrade 1991).

Baggley, J., *Festival Icons for the Christian Year* (New York 2000).

Bakalova, E., 'Към Вы і Роса за Отраженной! На Исихазма върху Изкуството 1371–1971', in P. Rusev et al (eds), *Търновска Кяижовна Школа* (Sofia 1974) 373–389.

——, 'La Societe et l'Art en Bulgarie au XIVe siècle', 'L' Influence de l'Hesychasme sur l'Art', *Actes du XIV Congress International des Etudes Byzantines II* (Bucharest 1975) 33–38.

Bakić-Hayden, M., 'Two Methods of Contemplation: Yoga and Hesychast Prayer', *Гласник Етнографског Института САНУ*, vol. 56, no. 2 (2008) 149–157.

Baldwin Smith, E., *Architectural Symbolism of Imperial Rome and the Middle Ages* (Princeton 1956).

Balfour, D., 'Saint Gregory the Sinaite: Discourse on the Transfiguration', *Theologia*, vol. 52, no. 1 (1981–1983) 4–54.

——, 'Was St Gregory Palamas St Gregory the Sinaite's Pupil?', *St Vladimir's Theological Quarterly*, vol. 28 (1984) 116–30.

——, Discourse on the Transfiguration (St Bernardino 1986).

Barnard, K.M., 'Anastasis (The Anastasis): A Study of the Iconographical Development of the Anastasis in Monumental Mosaic and Fresco Decoration during the Macedonian, Comnenian, and Palaeologian Dynasties', MA thesis, Northern Illinois University (1982).

Barnard, L.W., 'The Emperor Cult and the Origins of the Iconoclastic Controversy', *Byzantion*, vol. 43 (1973) 13–29.

Barth, K., 'The Christian Life', *Church Dogmatics*, vol. 4, part 4 (Grand Rapids 1982).

Barthusis, M. et al., 'Days and Deeds of a Hesychast Saint: A Translation of the Greek Life of Saint Romylos', *Byzantine Studies/ Etudes Byzantines*, vol. 9, no. 1 (1982) 24–47.

Bartolo-Abela, C., *The Icon of the Divine Heart of God the Father* (Apostolate-The Divine Heart 2012).

Bauckham, R., '2 Petar and the Apokalipse of Peter', *The Fate of the Dead: Studies on the Jewish and Christian Apocalypses* (Leiden 1998).

Bemberger, J.E., 'Evagrius Ponticus: The Praktikos and Chapters on Prayer', *Cistercian Studies Series* 4 (Spencer 1970).

Beck, H.G., *Kirche und Theologisch Literatur im Byzantinischen Reich* (Munich 1959).

——, 'Intellectual Life in the Late Byzantine Church', in H. Jedin and J. Dolan (ed.), *From the High Middle Ages to the Eve of Reformation: Handbook of Church History* (New York 1968) 505–512.

——, 'Von der Fragwurdigkeit der Ikone', *Scripture Bulletin*, Philosophie & Historie, KL. vol. 7 (Munich 1975) 40–44.

Beckwith, J., *Early Christian and Byzantine Art* (Oxford 1993).

Beeley, C.A., *Gregory of Nazianzus on the Trinity and the Knowledge of God: In your Light we see Light* (Oxford 2008).

Belting, H., *Des Illuminierte Buch in der Spatbyzantinischen Gesellschaft* (Heidelberg 1970).

——, 'Le Peinture Manuel Eugenicos de Constantinople en Georgie', *Cahiers Archaeologique*, vol. 28 (1979) 103–114.

——, 'Image, Medium, Body: A New Approach to Iconology', *Critical Inquiry*, vol. 31, no. 2 (Winter 2005) 302–319.

Belting, H., et al., *The Mosaics and Frescoes of Scht. Mary Pammakaristos (Fethiye Camii) at Istanbul* (Washington D.C. 1978).

Benoît, P., 'L'Icône de la Trinité de Roublev', *Dans Renaissance de Fleury*, no. 101 (1978) 15–40.

Ben Schomaker, *Pseudo-Dionysius de Areopagiet: Over Mystieke Theologie* (Kampen 1990).

Bernabò, M. *Il Tetravangelo di Rabbula: Firenze, Biblioteca Medicea Laurenziana, Plut. 1.56: l'Illustrazione del Nuovo Testamento nella Siria del VI Secolo* (Roma 2008).

Betin, L.V., 'Митрополит Киприан к Феофан Грек', *Etudes Balkaniques*, vol. 1 (Sofia 1977) 109–115.

Beyer, H.V., 'Nichephoras Gregoras als Theologe und sein Crstes Auftreten Gegen die Hesychasten', *Jahurbuch Ostericichen Byzantinistik*, vol. 20 (1971) 171–188.

Bigham, S., *Studies in Orthodox Iconography* (Crestwood 1995).

Bilaniuk, 'The Mystery of Theosis or Divinization', in D. Nieman & M. Schatkin (ed.), *The Heritage of the Early Church. Essays in Honor of the Very Reverend Georges Vasilievich Florovsky*, Orientalia Christiana Analecta, vol. 195 (Rome 1973), 337–59.

Bishop Sylvester, *Опыт Православного Догматического Богословия* (Kiev 1892).

Blankoff, J., *André Roubliov et l'Art de la Russie Ancienne* (Brussels 1961).

Boespflug, F. & Zaluska, Y., 'Le Dogme Trinitarie et l'Essor de son Iconographie en Occident de l'Epoque Carolingienne au IVe Concile du Latran 1215', *Cahiers de Civilisation Medievale*, vol. 37 (1994) 181–240.

Bogdanovic, D., *Јован Лествичник у Византијској и Старој Српској Књижевности* (Belgrade 1968).

Bois, J., 'Le Synode Hesychaste de 1341', *Echoes d'Orient*, vol. 6 (1903) 5–60.

Bones, K., 'Gregory Palamas, der letze der Grossen Byzantinischen Theologen 1296–1359', *Theologia* (Athens 1979) 7–21.

Boonpitak, O., et al., 'Aspects of Symmetry', http://www.uic.edu/honors/learning/hc_aspects_4.pdf (accessed 02/02/2011).

Børtnes, J. & Häggws, T., *Gregory of Nazianzus: Images And Reflections* (Copenhagen 2006).

Bourdeau, L. & Chassé, S., 'Actes du Colloque Sites du Patrimoine et Tourisme, 2–4 Juin 2010, Québec, Canada', *Conference Proceedings World Heritage and Tourism: Managing the Global and the Local*, June 2–4, 2010 (Quebec City 2011) 621–622.

Breck, J., 'Reflection on the Problem of Chalcedonian Christology', *St Vladimir's Theological Quarterly*, vol. 33, no. 2 (1989).

Brehier, L., 'La Renovation Artistique sous les Paleologues et le Mouvement des Idees', in *Melanges Charles Diehl*, vol. 2 (Paris 1930) 1–10.

Brendel, O., 'Origin and Meaning of the Mandorla', *Gazette des. Beaux-Arts*, vol. 25 (1944) 5–24.

Brianchaninov, I. & Ware, K., *On the Prayer of Jesus* (Boston 2006).

Brightman, F.E., 'The Hystorica Mystagogica and other Commentaries on the Byzantine Liturgy', *Journal of Theological Studies*, vol. 9 (1908) 255–256, 390–394.

Briusova, V.G., *Бруисова Андрей Рублев и Московская Школа Иконописи* (Moscow 1998).

Brooks, S.T., *Byzantium, Faith and Power (1261–1557): Perspectives on Late Byzantine Art and Culture* (New York 2006).

Browning, R., *The Byzantine Empire* (Washington D.C. 1992).

Brubaker, L., *Vision and Meaning in Ninth Century Byzantium: Image as Exegesis in the Homilies of Gregory of Nazianzus* (Cambridge 1999).

Buchthal, H., *The Miniatures of the Paris Psalter: A Study in Middle Byzantine Painting* (London 1938).

——, 'Notes on Some Early Palaeologan Miniatures', *Kunsthistorischen Forschungen Otto Piicht zu Seinem 70* (Salzburg 1972) 36–43.

——, 'Toward a History of Palaeologan Illumination', in K. Weitzmann (ed.), *The Place of Book Illumination in Byzantine Art* (Princeton 1975) 143–178.

Bucur, B.G., 'The Theological Reception of Dionysian Apophaticism in the Christian East and West: Thomas Aquinas and Gregory Palamas', *The Downside Review*, vol. 125, no. 439 (April 2007) 131–146.

Bulgakov, S., *Благодатные Заветы Преподнаго Сергия Русскому Богословствованию* (Moscow 1926).

Bunge, G., *The Rublev Trinity: The Icon of the Trinity by the Monk–Painter Andrei Rublev* (Crestwood 2007).

Burrell, D. & Moulin, I., 'Albert, Aquinas, Dyonisus', *Modern Theology*, vol. 24, no. 4 (October 2008) 633–669.

Buschevitch, E.P., 'The Limits of Hesychasm: Some Notes on the Monastic Spirituality in Russia 1350–1500', *Forsch sur Osteurop Gesc*, vol. 38 (1986) 97–109.

Bychov, V.V., *The Aesthetic Face of Being: Art in the Theology of Pavel Florensky* (Crestwood 1993).

Bynum, C.W., *The Resurrection of the Body in Western Christianity, 200–1336* (1995).

Cage, J., *Color and Meaning: Art, Science and Symbolism* (University of California Press 2000).

Calian, C.S., *Theology without Boundaries: Encounters of Eastern Orthodoxy and Western Religion* (Louisville 1992).

Carile, A., *Η Θεσσαλονίκη ως Κέντρο Ορθοδόξου θεολογίας- Προοπτικές στη Ευρώπη Ευρώπη* (Thessaloniki 2000).

Carlton, C.E, 'Transfiguration and Resurrection', *Journal of Biblical Literature*, vol. 80, no. 3 (Sept. 1961) 233–240.

Carr, A.W., 'Two Manuscripts by Joasaph in the United State', *The Art Bulletin*, vol. 63, no. 2 (June 1981) 182–190.

Carter, F.S., 'Celestial Dance: A Search for Perfection, Dance Research', *The Journal of the Society for Dance Research*, vol. 5, no. 2 (Autumn 1987) 3–17.

Casey, M., *The Trinity of Rublev* (London 1981).

Cavarnos, C., *Byzantine Thought and Art* (Belmont 1986).

——, 'Byzantine Churches of Thessaloniki: An Illustrated Account of the Architecture and Iconographic Decoration of Seven Byzantine Churches of Thessaloniki, Together with Important Historical Data', MA thesis, Institute for Byzantine and Modern Greek Studies (Belmont 1995).

Caviness, H., 'Images of Divine Order and the Third Mode of Seeing', *Gesta*, vol. 11, no. 2 (1983) 99–120.

Chadd, L., 'From Byzantium to El Greco', MA thesis, Courtald Institute of Art (2004).

Chaillot, C., 'Contemplating Rublev's Icon: The Authority of the Trinity and the Community of Man and Women in the Church', *The Ecumenical Review*, vol. 60, no. 1–2 (Jan.–Apr. 2008) 137–144.

Charalampidis, C., 'The Representation of the Uncreated Light (Lux Increata) in the Byzantine Iconography of the Transfiguration of Christ', *Arte Mediveale*, vol. 1 (2003) 129–136.

Chatzidakis, M., *L'Icone Byzantine, Saggi e Memorie di Storia dell Annie*, vol. 2 (Venezia 1959), 11–40.

——, 'Classicisme et Tendances Populaires au XIVe Siecle: Recherches sur l'Evolution du Style', *XIVe Congres International des Études Byzantines, Bucarest, Septembre 1971, Actes I* (Bucharest 1971).

——, *Studies in Byzantine Art and Archaeology* (London 1972).

——, 'Classicisme et Tendances Populaires au XIVe Siecle', *Actes du XIVeme Congres International des Etudes Byzantines (Bucarest 1971)*, vol. 1 (Bucharest 1974) 153–188.

——, *Hellenike Techne: Byzantina Psephidota* (Athens 1994).

——, *The Mosaics of Hosios Loukas* (Athens 1997).

Chatzidakis, M. & Grabar, A., *Byzantine and Early Medieval Painting* (New York 1965).

Chemberas, P.A., 'The Transfiguration of Christ: A Study in the Patristic Exegesis of Scripture', *St Vladimirs Theological Quarterly*, vol. 14, no. 1–2 (1970) 48–65.

Cheremeteff, M., 'The Transformation of the Russian Sanctuary Barrier and the Role of Theophanes the Greek', PhD thesis (University of Oregon, 1987.

——, 'The Uncreated Light: Hesychasm, Theophanes the Greek and Russian Iconostasis', *Записки Русской Академической Группы в США* (Moscow 1988) 125–162.

——, 'The Transformation of the Russian Sanctuary Barrier and the Role of Theophanes the Greek', in A. Leong (ed.), *Millennium: Christianity and Russia, A.D. 988–1988* (Crestwood 1990) 107–121.

Chizhyevskiy, D., 'Житие Стефана Пермского, Епископа Пермского', *Apophoreta Slavica II* (Mouton 1959).

Christou, P., 'Double Knowledge According to Gregory Palamas', *Studia Patristica*, vol. 9 (Leuden 1966) 20–29.

——, 'The Teaching of Gregory Palamas on Man', *Myrobyblos: Online Library of the Church of Grace*, http://www.myriobiblos.gr/texts/english/christou_palamas.html.

Chryssavgis, J., *John Climacus: From the Egyptian Desert to the Sinaite Mountain* (London 2004).

Clucas, L.M., 'The Hesychast Controversy in Byzantium in the Fourteenth Century: A Consideration of the Basic Evidence', PhD thesis, University of California (1975).

——, 'Eschatological Theory of Byzantine Hesychasm: A Parallel to Joachim de Fiore', *Byzantinische Zeitschrift*, vol. 70, no. 2 (October 1977) 324–346.

Conceva, M., 'За Търновската Живописна Школа', *Търновска Книйовна Школа 1371–1971* (Sofia 1974).

Constan, E.C., *The Wall Paintings of the Panagia Olympiotissa at Elasson in Northern Thessaly*, vol. 1 (Athens 1992) 224–227.

Contenau, G., 'La Representation des Divinites Solaires en Babylonie', *Revue Biblique*, vol. 12 (1917).

Cooper, H.R., *Slavic Scriptures: The Formation of the Church Slavonic Version* (Boston 1981).

Cormack, R., *Byzantine Art* (Oxford 2000).

——, '... and the Word was God: Art and Orthodoxy', in A. Louth & A. Casiday (eds.), *Byzantine Orthodoxies: Papers from the Thirty-Sixth Spring Symposium of Byzantine Studies, University of Durham, 23–25 March 2002* (Aldershot 2006) 111–115.

Corneanu, N., 'The Jesus Prayer and Deification', *St Vladimir's Theological Quarterly*, vol. 39 (1995) 19.

Cotsonis, J., 'The Virgin with the Tongues of Fire on Byzantine Lead Seals', *Dumbarton Oaks Papers*, vol. 48 (1994) 221–227.

Cummings, C., 'The Name of Jesus', *Cistercian Studies Series*, vol. 44 (Kalamazoo 1978) 220–209.

Ćurčić, S., 'Medieval Royal Tombs in the Balkans: An Aspect of East, or West Question', *Greek Orthodox Theological Review*, vol. 29 (1984) 175–94.

——, 'Divine Light: Symbol and Matter in Byzantine art', lecture, Onasis Foundation, 2 Jul. 2007; http://www.onassis.gr/enim_deltio/foreign/08/lecture_07.php (accessed 25 Aug. 2010).

Ćurčić, S. & Mauriki, D., *The Twilight of Byzantium: Aspects of Cultural and Religious History in the Late Byzantine Empire: Papers from the Colloquium held at Princeton University* (Princton 1991).

Cutler, A., 'The Marginal Psalter in the Walters Art Gallery: A Reconsideration', *Journal of Walters Art Gallery*, vol. 35 (1977) 36–61.

——, 'Main Sources of Patronage in Byzantium', *Jahrbuch der Ostereichiscen Byzantinisk*, vol. 31 (Vienna 1981) 759–82.

Cvetković, B., 'Intentional Asymmetry in Byzantine Imagery: The Cvetkovićthe Apostles in St Sophia of Ohrid and later Instances', *Byzantion*, vol. 76 (2006) 74–96.

Dale, T.E.A., *Relics, Prayer, and Politics in Medieval Venetia: Romanesque Painting in the Crypt of Aquileia Cathedral* (Princeton 1997).

D'Alsace, P.B.D., *La Mount Tabor* (Paris 1900).

Danielou, J., *Theologie du Judeo-Christianisme* (Paris 1958).

Daniilia, S., et al., 'The Byzantine Wall Paintings from the Protaton Church on Mount Athos, Greece: Tradition and Science', *Journal of Archaeological Science*, vol. 34, no. 12 (December 2007) 1971–1984.

Danilova, I.E., 'Иконографический Состав Фресок Рождественской Церкви Ферапонтова Монастыря', *Истории Русского и Западноевропейского скусства Материалы и Исследования* (Moscow 1960) 103–117.

Darrouzes, J., (ed.), *Symeon the Nouveau Theologien: Chapitres Théologiques Gnostiques et Pratiques* (Paris 1951).

——, 'Lettre Inedite de Jean Cantacuzene Relative a la Controverse Palamite', *Revista Eclesiástica Brasileira,* 7 (1959) 7–50.

Dechow, J.F., *Dogma and Mysticism in Early Christianity: Epiphanius of Cyprus and the Legacy of Origen* (Macon 1988) 19–23.

Deletant, D.J., 'Some Aspects of the Byzantine Tradition in the Rumanian Principalities', *Slavonic and East European Review,* vol. 59, no. 1 (January 1981) 1–14.

Delvoye, S., 'Chronique Archaeologique', *Byzantion* 34 (1964) 135–160.

Demina, N.A., *Андрей Рублев и Художники его Круга* (Moscow 1963).

——, О Связях Андрея Рублева и Мастеров его Круга с Іскусством и Культурой Киевской и Владимиро —Суздальской Руси, *Андрей Рублев и его Эпоха* (1963) 125–141.

——, *Троица Андрея Рублева* (Moscow 1963).

de Muralt, E., *Catalogue des Manuscrits Grecs de la Bibliothèque Impériale Publique* (St Petersburg 1864).

Demus, O., *Byzantine Mosaic Decoration* (London 1948).

——, 'The Style of Kariye Djami and its Place in the Development of Palaeologan Art', in P. Underwood (ed.), *The Kariye Djami: Studies in the Art of Kariye Djami and its Intellectual Background* (Princeton 1975) 109–159.

Demus, O. & Diez, E. *Byzantine Mosaics in Greece,* Hosios Lucas & Daphni (Harvard 1931).

Demus, O. & Kessler, H.L., *The Mosaic Decoration of San Marco* (Venice 1988).

Dennis, G.T., 'The Deposition of the Patriarch Calecas', *Jahrbuch der Osterreichischen Byzantinistik,* vol. 9 (1960) 51–55.

de Régnon, T., *Etudes sur la Sainte Trinité,* vol. 1 (Paris 1892).

Devos, P., 'La Version Slave de la Vie de S. Romylos', Byzantium 31 (1961) 149–187.

Di Achille, A.M., 'Sur Iconographia Trinitaria Medievale: La Trinita del Santuario sul Monte Autore Presso Valapietra', *Arte Medievale,* vol. 2, no. 5 (1991) 49–73.

Didron, N., *Iconographie Chretienne. Historie di Dieu* (Paris 1843), E.J. Millington (trans), (New York 1851).

Dilke, O.A.W., 'Cartography in the Ancient Word: A Conclusion', in J.B. Harley & D. Woodward (eds), *History of Cartography*, vol. 1 (Chicago 1987) 276–279.

Dimitrieva, M., 'Rospisi Hrama Spasha Preobrazenija na Kovaleve (1380) v Novgorode', PhD thesis, Lomonosov Moscow State University (Moscow 2003).

Dinkler, E., *Das Apsismosaik von S. Apollinare in Classe* (Cologne 1964).

——, 'La Peinture Murale de Resava: Ses Origines et sa Place dans la Peinture Byzantine', *L'Ecole de la Morava et son Temps, Symposium de Resava 1968* (Belgrade 1972) 277–291.

——, *Византијске Фреске у Југославији* (Belgrade 1974).

——, 'La Peinture Murale Byzantine XIIe et XIIIe siècles', *Acts of 15th International Congress of Byzantine Studies Athens 1976*, vol. 10 (1979) 159–252.

Djordevic, I.M., 'The Dialogue Relationship between the Virgin and Christ in East Christian Art: Apropos of the Discovery of the Figures of the Virgin Mediatrix and Christ in Lesnovo', *Zograf*, vol. 38 (2000) 13–28.

Djurić, V.J., *Византијске фреске у Југославији* (Belgrade 1974).

——, *Манастир Раваница и Раванички Живопис 1381–1981* (Belgrade 1981).

——, 'Les Miniatures du Manuscript Parisinus Graecus 1242 et le Hesihasme', *L'Art de Théssaloniques et de Pays Balcaniques et les Courants Spirituals au XIVe Siecle: Recueil des Rapports du IVe Colloque Serbo-Grec* (Belgrade 1987) 89–94.

——, *Sopočani* (Belgrade 1991).

Dodd, E. C., *Medieval Painting in the Lebanon* (Reichert 2004).

Dodecanese, A., 'Ηεσυςηασμ ανδ τηε ΩαΛΛ Παιντινγσ ιν τηε Cηθρcη οφ Στ. Νικολασ, Cηελι, Νικοσ', *Αρcηαελογιcον Δελτον*, vol. 54 (1999).

D'Onofrio, G. & Struder, B., *The History of Theology: Middle Ages* (2008).

Downey, G., 'Description of the Church of the Holy Apostles at Constantinople', XVII, *Transactions of the American Philosophical Society*, vol. 47, part 6 (1957) 903–904.

——, 'The Tombs of the Byzantine Emperors at the Church of the Holy Apostles in Constantinople', *The Journal of Hellenic Studies* (The Society for the Promotion of Hellenic Studies 1979) 27–51.

Dragas, G.D., 'The Synodical Procedure followed in the Hesychastic Disputes', *The Greek Orthodox Theological Review*, vol. 45 (2000) 631–646.

Drpic, I., 'Art, Hesychasm and Visual Exegesis: Parisinus Graecus 1242 Revisited', *Dumbarton Oaks Papers*, vol. 62 (2008) 217–247.

Dufrenne, S., 'La Manifestation Divine dans l'Iconographie Byzantine de la Transfiguration, Nicee II, 787–1987', B. Boespflug & N. Lossky (eds), (Paris 1987).

Dulskis, R., 'Τρυσ Hεσυcηιjoσ Παкoπoσ, Vεδαvcιoσ I Aθτεvτισкα Kριкσcιovισкojo MαλδivγθμoKoкυβε, Λωγωσ', *A Journal of Religion, Philosophy, Comparative Cultural Studies and Art*, vol. 44 (2005) 50–58.

——, 'Hesychastic Ideas in the Oeuvre of St Andrei Rublev, *Logos-Vilnius* (2007) 126–142.

Dyadakova, K., *Science in Russia, Browsing through a Book: Monasteries in Russia* (Moscow 2003).

Dzuric, V.J., *Byzantinishen Fresken in Yougoslavien* (Munich 1976).

Eastmond, A., *Art and Identity in Thirteenth-Century Byzantium: Hagia Sophia and the Empire of Trebizond* (Oxford 2004).

Ekonomtsyev, I., Исихазм и Возрождение: Исихазм и Проблема Творчества, *Златоуст*, vol. 1 (Moscow 1992) 139–170.

Elsner, J., 'Image and Iconoclasm in Byzantium', *Art History* (1988) 471–491.

——, 'The Viewer and the Vision: The Case of the Sinai Apse', *Art History*, vol. 17, no. 1 (March 1994) 81–102.

——, *Art and the Roman Viewer* (Cambridge 1995).

Emchenko, E.B., *Стоглав: Исследование и Текст* (Moscow 2000).

Evdokimov, P., *L' Orthodoxie, Delachaux et Niestle* (Paris 1959).

——, 'The Icon of the Holy Trinity', *Lutheran World*, vol. 23, no. 3 (1976) 166–170.

——, *The Art of Icon: A Theology of Beauty* (Crestwood 1998).

Every, G., *The Time of the Spirit: Readings through the Christian Year* (Crestwood 1984).

Evseeva, L.M., 'Две Символические Композиции в Росписи XIV века Монастыря Зарзма', *Византийский Временник*, vol. 43 (1982) 134–140.

——, *Эсхатология 7000 Года и Возникновение Высокого Иконостаса* (Moscow 2000).

Farkansfalvy, D., 'The Ecclesial Setting of Pseudepigraphy in Second Peter', *The Second Century*, vol. 5, no. 1 (1985–1986) 3–29.

Featherstone, J.M., *Theodore Methochites's Poems to Himself* (Vienna 2000).

Fedorov, G.P., *The Russian Religious Mind* (Harvard 1946).

——, *The Russian Religious Mind: Kievan Christianity, The Tenth to the Thirteenth Centuries* (Harvard 1966).

Feldman, L.H., *Judaean Antiquities 1–4, Translation and Commentary* (Leiden 2000).

Fideler, D., *Jesus Christ, Sun of God: Ancient Cosmology and Early Christian Symbolism* (New York 1993).

Fiene, D.M., 'What is the Appearance of Divine Sophia?', *Slavic Review*, vol. 48, no. 3 (Autumn 1989) 449–476.

Filindash, L.V., 'Hesychasm and its Influence on Byzantine and Russian Iconography in XIV and XIV century', PhD thesis (Moscow 2005).

Florensky, P., 'Троице-Сергиевой Лавры. Сергиева монастыря и в России', *Троице-Сергиевой Лавры Сергиева монастыря* (Moscow 1919).

——, 'Иконостас', *Собрание Сочинений*, vol. 1 (Paris 1985).

——, 'St Gregory Palamas and the Tradition of the Fathers', *St Gregory Palamas: Collected Works*, vol. 1 (Vaduz 1987) 105–120.

——, *The Inverted Perspective and other Writings* (Bucharest 1997).

——, 'Reverse Perspective', in N. Misler (ed.), *Beyond Vision: Essays on the Perception of Art* (London 2002).

Florovsky, G., *О Почитании Софии Премудрости Божией в Византии и на Руси, Труды 5-го Съезда Пусских Академических Организаций за Границей* (Sofia 1932).

Forsyth, G.H. & Weitzmann, K., *The Monastery of Saint Catherine at Mount Sinai* (Princeton 1973).

Fortescue, A. 'Hesychasm', *The Catholic Encyclopedia*, http://www.newadvent.org/cathen/07301a.htm (accessed 25/11/2009).

Frazer, M.E., 'Church Doors and the Gates of Paradise: Byzantine Bronze Doors in Italy', *Dumbarton Oaks Papers*, vol. 27 (1973) 145–162.

Fryde, E., *The Early Palaeologan Renaissance 1261–1360* (Leiden 2000).

Fyeoktistov, L.A.A., *Города Россuu* (Moscow 2007).

Gabelic, S., *Manastir Lesnovo: Istorija i Slikarstvo* (Belgrade 1998).

Gabra, G., *The Treasures of Coptic Art and Architecture in the Coptic Musum and Churches of Old Cairo* (Cairo 2007).

Galavaris, C., *Studies in Manuscript Illumination* (Princeton 1969).

——, 'Στη μνήμη του Ανδρέα Γρηγ, Ξυγγόπουλου (1891–1979)', *Δελτίον ΧΑΕ*, vol. 10 (1980–1981) 85–94.

Gambero, L.S.M., *Mary and the Fathers of the Church: The Blessed Virgin Mary in Patristic Thought* (San Francisco 1999).

Gamillscheg, M.H., *Die Symbolik von Licht und Finsternis in der Orthodoxen Ikonographie* (Vienna 1979).

Gasparov, B. & Raevsky-Hughes, O., *Slavic Cultures in the Middle Ages* (Los Angeles 1993).

Gavryooshin, N.K., *Философия Русского Религиозного Искусства XVI–XXвв* (Moscow 1993).

Geanokoplos, D., *Constantinople and the West: Essays on The Late Byzantine (Palaeologan) and Italian Renaissances and The Byzantine and Roman Churches* (Wisconsin 1989).

Gelzer, H., 'Abriss der Byzantinischen Kaisergeschichte', in K. Krumbaker (ed.), *Geschichte der Byzantinischen Litteratur* (Munich 1897) 911–1067.

Georgios, I.M., 'Spiritual Life in Palamism', in J. Rait et al. (eds), *Christian Spirituality: High Middle Ages and Reformation*, vol. 17 (New York 1987) 208–222.

Gerke, F., *La Metamorphosi nell'Arte Protobyzantine*, vol. 7 (Rome 1960) 99–111.

Gerstel, S.E.J., 'Civic and Monastic Influences on Church Decoration in Late Byzantine Thessalonike: In Loving Memory of Thalia Gouma-Peterson', Symposium on Late Byzantine Thessalonike, *Dumbarton Oaks Papers*, vol. 57 (2003) 225–39.

——, 'The Chora Parekklesion, the Hope for a Peaceful Afterlife, and Monastic Devotional Practices', in H.A. Klein et all. (eds), *The Kariye Camii Reconsidered*, Istanbul Research Institute Symposium Series 1 (Istanbul 2011) 107–145.

Giakalis, A., *Images of the Divine: The Theology of Icons at the Seventh Ecumenical Council* (New York 1994).

Gianelli, G., *Un Progetto di Barlaam per l' Unione delle Chiese: Studi e Testi* (Vatican 1946).

——, 'Una "Edito Maior" delle "Quaestiones et Dubia" di S. Masimo il Confessore', a paper given at the Ninth International Congress of Byzantine Studies, Thessaloniki, 1953, *Scriptora Minora: Studi Byzantine et Neollenici*, vol. 10 (1963) 215–224.

Gillet, L. & Ware, K., *The Jesus Prayer* (Crestwood 1987).

Glebova, A. et al., 'Древнерусское Искусство в Собрании Вологодского Музея-Заповедника: Путеводитель по Экспозиции', *Северный Паломник*, vol. 11 (2004) 20–22.

Gligorijević-Maksimović, M., 'Classical Elements in the Serbian Painting of the Fourteenth Century', *Byzantine Studies*, vol. 47 (2007) 363–370.

Goldfrank, D.M., 'Burn, Baby, Burn: Popular Culture and Heresy in Late Medieval Russia', *The Journal of Popular Culture* 31, no. 4 (1998) 17–32.

——, *The Monastic Rule of Iosif Volotsky* (Kalamazoo 2000).

Goleizovskii, N.K., 'Пресвятая Троица и Домостроительство', *Журнал Московской Патриархии*, vol. 7 (1960) 32–40.

——, 'Заметки о Феофане Греке', *Византийский Временник*, vol. 24 (Moscow 1964).

——, 'Послание Иконописцу и Отголоски Исихазма в Русской Живописи на Рубеже XV–XVIвв', *Византийский Временник*, vol. 26 (1965) 219–238.

——, 'Исихазм и Русская Живопись XIV–XV', *Византийский Временник*, vol. 29 (1968) 196–210.

——, 'Факты, События, Люди: Живописец Дионисий и его Школы', *Вопросы Истории*, no. 3 (March 1968) 214–217.

——, 'Заметки о Творчестве Феофана Грека', *Византийский Временник*, vol. 24 (1969) 139–143.

——, 'Икона Живоначальной Троицы', *Журнал Московской Патриархии*, vol. 7 (1972) 69–76.

——, 'Искусство Феофана Грека и Учение Исихастов', *Византийский Временник* (1974) 139–149.

——, 'Воплощение Богословских Идей в Творчестве Преподобного Андрея Рублева', *Богословские Труды*, no. 22 (1983) 3–67.

Golubtsov, M., 'Пресвятая Троица и Домостроительство', *Журнал Московской Патриархии*, vol. 7 (1960) 37–50.

——, 'Икона Живоначальной Троицы', *Журнал Московской Патриархии*, vol. 7 (Moscow 1972) 69–76.

——, 'Воплощение Богословских Идей в Творчестве Преподобного Андрея Рублева', *Богословские Труды*, no 22 (1983) 3–67.

Gouma-Peterson, T., 'Christ as Ministrant and the Priest as Ministrant of Christ in a Palaeologan Program of 1303', *Dumbarton Oaks Papers*, vol. 32 (1978) 197–216.

——, 'Manuel and John Phokas and Artistic Personality in Late Byzantine Painting', *Gesta*, vol. 22, no. 2 (1983) 159–170.

Grabar, A., 'Les Frescoes de Ivanovo et le Art de la Palaeologes', in *Le Art de la Fin du l'Antiquiti at du Moyen Age* vol II (Paris 1968).

——, *Byzantium: Byzantine Art in the Middle Ages* (London 1966).

——, 'The Artistic Climate in Byzantium during Palaeologan Period', in P.A. Underwood (ed.), *The Kariye Djami*, vol. 4 (Princeton 1975) 7–8.

——, *Christian Iconography: A Study of its Origins* (Princeton 1986).

Grace, M., 'Spirit-Centred Eastern Fathers: Symeon the New Theologian and Gregory Palamas', *Diakonia*, vol. 31, no. 2 (1998) 129–38.

Grant, R.M., 'Greek Literature in the Treatise the Trinitate and Cyril Contra Julianum', *Journal of Theological Study*, vol. 15 (1964) 265–299.

Grigorii Camblak, *Похвала Слово за Евтимий [похвала за Евтимий]* (Sofia 1971).

Grotowski, L. & Skrzyniarz, S., 'Towards Rewriting? New Approaches to Byzantine Archaeology and Art', *Series Byzantina*, vol. 8 (2010) 45–65.

Grover, Z., 'Mandala Symbolism and Use in the Mysticsm of Hugh of St Victor', *History of Religions*, vol. 12, no. 4 (1973) 317.

Grozdanov, C., *Saint Sophia of Ohrid* (Zagreb 1991).

——, 'Христос Цар, Богородица Царица, Небесните Сили и Светите Воини во Живописот од XIV и XV век во Трескавец', *Културно Наследство 1985–86* (Skopje 1998) 5–20.

——, 'On the Conceptual and Thematic Foundations of the Fresco Paintings in the Diaconicon of the Church of Virgin Peribleptos in Ohrid', *Zograf*, vol. 33, (2009) 93–100.

Grozdanov, C. & Misguich, L.H., *Kurbinovo* (Belgrade 1992).

Grypeou, E. & Spurling, H., *The Exegetical Encounter Between Jews and Christians in Late Antiquity* (Leiden 2009).

Guéranger, Abbot D.P., *The Liturgical Year*, vol. 12 (Powers Lake 1983).

Guilland, R., 'Les Poésies Inédites de Théodore Métochite', *Byzantion*, vol. 3 (1937) 264–245.

Guillaumont, A., *Les Six Centuries des 'Kephalia Gnostica' d'Evagre le Pontique, Patrologia Orientalis* 28 (Paris 1958).

Guran, P., 'Jean VI Cantacuzène, l'Hésychasme et l'Empire: Les Miniatures du Codex Parisinus Graecus 1242', *Actes des Colloques Internationaux, L'Empereur Hagiograph: 13–14 Mars 2000 et 'Reliques et Miracles', 1–2 Novembre 2000 tenus au New Europe College* (Bucharest 2001) 73–121.

Guran, P. & Flusin, B., 'L'Empereur Hagiographe: Culte des Saints et Monarchie Byzantine et Post-Byzantine', *Actes des Colloques Internationaux, L'Empereur Hagiograph: 13–14 Mars 2000 et 'Reliques et Miracles', 1–2 Novembre 2000 tenus au New Europe College* (Bucharest 2001).

Hamann-McLean, R. & Hallensleben, H., *Die Monumen-Talmalerei in Serbien und Makedonien* (Giessen 1963).

Hamburger, J.F., *St John the Divine: The Deified Evangelist in Medieval Art and Theology* (Berkeley 2002).

Harries, R., *The Passion in Art* (Ashgate 2004).

Hart, T., 'Nicephoros Gregoras: Historian of the Hesychast Controversy', *Journal of Ecclesiastical History*, vol. 2 (1951) 169–179.

Hausherr, I., 'L'Hesychasm: Etude de Spiritualite', *Orientalia Christiana Periodica*, vol. 22 (1965) 5–40.

Haussig, H.W., *A History of Byzantine Civilization*, J.M Hussey (trans), (London 1971).

Hedrick, J.K.N.,'Visual Constructions in the Reign of Justinian: A Neo-Platonic Influence', *Journal of History and Social Science* (Spring 2010) 5–19.

Heil, G. & Ritter, A.M., *Pseudo-Dionysius Areopagita: De Coelesti Hierarchia, De Ecclesiastica Hierarchia, De Mystica Theologia, Epistulae* (Berlin 1991).

Heimann, A., 'L'Iconographie de la Trinite: L'Art Chretien', *Revue Mensuelle*, vol. 1 (September 1934) 37–54.

Hellmo, G., *Adventus Domini: Eschatological Thought in 4th-Century Apses and Catecheses* (Brill 1989).

Hennecke, E., *New Testament Apocrypha* (New York 1963).

Hepell, M., 'The Hesychast Movement in Bulgaria: The Turnovo School and its Relations with Constantinople', *Eastern Churches Review*, vol. 1 (1975) 9–20.

Hero, A.C., 'Some Notes on the Letters of Gregory Akindynos', *Dumbarton Oaks Papers*, vol. 36 (1982) 221–226.

Hillis, G.K., 'To Be Transformed by a Vision of Uncreated Light: A Survey on the Influence of the Existential Spirituality of Hesychasm on Eastern Orthodox History', http://www.arts.ualberta.ca/axismundi/2001/to_be_transformed_part1.php (accessed 15/03/2011).

Hills, J.V., *Parables, Pretenders and Prophecies: Translation and Interpretation in the Apocalypse of Peter 2, Revue Biblique*, vol. 98 (1991) 560–573.

Hisamatsu, E., 'The Significance of the Transfiguration for Hesychasm', *Kobe Kaisei Review*, vol. 44 (2005) 129–40.

Hjort, O., 'Oddities and Refinements: Aspects of Architecture, Space and Narrative in the Mosaics of Kariye Camii', in J.O. Rosenqvist (ed.), *Interaction and Isolation in Late Byzantine Culture, Papers Read at a Colloquium held at the Swedish Research Institute in Istanbul, 1–5 December, 1999* (Stockholm 2004) 27–44.

Hosking, G.A., *Russia and Russians* (Harvard 2003).

Hughes, L., 'Inventing Andrei: Soviet and Post-Soviet Views of Andrei Rublev and his Trinity Icon', *Slavonica*, vol. 9, no. 2 (Nov. 2003) 83–90.

——, 'Art and Liturgy in Russia: Rublev and his Successors', *The Cambridge History of Christianity*, vol. 5, *Eastern Christianity*, M. Angold (ed.), (Cambridge 2006).

Hulme, W.H., *The Middle-English Harrowing of Hell and Gospel of Nicodemus*, vol. 100 (Montana 1907).

Hunger, H., 'Herbert, Johannes Chortasmenos', *Wiener Byzantinische Studien*, vol. 7 (1969) 29–33.

Hunt, P., 'Andrei Rublev's Old Testament Trinity Icon: Problems of Meaning, Intertextuality, and Transmission', *A Journal of Russian (Religious) Thought*, vol. 7–12 (2002–2007) 15–46.

——, 'The Wisdom Iconography of Light: The Genesis, Meaning and Iconographic Realization of a Symbol', *Byzantinoslavica*, vol. 67, no. 1 (2009) 5–118.

——, 'Andrei Rublev's Old Testament Trinity Icon in Cultural Context', in V. Tsurikov (ed.), *The Trinity-Sergius Lavr in Russian History and Culture: Readings in Russian Religious Culture*, vol. 3 (Jordanville 2006) 99–122.

Ilin, M.A., *Искусство Московской Руси Эпохи Феофана Грека и Андрея Рублева: Проблемы, Хипотезы, Исследования* (Moscow 1976) 50–58.

Ioganson, I., 'Великий Русский Художник', *Правда* (14 Sept. 1960).

Ivanov, I., 'Bulgarskoto Българското Книжовно Влияние в Русия при Митрополит Киприан', *Izvestiya na Institut za Bulgarska Literature* (Sophia 1958).

James, M.R., *The Apocryphal New Testament* (Oxford 1924).

Janin, R., *Les Eglises et les Monastires des Grands Centres Byzantins Bithynie, Hellespont, Latros, Galesios, Tribizonde, Athines, Thessalonique* (Paris 1975).

Jazikova, I.K., 'Учение о Фаворском Свете и Иконография, Богословие Иконы: Учебное Пособие' (1995), http://nesusvet.narod.ru/ico/books/yazyk/yazyk9.htm (accessed 31/01/2012).

——, 'Богословие Иконы', http:www/wco /ru/ biblio/ books/ jazyk1/H09-Thm/ (accessed 15/ 9/2011).

Jeremias, M., *Die Holtur des Basilika S. Sabina in Rom* (Tubingen 1980).

Jevtic, A., 'Recontre de la Scholastique et de l'Hesychasme dans l'Oeuvre de le Nilus Cabasilas', *L'Art de Thessalonique et des Pays Balkaniques et les Courants Spirituels au XIVe Siècle Recueil des Rapports du IVe Colloque Serbo-Grec 1987, Éditions Spéciales: Balkanološki Institut*, vol. 31 (1987) 149–157.

——, *The Heavenly Kingdom in Serbia's Historic Destiny*. in B. Dorich & B.W.R Jenkins eds), (Kosovo 1992) 63–69.

Jolivet-Lévy, C., *Etudes Cappadociennes* (London 2002).

Jones, C., et al., *The Study of Spirituality* (Durham 1986).

Jones, J.D., (trans), *The Divine Names and Mystical Theology* (Wisconsin 1980).

Jordanov, S., *Skalniot Manastir Sv. Archangel Michael pri Selo Ivanovo* (Varna 2009).

Kallistos, W., 'The Human Person as an Icon of the Trinity', *Sobornost*, vol. 8, no. 2 (1986) 18.

Kalokyris, D., *The Essence of Orthodox Iconography* (Brookline 1971).

Kałužniack, E., 'Werke des Patriarchen von Bulgarien Euthymius (1375–1393)'; *Nach den besten Handschriften hrsg von Emil Kałužniacki* (Munich 1901).

Kantorowicz, E.H. & Jordan, W.C., *The King's Two Bodies: A Study in Mediaeval Political Theology* (Princeton 1997).

Karahan, A., 'The Palaeologan Iconography of the Chora Church and its Relation to Greek Antiquity', *Konsthistorisk Tidskrift: Journal of Art History*, vol. 2, no. 3 (1997) 89–95.

——, 'Byzantine Holy Images: Transcendence and Immanence', *Orientalia Lovaniensia Analecta*, vol. 176 (Leuven 2010) 109–138.

Kartsonis, A.A., *The Anastasis: The Making of an Image* (Princeton 1986).

——, *Treasures of Mount Athos* (Thessaloniki 1997).

Katsioti, A., 'Ηεσυcηασμ ανδ τηε ΩαλλΠαιντινγσ ιν τηε Cηθρcη οφ Στ. νικολασ, CηεΛι, Νικοσ', *Αρcηαελογιcον Δελτον*, vol. 54 (1999) 327–342.

Kazakova, N.A. & Lur'e, Ia. S., *Антифеодальные Еретические Движения на Руси Xiv-Начала Xvi века* (Moscow 1955).

Kenna, M.E., 'Icons in Theory and Practice: An Orthodox Christian Example', *Harvard Review*, vol. 24, no. 4 (1985) 344–359.

Kesich, V., 'Resurrection, Ascension, and the Giving of the Spirit', *The Greek Orthodox Theological Review*, vol. 25 (1980) 249–259.

Kessler, H.L., *Spiritual Seeing: Picturing God's Invisibility in Medieval Art* (Philadelphia 2000).

Kiselinkov, V.S., 'Житието на Св. Теодосий', *Търновски Като Исторически Паметник* (Sofija 1926).

Kitzinger, E., 'The Byzantine Contribution to Western Art of the Twelfth and Thirteenth Centuries', *Dumbarton Oaks Papers*, vol. 20 (1966) 25–47.

Klein, A., et al., 'The Chora Parekklesion, the Hope for a Peaceful Afterlife and Monastic Devotional Practices', *The Kariye Camii Reconsidered*, Istanbul Research Institute Symposium Series, vol. 1 (Istanbul 2011) 107–145.

Kluchevsky,.V.O., 'Значение Преподобного Сергия для Русского Народа и Государства', *Богословский Вестник* (November 1892) 190–204.

Kniazeff, A., 'La Theotocos dans le Offices du Temps Paschal', *Irenikon*, vol. 1 (1961).

Koester, H., *History, Culture And Religion of the Hellenistic Age* (Philadelphia 1982).

Komec, A.I., 'Роль Княжеского Заказа в Построении Софийского Собора в Киеве', *Древнерусское Искусство: Художественная Культура Домонгольской Руси* (Moscow 1972) 50–64.

Kondakov, N.P., *Histoire de l'Art Byzantin Considéré Principalement dans les Miniatures*, 2 vols. (Paris 1886–1891).

——, 'Лицевой Иконописный Подлинник', *Иконография Господа Бога нашего и Спаса Иисуса Христа* (St Petersburg 1905).

Konstantinova, K., 'Някои Моменти на Българо-Византийските Связи', *Старобългарска Литература* (Sofia 1971).

Kopylov, V., 'Hesychasm and Creative Activity of Andrei Rublev', paper given to the 16th International Patristic Byzantine Symposium in Thessaloniki 26th May 1999, *Patristic and Byzantine Review*, vol. 18–19 (1999) 41–47.

——, 'Hesychasm and Creative Work of Andrei Rublev', *Patristic and Byzantine Review*, vol. 18–19 (2000) 41–47.

Kornakov, D., 'Манастирот Зрзе', *Културно — Моментиисториско Наследство Наследство во Ср. Македония*, vol. 11 (1972) 15–19.

Kostic, D., 'Један Податак о Антиисихастичком Расположењу медју Србима Средином', *Хиландарски Зборник*, no. 10 (1998) 221–233.

Kovalevsky, O., *Saint Sergius and Russian Spirituality*, E.W. Jones (trans) (Crestwood 1976).

Kravyets, B. & Medvedeva, L.P., *Иосиф Волоцкий* (Moscow 1993).

Kristeller, P.O., *Renaissance Thought and the Arts: Collected Essays* (Princeton 1980).

Krivocheine, B., 'Аскетическое и Богословское Учение Святого Григория', *Seminarium Kondakovianum*, vol. 8 (Prague 1931) 99–116.

——, *In the Light of Christ: Saint Symeon the New Theologian* (Crestwood 1987).

Krivocheine, B. (ed.) *St Symeon the New Theologian* (Crestwood 1986).

Kroning, W., 'Zur Transfiguration der Cappella Palatina in Palermo', *ZKunstw*, vol. 9 (1956) 162–179.

Kuhlman, J., *Die Taten des Einfachen Gottes. Eine Römisch-Katholische Stellungnahme zum Palamismus* (Würzburg 1968).

Kuyumdzieva, M., 'The Face of God's Divinity: Some Remarks on the Origin, Models and Content of the Trinity Images of Synthronoi Type in Post-Byzantine Painting', *Scripta & e-Scripta*, vol. 5 (2007) 161–182.

Kuz'min, N., 'Андрей Рублев', *Новый Мир*, vol. 10 (Moscow 1960).

Kvlividze, V., et al., *Воскресение Иисуса Христа: Иконография, Православная Энциклопедия*, vol. 9 (Moscow 2005) 414–423.

——, 'La Methode d'Oraison Hesychaste', *Orientalia Christiana Periodica*, vol. 2, no. 2 (Rome 1927) 101–209.

Lane, B.C., 'Sinai and Tabor: Apophatic and Kataphatic Symbols in Tension', *Stoicorum Veterum Fragmenta*, no. 13–14 (1992–1993) 189–205.

Lange, R., *The Resurrection* (London 1967).

Laourdas, B., 'Φιλοqενοθ Πατριανρσοθ Κωνσταντινοπονλεω': Δεγκωνμιον εij' το;ν 'Αγιον Δημηντριον', *Μακεδονικαν*, vol. 2 (1941–1952) 558–582.

——, *Νικολάου Καβάσιλα προσφώνημα καὶ ἐπιγράμματα εἰς ἅγιον Δημήτριον* (Athens 1952).

Latash, M.L., *Synergy* (New York 2008).

Lawrence et al., 'Anastasis: Icon, Text and Theological Vision', *Australian EJournal of Theology*, vol. 7 (2006), http://dlibrary.acu.edu.au/research/theology/ejournal/aejt_7/cross.htm.

Lazarev, V.N., 'Byzantine Ikons of the Fourteenth and Fifteenth Centuries', *The Burlingtone Magazine for Connoisseurs*, vol. 71, no. 417 (Dec. 1937) 249–261.

——, *История Византийской Живописи*, 2 vols. (Moscow 1947–1948).

——, *Живопись Пскова: История Русского Искусства*, vol. 2 (Moscow 1954).

——, *Дионисий и его Школа* (Moscow 1955).

——, *Феофан Грек и его Школа* (Moscow 1961).

——, *Andrej Rublev* (Milan 1966).

——, *Андрей Рублев и его Школа* (Moscow 1966).

——, *Storia Della Pittura Bizantina* (Torino 1967).

——, *Страницы Истории Новгородской Живописи* (Moscow 1977).

——, *History of Byzantine Art* (Moscow 1986).

——, 'История Византийской Живописи', *Искусство* (1986) 117–118.

——, 'Русская Иконопись от Истоков до Начала XVI века', *Искусство*, no. 83 (2000) 79–80.

Lebedev, A., *Ветхозаветное Вероучение во Времена Патриархов* (St Petersburg 1886).

Lebedev, L.L. 'Кто Изображен на Иконе Троица Андрея Рублева?', *Наука и Религия*, vol. 10 (1988) 60–64.

Lee, D.A., *Transfiguration* (Chicago 2004).

Leonidovna, K. *Русская икона XIV–XVI веков* (Moscow 1988).

La Methode d'Oraison Hesychaste', *Orientalia Christiana Periodica*, I. Hausherr (ed.), vol. 2, no. 2 (Rome 1927) 101–209.

Likhachyov, D., *Культура Руси Времени Андрея Рублева и Епифания Премудрого Конец XIV–Начало XV в* (St Petersburg 1962).

Lin'kov, A., 'Коллекция А.В. Морозова', *Литературная Россия*, no. 33 (1978).

Lison, J., 'La Divination selon Grégoire Palamas: Un Sommet de la Théologie Orthodoxe', *Irenikon*, vol. 67, no. 1 (1994) 59–70.

Lixačev, D.S., *Некоторые Задачи Изучения Второго Южнославянского Влияния в России: Исследования по Славянскому Литературоведению и Фольклористик* (Moscow 1960).

——, *Nekotorye Zadachi Izucheniia Vtorogo Iuzhnoslavianskogo Vliianiia v Rossii, Issledovaniia po Slavianskomu Literaturovedeniiu i Fol'kloristike* (Moscow 1960).

——, *Культура Руси Времени Андрея Рублева и Епифания Премудрого* (Moscow 1962).

——, 'The Illuminations of the Greek Manuscript of the Akathistos Hymn (State Historical Museum Synodal Gr. 429)', *Dumbarton Oaks Papers*, vol. 26 (1972) 253–262.

——, *Vizantitskaia Miniatiura* (Moscow 1977).

Lock, C., 'The Space of Hospitality: On the Icon of the Trinity Ascribed to Andrei Rublev', *Sobornost: Incorporating Eastern Churches Review*, vol. 30, no.1 (2008) 23–53.

Loerke, C., 'Observations on the Representation of Doxa in the Mosaics of S. Maria Maggiore, Rome, and St Catherine's, Sinai; Essays in Honor of Harry Bober', *Gesta*, vol. 20, no. 1 (1981) 15–22.

Lossky, V., 'La Théologie Négative dans la Doctrine de Denys l'Aréopagite', *Revue des Sciences Philosophiques et Théologiques*, vol. 28 (1939) 204–221.

——, *The Mystical Theology of the Eastern Church* (Crestwood 1957).

——, *The Vision of God* (Beds 1963).

——, *Мистическое Богословие* (Kiew 1991).

——, *Theology of the Icon* (New York 1996).

Louth, A., *Denys the Areopagite* (London 1989).

——, 'Light, Vision and Religious Experience in Byzantiun', *The Presence of Light: Divine Radiance and Religious Experience* (Chicago 2004) 85–103.

——, 'The Oak of Mamre, the Fathers and St Andrei Rublev: Patrisitc Interpretation of the Hospitality of Abraham and Rublev's Icon of the Trinity', in V. Tsurikov (ed.), *The Trinity Sergius Lavra in Russian History and Culture* (London 2005) 91–96.

Macarios of Corinth & Nicodemos of the Holy Mountain, in G.E.H. Palmer (ed.), *The Philokalia: The Eastern Christian Spiritual Texts*, vol. 4 (Athens 1961) 121–131.

Mackenzie, D., *Migration of Symbols* (Whitefish 2003).

Macculloch, J.A., *The Harrowing of Hell: A Comparative Study of an Early Christian Doctrine* (Edinburgh 1930).

Maglenovski, J.D., 'The Virgin as the Fountain of Life: Gems of a Late and Post-Byzantine Motif', *Zbornik Matice Srpske za Likovne Umetnosti*, vol. 1, no. 32–33 (2002) 183–192.

——, *Theotokos-Zivonosni Istocnik: Dragulj Jedne Kasne I Postvizantiske Teme* (Belgrade 2003) 188–192.

Maguire, H., 'The Mosaics of Nea Moni: An Imperial Reading', *Dumbarton Oaks Papers*, vol. 46, *Homo Byzantinus: Papers in Honor of Alexander Kazhdan* (1992) 205–214.

Majeska, G.P., *Russian Travelers to Constantinople in the Fourteenth and Fifteenth Centuries* (Washington D.C. 1984).

Makaryk, I. R., *About the Harrowing of Hell* (Kiev 1989).

Makseliene, S., 'The Glory of God and its Byzantine Iconography', MA thesis, The Central European University Budapest (1998).

Malickii, K.N., 'Панагия Русского Музея с Изображением Троицы', *Материалы по Русскому Искусству*, vol. 1 (St Petersburg 1928).

——, 'К Истории Композиций Ветхозаветной Троицы', *Seminarium Kondakovianum*, vol. 2 (Prague 1928) 33–45.

Maloney, G., *Russian Hesychasm: The Spirituality of Nil Sorsky* (Hague 1973).

——, *Pseudo-Macarius: The Fifty Spiritual Homilies and the Great Letter* (New York 1992).

Marcel, R., *Répertoire des Bibliothèques et des et des Cataloguesdes Manuscripts Grecs*, 2nd ed. (Paris 1958).

Markovic, M., 'Илустрације Патеричких Прича у Припрати Хиландарског Католикона', *Осам Векова Хиландара* (Belgrade 2000).

Mathews, T., *Byzantine Aesthetics* (New York 1971).

Mauck, B., 'The Mosaic of the Triumphal Arch of S. Prassede: A Liturgical Interpretation', *Speculum*, vol. 62, no. 4 (October 1987) 813–828.

Mauropoulou-Tsioumē, C., *Buzantinhv Qessa* (Paris 1927).

——, *Vlatadon Monastery* (Thessaloniki 1987).

Mavrodinova, L., *Stenata Zivopis v Balgaria do Kraja na XI vek-Sofija* (Sofia 1996).

Mayer, M.J., *Die Realenzyklopädie fur Protestantishe Theologie und Kirche*, vol. 14 (1904).

M.B., 'Hesychasm: Its Development and Basic Characteristics', *Canadian Catholic Review* (June 1988) 228–232.

McGinn, J.A., *The Transfiguration of Christ in Scripture and Tradition* (Lewiston 1986).

——, 'Trinity Higher than any Being! Imagining the Invisible Trinity', *Aesthetic des Unsichtbaren* (Erschienen 2004) 77–93.

McKenna, S., 'Saint Augustine: The Trinity', *The Fathers of the Church*, vol. 46 (Washington D.C. 1963).

Meiner, F., (ed.), *De Trinitat: (Bucher VIII–XI, XIV–XV, Anhang Buch V): Lateinisch-deutsch* (San Francisco 2001).

Medakovic, D., 'Bogorodica Zivonosni Istocnik u Srpskoj Umetnosti', *Zbornik Radova Vizantološkog Instituta*, vol. 5 (Belgrade 1958) 201–218.

Medvedev, I.P., *Sovremenaя Bibliografiя Isihastshih Sporov v Vizantii 14go Veka* (1973).

Metropolitan Hierotheos of Nafpaktos, Οἱ Δεσποτικες Εορτές: *The feasts of the Lord* (Lebadeia 1995).

——, 'Saint Gregory Palamas as a Hagiorite', http://www.pelagia.org/htm/b16.en.saint_gregory_palamas_as_a_hagiorite.03.htm, (accessed 24/10/2010).

Metropolitan Hierotheos of Nafpaktos & E.E. Cunningham-Williams, *Orthodox Psychoterapy* (Athens 2005).

Metropolitan Tseemee, 'Βυζαντινή Θεσσαλονίκη', *Θεσσαλονίκη: ΡΕΚΟΣ, Γέκδοση* (1996) 130–132.

Meyendorff, J., 'Les Debutes de la Controverse Hesychaste', *Byzantion*, vol. 23 (1953) 104–108.

——, 'L'Origine de la Controverse Palamite: La Premiere Lettre de Palamas a Akindynos', *Theologia*, vol. 25 (1954) 602–630.

——, 'La Première Lettre de Palamas à Akindynos, *Theologia*, vol. 25 (Athens 1955) 602–630.

——, 'Humanisme Nominaliste et Mystique Cretienne a Byzance au XIVe Siecle', *Nouvelle Revue Theologique*, vol. 79, no. 9 (Louvain 1957) 905–914.

——, 'Introduction à l'Etude de Grégoire Palamas', *Patristica Sorbonensia*, vol. 3, no. 38 (Paris 1959).

——, 'Introduction', *Defense de Saints Hesychasts, Texte Critique, Traduction et Notes*, 2 vols (Louvain 1959).

——, 'L'Iconographie de la Sagesse Divine dans la Tradition Byzantine', *Cahiers Archeologiques*, vol. 10 (Paris 1959) 259–277.

——, *A Study of Gregory Palamas*, G. Lawrence (trans), (London 1964).

——, 'Spiritual Trends in Byzantium in the Late Thirteenth and Early Fourteenth Centuries', *Arte et Societé à Byzance sous les Paleologues: Acts du Colloque Organise par l'Association Internationale des Etudes Byzantines in Venice en Septembre 1968* (Venice 1971).

——, 'Spiritual Trends in Byzantium in the Late Thirteenth and Early Fourteenth Centuries', in P. Underwood (ed.), *Kariye Dzami* (Princeton 1975) 103–106.

——, 'Le Theme du Retour en Soi dans le Doctrine Palamite du XIV siecle', *Byzantine Hesychasm: Historical, Theological and Social Problems* (London 1972) 204–206.

——, *Gregorie Palamas: Defense des Saint Hesychastes*, 2nd edn (Louvain 1973) 596–569.

——, 'L'Hésychasme: Problêmes de Sémantique', in *Mélanges D'Histoire des Religions Offerts à H.-Ch. Puech* (Paris 1973), 543–47.

——, *Byzantine Hesychasm: Historical, Theological and Social Problems: Collected Studies* (London 1974),.

——, 'О Византийском Исихазме и его Роли в Культурном Историческом Развитии Восточной Европы: История Церкви и Восточно-Христианская Мистика', *Труды Отдела Древнерусской Литературы*, vol. 29 (Moscow 1974) 291–305.

——, 'Society and Culture in the Fourteenth Century: Religious Problems', in M. Berza & E. Stanescu (eds), *Actes du XIV Congres International des Etudes Byzantines, Bucarest, 6–12 Septembre, 1971* (Bucharest 1974) 111–124.

——, *St Gregory Palamas and Orthodox Spirituality*, A. Fiske (trans), (New York 1974).

——, 'Spiritual Trends in Byzantium in the Late Thirteenth and Early Fourteenth Centuries', in P. Underwood (ed.), *Kariye Dzami*, (Princeton 1975) 103–106.

——, *Orthodox Theology in the Modern World* (New York 1981).

——, *Byzantine Theology: Historical Trends and Doctrinal Themes* (New York 1983).

——, 'Is "Hesychasm" the Right Word? Remarks on Religious Ideology in the Fourteenth Century', *Harvard Ukrainian Studies*, vol. 7 (1983) 447–457.

——, 'Wisdom-Sophia: Contrasting Approaches to a Complex Theme', *Studies on Art and Archeology in Honor of Ernst Kitzinger on His Seventy-Fifth Birthday*, vol. 41 (1987) 391–401.

——, 'Mount Athos in the Fourtheenth Century, Spiritual and Intellectual Legacy', *Dumbarton Oaks Papers*, vol. 42 (1988) 157–65.

——, *Byzantium and the Rise of Russia: A Study of Byzantino-Russian Relations in the Fourteenth Century* (Crestwood 1989).

——, 'New Life in Christ: Salvation in Orthodox Theolcgy', *Theological Studies*, vol. 50 (1989) 481–499.

——, 'О Византийском Исихазме и его Роли в Культурном Историческом Развитии Восточной Европы', *История Церкви и Восточно-Христианская Мистика* (Moscow 2003).

Meyendorff, P., *St Germanus of Constantinople: On the Divine Liturgy, Trans., Introduction and Commentary* (Crestwood 1984).

Miklosich, F.R.V., *Monumenta Serbica: Spectantia Historiam Serbiae Bosnae Ragusii* (Vienna 1858).

Miller, D., 'Rublev's Old Testament Trinity or the Appearance of the Holy Mother of. God to Saint Sergius: Dual Iconographic Signifiers of the Holy Trinity, Monastery in the First Centuries of its Existence', PhD thesis (1992).

Millet, G., *Recueil des Inscriptions Chrétiennes de l'Athos Paris* (Paris 1904).

——, *Monuments Byzantins de Mistra* (Paris 1910).

——, *La Peinture du Moyen-Age en Yougoslavie* (Paris 1954).

——, *Recherches sur l'Iconographie de l'Evangile aux XIVe, XVe et XVIe Siecles d'Après les Monuments de Mistra, de la Macedoine et du Mont Athos* (Paris 1968).

Millet, G. & Frolow, A., *La Peinture du Moyen Âge en Yougoslavie: Serbie, Macédoine, et Monténégro*, vol. 3 (Paris 1962).

Millet, G. & Velmans, T., *La Peinture du Moyen Age en Yougoslavie: Serbie, Macédoine et Monténégro*, vol. 4 (Paris 1969).

Milosavljevic, B., 'Basic Philosophical Texts in Medieval Serbia', www.doiserbia.nb.rs/ft.aspx?id=0350-76530839079M (accessed 11/01/2012).

Miner, E., 'The Monastic Psalter of the Walters Art Gallery', in Weitzmann et al. (eds), *Late Classical and Mediaeval Studies in Honor of Albert Mathias Friend* (Princeton 1955).

Miquel, D.P., 'Gregoire Palamas, Docteur de l' Experience', *Irenikon*, vol. 37 (1964) 227–237.

——, 'L'Experience Sacrementelle selon Nicolas Kabasilas', *Irenikon*, vol. 2 (1965) 130.

Misguich, L., *Kurbinovo: Les Fresques de Saint-Georges et la Peinture Byzantine du XIIe Siècle* (Brussels 1975).

Mitrovic, L.W. & Okunev, N., 'La Dormition de la Sainte Vierge dans la Peinture Orthodoxe', *Byzanlinoslavica*, vol. 3 (1931) 134–174.

Miziolek, J., 'Transfiguratio Domini in the Apse at Mount Sinai and the Symbolism of Light', *Journal of the Warburg and Courtauld Institutes*, vol. 53 (1990) 42–60.

Moore, A.C., *Iconography of Religions: An Introduction* (Minneapolis 1977).

Moraru, A., 'Bulgarian Hesychasts in the XIVth Century and Romanian Monasticism Publication: Studia Universitatis Babes-Bolyai', *Orthodox Theology*, vol. 1–2 (1998) 53–60.

Moroziuk, R.P., 'Origen and Apophaticism: The Case of Asomaton in I, 1.1–9 of the Peri Archon', *Logos*, no. 34 (1993) 587–600.

Moshin, V.A., 'O Периодизации Пусско-Южнославянских Литературных Связей X-XV вв', *Труды Отдела Древнерусской Литературы* (St Petersburg 1963) 28–106.

Mouriki, D., 'Αφηγηματική Σκηνή ή Εικονιστική Παράσταση', *Δελτίον της Χριστιανικης Αρχαιολογικης Εταιρείας*, vol. 4, no. 3 (1962–1963) 87–114.

Muller, L., 'Epiphanius, Die Legenden des Heiligen Sergij von Radonez', *Slavische Propylaen*, vol. 17 (Munich 1967) 40–49.

Myslivec, J., 'Verklarung Christi', in E. Kirschbaum & W. Braunfels (eds), *Lexikon der Christlichen Ikonographie*, vol. 4 (Wien 1959) 416–421.

Nadal, J.S., 'La Critique par Akindynos de l'Herméneutique Patristique de Palamas', *Istina*, vol. 19 (1974) 297–328.

——, *Gregorii Acindyni Refutationes duae Operis Gregorii Palamae cui titulus Dialogus inter Orthodoxum et Barlaamitam* (Louvain 1995).

Nasr, S.H. 'The Prayer of the Heart in Hesychasm and Sufism', *Greek Orthodox Theological Review*, vol. 31, no. 1–2 (1986).

Necipoğlu, N., *Byzantine Constantinople* (Brill 2001).

Nellas, P., *Deification in Christ: The Nature of Human Person*, N. Russell (trans), (New York 1987).

Nelson, R. 'Taxation with Representation': Visual Narrative and the Political Field of the Kariye Camii', *Art History*, vol. 22, no. 1 (1976) 156–182.

——, *Visuality Before and Beyond the Renaissance: Seeing as Others Saw* (Cambridge 2000).

——, *Later Byzantine Painting: Art, Agency and Appreciation* (Ashgate 2007).

Nelson, R.S. & Lowden, J., 'The Palaeologina Group: Additional Manuscripts and New Questions', *Dumbarton Oaks Papers*, vol. 45 (1991) 59–68.

Nes, S., *The Uncreated Light: An Iconographical Study of the Transfiguration in the Eastern Church* (Edinburgh 2007).

Nicol, D.M., *The Byzantine Family of Kantakouzenos (Cantacuzenus) ca. 1100–1460: A Genealogical and Prosopographical Study* (Washington, DC 1968).

——, 'The Byzantine Church and Hellenic Learning in the Fourteenth Century', *Studies in Church History* (Leiden 1969) 23–57.

——, 'Thessalonica as a Cultural Centre in the Fourteenth Century', *Studies in Late Byzantine History and Prosopography* (London 1986).

——, *The Reluctant Emperor: A Biography of John Cantacuzene, Byzantine Emperor and Monk, c. 1295–1383* (Cambridge 1996).

——, *The Last Centuries of Byzantium 1261–1453* (Cambridge 1972).

Nicoletta, I., 'Chorós: Dancing into Sacred Space of Chora', *Byzantion*, vol. 75 (2005) 199–224.

Nikeforov, N., 'Икона Святой Троицы Преподобного Андрея Рублева', *Источник: Православная Жизнь*, vol. 51, no. 5 (1955).

Nikitin, A., 'Кто Написал Троицу Рублева?', *Наука и Религия*, vol. 10 (1988) 44–48.

Nikolova, B., *Православните Църкви през Българското Средновековие IX–XIV* (Sofia 2002).

Obolensky, D., *The Byzantine Commonwealth: Eastern Europe 500–1453* (Crestwood 1971).

——, *Bogomils: A Study of Balkans Neo-Manichaeism* (Cambridge 2004).

Okunev, N.L., 'Црква Св. Ђорђе у Старом Нагорићану', *Гласник Скопског Научног Друштво*, vol. 5 (1919).

——, 'Арилье, Памятник Сербского Искусства XIII в', *Seminarium Kondakovianum*, vol. 8 (Prague 1936) 221–258.

——, 'Lesnovo', P. Lemerle (trans), *L'Art Byzantin Chez les Slaves, Les Balkans: Mélanges Théodore Uspenskij*, vol. 1 (Paris 1930) 222–263.

Omont, A., *Miniatures des Plus Anciens Manuscripts Grecs de la Bibliotheque Nationale du VIe au XIVe Siecle* (Paris 1929) 58–59.

——, *Inventaire Sommaire des Manuscrits Grecs de la Bibliothèque Nationale* (Paris 1886).

Onasch, K., *Icons* (New York 1969).

Opie, J.L., 'The Trinity in Andrei Rublev's Icon of the Holy Trinity', *Il Mondo e il Sovramondo del'Icona* (Florence 1998) 197–209.

Orange, H.P.L., 'Lux Aeterne: La Adorozione della Luce nell'Arte Tardoanica el Alto Mediveale', *Randiconti della Pontifica Accademia Romana di Archaeologia*, vol. 67 (Roma 1974–1975) 78–142.

Orthodox Spirituality (Crestwood, N.Y. 1997).

Ostashenko, E.I. 'Троица Ветхозаветная', *Сергиево-Посадского Музея-Заповедника и Проблема Стиля Живописи Первой Трети* (St Petersburg 2002).

Ostrogorsky, G.A., 'Афонские Исихасты и их Противники', *Записки Русского Научного Института Белграде* (Belgrade 1931).

——, *History of the Byzantine State*, J. Hussey (trans), (New Brunswick 1969).

Otis, B., 'Gregory of Nyssa and the Cappadocian Conception of Time', *Studia Patristica*, vol. 117 (1976) 339–241.

Oulsufiev, Y., 'The Development of Russian Icon Painting from the Twelfth to the Ninthenth Century', *Art Bulletin*, vol. 12, no. 4 (December 1930) 347–373.

Ouspensky, L., *Ocerki po Istorii Vizantiskoi Obrazovanosti* (St Petersburg 1982).

——, *The Theology of the Icon* (Crestwood 1992).

Ouspensky, L. & Lossky, V., *The Meaning of Icons* (1982)

Ousterhout, R. 'Temporal Structuring in the Chora Parekklesion', *Gesta*, vol. 34, no. 1 (1995) 63–76.

Panayotidi, M., 'Les Tendances de la Peinture de Thessalonique en Comparaison avec Celles de Constantinople comme Expression de la Situation Politico–Economique de ces Villes Pendant le XIV siecle', *National Hellenic Research Foundation, Institute of Byzantine Research, International Symposiums*, vol. 3 (Athens 1996) 351–362.

Panofsky, E., *Studies in Iconology: Humanistic Themes in the Art of the Renaissance* (Oxford 1939).

Papadopoulos, S., 'Essai d'Interprétation du Thème Iconographique de la Paternité dans l'Art Byzantin', *Cahiers Archéologiques*, vol. 17 (1968) 121–136.

Papamichael, O., *St Gregory Palamas, Archbishop of Thessaloniki* (Alexandria 1911).

Papanikolaou, D., 'Divine Energies or Divine Personhood: Vladimir Lossky and John Zizioulas on Conceiving the Transcendent and Immanent God', *Modern Theology*, vol. 19, no. 3 (July 2003) 359.

Parani, M.G., *Reconstructing the Reality of Images: Byzantine Material Culture* (2003).

Parry, K., 'Theodore Studites and Patriarch Nicephoros', *Byzantion*, vol. 59 (1989) 164–183.

——, *Depicting the Word: Byzantine Iconophile Thought of the Eighth and Ninth Centuries* (Leiden 1996).

Paschos, P.B., 'La Θεολογίας de la Μεταμόρφωση', *Ερως Ορθοδοξίας εκδ Αποστολικής Διακονίας* (Athens 1978) 51–57.

Patterson, J., 'Hesychast Thought as Revealed in Byzantine, Greek and Romanian Church Frescoes: A Theory of Origin and Difussion', *Revue Études Sud-Est Européenes*, vol. 16, no. 4 (1978) 663–670.

Payne, D., 'The Revival of Political Hesychasm in Greek Orthodox Thought: A Study of the Hesychast Basis of the Thought of John S. Romanides and Christos Yannaras', PhD thesis, Baylor University (2006).

Pedoe, D., *Geometry and the Liberal Arts* (Harmondsworth 1976).

Pelekanidis, S.M., *The Treasures of Mount Athos Illuminated Manuscripts Miniatures — Headpieces — Initial Letters* (no year of publication assigned).

Pelikan, J., 'Council of Father or Scripture: The Concept of Authority in the Theology of St Maximus the Confessor', in D. Neiman & M. Schatkin (eds), *The Heritage of the Early Church*, Orientalia Christiana Analecta 195, (Roma 1973) 227–288.

Peltomaa, L.M., 'The Image of the Virgin Mary in the Akathistos Hymn', *Medieval Mediterranean*, vol. 35 (Leiden 2001).

Percival, R., *The Seven Ecumenical Councils, Nicene and Post-Nicene Fathers*, vol. 14 (1956), http://www.ccel.org/ccel/schaff/npnf214.txt (accessed 20/02/2012).

Perl, E.D., 'Grégoire Appuie sa Spiritualité sur une Métaphysique Cohérente, plus Cohérente Même que Celle de Thomas d'Aquin en ce qui Découle du Néo-platonisme', *Dionysius*, vol. 14 (1990) 105–130.

Peterson, T.G., 'The Parekklesion of St Euthymius in Thessalonica: Art and Monastic Policy under Andronicus II', *Art Bulletin*, vol. 58 (1976).

——, 'Manuel and John Phokas and Artistic Personality in Late Byzantine Painting', *Gesta*, vol. 22, no. 2 (1983) 159–170.

Petkovic, S., *La Peinture Serbe du Moyen Age II* (Belgrade 1930).

——, 'Serbian Painting at the Time of George Brankovic (1427–1456)', *Jahrbuch der Osterreichischen Byzantinistik*, vol. 32, no. 5 (1982) 195–203.

——, 'The Lives of Hermits in the Wall Painting of the Katolikon of the Monastery at Josanica', in C. Moss & K. Kiefer (eds), *Byzantine East and Latin West, Art Historical Studies in Honor of Kurt Weitzmann* (Princeton 1995) 289–98.

Petrov, V. & Pryanishnicov, N., 'The Formulas of Beautiful Proportions', *Number and Thought*, vol. 2 (Moscow 1979) 72–92.

Phillips, G., 'La Grâce chez les Orientaux', *Ephemerides Theologicae Lovanienses*, vol. 48 (1972) 38–47.

Picchio, R., 'Hesychastic Components in Gregory Camblak's Eulogy of Patriarch Euthymius of Trnovo', in R. Lenček et al. (eds), *Proceedings of the Symposium on Slavic Cultures, Columbia University, November 14, 1980* (Sofia 1983)
132–143.

Pierce, S., *From Abacus to Zeus: A Handbook of Art History* (Englewood Cliffs 1977).

Plamondon, L.P., 'Divine Illumination: Light as Mystical Imagery in Transfiguration and Anastasis Scenes of Byzantine Iconography', MA thesis, Northern Illinois University (1998).

Plugin, V.A., 'О Происхождении Троицы Рублева', *История СССР*, vol. 2 (Moscow 1987) 64–79.

——, 'Сергий Радонежский, Дмитрий Донской, Андрей Рублев', *История СССР* (Moscow 1989) 71–88.

——, 'Мастер Святой Троицы', *Труды и Дни Андрея Рублева* (Moscow 2001).

Podskalsky, G., 'Gottesschau und Inkarnation, zur Bedeutung der Heilsgeschichte bei Gregorios Palamas', *Orientali Christiana Periodica*, vol. 35 (1969) 124–157.

——, *Theologie and Philosophie in Byzanz* (Munich 1977).

——, 'Review of Theosis bei Palamas und Luther', *Byzantinische Zeitschrift*, vol. 91 (1998) 118–120.

Pokrovsky, N.V., *Notes on Monuments of of Russian Iconography and Art* (St Petersburg 1900).

Polemēs, I., *Theophanes of Nicaea: His Life and Works*, vol. 20 (Vienna 1996).

Politis, K., 'Jean-Joasaph Cantacuzène fut-il Copiste?', *Revue des Études Byzantines*, vol. 14 (1956) 195–199.

Polyvios, K., 'From the Resurrection to the Ascension: Christ's Post-Resurrection Appearances in Byzantine Art', PhD thesis, University of Birmingham (2010).

Pomyalovskiy, I.V., *Житие Святого Григория Синаита: Записки Ист.-Филол. Фак* (St Petersburg 1894–1896).

Popov, G.V., *Živopis i Minijatjura Moskvi Seredini XV Načala XVI Veka* (Moscow 1975).

——, 'Икона Григория Паламы из ГМИИ и Живопись Фессалоник Поздне-Византийского Периода', *Искусство Западной Европы и Византии* (Moscow 1978).

Popova, O.S., *Russian Illuminated Manuscripts* (London 1984).

——, *Особенности Искусства Пскова. из Кн. Отблески Христианского Востока на Руси* (Milan 1993).

——, 'Medieval Russian Painting and Byzantium', in R. Grierson (ed.), *Gates of Mystery: The Art of Holy Russia* (Fort Worth 1992).

Popovich, L.D., *Personification in Palaeologan Painting 1261–1453* (Bryn Mawar Colledge 1963).

Pospielovsky, D., *The Orthodox Church in the History of Russia* (Crestwood N.Y. 1998).

Pribitkov, V.S., 'Сквозь Жар Души: О Трех Древнерус', *Живописцах: А. Рублеве, Дионисии, С. Ушакове* (Moscow 1968) 22–25.

Prokhorov, G.M., 'Публицистика Иоанна Кантакузина 1367–1371', *Византийский Временник*, no. 27 (1968) 318–341.

——, 'Исихазм и Общественная Мысль в Восточной Европев 14в', *Литературные Связи Древних Славян*, vol. 23 (1968) 86–108.

——, *Памятники Литературы Византийско-Русского Общественного Движения Эпохи Куликовской Битвы* (St Petersburg 1977).

——, 'L' Hésychasme et la Pensée Sociale en Europe Orientale au XIV Siècle', *Revue Francaise de l'Orthodoxie Paris*, vol.31, no. 105 (1979) 25–63.

——, 'Гимны на Ратные Темы Эпохи Куликовской Битвы', *Труды Отдела Древнерусской Литературы*, vol. 37 (Moscow 1983) 286–304.

——, 'Послание Титу-Иерарху Дионисия Ареопагита в Славянском Переводе и Иконография Премудрость Созда Себе Дом', *Труды Отдела Древнерусской Литературы*, vol. 38 (1985) 11–12.

——, *Памятники Переводной и Русской Литературы XIV–XV веко* (Leningrad 1987).

——, 'John Kantacuzenos, Диалог с Иудеем', *Труды Отдела Древнерусской Литературы*, vol. 41 (1988) 331–346, vol. 42 (1989) 200–227, vol. 43 (1990) 305–323.

——, 'Pakhomii Serb', in D.S. Lixačev (ed.), *Slovar' Knizhnikov i Knizhnosti Drevnei Rusi*, vol. 2, (Moscow 1987–1993) 167–177.

——, *Dionisii Aeropagit* (St Petersburg 1995).

Prolovic, J., 'Списки рукописи XIII и XIV века у Бечу и Монастир Хиландар', *Хиландарски Сборник* (Beograd 1986) 213–215.

Quenot, M., *The Resurrection and the Icon* (New York 1997).

Radchenko, K.F., *Religioznoe i Kul'turnoe Dvizhenie v Bolgarii v Epokhu pered Turetskim Zavoevaniem* (Kiev 1898).

Radovanovic, J., *Ikonografska Istrazivanja Srpskog Slikarstva XIII i XIV Veka* (Belgrade 1988).

Rahner, H., *Griechische Mythen in Christlicher Deutung. Greek Myths and Christian Mystery*, B. Battershaw (trans.), (London 1963).

——, 'The Christian Mystery of the Sun and Moon', *Greek Myths and Christian Mystery*, B. Buttershaw (trans.) (London 1963).

Raushenbah, M.L., *Пространственные Построения в Живописи* (Moscow 1980).

Rautman, M.L., 'The Church of the Holy Apostles in Thessaloniki', PhD thesis, University of Indiana (1984).

Raya, J. & De Vinck, J., Byzantine Daily Worship; With Byzantine Breviary, the Three Liturgies, Propers of the Day and Various Offices (Allendale 1969).

Reimer, J., 'The Spirituality of Andrei Rublev's Icon of the Holy Trinity', *Acta Theologica Supplementum*, vol. 11 (2008) 167–169.

Reste, M., *Byzantine Wall Painting in Asia Minor*, vol. 1 (New York 1984).

Reynolds, M.A., 'The Octagon in Leonardo's Drawings', http://markareynolds.com/?p=89 (accessed 10/03/2012).

Riasanovsky, V. & Steinberg, M. D., *A History of Russia* (New York 2005).

Richardson, C.R.D., 'The Doctrine of the Trinity: Its Development, Difficulties and Value', *The Harvard Theological Review*, vol. 36, no. 2 (April 1943) 109–134.

Rigo, A. 'Grigorio il Sinaita', in G. Conticello & V. Conticello (eds), *La Theologie Byzantine* (Turnhout 2002) 30–130.

Rist, J.M., *Augustine: Ancient Thought Baptized* (Cambridge 1996).

Rizhov, Y., 'Философия Иконы в Традициях Востока и Запада', http://www.gumer.info/ryjov_filikon.php (accessed 23/06/2011).

Robertson, A., *The Bible of St Mark, St Mark's Church the Altar and Throne of Venice* (Venice 1898).

Rogich, D., 'Homily 34 of Gregory Palamas', *The Greek Orthodox Theological Review*, vol. 33, no. 2 (1988) 135–166.

Romanides, J.S., 'Notes on Palamite Controversy and Related Topics', *The Greek Orthodox Theological Review*, vol. 6, no. 2 (1960/61) 186–205; vol. 9, no. 2 (Winter 1963/64) 225–270.

——, 'Saint Gregory Palamas 1296–1359: Introduction to the Theology of the Romans against the Franks', in J. Romanides & D.D. Kontostergios (eds), *Romans and Roman Fathers of the Church* (Thessaloniki 1984).

Rorem, P., *Pseudo-Dionysius: A Commentary on the Texts and an Introduction to their Influence* (New York 1993).

Ross, L.E., *Medieval Art: A Topical Dictionary* (Greenwood 1996) 10–11.

Rossum, J., 'The Logoi of Creation and the Divine Energies in Maximus the Confessor and Gregory Palamas', *Studia Patristica*, vol. 27 (1993) 212–217.

Roussanova, T.B., 'Painted Messages of Salvation: Monumental Programs of the Subsidiary Spaces of Late Byzantine Monastic Churches in Macedonia', PhD thesis, University of Maryland (2005).

Rudolph, K., *Gnosis* (San Francisco 1985).

Runciman, S., *The Last Byzantine Renaissance* (Cambridge 1970).

Rusev, P., et al., *Похвално Слово за Евтимий от Григорий Цамблак* (Sofia 1973).

——,Търновска Книжовна Школа 1371–1971', *Международен Симпозиум Велико Търново, 11–14 Октомври 1971* (Sofia 1974).

Russell, N., 'Prochoros Cydones and the Fourteenth-Century Understanding of Orthodoxy', in A. Louth & A. Casiday (eds), *Byzantine Orthodoxies* (Durham 2006) 75–91.

Ruzsa, G., 'Une Icone Inconnue Representant les Apotres Pierre et Paul et la Question de l' Hesychasme', *Jahrbuch der Osterreichischen Byzantinistik*, vol. 32, no. 5 (1982) 545–549.

Sandmel, S., *Philos's Place in Judaism: A Study of Conceptions of Abraham in Jewish Literature* (Jersey City, NJ 1972).

Sakovic, A.G., *Narodnaja Gravirovannaja Kniga Vasilija Korenja 1692–1696* (Moscow 1983).

Saltykov, A.A., 'Иконография Троицы Андрея Рублева', *Древнерусское Искусство XIV–XV* (Moscow 1984) 77–85.

——, *Музей Древнерусского Искусства Имени Андрея Рублева* (St Petersburg 1989).

Schaff, P. & Wace, H., 'Justin Martyr: Second Apology (Dialogue with Trypho)', from *Ante-Nicene Fathers*, vol. I (Grand Rapids 1955) 188–270.

Schiller, G., *Iconography of Christian Art*, J. Seligman (trans), 2 vols (London 1971).

Schmidt, D.H., 'The Peters Writing: Their Redactors and their Relationships', PhD thesis, Northwestern University 1972.

——, *God Seekers: Twenty Centuries of Christian Spiritualities* (Grand Rapids 2008).

Schwartz, E.B., *The Wolfenbüttel Sketchbook Reconsidered* (New York 1973).

SedRajna, G., *L'Art Juif: Orient et Occident* (Paris 1975).

Serracino Inglott, P., 'La Trasfigurazione come Epiphania Monarchica', *Arta Christiana*, vol. 60 (1971) 67–96.

Setton, K.M. 'The Byzantine Background to the Italian Renaissance', *Proceedings of the American Philosophical Society*, no. 100 (1956) 1–76.

Ševčenko, I., 'The Decline of Byzantium seen Through the Eyes of its Intellectuals', *Dumbarton Oaks Papers*, vol. 15 (1961) 167–186.

——, 'Theodore Metochites, the Chora, and the Intellectual Trends of his Time', in P. Underwood (ed.), *The Kariye Djami* (London 1967) 17–91.

——, *Society and Intellectual Life in Late Byzantium* (London 1981).

——, 'The Decline of Byzantium Seen through the Eyes of its Intellectuals', *Society and Intellectual Life in Late Byzantium* (London 1981) 171–172.

Sinkewicz, R.E., 'A New Interpretation of the First Episode in the Controversy Between Barlaam the Calabrian and Gregory Palamas', *Journal of Theological Studies*, no. 31 (1980) 489–490.

——, 'The Doctrine of the Knowledge of God in the Early Writings of Barlaam the Calabrian', *Mediaeval Studies*, vol. 44 (1982) 181–242.

——, 'Christian Theology and the Renewal of Philosophical and Scientific Studies in the Early Fourteenth Century: The Capita 150 of Gregory Palamas', *Pontifical Institute of Mediaeval Studies*, vol. 48 (1986) 334–351.

——, *Saint Gregory Palamas: The One Hundred and Fifty Chapters* (Toronto 1988).

Simić-Lazar, D., 'Observations Sur le Rapport Entre les Décors de Kalenić, de Kahrié Djami et de Curtea de Argeş', *Cahiers Archéologiques*, no. 34 (1986) 143–160.

——, *Kalenić et la Dernière Période de la Peinture Byzantine* (Paris 1995).

Sirku, P., *Литургические Труды Патриарха Евфимия* (St Petersburg 1890).

——, 'К Истории Исправления Книг в Болгарии в XIV веке' (St Petersburg 1898).

——, *Житие Григория Синаита Составленное Константинопольским Патриархо Каллистом, Жития по Рукописи XVIв. С. Истор-Археологические Вовед* (St Petersburg 1909).

Skliris, S., 'The Person of Christ and the Style of Icons, A Mystery Great and Wondrous', *Byzantine and Christian Museum. Exhibition of Icons and Ecclesiastical Treasures 28 May – 31 July 2001* (Athens 2001).

Skorobogaceva, E.A., 'Троице Сергиева Лавра и Иконография "Троица Ветхозаветная" в Северных Письмах XVII века', *Троице-Сергиева Лавра в Истории, Культуре и Духовной Жизни России, Матерıалы IV Международной Конференции 20 Сентября – 1 Октября 2004 Года* (Moscow 2007) 228–243.

Sjögren, P.O., *The Jesus Prayer: Lord Jesus Christ, Son of God, Have Mercy upon Me* (Minneapolis 1975).

Smirnova, E. S., 'Иконы XIV – Начала XVI века', http://rus-icons.ru/publication/detail.php?ID=256] (accessed 4/08/2011).

——, *Litsevye Rukopisi Velikogo Novgoroda XV Vek* (Moscow 1994).

——,'Иконографический Вариант 'Сошествия во Ад Ростов, Москва, Север', *Иконы Русского Севера: Двинская земля, Онега, Каргополье, Поморье, Статьи Материалы* (Moscow 2005) 141–161.

Smith, M., 'The Origins and Significance of the Transfiguration Story', *Union Seminary Quarterly Review*, vol. 36 (1980) 39–44.

Smolčić-Makuljević, S., 'The Treskavac Monastery in the 15th Century and the Programme of Fresco Painting of the Nave in the Church of the Dormition of the Mother of God', *Zbornik Matice Srpske za Likovne Umetnosti*, vol. 37 (2009) 43–79.

Snyman, D., 'In the Gaze of God: Aspects of the Spiritual Significance of Rublev's Holy Trinity', MA thesis, Rhodes University (2001).

Sokolov, I.I., *Житие Иже во Святых Отца Нашего Григория Синаита* (Moscow 1904).

Sokolova, N.I., *Selected Works of Russian Art: Architecture, Sculpture, Painting, Graphic Art:11th – Early 20th Century* (St Petersburg 1976).

Spatharakis, J., *The Portrait in Byzantine Illuminated Manuscripts* (Leiden 1976).

——, *The Left-Handed Evangelist: A Contribution to Palaeologan Iconography* (Pindar 1998).

Specieris, K., *Изображения Эллинских Философов в Церквах* (Athens 1964).

Spieser, M., 'Le Programme Iconographique des Portes de Sainte-Sabinem', *Journal des Savants* (1991) 47–81.

Stikas, E.G., 'Une Église des Paléologues aux Environs de Castoria', *Byzantinische Zeitschrift*, vol. 51 (1958) 100–112.

Starodubcev, D., 'Богородица Живоносни Источник у Раваници: Питања Порекла Слике' (unpublished paper) accessed 5/06/2011, in situ (Belgrade 2011).

Steenberg, M.C., 'The Nativity of the Paschal Christ', http://www.monachos.net/content/liturgics/liturgical-reflections/434-nativity-of (accessed 15/02/2012).

Steiner, G., *Real Presences* (University of Chicago 1991).

Stiernon, D., 'Bulletin sur le Palamisme', *Revue des Etudes Byzantines*, vol. 30 (1972) 231–341.

Stikas, G., 'Une Église des Paléologues aux Environs de Castoria', *Byzantinische Zeitschrift*, vol. 51 (1958) 100–112.

Stojanović, S., 'Настанак, Ширење и Прихватање Исихазма у Средњовековне Србије' (accessed 3/11/2009).

Strezova, A., 'Knowledge and Vision of God in the Cappadocian Fathers', *Theandros*, vol. 5, no. 1 (2007) http://www.theandros.com/cappavision.html (accessed 20/3/109).

——,'Relations of Image to its Prototype in Byzantine Iconophile Theology', *Byzantinoslavica*, vol. 66, no. 1–2 (2008) 87–106.

Subotic, G., *Ohridskata Slikarska Skola od XV Vek* (Ohrid 1980).

Tachiaos, L., 'Le Mouvement Hesychaste Pendant les Dernières Décennies du XlVe Siècle', *Kleronomia*, vol. 6, no. 1 (1974) 122–125.

——, 'Hesychasm as a Creative Force in the Fields of Art and Literature', *L'Art de Thessalonique et des Pays Balkaniques et les Courants Spirituels au XIVe Siècle*, (Belgrade 1987) 117–123.

Taft, R.F., 'The Living Icon: Touching the Transcendent in Palaeologan Iconography and Liturgy', in S. Brooks (ed.), *Byzantium: Faith and Power 1261–1557 Perspectives of Late Byzantine Art and Culture* (New York 2007) 54–62.

Talbot-Rice, D., *Art of Byzantine Era* (London 1963).

——, *Byzantine Painting:The Last Phase* (London 1968).

——, *Byzantine Art and its Influences* (London 1973).

Talbot-Rice, D. & Talbot-Rice, T., *Icons and their History* (Overlook Press 1974).

Talbot, M.A., 'Epigrams of Manuel Philes on the Theotokos tes Peges and its Art', *Dumbarton Oaks Papers*, vol. 48 (1994) 131–165.

Tatic-Djuric, M., 'Image et Message de la Theotokos Sorce de Vie', *Association Internationale d'Etudes du Sud-Est European Bulletin*, vol. 9–23, no. 1–2 (Bucharest 1993) 31–47.

Teholiz, L., 'Religious Mysticism and Socialist Realism: The Soviet Union Pays Homage to the Icon Painter', *Art Journal*, vol. 21, no. 2 (Winter 1961–1962) 72–78.

Teitelbaum, B., 'The Knowledge of God', *Eirenikon*, vol. 3, 1 (Fall 1982) 40–47.

Terzian, E., *The Aesthetics and Poetics of Art in Eastern Christian Iconography: A Mythopoetic Perspective* (Carpentaria 2003).

Teteriatnikov, N., 'New Artistic and Spiritual Trends in the Proskynetaria Fresco Icons of Manuel Panselinos, the Protaton', in L. Mavromates (ed.), *Manuel Panselinos and his Age* (Athens 1999) 101–125.

Thomson, F.J., 'Corpus Slavonic Translations Available in Muscovy: The Cause of Old Russia's Intellectual Silence and a Contributory Factor to Muscovite Cultural Autarky', in *Christianity and the Eastern Slavs*, vol. 1, B. Gasparov & O. Raevsky-Hughes (eds), *Slavic Cultures in the Middle Ages* (Los Angeles 1993) 179–215.

Thundberg, L., *Microcosm and Mediator: The Theological Anthropology of Maximus the Confessor* (Chicago 1965) 137–139.

——, 'The Human Person as an Image of God', *Christian Spirituality*, vol. 16 (1985) 291–311.

Thuren, L., 'Style Never Goes out of Fashion: 2 Peter Reevaluated', in S.T. Porter & H. Olbricht (eds), *Rhetoric, Scripture and Theology: Essays from the 1994 Pretoria Conference* (Sheffield 1996).

Tikhomirov, M.N., *Андрей Рублев и его Эпоха: Вопросы История* (Moscow 1967).

Titz, A., 'Some General Features of the Compositions of the Icons of Rublyov and His School', *Ancient Russian Art of the Fifteenth and Early Sixteenth Centuries* (Moscow 1963) 22–53.

Tkacz, C.B., *The Key to the Brescia Casket* (Paris 2001).

——, *Государственныї Русскиї Музеї, Санкт-Петербург: Живопис ХИИ — начала XX Века, Изобразителное Искусство* (St Petersburg 1993).

Todic, B., Gračanica: Slikarstvo (Belgrade 1988).

——,*Staro Nagoricano* (Belgrade 1993).

——, *Serbian Medieval Painting: The Age of King Milutin* (Belgrade 1999).

Todorova, R.G., 'Mandorla in Eastern Orthodox Iconography — Light or Space', http://www.sustz.com/Proceeding08/Papers/THEOLOGICAL%20 STUDIES/Todorova_Rostislava.pdf (accessed 10/03/2011).

——, 'New Religion — New Symbolism: Adoption of Mandorla in Christian Iconography', *Collection of Scientific Works*, Ninth Symposium Niš and Byzantium, 3–5 June 2010, vol. 9 (Niš 2011) 47–64.

Toti, M., 'Anthropological Significance of the Hesychastic Method of Prayer, Some Historico-Religious Aspects of Morphology of the Ascetic Praktiké', *Archaeus: Studies in History of Religions*, vol. 11–12 (2007–2008) 117–132.

Touraille, J., *Philocalie Des Peres Neptiques: Fascicule 7 Thalassius l'African, Jean Damascene, Abbe Philemon, Theognoste, Philothee le Sinaite, Elie l'Ecdicos, Theophane le Climaque* (Kidderminster 1991).

Treadgold, W., *Renaissance before the Renaissance: Cultural Revivals of Late Antiquity and the Middle Ages* (Stanford 1984).

Treadwell, P., *The Resurrection of Eve: A Study of the Anastasis in the Kariye Camii* (London 1988).

Trites, A.A., *The Transfiguration of Christ: A Hinge of Holy History* (Lancelot 1994).

Troizky, I.E, *Arsenius and the Arsenites* (St Petersburg 1873).

Trubetskoi, E.N., *Умозрение в Красках: Три Очерка о Русской Иконе* (Moscow 1991).

Tselengidis, D., 'The Contribution of Saint Gregory Palamas to Hesychasm: Theological Pressumposition of the Life in the Holy Spirit', http://www.saintnicodemos.org/documents/Final_Tselengides_Word.pdf (accessed 10/07/2010).

Tsirpanlis, C.N., 'Byzantine Humanism and Hesychasm in the Thirteenth and Fourteenth Centuries: Synthesis or Antithesis, Reformation or Revolution', *The Patristic and Byzantine Review*, vol. 5, no. 12 (1993), 13–23.

——, 'Epistemology, Theognosis, the Trinity and Grace in St Gregory Palamas', *Patristic and Byzantine Review*, vol. 13, no. 1 (1994) 5–27.

Tugwell, S., *Chapters on Prayer* (Oxford 1981).

Turner, P. & Coffey, K., *Understanding the Revised Mass Texts* (Chicago 2010).

Uliyanov, O.G., 'В Филоксения Авраама: Библейская Святыня и Догматический Образ', *Богословские Труды*, vol. 35 (1999) 225–229.

——, *Воплощение Тринитарного Догмата в Иконе 'Архангел Михаил с Деяниями' из Собрания Музеев Московского Кремля, Троицкие Чтения 2003–2004 гг* (Moscow 2004) 141–142.

——, *О Месте Иконы Живоначальной Троицы в Праздничном Ряду Русского Иконостаса Троицкие Чтения 2003–2004 гг. Большие Вяземы* (Moscow 2004).

——, 'Была ли Литургическая Реформа при Митрополите Алексии в Русской Православной Церкви', in V.T. Pashuto & A.A. Zemina (eds), *Восточная Европа в Древности и Средневековье, Проблемы Источниковедения: XVII Чтения памяти* (Moscow 2005) 268–271.

Underwood, P.A., 'The Fountain of Life in Manuscripts of the Gospels', *Dumbarton Oaks Papers*, vol. 5 (1950) 43–138.

——, 'First Preliminary Report on the Restoration of the Frescoes in the Kariye Camii at Istanbul by the Byzantine Institute 1952–54', *Dumbarton Oaks Papers*, vol. 9 (1956) 253–288.

——, 'Notes on the Work of the Byzantine Institute in Istanbul: 1955–1956', *Dumbarton Oaks Papers*, vol. 12, (1958) 269–287.

——, *The Kariye Djami*, vol. 2 (New York 1966).

Ungureanu, C., 'Dialogue between Sphere and Cube: The Secrete Geometry of Byzantine Icons', *Cultura: International Journal of Philosophy of Culture and Axiology*, vol. 6 (2006) 82–96.

Upadhya, O., *The Art of Ajanta and Sopoćani: A Comparative Study: an Enquiry in Prāna Aesthetics* (1994).

Uspenskiĭ, A., *Semiotics of the Russian Icon* (Philadelphia 1976).

Van Antwerp Fine, J. *The Late Medieval Balkans: A Critical Survey from the Late Twelfth Century* (Michigan 1994).

Van Rosum, J., *Palamism and Church Tradition: Palamism, its Use of Patristic Tradition, and its Relationship with Thomistic Though* (New York 1985).

Van Unnik, V.C., *Patristica, Gnostica, Liturgica* (Leiden 1983).

Vasic, M.M., *Жича и Лазарица: Студије из Српске Уметности Средњег Века* (Belgrade 1928).

——, 'L'Hésychasme dans l'Eglise et l'Art des Serbes du Moyen Age', *L'Art Byzantin Chez les Slaves, Les Balkans: Mélanges Théodore Uspenskij,* vol. 1 (Paris, 1930) 110–123.

Vasileva, O.A., *Иконы Пскова* (Moscow 2006).

Veletev, A., 'Богословское Содержание Иконы: Святая Троица Андрея Рублева', *Журнал Московской Патриархии,* no. 8 (1972) 63–75; no. 10 (1974) 62–65.

Velimirović, N., *The Life of St Sava* (Platina 1989).

Velmans, T., 'Les Fresques d'Ivanovo et la Peinture Byzantine à la fin du Moyen Âge', *Journal des Savants,* no. 1 (1965) 358–412.

——, 'Les fresques de Saint-Nicolas Orphanos à Salonique et la Decoration Monumentale au XIVe Siècle', *Cahiers Archéologiques,* vol. 16 (1966) 145–148.

——, 'L'Iconographie de la Fontaine de Vie dans la Tradition Byzantine a la fin du Moyen Age', *Synthronon: Bibliotheque des Cahiers Archeologiques,* vol. 2 (Paris 1968) 119–134.

——, 'Le Portrait dans l'Art Religieux à l'Époque des Paléologues et son Témoignage sur la Société Byzantine', *Art et Société à Byzance sous les Paléologues: Actes du Colloque Organisé par l'Association Internationale des Études Byzantines à Venice en Septembre 1968* (Venice 1971) 93–148.

——, 'Infiltrations Occidentales dans la Peinture Murale Byzantine au XIVe et au Début du XVe siècle au XIV et au Debut du XVe Siecle', in V. Duric (ed.), *L'École de la Morava et son Temps: Symposium de Résava 1968* (Belgrade 1972) 37–48.

——, 'La Peinture Murale Byzantine a la Fin du Moyen Age', *Bibliotheque des Cahiers Archeologiques*, vol. 1, no. 1 (Paris 1977) 242–246.

——, 'Le Rôle de l'Hésychasme dans la Peinture Murale Byzantine du XIVe et XVe Siècles', in P. Armstrong (ed.), *Ritual and Art: Byzantine Essays for Christopher Walter* (London 2006) 182–226.

——, Art et Mentalité à Byzance (Paris 2009).

Velnee, G., 'Οι Άγιοι Απόστολοι Θεσσαλονίκης και η Σχολή της Κωνσταντινούπολης', *Akten des XVI International Byzantinistenkongress*, vol. 2, no. 4 (Vienna 4–9 October), *Jahrbuch der Österreichischen Byzantinistik*, vol. 32, no. 4 (1981) 457–467.

Vigne, D., 'La Théologie Apophatique de Saint Grégoire Palamas', *Bulletin de Littérature Ecclésiastique*, vol. 106, no. 4 (2005) 349–364.

Vikan, G. (ed.), *Illuminated Greek Manuscripts from American Collections* (Princeton 1973).

Voloshinov, A.V., 'The Old Testament Trinity of Andrey Rublyov: Geometry and Philosophy', *Leonardo*, vol. 32, no. 2 (1999) 103–112.

Voordeckers, E., 'Examen Codicologique du Codex Parisinus Graecus 1242', *Scriptorum*, vol. 21 (1967) 288–294.

Vopovz, O., *Ascesi e Trasfigurazione: Immagini dell'Arte Bizantina e Russa nel XIV Secolo* (Milan 1996).

Voronov, L., 'Андрей Рублев-Великий Художник Древней Руси', *Богословские Труды*, no. 14 (1975) 83–86.

Vzdornov, G.I., 'Новооткрытая Икона 'Троицы' из Троице-Сергиевой Лавры', *Троица Андрея Рублева: Антология* (Moscow 1970) 129–132.

——, *Фрески Феофана Грека в Церкви Спаса Преображения в Новгороде* (Moscow 1976).

——, *The Frescoes of Theophanes the Greek in the Church of the Transfiguration in Novgorod* (Moscow 1976).

Walther, F.I., *Codices Illustres: The World's Most Famous Illuminated Manuscripts 400 to 1600* (Cologne 2005).

Walzl, F., 'The Liturgy of the Epiphany Season and the Epiphanies of Joyce', *Publications of the Modern Language Association of America*, vol. 80, no. 4 (Sept. 1965) 436–450.

Ware, K., 'The Jesus Prayer in St Gregory the Sinai', *Eastern Churches Review*, vol. 4, 1 (1972) 3–21.

——, 'God Hidden and Revealed: The Apophatic Way and the Essence–Energies Distinction', *Eastern Churches Review*, vol. 7, no. 2 (1975) 132–145.

——, *Act out of Stillness: The Influence of Fourteenth-Century Hesychasm on Byzantine and Slavic Civilisation* (Toronto 1995).

——, *The Inner Kingdom: The Collected Works* (Crestwood 2000).

——, 'La Transfiguration du Christ et la Souffrance du Monde', *Soperim*, no. 294 (January 2005) 20–26.

Ware, K. & Dillon, J.M., 'The Value of the Material Creation', *Symbolae Osloenses: Norwegian Journal of Greek and Latin Studies*, vol. 6, no. 3 (Summer 1971) 154–165.

——, *The Orthodox Way* (Crestwood 1995).

——, *Dionysius the Areopagite and the Neoplatonist Tradition: Despoiling the Hellenes* (Crestwood 2007).

Waring, L.F., 'Art in the Life of the Yugoslavs', *The Slavonic and East European Review*, vol. 24, no. 63 (January 1946) 180–188.

Weiss, G., *Joannes Kantakuzenos: Aristokrat, Staatsmann, Kaiser und Mönch, in der Gesell Schaftsentwicklung on Byzanz im 14* (Munchen 1969).

Weitzmann, K., 'The Selection of Texts for Cyclical Illustration in Byzantine Manuscripts', *Byzantine Books and Bookmen: A Dumbarton Oaks Colloquium* (Washington D.C 1975) 69–109.

——, *The Icon: Holy Images—Sixth to Fourteenth Century* (New York 1978).

Wice, H. & Smith, W., *A Dictionary of Christian Biography, Literature, Sects and Doctrines* (1880) 258–261.

Wilberding, E., 'A *Defense* of Dionysius the Areopagite by Rubens', *Journal of the History of Ideas*, vol. 52, no. 1 (Jan.–Mar., 1991) 19–34.

Williams, J., 'The Apophatic Theology of Dionysius the Pseudo-Areopagite', *Downside Review*, vol. 117 (1999) 157–172.

Williams, R., *The Dwelling of the Light: Praying with Icons of Jesus* (Norwich 2003).

Wilson, J.F., *The Story of Caesarea Philippi, Lost City of Pan* (London 2004).

Winkelmann, F., 'Andrei's Icon of the Old Testament Trinity: Observation on its Interpretation', *Byzantinoslavica*, vol. 50, no. 2 (1989) 197–202.

——, 'Die Trinitatsikone Andrei Rubljovs', Bemerkungen zu Ihrer Interpretation, vol. 50, no. 2 (1989) 197–202.

Wright, N.T., 'Jesus's Resurrection in the Early Christian Texts: An Engagement', *Journal for the Study of the Historical Jesus*, vol. 3, no. 2 (2005) 197–208.

Wybrew, H., *The Orthodox Liturgy: The Development of the Eucharistic Liturgy in the Byzantine Rite* (Crestwood 1990).

Xyngopoulos, A., *The Mosaic Decoration of the Church of the Holy Apostles in Thessaloniki* (Thessaloniki 1953).

——, 'Seint Demetre le Grand Duc Apocafkos', *Ellenica*, vol. 15 (Thessalonica 1957) 127–128.

——, *The Wall Paintings of St Nicholas Orphanos in Thessaloniki* (Athens 1964).

——, 'Les Fresques de l'Église des Saints-Apotres a Thessalonique', *Art et Societe a' Byzance sous les Paleologues: Bibliothkque de l'Institut Hellinique d'Études Byzantines et Postbyzantines de Venice*, vol. 4 (Venice 1971) 83–89.

Yadim, S., 'The Italo-Cretan Religious Painting and the Byzantine-Palaeologan Legacy', *Edebiyat Fakültesi Dergisi: Journal of Faculty of Letters*, vol. 25, no. 1 (June 2008) 267–279.

Yangazoglou, S., 'Philosophy and Theology: The Demonstrative Method in the Theology of Saint Gregory Palamas', *The Greek Orthodox Theological Review*, vol. 41, no. 1 (1996) 1–18.

Yannaras, C., 'The Distinction between Essence and Energies and its Importance for Theology', *St Vladimir's Theological Quarterly*, vol. 19 (Summer 1975) 232–245.

Young, M., *Biblical Exegesis and the Formation of Christian Culture* (Cambridge 1997).

Young, S.H., 'Relations between Byzantine Mosaic and Fresco Technique', *Jahrbuch der Osterreichischen Byzantinistik*, vol. 25 (1976) 269–278.

Žikić, B.,'Културни Херој као Морални Трикстер: Свети Сава у Усменом Предању Срба из БиХ', *Bulletin of the Ethnographical Institute SASA*, vol. 46 (1997), 122–128.

Zlatarski, V.N., *Житие на Теодосий Търновски* (Sofia 1962).

Zotov, A., 'Народность Искусства Андрея Рублева', *Искусство*, vol. 9 (1960) 60–63.

Zvonok, N.S., 'Исихазм как Духовный Источник Русской Иконы', http://www.nbuv.gov.ua/e-journals/vsunud/2008-1E/08znsiri.htm (accessed 8/07/2011).

Index

www.ingramcontent.com/pod-product-compliance
Lightning Source LLC
LaVergne TN
LVHW060622110826
845147LV00015B/914

* 9 7 8 1 9 2 5 0 2 1 8 3 7 *